Charles County Public Library
www.ccplonline.org

The JOURNEY *to the* MAYFLOWER

The
JOURNEY
to the MAYFLOWER

GOD'S OUTLAWS AND THE INVENTION OF FREEDOM

STEPHEN TOMKINS

PEGASUS BOOKS

NEW YORK LONDON

THE JOURNEY TO THE MAYFLOWER

Pegasus Books, Ltd.
148 West 37th Street, 13th Floor
New York, NY 10018

Copyright © 2020 by Stephen Tompkins

First Pegasus Books hardcover edition January 2020

ISBN: 978-1-64313-367-6

10 9 8 7 6 5 4 3 2 1

Printed in the United States of America
Distributed by W. W. Norton & Company

To my dad,
across the main ocean

Contents

Introduction

I N 1648, THE Governor of Plymouth, New England, William Brad-ford, was depressed. As a founder of the colony, one of the pilgrims who sailed on the *Mayflower* in 1620, Bradford had seen the settlement overcome huge threats to its survival and grow – but, he feared, it had lost its vision. The younger generation failed to grasp the ideals that their community was founded on, and did not see the value of the religion that Bradford's generation had sacrificed so much to practise in freedom. As Plymouth struggled economically and newer settlements outpaced them, many young people moved away in search of more and better land. Those that stayed saddened Bradford with their moral decline.

Bradford's solution was to tell them a story. To explain what Plymouth was, he wrote a booklet in the form of a conversation between the young men of New England and the 'ancient men' from 'Old England', in which the ancients set out the story of their movement. It was not an account of their twenty-eight years in America, or of their sea voyage to get there, but the longer story behind that, which he hoped would make sense of what they were doing there.

The tale Bradford told stretched back ninety-five years, to the creation of an underground Protestant church during Queen Mary's reign of fire. It then made its way through decades of persecution, not from Catholics but from the Protestant Church of England. The underground church was recreated to resist this surprising new enemy, and faced imprisonments, executions, foreign exile and grinding poverty, all because men and women would not bow to authorities who demanded they disobey the word of God as they understood it. Bradford told of heroic stands and an ignominious capitulation, amazing conversions and embarrassing splits. His cast stretched from the Queen of England to an outlaw shoemaker. His setting was first England, and then the Netherlands where the English were strangers and pilgrims – though as godly pioneers they had been strangers and pilgrims in their home country too. His moral was that these people had created a beautiful community at great cost to themselves, and so deserved to be remembered and imitated by their children.

That story of Bradford's is the story of this book, told here at rather greater length since a lot more information is now available, and not necessarily reaching precisely the same conclusions. The sailing of the *Mayflower* was not just an American beginning but one of the numerous remarkable outcomes, the many flowers, of an illegal religious movement in Elizabethan and Jacobean England. This movement is about as forgotten in Britain as the *Mayflower* is remembered in the United States, though its members are the fathers and mothers of Christian Churches that today have tens of millions of members.

These men and women are generally known today as the Separatists, because they separated from the Church of England. They themselves disliked the name, although they were happy with 'the churches of the separation'. In their own day they were most often called Brownists, after their most notorious leader – a name they utterly abhorred, which of course made it stick. The small number of them who sailed on the *Mayflower* have become known as the pilgrims, but all the Separatists would have owned that name: they became pilgrims when they realised they did not belong in the national church they had been born into. They made many journeys, literal and spiritual, before that celebrated one of 1620; and on earth itself they considered themselves 'Christian pilgrims who here have no biding city'.[1]

This is the story of people, but it is also the story of an idea: that religion should be free, and that the church of Christ is a voluntary community, not an entire church state. This was a truly dangerous and frightening idea, one that Separatists variously groped towards, stumbled over, retreated from and proclaimed from the rooftops. There are people in this story who were willing to give their lives for it, and others who were ready to take them. It was a difficult idea, but a good one, and the Western world owes it a great deal.

This book has some family resemblance to the PhD thesis I wrote twenty years ago on the thinking of the Separatist movement – a resemblance much like the second generation at Plymouth had to the first. The completed thesis was accepted by an excitingly prestigious publisher, on the condition of a few revisions that I was too sick of the whole thing to get around to making. The world doesn't know what it missed. This new book is very far indeed from being an adaptation of that thesis, more a story that manages to rescue a few of its insights from oblivion. Still, it is quite a treat, after all these years, to see that work have some use for the first time. I again have to thank Meic Pearse, whose teaching and supervision were a joy, and who will doubtless find his theological DNA all over this book, should he care to look, along, I trust, with plenty to violently disagree with, and none of his politics at all.

I'd also like to thank Katherine Venn at Hodder & Stoughton for her enthusiasm and encouragement, and for being persuaded to take a chance on the book in the first place. It is a privilege to have the book indexed by Caroline Jones, a descendant of Peregrine White, the first child born to the pilgrims in the New World, while the *May-flower* was anchored off Cape Cod. Heartfelt thanks to Dr Williams's Library, Marsh's Library, Lambeth Palace Library and the British Library. Also to the United Reformed Church, for their flexibility as employers, which saved me from having to write the book entirely over lunch, in bed and on the bus, and for keeping the light burning. And to my pals at the Mayflower pub in Rotherhithe, who made no contribution at all but asked quite nicely.

Spelling and punctuation have been modernised in quotations from sixteenth- and seventeenth-century sources, but not book titles. Dates are given in the modern style, so 6 February 1571/2 is given as 6 February 1572; and according to the local calendar, so 6 February in London would be 16 February in Amsterdam. The words 'Brownist' and 'Barrowist' are sometimes used by modern writers to distinguish between two distinct streams of Separatism; I use 'Brownist' as it was used at the time, to denote any member of the Separatist movement from Browne's day onwards, not just one who identified as a follower of Browne.

PART ONE

The bloody beast's gear

I

Burning sermons

Iɴ Aᴜɢᴜsᴛ 1553, the Bishop of Gloucester and Worcester was summoned to London. The Privy Council told him he was in trouble
over a debt to the crown of £509 5s 5d in unpaid first fruits, but
everyone knew the truth: the Queen wanted him burned alive.

The Catholic establishment was not in the habit of having its bishops executed, but the Protestant Reformation had changed things,
in Queen Mary's eyes. Under her half-brother Edward's six years
of Protestant rule in England, churches had been stripped, services
rewritten, faithful bishops deposed, and Catholic teachings denounced
and insulted from the pulpit and contradicted in the Prayer Book.
Now, after Edward's premature death, Mary embarked on a Catholic
spring-clean, and those who had assaulted the Church and blasphemed
its faith, even in its highest places, would be punished and purged.

The Bishop of Gloucester and Worcester, John Hooper, was high
on the list. Not only had he been involved in unseating traditionalist
bishops in Edward's time – bishops who were now back in power
with vengeance – but he was one of the most radical Protestants in
public life, even refusing where possible to wear the traditional episcopal vestments. He was, you might say, an early puritan.

Hooper was imprisoned in the Fleet for a year and a half, and
relieved of his bishopric. He paid the fee for freedom to move around
inside the prison, but was kept in close confinement anyway. The
cell was positioned, as he put it, between 'the sink and filth of all
the house' and the street gutter, and he became ill, suffering sciatica
and a bloated torso. Attempts were made to convert him, including
exorcism, but Hooper was prepared to die for his faith. The authorities had given him the chance to flee the country, and Hooper's
friends had urged him to return to exile in Switzerland, where he had

gone six years earlier to escape Henry VIII's erratic anti-Protestant backlash. But back then he had been a mere scholar, now he was a bishop. 'Once I did flee, and take me to my feet; but now, because I am called to this place and vocation, I am thoroughly persuaded to tarry, and to live and die with my sheep.'[1]

Interrogated in January 1555 in St Saviour's Church, Southwark, by the Bishop of Winchester (whose diocese extended from Hampshire to London Bridge), Hooper was found guilty of heresy and taken by night to Newgate, the bishop's men going ahead to dowse the costermongers' candles so that he would not be recognised. On Monday 4 February, refusing to recant, Hooper was defrocked – a literal term in those days – and at four the following morning was woken to start his last journey back to Gloucester, hooded to avoid exciting the public.

Hooper had been loved and hated in Gloucestershire. He was perhaps the most popular preacher in England, performing (the word does justice to the entertainment value of Tudor sermons) two or three times a day to overflowing churches. He had been a driven reformer, especially after his first survey of the diocese revealed, according to one count, that fewer than half of the 311 clergy interviewed were able to list the ten commandments, thirty failed to recite the Lord's Prayer in English, and 27 could not tell him who composed it. He even demanded a minimum religious educational standard from the laity, making one John Trigg do public penance for not knowing any of the ten commandments.

The execution of Bishop Hooper

Whether to pay loving tribute to their martyr pastor, or to enjoy a religious tyrant's comeuppance, vast crowds gathered on the Saturday morning around St Mary's Knapp, some perching in the great elm, to see Hooper's gospel in the crucible. John Foxe, the chronicler of the Marian burnings, claims that 7,000 were there – an impressive head count considering the population of the city was about half that, though attractions like a market or feast would bring large numbers from the surrounding villages.

Understandably, Mary insisted the golden-tongued preacher 'be led quietly and in silence' and open not his mouth, but, while the sheriffs forbade him to address the crowd, they allowed him to pray aloud. Hooper in his prayer confessed to being swill, and a sink of sin, but publicly reminded the Lord that he was dying not for his offences but for his refusal to deny the gospel as he understood it, which he briefly recapitulated; the Mayor chased away two people taking notes. Hooper prayed for the patience to endure the fire, or, if it were God's will, for the supernatural anaesthesia that ancient tradition said was granted to martyrs in their hour of death. The former request was indeed granted.

Hooper was shown a pardon from the Queen, to take effect if he would abjure his heresy even now, but he cried, 'If you love my soul, away with it!' He was stripped to his shirt, and the sheriffs divided up his clothes among them. Standing on a stool, he was fastened to the stake by a metal band, which the soldiers had trouble fitting around his swollen waist. The faggots and reeds were placed about his feet and lit, the wood being green to prolong his dying, but the wind was so strong that when the fire was spent, he was hurt but very much alive. The executioners kindled a second fire, which again, Foxe says, 'burned at the nether parts, but had small power above, because of the wind, saving that it did burn his hair and scorch his skin a little'. 'For God's love, good people,' Hooper cried from the unconsuming flames, 'let me have more fire!'[2]

A third bundle was lit, and this finally did the job. Hooper called out repeatedly, 'Lord Jesus, have mercy upon me! Lord Jesus receive my spirit!' Foxe concludes:

> When he was black in the mouth, and his tongue swollen, that he could not speak, yet his lips went till they were shrunk to the gums: and he knocked his breast with his hands till one of his arms fell off, and then knocked still with the other, what time the fat, water, and blood, dropped out at his fingers' ends, until by renewing of the fire, his strength was gone, and his hand did cleave fast, in knocking, to the iron upon his breast. So immediately, bowing forwards, he yielded up his spirit.[3]

He had been three-quarters of an hour in the fire.

Between 280 and 300 men and women died on Mary's bonfires in the course of four years, including bricklayers and gentlefolk, university fellows and illiterate workers, a 'blind boy' and an 'aged woman', and five bishops including the Archbishop of Canterbury. The theory behind burning heretics was that it intimidated their fellow travellers while edifying the faithful, giving both a tangible sense of the hellishness of false doctrine. But as Peter Marshall puts it, 'the meaning of those deaths could never be entirely controlled by the oppressors'. Mary's spectacles seemed to leave much of the audience with the disastrous impression that saints had been martyred. Foxe's stories, compelling works of Protestant propaganda published in 1563 as the *Book of Martyrs*, naturally tend to present the victims as brave heroes roasting joyfully before tearful, admiring crowds, but Catholic observers painted much the same picture. Witnessing the first burning, that of John Rogers the Bible translator, in Smithfield five days before Hooper's, the French ambassador said Rogers went to his death 'as if he had been led to a wedding', accompanied by his children and cheered on by the crowd. Mary's Spanish chaplain Simon Renard reported the same event: 'Some of the onlookers wept, others prayed to God to give him strength, perseverance, and patience to bear the pain and not to recant, others gathered the ashes and bones and wrapped them up in paper to preserve them, yet others threatening the bishops.'[4]

As a more recent commentator, Ted Hughes, put it, in a poem about the execution of the Bishop of St David's the following month:

> *No pulpit*
> *Of his ever held their eyes so still,*
> ...
> *Out of his mouth, fire like a glory broke,*
> *And smoke burned his sermon into the skies.*[5]

'The blood of Christians is seed', exulted the second-century apologist Tertullian when the faithful were being killed by Rome fourteen centuries previously, and now once again there went out a sower to sow.

The Marian burnings

This is where the story of the Pilgrim Fathers starts, with Mary's campaign to burn Protestantism out of England. It was this more than anything that ignited the first puritan movement and lit the pilgrims' way into the religious underground, into exile and into the New World. Always, behind all their passions, their longings and hatreds, their dreams and sacrifices, and their wranglings over theological trivia, there is the heat of Mary's fires. The founders of the Separatist movement that would take them to the Netherlands and North America lived and hid and prayed through this assault, and it changed their view of the world. It gave them an arch-enemy and divided the world into two bodies: of Christ and antichrist. It forced them to choose whether they would stay true, despite the danger, to the gospel they had embraced or bend the knee to another lord; and in so doing it made religion what a millennium of Christian rule over Europe had, at all costs, prevented it from being: a matter of choice. Their revolutionary, pioneering, fanatical movement was forged in these fires.

The motive that persuaded Mary, by nature the mildest of Tudor monarchs, to execute her subjects for their crimes of belief was above all a hatred of the religion that had wrecked her life. When, in her adolescence, it became clear that she would be Henry VIII and Catherine of Aragon's only surviving child, Henry feared his failure to produce an heir would destroy the young Tudor dynasty and plunge England back into civil war. A papal dispensation overruling canon law had allowed Henry to marry Catherine in the first place, but now Pope Clement VII was controlled by the Catholic Emperor Charles V, Catherine's nephew, and could not oblige. Thus it was, for every reason except religion, that Henry turned to Protestantism. Taking the church away from Rome solved his marital problems, and confiscating the houses and vast lands of the monks solved his financial problems for a while. He took the title 'Supreme Head of the Church of England' but continued to enforce Catholic worship and doctrine, executing both Protestants and Catholics who opposed him. It was a reformation unlike any other in Europe, one entirely steered by the whim of the monarch.

When Parliament declared Catherine unqueened in 1534, Mary became illegitimate and unmarriageable, was banished from court and excluded from succession to the throne (until she was eventually reconciled to Henry), and she never saw her mother again.

Her Protestant stepmother Anne Boleyn humiliated her and pressed Henry to have her killed, but instead Mary was made a servant to her baby half-sister Elizabeth. She threw herself into piety and was perpetually unwell. During her brother's Protestant reign, a diplomat reported that Mary would constantly repeat, '*Si deus est pro nobis, quis contra nos?*' If God is for us, who can be against us?

This text was proved true when the dying Edward was persuaded to exclude Mary once again from the royal succession, this time in favour of his adviser's daughter-in-law Jane Grey. Against the warnings of her most trusted counsellors, Mary raised an army, successfully seized the throne and received a rapturous welcome from crowds hailing the legitimate sovereign. God was for her; she was to rule by and for God.

Mary's assault on Protestants was not a matter of political expediency then, but a crusade against evil and a war on error. Rome had condemned Protestant teachings as 'pernicious poison' to be purged, and she had the divine anointing to administer the purgation. Fire had been the Catholic defence against heresy for centuries, and the English laws requiring it had only been repealed under Henry and Edward. Mary's third Parliament eventually agreed to reinstate the heresy laws, and she started immediately. Mary's more worldly advisers, including her trusted chaplain Renard, implored her to restrain herself, fearing that public cruelty would squander the goodwill of the people and provoke an uprising, but she would not be tempted. She believed in forgiving crimes against herself wherever possible, but heresy only became a crime to be forgiven after a heretic recanted. Till then it was a disease to be cured.

The rationale for persecution

Mary had every reason to believe she could overcome faith with fire. Public judicial murder did not revolt sixteenth-century viewers or discredit the persecutor. Thousands of people were executed every year in England and Wales, to the great diversion of the public, and torture and mutilation were standard acts of justice. Mary's heretics probably increased the annual total of executions by no more than

3 per cent. Burning was a cruel punishment to be sure, but no more so than the hanging, drawing and quartering of traitors. The burnings of Protestants in Spain were hugely popular cruelties; they burned no sermons into the skies, but successfully eradicated Spanish Protestantism, just as holy fire had destroyed earlier movements. The blood of martyrs is not always seed; sometimes it is just blood.

Neither were most viewers shocked that victims were killed for their religious beliefs. The whole of western and central Europe had been united in the one Christian faith for a millennium before Protestantism had appeared thirty-five years ago, so agreement seemed obviously possible and natural, as well as desirable. Religious dissent threatened the fabric of society and lured people into hell. It was as widely understood that the population must be united in one religion as it is, by us today, that citizens must all be subject to the same laws; and it was as vital to stamp out wrong religion as it is to stop medical malpractice.

Protestantism had in it the seeds that could in time grow to overturn such preconceptions: its fundamental innovation was to enthrone the principle that a person has the responsibility to listen to their own conscience, and the right to follow their own mind, as Martin Luther had demonstrated unforgettably at Worms. But other forces pulled the movement in the opposite direction. One was the millennium of experience in which church was a whole Christian society, making it hard to think of church in any other way. In this arrangement, religious leaders and thinkers had power over the whole population, power that they were in no hurry to throw away now. And there was the conviction that eternal souls were at stake and false beliefs would damn them, so no punishment could be crueller than allowing religious misinformation to thrive.

Protestants, while condemning Catholicism as a creed of persecution, could be as ruthless with heretics as Catholics were. Bishops that Mary burned had themselves, during Edward's reign, approved the execution of a man who denied the deity of Christ and a woman who believed that Jesus grew in Mary's womb without taking her flesh; other radicals had recanted when threatened with violence. The main difference between Catholics and Protestants on the issue of heresies was whether Protestantism was one. Almost the only Christians who disapproved of persecution per se were the radical Protestant spin-off the Anabaptists, who denounced the very idea of a state church – and therefore were killed, eradicated as a religious and political plague, by almost any authority, Protestant or Catholic, who found Anabaptists in their realm. The number of Anabaptists in England was minuscule, and the real extremism of the movement had been distorted into horrible proportions in the minds of others by the Anabaptist revolution in Münster in the 1530s, which had involved communism and polygamy among other scandals, so Anabaptists were seen not as a movement to be engaged with but as mere monsters. This is why the English Separatists' hesitant, uncertain vision of a society where religion is a matter of choice, of voluntary churches for believers only, had to be discovered from scratch, rather than learned from the Anabaptists, and why it would be so dangerously radical it would make them outlaws.

The failure of persecution

And yet Mary's executions, instead of exterminating English Protestantism, give birth to puritanism, its most uncompromising manifestation. She underestimated Protestants, convinced they were fools who just needed to be shown their error, or knaves who would recant to save their skins; she expected to kill a few anyway, and then to see the whole movement fall apart. This strategy worked in Spain, and perhaps if the first few in England had recanted it would have worked here; but when Rogers, Hooper and others went into the flames unflinching, a precedent was set. Protestantism was glorified by martyrdom, and by the summer of 1558 the organisers of the burnings were having to send their convicts 'into odd corners of the country' to die, because the supposedly intimidating display was having the opposite effect.[6]

Another problem for Mary's policy was that Protestants, unlike in Spain, had become a substantial minority in England. They had been the party of government and the established church was full of them, from archbishop down to parish priest. The Queen was assaulting not some alien teaching smuggled around the country by a sinister underground movement, but the religion of the English Prayer Book and the pastors of the English people. She only emphasised this by sending men like Hooper home to die in front of their flocks. This was not simply the church destroying a false teaching, but a contest between two churches as to which was the true one.

Equally counterproductive was Mary's marriage to Emperor Philip II of Spain in 1554. It was feared and resented by many English subjects, who foresaw England being absorbed into the Habsburg empire. Such an abomination against the natural order was this, that on Philip's arrival in London a second sun appeared in the sky, with an upside-down rainbow, Foxe tells us. Spaniards were said to be cruel, acquisitive, ruttish and growing rich on their American colonies. Spain was also the most aggressively Catholic nation in Europe. Suddenly Mary's fiery reforms started to look like an invasion. In the space of just four years she achieved the colossal feat of making Roman Catholicism – the religion of most English people, as it had been for a millennium – seem to many people alien and threatening, and Protestantism – an import from Germany and Switzerland – seem patriotic.

Above all, Mary failed by dying in 1558, after only five years' rule, and England would not see another Catholic monarch for a hundred years, by which time Protestantism was so irremovably entrenched that the king's faith was the best-kept secret in the kingdom. Mary's heated arguments just did not have time to convince the heretics; Foxe's version of events, where the flaming weapons of antichrist failed to break the saints, had all the time it needed. The day of Mary's death and England's deliverance was a public holiday for the better part of two hundred years.

2

Going underground

FOXE WAS A man of means, and was able to work on his martyr-ology in exile in Strasbourg, having fled from home with his pregnant wife, pursued by the officers of the Bishop of Winchester. Eight hundred other Protestants went abroad too, but most did not leave the country and so spent several years under sentence of death. Robert Harrison, who was to become a Separatist leader in the 1580s, was a child in Norfolk in these years, a county where ten people were burned. Writing in 1583, he recalled the time

> when the fiery sword did hang over our heads in the days of Queen Mary, and that by so weak a thread that we looked every hour when it should fall upon us; when we, being strangers from our own houses, walked from house to house, at such time as the owls and backs [i.e. bats] look forth and fly: and we thought it well if we might live so without house or land, or ought else save bare bread for life.[1]

The underground church

The Protestant outlaws met for worship in cellars and clothworkers' lofts, in woods and ships, in inns and private houses. They were spied on and reported. Once when they were besieged in a house on the Thames, one of them swam out, brought a boat and ferried the wor-shippers to safety, using his shoes as oars.

There were such meetings throughout the country, from Devon to Lancashire and from Wales to East Anglia, but the largest congre-gation and the one we know most about was in London, claimed as an ancestor by the Separatist church in England and America. It was formed early in Mary's reign with about twenty people and continued till her death, by which time it was sometimes more than two hundred-strong. The church evaded capture by constantly shifting around the city and the surrounding area, meeting at all times of day and night, and, though many were arrested, it was never destroyed.

Reports from witnesses including the landlady of the King's Head in Ratcliffe say that the Protestants met in a back room of the inn, ordered a fire, beer and a roasted pig, and then sat and stood around the table, while one read a selection of psalms and the minister preached and shared bread and wine. The staff also noticed that deacons collected money for the poor and prisoners, and that members called each other 'brother'. They liked to meet where there was a play or May Day celebrations or suchlike to provide cover – and unlike later generations of puritans had no scruples about joining these entertainments afterwards. They also shared letters and books sent by the exiles on the continent.

The company included a number of foreigners, Dutch, French and Scottish Protestants, who were numerous in London. Worshippers sometimes met at the house of one Mr Frog, a Dutch shoemaker. Before Mary's time, foreigners had been allowed 'stranger churches' in the capital, giving Londoners an enticing glimpse of the more progressive Protestantism of the continent.

The London underground church read the English Bible in their meetings and discussed it, and used the second Prayer Book that Archbishop Cranmer had introduced into churches under King Edward, the more progressive of the two. These Londoners were said by a young contemporary to have chosen their own ministers 'by common consent'[2]; elsewhere some congregations had no clergy, but still worshipped privately, with or without the Prayer Book. Some laymen even preached, as one of them, the Kent miller Edmund Allin, explained to his captor: 'Why are we called Christians, if we do not follow Christ, if we do not read his law, if we do not interpret it to others that have not so much understanding?'[3] Allin and his wife were burned with five others in Maidstone. Thomas Hudson, a poor glover from Aylsham in Norfolk, held meetings in his house at which he prayed and preached. He built a permanent hiding place in his woodpile, but died on Mary's faggots after he turned street preacher.

Some people had the perilous job of smuggling correspondence between London and the exiles on the continent, and bringing their books back. One smuggler, Elizabeth Young, was arrested in London carrying a tract printed in Frankfurt called *Antichrist*. She was kept permanently in the stocks, interrogated thirteen times for information on her contacts, threatened with torture, and eventually released. Another was Thomas Sprat, a tanner, who once, landing at Dover and walking north, had the bad luck to meet his former employer on the road, an ardent Catholic magistrate by the name of Brent. Brent had ten men on horseback with him, and recognised the outlaw, but Sprat fled on foot, and by crawling through a hedge, running down a hillside too steep for horses, and disappearing into a wood, evaded capture.

Rose, Rough and Symson

One early leader of the London underground church was Thomas Rose, a clergyman who had gone abroad to escape Henry VIII's anti-Protestant zeal and, like Bishop Hooper, decided not to flee a second time. Removed from his church in West Ham, for a year he led secret services around London, until the congregation was betrayed to the authorities. Rose was leading worship in a sheep-shearer's house in Bow churchyard on the night of 1 January 1555 when the bishop's men raided the service and arrested thirty-six people. Rose was interviewed repeatedly by the Bishops of Winchester and Norwich (Rose having previously lived in East Anglia), who threatened to rack him and to have him hanged, drawn and quartered as a traitor, for praying that God would remove Mary's yoke from the necks of the godly. Eventually he was released into the keeping of his friend, the MP for Great Yarmouth. According to the constables, Rose earned this transfer by recanting the Protestant understanding of the Eucharist; Rose claimed they had wilfully misunderstood his statement, and wanted to be rid of him because they feared the Queen was about to die in childbirth and so did not want to provoke Protestants. Rose escaped, hid for three weeks in the cottage of a local woman until the search for him cooled off, and then fled to Frankfurt.

In 1557, the London congregation was infiltrated by a Catholic spy, the tailor Roger Sergeant. On his information, on Sunday 12 December, the Vice Chamberlain's men caught worshippers at the Saracen's Head in Islington, where they were supposed to be seeing a play, but were in fact about to celebrate Communion. The new minister John Rough and the deacon Cutbert Symson were arrested, along with two other members, John Devenish and Hugh Foxe.

Rough was a Scot who, before his conversion, had been a Dominican friar and chaplain to the Earl of Arran, and afterwards had become a successful Protestant preacher in Scotland and the north of England. He persuaded John Knox to become a preacher, addressing him directly in a sermon and reducing him to tears. On Mary's accession, Rough and his wife Kate went into exile in Norden in Friesland, in the Netherlands, knitting caps. Foxe says that John Rough came to London to get yarn in November 1557, discovered the underground church, and stayed as its minister, though some have thought he must have been sent by the English Protestants in exile to lead the church. Foxe also says that Rough attended the burning of James and Margaret Austoo in Smithfield, telling a friend he had gone 'to learn the way', though there is a clash of dates here as the Austoos were executed on 17 September.

Shortly after Rough and Symson were taken into custody, a former member of their church, Margaret Mearing, was also arrested. Rough had excommunicated her only days before this on suspicion of being a spy, because she kept bringing strangers to church with her and talked too much. He had got the wrong person however, and she, as Foxe puts it, 'did not well take it, nor in good part', bitterly protesting her unfair treatment. And yet when none of Rough's friends were allowed to visit him, she pretended to be his sister and took him a clean shirt. She then went to Sergeant's house and berated him as Judas, and was arrested by the Bishop of London's summoner days later.

Mearing and Rough were burned together in Smithfield on 22 December 1557. Rough left behind his wife and a two-year-old daughter, Rachel; Mearing left a husband, James. On the day of his condemnation, Rough had written to his congregation, saying he had been under great temptation until he heard the voice of God saying, 'He that will not suffer with Christ, shall not reign with him.' He told them, 'I have chosen the death, to confirm the truth by me taught … It is no time, for the loss of one man in the battle, for the camp to turn back. Up with men's hearts; blow down the daubed walls of heresy. Let one take the banner, and the other the trumpet.'[4]

Symson was kept alive longer because he had information. As deacon, he kept accounts of the money given by each church member for prisoners and others in need, so he was tortured, including repeated racking in three-hour sessions, to persuade him to give names, which he successfully withheld. Foxe tells us that he had been in the habit of carrying his account book about, until the Friday before their arrest, when Rough was warned of the danger in a dream. He asked Symson to hide the book, but Symson replied that dreams 'were but fantasies'. Rough insisted though, and Symson hid the book, and the church was saved. Later, while Symson was in the stocks in the Bishop of London's coalhouse, he had his own dream or vision, in which a glowing man appeared to him, said 'Ha', and disappeared, which Symson apparently found a great comfort. Symson was finally executed at Smithfield, on 28 March 1558, along with his fellow church members John Devenish and Hugh Foxe.

Bernher and Bentham

After Rough's death, John Foxe tells us that the London underground church was led by Augustine Bernher, a Swiss man whose survival throughout Mary's reign was remarkable, considering that he smuggled writing materials in to prisoners, including his former employer Hugh Latimer, smuggled their writings out, got their works printed abroad, and accompanied them as they were led to the stake.

The Oxford academic and Bible translator Thomas Bentham returned from exile in Frankfurt to become the main minister of the London church, and under his leadership its numbers grew. Bentham distinguished himself at a burning of seven in Smithfield in June 1558 when he flouted a decree forbidding audiences to shout encouragement or to pray for the convict. As the decree was read out, he cried, 'Almighty God, for Christ's sake strengthen them', and the roar of approval from the crowd was so great that the outnumbered soldiers took no action. Bentham also had a narrow escape when he was required to take part in an inquest, where he was supposed to swear on a Roman Catholic primer. On his refusal, he was arrested, but escaped when the inquest was cancelled. Bentham wrote to his friend Thomas Lever, who was in exile in Aarau, that, despite 'being every moment of an hour in danger of taking, and fear of bodily death', he was happier and more at peace than he had been in the safety of Germany, 'seeing the fervent zeal of so many, and such increase of our congregation, in the midst of this cruel and violent persecution'.[5]

This covert London congregation was what the later Separatist underground and the New England pilgrims would look back to as their genesis, the first steps taken on their own path. William Bradford, Governor of Plymouth colony from 1621, wrote for the younger generation there about the church 'in the time of Queen Mary of which Mr Rough was pastor or teacher and Cudbert Simson a deacon, who ... professed and practised [our] cause'.[6]

Spiritual subterfuge brought a new religious experience for many laypeople. Not only had their religion never been so dangerous, but they had never exercised so much control over it, never such choice or personal involvement. This was not Christianity as a national way of life binding the whole people together, so much as a chosen path and a collaborative endeavour. How easy would it be to hand that freedom back to the state when England became Protestant again – especially if its Protestantism had a flavour that was hard to stomach?

3

A new hope

LATER SEPARATISTS WOULD look back on the supposed Protestant conversion of the English Church at Elizabeth's accession with derision and disgust: one moment England had been a nation of blasphemers, every parish disobeying God to join in with the anti-christian idol worship of Rome; then, as the Separatist leader Henry Barrow put it, with typical sarcasm, 'All this people, with all these manners, were in one day, with the blast of Queen Elizabeth's trumpet, of ignorant papists and gross idolaters, made faithful Christians.'[1] This was partly puritan disappointment talking, and more particularly the Separatists' novel idea that religion is a matter of individual choice, not of state legislation. Either way, such an attitude is a long way from the joy and thankful optimism English Protestants felt at the time.

A Protestant Queen

Being the daughter of Henry VIII's remarriage, which under Catholic rules made her illegitimate with no right to the throne, Elizabeth could hardly be anything but Protestant. When she was proclaimed Queen in London on 17 November 1558, all the bells of the capital rang, people danced and bonfire parties – despite their grim associations – filled the streets long into the night. It would be a great exaggeration to see this as a token of England's delight in throwing off the Catholic yoke. If Londoners were celebrating deliverance from Mary, it by no means followed that the rest of the country felt the same. Crowded cosmopolitan London was a hotbed of Protestantism, and when combined with the neighbouring counties of Kent and Essex had provided more than half of Mary's martyrs. The religious outlook of the mass of English people in these years is hard to gauge, but it is likely that a large majority would have been happy for their parish church to continue to supply the Catholic ritual they had grown up with, rather than undergo a third reinvention. The Spanish ambassador estimated that two-thirds of England remained Roman Catholic, which is no more than a guess, but plausible.

Our story, however, concerns the Protestants, and their feelings are clear. Robert Harrison, though he had not been part of the literal exile, saw Mary's regime as taking the whole land into exile, re-enacting the oppression of the Israelites' in the hostile godless empire of Egypt:

> Now, when we sighed and cried for the bondage, and the cry for our bondage came up unto God, and God heard our moan and remembered his covenant, then he brought [us] again [from] our captivity, as he did of Jacob; then were we like unto them that dreamed, even, for sudden joy, doubting whether we dreamed those happy tidings or no. Then was our mouth filled with laughter and our tongue with joy.[2]

It was not to last.

The reports that filtered down to Elizabeth's Protestant subjects in these early months seemed reassuring. She dismissed Catholic councillors and staff, and publicly humiliated the Bishop of London, known as 'Bloody Bonner' or 'Bitesheep Bonner', who would be the arch-villain of Foxe's *Book of Martyrs*. At Christmas, Elizabeth walked out of the chapel royal when the Bishop of Carlisle insisted on raising the wafer and wine during Mass – an action symbolising their adoration as the body and blood of Christ, the blasphemy that Protestants hated more than anything else in Catholicism. Her coronation was a spectacular display of Protestant pageantry, and when the Queen returned to Westminster for her first Parliament in January 1559, she shunned the monks who greeted her with lighted tapers: 'Away with those torches, for we see very well.'

And yet the Queen's Protestantism, though emphatic and sincere, was idiosyncratic and unusually moderate, and she was thoroughly attached to some of the traditional forms of Catholic worship, to the grandeur, the ceremony, the ornamentation, the music; she was even in favour of clerical celibacy, though she never imposed it. Her uniquely backward-looking version of Reformed Protestantism was Protestant enough to appal Catholics, while also profoundly disappointing Protestants. Before Mary's reign, a church of the kind that Elizabeth was planning would have been easier to impose on England. But most of the influential Protestants that survived Mary's inferno had done so in exile among the Reformed churches of Germany and Switzerland – Frankfurt, Zurich, Strasbourg, Geneva – where they had encountered ways of worship and church life that went further than England had yet seen. The exiles disagreed about whether to imitate their hosts' worship or to stick loyally with the form of service sanctioned under King Edward, but either way they rejoiced to belong to something bigger than their own church. The Reformed churches were not simply isolated state churches, but an international fellowship that England was expected to be part of. Many exiles returned home with a new vision of the holy purity of the true gospel. A battle loomed.

Puritans and bishops

The shape of the Elizabethan Church and its worship was set out in 1559 in the laws of Supremacy and Uniformity and the Royal Injunctions. The church they described was to be much the same as that left behind by Edward VI, the church of Cranmer's second Prayer Book, but with some modifications, all in a conservative direction. Most noticeably, Elizabeth restored some of the traditional priestly robes: the alb, surplice and cope. The bread at Holy Communion was replaced by the traditional wafer, and the crucial words with which the minister delivered it to worshippers became ambiguous, allowing individuals to decide for themselves whether what they ate was mysteriously transubstantiated or merely symbolic. Anti-Catholic insults disappeared from prayers. Most English Protestants had been thinking in terms of how much closer their church would be brought into line with the continental Reformed churches than it had been at Edward's death, only the most conservative being content to restore Edwardian religion unchanged; and yet the settlement imposed on them in 1559 did neither, taking it in the opposite direction.

Moderate Protestants could accept the church settlement, however disappointing, but others had grave misgivings, and became campaigners or supporters of the campaign for further change – and so we have puritanism. The puritans were dissatisfied with the Elizabethan Church and fought its leaders for further Protestant reform, to purify it of 'the relics of papistry'. In these early years, 'puritan' had none of the associations of killjoy morality that have since become its main meaning. Puritans were also, and at first more commonly, known as 'precisians', wanting the church more precisely to model itself on the Bible.

Puritanism was nothing so concrete as a party or a sect, but rather a climate of opinion, a mood of discontent. Moderate puritans would have been content simply to be rid of the priestly robes; the more radical puritans had conceived such a horror of the saint-torturing regime they had lived through that they insisted on the abolition of all church ceremonies that had originated in Catholicism rather than the Bible: saints' days, kneeling, the sign of the cross at baptism, confirmation, wafers. Many such traditional aspects of worship had developed in the church after the Bible was written, and for radical puritans this made them the creation of a hierarchy disobedient to Christ, the work of antichrist. These puritans objected to wedding rings as godless ritual, while the phrase from the wedding service 'with my body I thee worship' was horrifying. Insisting that the church should use precisely biblical forms of worship, they condemned organs and singing in parts – though they did not take this to its logical conclusion by reintroducing the harps, trumpets, psaltries and loud cymbals of the book of Psalms. Some radicals complained that the Prayer Book service was too long, leaving too little room for a good meaty sermon, and that its prayers were worldly, asking for material gain.

Elizabeth would have found it much easier to quench Protestant opposition if she had managed to keep a good number of Mary's bishops. She hoped that half of them would accept her regime, but with two inglorious exceptions they all rejected her as Supreme Governor of the Church, and so were dismissed. Two-thirds of the new appointments were offered to returning exiles.

This placed the exiles themselves in a ticklish position. Should they take posts that required them to enforce a defective form of religion, or shun the appointments and risk their going to crypto-Catholics? They did not assume the present religious rules were permanent: Protestantism had so far been a gradual process of purifying the Church of England, so one would expect the reformation to continue. As the Act of Uniformity said, the ceremonies it imposed were to be retained 'until other order shall be therein taken'. There was no assuming Elizabeth would grow old – she nearly died of smallpox in 1562 – or that she would remain her own master. That she would rule for forty-five years unmarried, allowing no further reformation whatsoever, and that the 1559 settlement would, essentially, survive into the twentieth century, was an unlikely prospect to say the least.

Weighing such considerations, and advised by the leaders of other Reformed churches, the majority of Protestant clergy saw their way clear to accepting whatever office was offered – or as Barrow would later put it, 'These hungry priests, like ravening wolves and greedy foxes, flew to divide the prey.'[3] The new Archbishop of Canterbury was Matthew Parker, a very conservative Protestant who had survived Mary's regime not by leaving the country but by keeping his head down. The man who replaced Bitesheep Bonner as Bishop of London was Edmund Grindal, who had been in exile in Strasbourg, and had a lot more sympathy than Parker for puritan scruples. The minister of the underground London congregation, Thomas Bentham, became Bishop of Coventry and Lichfield, and Edmund Scambler, whom Foxe names as the first minister of the underground congregation, became the Bishop of Peterborough.

The underground congregation itself had continued meeting after Elizabeth's succession so long as Catholic Mass continued in parish churches, though since Mary's death they could afford to do so far more openly. One of the most fervent returning refugees, Thomas Lever, joined with them and sent a report back to Zurich in August 1559, saying that amid dismal scenes of continued popery this one congregation, which had met in private throughout the persecution, continued to offer sound worship and preaching. Though technically the group was still illegal, he said, the authorities winked at their meetings. Safety swelled their numbers more than ever, as former members who had bowed to Mary's religion to save their lives repented. 'I have frequently been present on such occasions,' said Lever, 'and have seen many returning with tears, and many too in like manner with tears receiving such persons into communion; so that nothing could be more delightful than the mutual tears of all parties.'[4]

Now that the reformation of the Church of England had been agreed by Parliament and the minister of the underground church made Bishop of Coventry, it was time for the congregation to wrap up its business. Just in case any of its members failed to appreciate this, the Queen issued a proclamation in 1560 commanding 'on pain of imprisonment that no minister or other person make any conventicles or secret congregations either to read or preach or to minister the sacraments or to use any manner of divine service'. There would be no worship allowed, Protestant or Catholic, except by the Prayer Book, led by authorised ministers. Not without a certain ambivalence, the congregation dispersed to join in with the diluted Protestantism of the parish churches. Their exile was over.

Puritan nonconformity

The next few years were promising ones for the puritans. The government was more worried about Roman Catholicism than about Protestant dissent: Catholics had greater numbers, their religion was much more seriously disabled by the 1559 settlement, and they had more dangerous foreign connections, such as Queen Mary of Scotland and Philip II the Spanish emperor, widower of Queen Mary of England. Puritan clergy found they were free to interpret the instructions of the Act of Uniformity with a surprising degree of creativity. Some wore the robes, some did not; some distributed eucharistic wine from a chalice, some used an ordinary cup; some baptised babies using the sign of the cross, some omitted it. And the more they got away with this piecemeal reformation, the more widespread it became.

Some who had refused or been refused parishes found themselves 'lectureships' – posts where their only job was to preach, not to lead services. Such jobs could provide extra work for vicars, but, as they did not involve following the Prayer Book, they also provided pulpits for men too radical to be ministers. Some lecturers were itinerant preachers paid by patrons: before he was eventually found an official post, John Foxe was employed by the Duke of Norfolk, while Miles Coverdale – the grand old man of the Reformation who had been Bishop of Exeter back in John Hooper's day, and a Bible translator – was employed by the puritan Duchess of Suffolk. Other lecturers were paid by town councils, such as Thomas Lever in Coventry, where he later became Archdeacon.

In London, St Antholin's Church had three lecturers, in addition to its minister, offering sermons and psalm-singing every day before work. Holy Trinity, Minories – one of Father Coverdale's haunts just outside the east wall of London – not only enjoyed extracurricular sermons but the rare privilege, thanks to a quirk of its history, of electing its own ministers. These churches became puritan anti-cathedrals, attracting ardent Protestants from all over London and its environs. The best-loved preachers attracted groups of devotees who followed them from church to church, where they preached without fear sermons that would have cost them their lives a few years previously, free from the uniform and paraphernalia of their persecuting enemy.

To most of us in the twenty-first century, the variety of religion that characterised these years will seem unobjectionable and far more natural than trying to impose one form of religion on an entire nation. For Elizabethans, it was unprecedented chaos. They did not generally have or expect anything like the freedom of choice that characterises the modern West, in their careers, partners, places of living, meals, rulers or religion, and whereas we tend today to assume that the main quality of a good society is freedom, to Tudor minds (that is to the classes of Tudor people whose opinions have been preserved) the main quality of a good society was order. The received wisdom, on every side, was that God had designed and constructed society, just as he ordered the human body and the material universe, everything with its proper place and function. In Bishop Hooker's words: 'If the moon should wander from her beaten way, the times and seasons of the year blend themselves by disordered and confused mixture … what would become of man himself whom these things now do all serve? See we not plainly that obedience of creatures unto the law of nature is the stay of the whole world?'[5] Given this outlook, the government could not be expected to tolerate the present degree of religious pluralism for long. So long as there was diversity, the Act of Uniformity was not being observed. Dissent would have to be dealt with.

The puritans themselves, radicals though they were, were no more tolerant at heart than the government. As much as they appreciated being tolerated for now, toleration was not what they wanted, either for themselves or for anyone else. The epithet was accurate: puritans wanted purity, not freedom or diversity. They wanted true reformed religion to be imposed on the whole realm, and unreformed religion to be eradicated. John Gough, the rector of St Peter's Cornhill and one of the preachers at St Antholin's, far from celebrating his own personal freedom of religion in these years of diversity, bewailed the toleration of papistry, looking ahead to the 'perfection of [Christ's] most holy and sincere religion and the flourishing thereof, with the utter overthrow of antichrist, and all his dirty dregs and sink of devilish dreams and filthy ceremonies'.[6] No concept here of simply providing reformed worship for those who want it: puritans agreed with Mary, you cannot provide good health without banishing the disease. Even while the puritans were refusing to conform, they complained about the lack of uniformity: since some wore a cap and surplice and some did not, complained Thomas Lever in Coventry, the attempt to impose them had created 'dissension and division in the body of Christ'. The vestiarian controversy was not a battle between freedom and authoritarianism, but between two uniformities.

Book of Martyrs

It was now, in 1563, that Foxe's phenomenal *Book of Martyrs* was published in English, after earlier, shorter versions in Latin. Formally known as *Acts and Monuments*, it was a masterpiece of Protestant propaganda, ensuring that Mary's burnings were not just a failure but catastrophically counterproductive. It not only documented the martyrdoms meticulously, its heroes dying with miraculous fortitude for the one true faith, but it set them as the culmination of a noble pageant of Christians who had been killed for their faith from the apostles onwards. Foxe showed readers that children of light always had been and always would be bloodily attacked by the powers of darkness. It has been called 'the most radical piece of historical revisionism ever undertaken',[7] turning upside-down the traditional understanding that the burning of heretics was a defence of the true church. Foxe showed that the Roman Catholic Church, itself riddled with evil and mired in false teaching, had always murdered true believers, taking up where the ancient Jews and Romans had left off. Hooper and his brothers and sisters had followed in the footsteps of Peter and Paul, and the Pope was the new Nero.

Foxe had been working on the subject for a decade and the book was 1,800 folio pages long; the second edition of 1570 was 2,300 pages and so outstripped the printer's paper supply that he had to paste together smaller pages to complete it. Despite its size the *Book of Martyrs* sold very well, and eventually every Elizabethan church was required to have a copy, making it the most widely available book to English readers besides the Bible and Prayer Book – and to non-readers it offered vivid, graphic illustrations. It went on to become a second Bible in English homes, ensuring that the Catholic Church has so far never again been quite at home on English soil. It turned Mary's fires against her and scorched the earth.

The *Book of Martyrs* played a key part in Elizabeth's strategy to sell Protestantism to the English, stoking abhorrence of Catholicism. It showed that the religion of Mary was not just a false teaching to be corrected, but the antichrist, its advocates not just traditionalists but the army of the apocalyptic beast. This was a useful idea for Elizabeth, but it also caused her a huge amount of trouble, reinforcing the belief that every last vestige of popish tradition must be stripped from the church.

Foxe's story had other less deliberate morals to it too. One was that religion is not simply a national way of life after all, but a matter of personal allegiance. The *Book of Martyrs* told story after story of holy heroes who followed their own conscience against the authority of the church of their day, and the implication was clear that in

the same position we ought to do the same. Foxe was as committed
to the ideal of a monolithic church state as Elizabeth and Mary, but
his stories in effect made religion something more personal than
that; like Mary's fires, his stories demanded that every individual
make their own choice between the two churches that were vying
for their souls.

The *Book of Martyrs* also gave readers and hearers the impression
that real Christians do not persecute. This was the contradiction at
the heart of mainstream Protestantism. Foxe hated religious violence
and his number-one argument against the Church of Rome was that
it could not be the church described in the Bible because it had
been the scene of 'such killing and slaying, such cruelty and tyranny
shewed, such burning and spilling of Christian blood'.[8] And yet his
Protestantism was inescapably attached to the ideal of the state church
embracing an entire population. If you are committed to uniting
the nation in one faith, there comes a point when that is impossible
without coercion. If true Christian faith is obligatory, but it is antichristian to persecute, something has to give. The Separatists were to
find themselves on the sharp end of that contradiction and came up
with a solution.

Parker's Advertisements

The year 1563 brought a highwater mark in the fortunes of this first
wave of puritanism, with the Convocation of Canterbury. There was
considerable support among bishops and clergy for a motion to abolish all priestly robes, saints' days, organs, singing in parts and the sign
of the cross, and to deter worshippers from kneeling. It failed by one
vote, thanks to the manoeuvres of Archbishop Parker.

Then the Queen took the offensive. In January 1565, she instructed
Parker to take action against the religious 'varieties, novelties and
diversities' that were afflicting the realm. The archbishop compiled
a book of instructions for the church, insisting on strict adherence
to the Prayer Book everywhere, and that dissident ministers be disciplined. These rules had very little legal authority in Parker's own
name, so he needed the Queen to issue them in hers, but she did

not feel strong enough to attach her name to such an unpopular policy, and left him to publish them himself in 1566, under the conspicuously wimpish title *Advertisements* (i.e. 'notices'). These instructions cancelled all preaching licences but the most recent, so that they could be reissued to conformists only, and they required all ministers to declare their acceptance of the robes or be dismissed.

In March 1566, Parker along with Grindal, the Bishop of London, gathered the London clergy at Lambeth. (Grindal had negotiated a generous compromise with London puritans, but Parker overrode it.) The archbishop dressed a minister in regulation robes, set him on the ecclesiastical catwalk, and told each cleric to choose: conform to the model set before them or be discharged from ministry. Thirty-seven out of 110 refused to conform, and were suspended for a three-month cooling-off period.

There was uproar throughout the city. Some churches had lost all clergy three weeks before Easter. St Antholin's lost all its lecturers. Coverdale – whom Grindal had eventually taken pity on and given a post at St Magnus Bridgefoot – was one of nine or ten who had managed to absent themselves from the meeting and escape suspension, but Foxe seems to have been suspended. Even Parker himself lamented that London had lost its best ministers, as well as plenty who were 'but zealous, and of little learning and judgment'.[9]

The suspended Vicar of St Giles Cripplegate and St Antholin's lecturer, Robert Crowley, was arrested on 2 April for preventing lay clerks from entering St Giles in robes for a funeral service. A lecturer there, John Bartlett, was put under house arrest for refusing to stop preaching, whereupon sixty women went to Grindal's house to complain; he told them 'to send half-a-dozen of their husbands, and with them I would talk'. Women led lay protests against the suspensions: Grindal mentioned to Parker his problems with the 'womanish brabble', and was told that he had brought it on himself by his 'tolerations'.

On Palm Sunday, a member of the congregation at St Mary Magdalen's on Milk Street stole the wafer and wine while the minister was reading the lesson, to stop him presiding in his vestments. On the same day, at Little All Hallows on Thames Street, one of the main roads across London, a fight broke out. Other churches cancelled

Easter services to avoid such scenes. Parishioners of St Mildred's Bread Street, whose minister Thomas Earle was suspended, shipped in a non-puritan minister from elsewhere to serve Communion on the Sunday after Easter, and, when Earle and other local puritans tried to remove him, formed a bodyguard around him until he was finished. Grindal feared that 'many of the more learned clergy seemed to be on the point of forsaking their ministry'.[10]

Puritans issued a volley of tracts in protest at their oppression. Crowley wrote arguing that the monarch's job is to enforce God's law as set out in the Bible, so if she commands something that God has not commanded it is up to us to weigh up whether it is good or bad, and if bad – as in the vestments – to disobey and face the consequences. For this tract, Crowley's printer was put in prison.

Protestant leaders who watched the faltering progress of the English Reformation from abroad were dismayed. 'Where did such a Babylon ever exist?' wrote Beza, the Genevan church leader. Gualter of Zurich admonished the Bishop of Norwich, comparing the bishops to 'the faithless steward, who when he ought to have been feeding his household, riots and sports with the drunken and smites his fellow servants'. But these commentators did not necessarily support the suspended ministers either. Though the General Assembly of the Scottish Kirk urged English bishops not 'to trouble the godly for such vanities', Bullinger wrote from Zurich to bishops and puritans alike, saying that much as he disliked the vestments, he did not consider them prohibited to Christian ministers, so it was better to wear them than quit the work and leave it to less conscientious and more traditional ministers.[11]

As the three months wore on, as Parker had predicted, the suspended ministers and their families grew hungry. Grindal published Bullinger's letter saying the vestments were lawful, which eased consciences. Eventually twenty-three rebel ministers submitted, leaving fourteen permanently deprived. Crowley quit the ministry, while Earle bowed to its vestiarian demands, saying, 'We are killed in the soul of our souls for this pollution of ours.'[12] John Gough and his fellow St Antholin's lecturer John Philpot were taken forcibly to Winchester, cheered out of London by two or three hundred female supporters, who loaded them down with gifts of gold, silver, sugar and spice. One erstwhile

ardent puritan who had submitted went to preach at St Margaret Pat-
tens, Rood Lane, in his new surplice, on the evening of 3 June, 'and
a certain number of wives threw stones at him, and pulled him forth
of the pulpit, renting his surplice, and scratching his face'.[13] Coverdale,
having escaped suspension, quit his London church in order to keep
out of the firing line, but continued his lecturing in and around the
city. Some lay puritans, deprived of all other acceptable preachers, tried
to follow Coverdale from church to church. They called at his house
to find out where he would be preaching next, but such irregularity
alarmed him and he refused to tell them. Meanwhile, the church courts
fined these wanderers for not attending their parish churches.

The Parliament that met towards the end of 1566 might well have
pressed for a change in the vestments, except that all its energies went
into the more fundamental task of trying to persuade the Queen to
settle the questions of her marriage and her heir, in order to ensure
a Protestant succession. And so the conflict continued. Grindal felt
relieved to have reduced the rebellion of so many serious and celebrated clergy to more manageable proportions, but the movement
was not defeated. Arriving to preach at St Margaret Moses, Old Fish
Street, one Sunday in January 1567, the bishop was greeted by a crowd
of women who 'unreverently hooted at him with many opprobrious
words, and cried "Ware horns", for that he ware a cornered cap'. Mrs
Symsone, a woman whose husband was a tinker, was punished for
these insults by being made to sit for an hour on a pair of ladders set
in front of the church, but onlookers 'animated the lewd woman to
rejoice and praise the Lord for that he had made her worthy to suffer
persecution for righteousness'.[14]

The problem with vestments

'It is scarcely credible how much this controversy about things of no
importance has disturbed our churches,' said Grindal,[15] and modern
readers will tend to agree. What could possess puritans to make such
a fuss about a dress code?

One theory is that they were wrongfooted by the Queen: puritans
had all kinds of complaints about the church, but she chose vestments

as the battleground, to make their stand seem trivial. It did indeed suit Elizabeth to make the puritans look petty, but she did not do so without their help: by the time Parker told the London clergy to conform or depart, their protest was seven years old, and in that time they had chosen to focus a great deal of it on the vestments. One puritan boasted in 1563 that he had already preached against them six times.

One factor in the hatred of vestments was that they were the most inescapable part of Elizabethan religion. Unlike an objectionable phrase in the liturgy or a stained-glass image, the vestments were what congregations looked at throughout the whole time their minister was preaching, presiding, praying or baptising, and contaminated every moment of the service. Also, Protestantism was relentlessly forward looking and the alb and cope had been removed from churches once already. One might tolerate delays in reformation, but turning back was the grave sin of apostasy.

Another factor was, once again, Mary's bonfires. Throughout all the protests against 'the bloody beast's gear', we hear the impact of the three years of violence Protestants had lived through. For puritans, that persecution now defined Catholicism, and they allowed their own religion to become defined in opposition to Catholicism. They did not generally hate Catholic people, as a rule, or petition the government for reprisals, but they abhorred the religion itself to the pit of their being. Getting religion right for puritans was about eradicating every element of popery that had insinuated itself into the Christian tradition. The historian Michael Watts compared the offence of vestments to the way German Jews might feel returning home after the defeat of Nazism to find police officers dressed in SS uniforms. That is a great exaggeration, but it illustrates the truth that clothes are not just clothes, any more than a flag is just a cloth. Parker was asking his ministers to express mixed allegiances and submit to a double identity; and if they did so, this would make it harder to take a stand against him on other controversial matters.

Their abhorrence was magnified by a less obvious but very powerful factor: the apocalyptic outlook of Protestantism. The Bible seems to look forward to a final conflict between Christ and antichrist, the saints and the beast, in which, though Christ's victory is ultimately certain, antichrist's power will for a time be terrifying. It was a commonplace of Protestants that their own struggle fulfilled that prophecy. Bishop Grindal called the Pope 'the very antichrist and son of perdition of whom Paul speaks'. Gualter, the reformer of Zurich, told Queen Elizabeth on her accession that 'in this last time, wherein antichrist is putting forth all his powers in his last struggle', the Lord had sent Elizabeth, 'according to the prediction of the prophet'.[16] It took some theological nuance to see oneself fighting in the final, global, cosmic battle between God and Satan and yet to be comfortable wearing some of the uniform of the enemy – nuance of which the bishops were capable and the puritans were not.

The bishops submitted to the Queen for the sake of the unity and stability of the church. The puritans also wanted unity, but thought that it should happen through the government acting as a tool of religion, rather than vice versa. As they saw it, firmly in the Reformed tradition, the point of the state was to enforce Christian life and faith, to serve the interests of true religion; but every time they looked at a pastor in priest's clothing they saw the church being made subservient to political ends, God's religion being overwritten by the state, instead of enforced by it.

What were radical puritans to do then, those who could still not accept the vestments? They had lost many of their leaders: not only did the more fiery lay puritans reject the ministers who had conformed, but the ministers themselves seemed to find that once they were preaching in Parker's robes their own fires of nonconformity were somewhat dampened. Many puritans just continued to complain and campaign and pray for better times, and the majority of the deprived ministers accepted being silenced. But the most radical London puritans turned to a more extreme solution: the underground.

Their very idea of what a church is was subtly changing. For most people in England, as elsewhere, the church was the local building where people gathered for services, following the same pattern as every other parish in the land. But for London Protestants, that tie between church and the parish services had been weakened: they had quit those buildings in Mary's time, making church in taverns, ships and private houses, wherever true believers could gather together; and even since Elizabeth's accession they had neglected their own parishes and travelled about the city to find church wherever they could hear acceptable preachers. What was essential to church, it now seemed, was not place or building or state sanction; it was preaching, sacraments and pure worship – and the underground offered one more of those things than the parish church. Now that there were no undefiled ministers in the parish churches, the only way they could meet as a pure Christian church, free from the bloody beast's gear, was to arrange it themselves, preachers and people meeting illegally in private. As one of them, John Smith, would later have to explain to Bishop Grindal: 'When it came to this point, that all our preachers were displaced by your law … Then we bethought us what were best to do; and we remembered that there was a congregation of us in this city in Queen Mary's days.'[17]

And so the London underground church was revived, not to hold out against the flames of Rome this time, but against the Church of England.

4

A phoney wedding

A YEAR AFTER Archbishop Parker's rout of the puritan clergy of London, Thomas Bowland of Thames Street hired Plumbers' Hall on Anchor Lane, a narrow way running from Thames Street down to the river. Bowland booked the hall ostensibly for a wedding to be celebrated on Thursday 19 June 1567, but the sheriff had information that Bowland had a far more sinister purpose. He sent his men to investigate on the day, and sure enough they found neither bride nor groom, but a congregation of over a hundred people at prayer, using not the Elizabethan Prayer Book, but the Genevan Prayer Book written by the more progressive English church leaders in exile. About seventeen leading worshippers were arrested, the rest dispersed.

The Plumbers' Hall interview

The following day, Bishop Grindal interviewed seven or eight of the conventiclers, with the Lord Mayor, the Dean of Westminster and some aldermen. Afterwards, one of the men, William Nixon of Queenhithe, wrote up the encounter, the first known writing of the Separatist movement, and because of this the Plumbers' Hall meeting has become known as a foundational event in Separatist history. It was by no means the first though: Grindal told them, 'you have gathered together and made assemblies … many times'. The Privy Council had heard about the privy churches, and had instructed Grindal to take action against them. During the suspension crisis a year before, the bishop had been aware that 'many of the people … had it in contemplation to withdraw from us and set up private meetings', and although the outcome was not as bad as feared, he could only tell Bullinger back in August 1566 that 'most of them', not all, 'have now returned to a better mind'. It seems likely that ejected ministers started holding small meetings in their homes and the homes of their followers straightaway, and now a year later, their numbers having grown so large that they were hiring a hall, they were becoming hard to ignore. A late source, but one that might be citing reliable information, tells us that a month before the Plumbers' Hall arrests 'a congregation, with Richard Fitz their minister, was surprised ... and committed to Bridewell'.[1] It was only the prisoners from Plumbers' Hall who kept a record of their interview with Grindal though.

The three prisoners that talked most in the interview were Robert Hawkins, William White who was a well-to-do baker of St John's Street in the north-west corner of London, and Nixon, 'a busy fellow' and 'full of talk', according to Grindal.

For the first few minutes of the interview, Grindal, in the transcript, sounds like the lord of the realm that he is, dealing with offenders, but he soon reverts to his preferred tone, that of a pastor, as he calls back his lost sheep. Above all, he sounds like a moderate trying to reason with extremists who is continually outpaced not so much by their arguments as by the sheer force of their beliefs. He was caught unhappily between practices that he did not much like but accepted out of respect for his godly Queen, and unruly radicals who, sharing his dislike of these practices, considered him to have struck a bargain with antichrist. He was uncomfortably aware that the men before him were brothers who had kept faith through the ascendancy of the bloody bishops of Rome, and that he had become the persecuting bishop himself. The prisoners did not miss the irony either.

Grindal tried to get the 'ancientest' to speak for them, John Smith of Distaff Lane, who had been a member of the London underground in Mary's time, but the younger hotheads took over, complaining that their parish churches were polluted by superstitious popish uniforms. Grindal replied that he personally disliked the cope and surplice too, but they were 'things indifferent', neither commanded nor forbidden by God. Puritans in general were suspicious of the concept of anything being indifferent – if the Bible is God's blueprint for the church then anything not commanded is unchristian. These interviewees argued that even if the vestments had originally been indifferent in themselves, the church authorities had silenced those who would not wear them, and so revered clothes more than the word of God, making them idols.

Hawkins reminded the bishop that Christians must disobey laws that contradict God's law. He referred Grindal to the revered heroes of Foxe's *Book of Martyrs*: they 'died for standing against popery, as we do now'. The puritans complained that the Church of England had turned from the ways of the Reformed churches in Germany, Switzerland and elsewhere. Grindal pointed out that these Reformed churches remained in solidarity with the Church of England, so it was the conventiclers who were out on a limb. The prisoners changed tack: foreign churches are irrelevant; the Bible must overrule any human authority.

'Will you be judged by the learned in Geneva?' asked Grindal, citing the most progressive. 'They are against you.'

'We will be judged by the word of God,' replied Hawkins.

Grindal responded that even heretics support their errors from their own reading of Scripture, but to the puritans' ears, the bishop was simply repeating what his predecessor said to Protestants when he burned them for believing the Bible. 'When [popish bishops] cannot maintain their doings by the scriptures ... then they make the mayor and aldermen their servants and butchers, to punish them that they cannot overcome by scripture,' said Nixon, leaving the bishop, mayor and aldermen present to draw the obvious conclusion.

'Good Lord,' cried the mayor, 'how unreverently do you speak!' Grindal said he had heard no one address officials with less respect in his eight years as bishop.

We see the narcissism of small differences here. Despite the multitude of differences between Reformed and Catholic Christianity – theological, structural, ideological, political – and the fact that the single point of issue between the Church of England and other Reformed churches was some clothing, this one difference put the Church of England on the Catholic side of the chasm, in the eyes of these conventiclers. They use the words 'pope' or 'popish' eleven times in the recorded interview; in one case they are referring to the Roman Catholic Church, in every other they refer to the Church of

England. Their view of religion was so free of shades of grey that this one spot turned white to black.

Similarly, their experience of prison, rather than making them rethink their separation, had confirmed that they were still dealing with antichrist: now, just as under Mary, 'the saints are persecuted'. And yet, compared to Mary's regime, or to the extermination of Protestants now being visited on the Netherlands by the Spanish, Grindal was slow to anger and abundant in mercy. He was instructed by the Privy Council, and by his own inclinations, to try 'to move [them] to be conformable by gentleness', but all the prisoners themselves experienced was another attempt to force them to bow the knee to antichrist.[2]

Historians have debated whether these conventiclers had written off the Church of England as a false church or remained a nonconformist part of it – whether they were strictly speaking Separatists or not. There is not enough data to be definite, but my impression is that the movement drifted or hardened from puritanism into Separatism over time. When later Separatists such as Robert Browne and Robert Harrison and their followers founded a church, it was clear to all concerned that they were deliberately rejecting the Church of England as a false church and joining the true church. In contrast, the London ministers who started leading secret meetings in 1566 had held on to their livings in the Church of England for as long as possible before being forced out of them. And where later Separatists such as John Greenwood renounced their ordination in the antichristian Church of England and were ordained in the true Separatist church, the radicals of 1566 simply took their existing ministry underground.

And yet, although meeting privately did not necessarily entail writing off the whole Church of England, it seems clear that the longer they kept at it, the harder it became to imagine rejoining the unreformed parish churches, and the more antichristian that whole system seemed. Radical thought followed radical action. We see a flash of this in the Plumbers' Hall interview. Hawkins tells the bishop, with hearty approval, that he heard one deprived minister say 'that he had rather be torn in a hundred pieces than to communicate with you'.[3] Being out of communion with the Church of England meant rejecting it as a false church, so this was thoroughly Separatist language. It was the only instance of such language in their whole conversation, so we seem to see the radicalism that would later dominate their thinking creeping in here.

The bishop and the Privy Council were torn about how to deal with the conventiclers. Neither wanted to be persecuting anyone, certainly not Protestants. They believed they were better than that, and this was one of their best proofs that the Protestant faith was the true one. And yet the job of the church was to unite society in that faith, so if some refused to be united they had to be forced. The interviewees were taken back to prison, but released some time later that year.

John Browne and Mr Pattenson

The meeting at Plumbers' Hall, however, was just one manifestation of an epidemic. The underground worshippers continued to meet in large numbers in fields, houses and warehouses. One service was surprised on a ship in St Katherine's Pool, to the east of the Tower of London.

Grindal reckoned the ringleaders were four or five of the London ministers who had been deprived in 1566 and that they ordained new ministers too, perhaps because their ministers were increasingly in prison. Further arrests brought in two more ministers, John Browne and Mr Pattenson, men who, like Coverdale, were sponsored by Katherine Bertie, the Duchess of Suffolk and resident of the Minories. The Duchess had been an exile in Queen Mary's time, fleeing the country in disguise, pursued through Germany by the Queen's agent, ending up a guest of the King of Poland, her 'calamity' later preserved in a ballad that was still sung in the eighteenth century, and she returned to England in 1559 as a fierce critic of Elizabethan religious policy. Browne and Pattenson are thought to have been in Strasbourg with her. Browne – not to be confused with the Robert Browne who will be a major character later in our story – seems to have emerged as a leading figure in the underground church, if the Elizabethan chronicler John Stow was right in saying the conventiclers were called Brownings after him. Browne's arrest was made while he was leading worship in a chopper's house in Thames Street, Stow tells us, and the chopper was taken too.

We do not know in what circumstances Pattenson was seized, but he had hardly gone to great lengths to avoid the risk, having sent a letter to Grindal calling him 'an antichrist, and a traitor to God and [his] prince, and an heretic'. Like the Plumbers' Hall prisoners, Pattenson was good enough to leave us a record of his interview with the bishop, which took place in September 1567. The report tells us that Grindal reminded Pattenson that Archbishop Parker had suspended his licence to preach. 'But the archbishop of archbishops hath not suspended me from preaching, but continueth his commandments to me still,' replied Pattenson. 'I may not disobey him to obey you.' When Grindal confronted Pattenson about the irregularity of preaching without a parish, Pattenson's reply was the same as John Wesley's to the same accusation two centuries later – 'The world is my parish' – if not so quotably worded: he said that his cure was 'wheresoever I do meet with a congregation that are willing to hear the word of God preached at my mouth'. Before this interview, the Duchess of Suffolk had visited Pattenson and told him she would petition Grindal for his release. The bishop now told Pattenson his release depended on an undertaking to stop preaching and administering sacraments. Pattenson angrily refused, and Grindal warned him, 'I could keep you in prison this seven years and I list, for saying I am a traitor to God and to my prince.' 'You know not,' said Pattenson, 'whether you shall live seven days or not.' Pattenson was returned to the Gatehouse jail in Westminster, now in close confinement; that is, with the freedom to move around the prison rescinded.

Pattenson's enmity towards Grindal was greater than anything we see in the Plumbers' Hall interview. For the Plumbers' Hall prisoners, it was simply the vestments and rituals of the Church of England that were antichristian; for Pattenson this made Grindal antichristian himself: 'You use things accursed and abominable, whereby you yourself are made abominable before God also.' He even refused to drink Grindal's wine, explaining, 'I thought him to be accursed before God, and therefore I ought not to eat or drink in such a man's house.' Pattenson's attitude to the episcopal office is in stark contrast with White's, who in 1571 was willing to address Bishop Jewel as 'beloved father in the Lord Jesus', though not as 'my lord'. And yet despite the extremity of Pattenson's attitude to Grindal himself, he had not developed a fully Separatist stance towards the church. He had not renounced his ordination – by Grindal – but, on the contrary, cited it as his ministerial credentials, and talked about his ministry as if he were a kind of unofficial special-category pioneer minister within the Church of England.[4]

Further arrests

In late 1567 or early 1568, a meeting was discovered in a minister's house in a hidden alley off Pudding Lane, and seven people were committed to the Compter in the Poultry, one of two London prisons by that name (also written as 'Counter'). In February 1568, news reached the Spanish ambassador, Don Diego Guzmán de Silva, of this 'newly invented sect, called by those who belong to it "the pure or stainless religion"': a meeting of 150 people had been raided by 40 soldiers. According to de Silva's account, the preacher wore a white cloth – odd for a movement whose defining point was hatred of white robes – and spoke from a makeshift pulpit of half a tub. Worshippers brought food and divided it among poorer members, as the first church had done in the book of Acts. Only five were arrested, and the bishop appointed a couple of more reliable ministers to visit them in prison and try to convert them. A few weeks later, the ambassador heard the news that six more had been arrested at an equally large service, recording (very generous) estimates that the underground church had five thousand members.

The ambassador found Grindal's lenience remarkable. He ascribed it to the scandal that would be caused if London's jails were crammed with hundreds of Protestants, and to the influence of the dissenters' friends in high places. He might also have mentioned the fact that Grindal himself had only ten years ago been in exile in Germany, escaping the Bishop of London's attacks on Reformed believers, and was profoundly unhappy to find himself playing Bloody Bonner, persecuting men and women who were not even heretics but his brothers and sisters – some of them his fellow former exiles – and persecuting them in defence not of the gospel but of popish paraphernalia. On the Sunday before Lent, 29 February, the bishop was told that the conventiclers were meeting at Mountjoy Place, and declined even to interrupt their service.

On Tuesday 4 March, one day after a service was discovered in Westminster, the sheriff's men found seventy-seven people at prayer in the house of James Tynne, a goldsmith who lived a mile to the west of London near the Strand in the parish of St Martin-in-the-Fields. They included William White and William Nixon from the Plumbers' Hall crowd, John Smith the 'ancientest' of that group, and Thomas Bowland who had booked the hall – most of those interviewees in fact, apart from Robert Hawkins. According to Stow, just three of the worshippers were jailed, in the Gatehouse, Westminster; but if so, the others were arrested again soon afterwards, because Grindal says that by April 1569 this group had been in prison for a year.

The worshippers found at Tynne's house also included a man whose previous persecutions had been immortalised in Foxe's *Book of Martyrs*: John Bolton, a silk weaver from Reading. Foxe said Bolton had been arrested in the first year of Mary's reign, because being openly Protestant he was wrongly suspected of nailing an attack on the Mass to the church door. He had been brought before Stephen Gardiner, the Bishop of Winchester, who tried to dissuade him from his heresies, but Bolton 'most boldly reproved the said bishop to his face'. As a result, he was put on bread and water, and kept in a dungeon with 'a marvellous evil scent'. He was locked in the stocks for days on end, and chained for good measure, and the jailer's family repeatedly threw fireworks into the cell. His neighbours brought food and drink for him, which the jailer either ate with his family or gave to the dogs before his eyes, 'whereby the said poor John Bolton was enforced (alas! the pity) to eat what cannot be named for hunger'. A collar maker who had been mentally damaged by his imprisonment attacked Bolton with his awl and scarred him permanently, and Bolton himself finally succumbed to 'ravings and strange fantasies'. He was released, as a result, after sixty-two weeks, and joined the exiles in Geneva. Foxe had some of his account from Bolton himself, finding him still 'weak and feeble' from his sufferings. (An alternative version of Bolton's story came from a Catholic priest in Reading, Thomas Thackham, who said Bolton was arrested for insulting the Queen while feigning madness, and that he (Thackham) paid the bail, which Bolton skipped. A third version, from the actual writer of the attack for which Bolton was arrested, John Moyer, is that Thackham got Bolton released by persuading him to submit to Catholicism, after which Bolton fled to Geneva in shame – a proleptic accusation, as his later story will show.) In 1568, Bolton lived in Long Lane, Smithfield, just outside the city walls to the north.[5]

A visit to Scotland

The movement was not, as the Privy Council had hoped, being overcome by gentleness, and early in 1568 it seems that Grindal came up with a promising idea to get rid of it: it could go to Scotland. When the bishop had interviewed the Plumbers' Hall conventiclers, he argued that the foreign Reformed churches shared some of the Church of England's alleged imperfections, and White replied, 'The Church of Scotland hath the word truly preached, the sacraments truly ministered, and discipline according to the word of God.' Grindal had no answer to that. After the latest arrest, though, it seems he had come up with one: go there then.

The prisoners were interviewed by William Cecil, the Queen's chief minister, and then, so de Silva reports, were banished from England. Grindal's biographer John Strype, who had access to the bishop's papers, says the arrangement was consensual, the conventiclers being 'encouraged to go and preach the Gospel in Scotland' and given references commending their fervent Protestantism to the Scottish government. From the perspective of the conventiclers themselves, perhaps they went considering the possibilities – ten years after the end of the last great English Protestant exile – of another exile to a country with a properly reformed church, escaping persecution as in Queen Mary's time, and ready to report to their fellow worshippers whether they should emigrate en masse. The results were disappointing for everyone.

The Scottish Church had been reformed in 1560 under the leadership of John Knox, who was by then no longer welcome in Elizabeth's England, thanks to his spectacularly ill-timed treatise *The first blast of the trumpet against the monstruous regiment of women*, which urged subjects to rise up against the unnatural rule of the queens of England and Scotland (both Catholic), but was published months before Elizabeth's accession. Knox therefore returned to Scotland and took part in a successful uprising against Mary Stuart. He helped to direct Parliament's reform of the church, applying the presbyterian system of Calvin's Geneva – an egalitarian network of local preachers and lay elders – to the entire national church, and outlawing the Catholic traditions that puritans were protesting about in England.

The English dissidents went to Scotland in March 1568, but did not feel the call into exile. Arriving shortly before Easter, they enjoyed a friendly personal welcome from Knox, whom they had already written to from prison, but were disgusted to see Scots going to church in Dunbar with bare feet on Good Friday, to 'creep to the cross', a tradition banned in England. According to Strype, the English could not stand the cold. For whatever reason, they were back in London in the first week of May, and never returned. Their Scottish exile had lasted about a month. The London conventicles carried on as ever and the usual suspects were soon back in prison. Grindal suggested to Cecil that it might be time for them 'to be called again before you'.

The conventiclers were surprised to receive a letter from Knox on their return from Scotland, telling them that he disapproved of their separation from the Church of England and wished that their 'consciences had a better ground'. Though he was noted for his outspoken candour in theological disagreement, Knox had waited until the English left before criticising them – perhaps expecting to have more time with them in Scotland, perhaps needing time to get his head around the novel theological problem of those who had an immoderate attachment to his own principles of pure reformed worship. Knox said he agreed in abominating the 'knackles of popery' and their imposition on English Protestant ministers; but given that they were in fact imposed, the question was then whether we should remain in fellowship with all who preach the truth or should 'refuse to hear the message of salvation at such men's mouths as please not us in all things'.

One of the Londoners, unnamed, replied on behalf of their congregation, denying that they led people away from hearing the message of salvation – they heard it in their own services, he said. Since the conventiclers had among themselves a properly reformed congregation, he said, 'to come back from an Apostolical Church', 'to go back to mixtures', would be a retrograde step, putting a hand to the plough and then turning back. The writer was clearly saddened by Knox's letter, and told him 'if I had known the tenor of it, when I was with you, I would have said many words that I never spake', but concluded that when the approbation of God was to be had or lost, the approbation of men was of no account.

The letter to Knox, nine or ten months after the Plumbers' Hall incident, gives us the first explicit statement of full separation from the Church of England in the writings of the movement. The writer says 'we [do] not communicate with other churches' in England and 'we utterly refuse to hear … all those that do maintain this mingle-mangle ministry'. They were no longer just meeting separately to avoid the impurities accepted in other English churches, but were a Separatist church that rejected the Church of England as a false church.

The trip to Scotland was not a complete failure from Grindal's point of view. The experience led one member, John Evans, to rethink his Separatism. He quarrelled violently with the other Separatists, and they excommunicated him. This seems like another exhibition of fully-fledged Separatism, if the church excommunicated Evans for returning to the Church of England. Evans made his peace with the state church and, says the writer to Knox, 'now is in great favour of the bishop, which never was before, and hath told him and all others that you are flat against us and condemn all our doings'. 'Since our departure from you,' he told Knox, 'more enemies we have a great many.'[6]

Even while this Scottish trip was taking place, it had brought no peace to Grindal's watch. On Easter Sunday, a meeting of 140 conventiclers was surprised in the home of the bishop's own servant, which must have surprised the bishop himself. A week afterwards, more were found in a carpenter's house in Aldermanbury.

In June 1568, the Spanish ambassador reported that as many as four hundred were discovered in one meeting, but once again only six were arrested. That month the Lord Mayor told his constables to arrest unlicensed preachers.

The chronicler William Camden mentions the private churches existing in 1568, suggesting that the movement was led by four men named Colman, Button, Hallingham and Benson, who he says were imprisoned for their dissent. The only other thing we know about any of those four is that Christopher Colman and John Benson appear on a list of thirty-one conventiclers released from Bridewell prison in April 1569.

William White wrote a tract justifying the illegal conventicles of the underground church, *A brief of such things as obscure Gods glory*. It exists only in manuscript in a collection of puritan and Separatist writings called *The Seconde Parte of a Register*, which is undated, and its argument is strikingly similar to that of Robert Browne's celebrated Separatist work of 1582, *A Treatise of Reformation without Tarying for Anie*. After the standard puritan complaints about 'the remnants of antichrist's priesthood' in the Church of England, he imagined a reader agreeing that reformation is commanded by God, then adding, 'but it must be done of the preachers and magistrates; but the common people must not meddle therewith'. White asked whether Christians are exempted from God's commands if preachers and magistrates do not lead the way.

> Shall we be excused by saying the magistrates would not suffer us to do his will? All this will be none excuse for us, it will be said to us: 'Search the scriptures, for in them you think you have eternal life and they are they which testify of me,' and we shall not be judged by our magistrates by the words that they speak.[7]

This argument, that religious obedience is owed to God, not the Queen, was a ground on which the Elizabethan bishops themselves had dissented from the Catholic state of Mary and separated from her church, so the Protestant state church had its work cut out trying to reason its own dissenters out of their dissent. White was arrested again early in the summer of 1568 and this time kept there for nearly a year.

Grindal reported the crisis to Bullinger, the church leader in Zurich, in June 1568:

> Some London citizens of the lowest order together with four or five ministers, remarkable neither for judgment or learning, have openly separated from us; and sometimes in private houses, sometimes in the

fields, and occasionally even in ships, they have held their meetings and administered the sacraments. Besides this, they have ordained ministers, elders, and deacons, after their own way, and have even excommunicated some who had seceded from their church.[8]

However many had 'returned to a better mind', the bishop now had a full-scale Separatist movement on his hands.

5

'Unspotted lambs of the Lord'

WHO WERE THESE conventiclers? Our evidence is sketchy and often contradictory. Grindal told Bullinger that they numbered 200; the Spanish ambassador said 5,000. Grindal was the better informed, but was clearly playing down the defection, just as de Silva repeated gloating exaggeration of the Protestant Church's troubles. More credibly, the Separatist who wrote to Knox spoke of their being 'many a hundred', and another in later years recalled their being 'at least a thousand'.[1] Robert Harrison, looking back in 1582, said that a large number joined the movement at first, but that persecution 'discouraged many'.

Demographics

Though Grindal said they were citizens of the lowest order, the few of their jobs we know of tend to suggest the class of artisan rather than unskilled worker – goldsmith, carpenter, baker, weaver. His own servant would hardly be of the lowest order either, though a chopper might. William White was sufficiently wealthy to procure several lecturers for his parish. On a 1571 petition, a third of the twenty-seven supplicants could write their own name, which puts the conventiclers well above the national average for literacy, when only one English person in eight could do so.

Grindal said that they consist of 'more women than men'. This was yet another way of playing down the significance of the movement, and though female protesters had played an important role in the vestments controversy, we do not see much difference between the numbers of men and women here. The one full list of people found at an illegal service, at James Tynne's house, contains about thirty-eight women and thirty-nine men, though the names are not all clear. The one list any of them made of their own names, on a petition to the Queen from Richard Fitz's congregation, contains approximately fourteen women and twelve men, while also mentioning three men in prison.

Contemporaries did not agree on what to call the movement. In their own writings they generally called themselves the true church – this is why the naming of most new denominations falls to their detractors – or 'the privy [i.e. private] church'. Others apparently called them 'Brownings', or, reflecting the way they talked about themselves, 'the apostolic religion', 'the pure or stainless religion'. Most commonly, they were called 'puritans'; most colourfully, Stow calls them 'unspotted lambs of the Lord'.

Stow also called them 'Anabaptists', lumping them together with the continental radicals who denied the very concept of the state church. This was an inaccurate term of abuse, because the London conventiclers merely wanted the state church to be reformed, not abolished. They looked like Anabaptists from a hostile distance, because they met privately and voluntarily; but they did so not on principle. They did not believe that religion was a private matter. Even at their very hottest, their condemnations of the English Church never once questioned the concept of a state church itself. Though they condemned Grindal's persecution, that is because it was directed at true Christians; we can be sure, in the unlikely event they were put in charge of reforming the church themselves, they would resort to coercion. In the oft-quoted phrase of the historian B.R. White, they were 'hasty puritans', wanting the same kind of national church as other puritans, but starting without them. Even the most radical of Separatists were keen to distinguish themselves from the detested Anabaptists.

Considering so much of our information about the Separatists comes from reports of their services being disturbed by the authorities, even these are extremely incomplete. The reports come to us largely through three sources: state papers (which mention two occasions); the Spanish ambassador's dispatches (three); and the *Memoranda* of John Stow (seven). Across those three sources there is a clear duplication of only one event – the state papers and Stow both mention the arrests at James Tynne's house – and here they differ on the date and number of attendees: Stow is a day late, and numbers them at '60 and odd' while the state papers list seventy-seven by name. The ambassador's accounts are clearly exaggerated and depend on hostile hearsay. Stow had connections with the ambassador – in 1569 he was questioned by the Lord Mayor about distributing a manifesto against the Queen, which de Silva had printed – but they are obviously independent sources, and, though Stow clearly enjoyed stories about puritans behaving badly, his accounts of these conventicles are restrained, erring, in the example we know of, on the side of understatement. Considering this restraint and the small overlap in their accounts, it seems likely that they fail to capture the full scale of the movement and that there were plenty of interrupted services that none of our sources reported, and of course many more services that never came to the attention of the authorities at all.

What connection these various worship meetings had with each other is uncertain, but the belief of twentieth-century historians that they were divided into distinct congregations from the start seems to be incorrect. Albert Peel argued that Pattenson must have pastored a different congregation to the one found at Plumbers' Hall, because their conversation with Grindal included no mention of their having a minister, which 'can hardly be imagined' if they had one. This conclusion from silence is contradicted by what Grindal did say (and the group's scribe accepted): 'You have gathered together and made assemblies … ministering the sacraments among yourselves.' Since there were evidently ministers in this network administering sacraments, the fact that Pattenson was a minister is no evidence that he led a separate group.[2]

Another reason for seeing the movement as a single network is that when the authorities took the names and addresses of the seventy-seven people found at Tynne's house, they came from across the whole spread of London, and beyond the city walls in every direction – from Islington to Southwark, from St Katherine's Pool to St Martin-in-the-Fields – and include a number of people on either side of their later theological divide, so it seems that at this point there was one community of dissidents across London and the surrounding area, meeting in different places, hearing different preachers, but drawing from a single pool.

Bonham and Crane

By April 1569, some of the conventiclers had been in prison for a year. At last, some, including White, were formally charged under the Act of Uniformity, and, White says, 'almost outlawed'. But it seemed obvious to Grindal that persecution was doing nothing to teach them conformity, and, discussing the matter with less radical puritans, he was urged, and in turn he urged the Privy Council, to try gentleness again and release the prisoners without conditions, on the conviction 'that taste of liberty and experience of your clemency should in time work good obedience in them, which by compulsion of imprisonment could not be wrought'. The Council consented, so long as Grindal made it clear to the conventiclers that if they reoffended they would face exemplary punishment.[3]

So, in April 1569, Grindal once more released all of them that were in Bridewell, twenty-four men and seven women, including Smith, White, Bowland, Hawkins, Nixon, Colman, Benson and Bolton. There seems to have been a major miscommunication over this though, or at least each party told very different stories to the Privy Council. The bishop said he had made it clear that they were freed on the understanding that they would give up their underground religion, while the Separatists insisted that he had appointed two preachers to lead them, assured them of toleration and given them permission to baptise in their own way. The two preachers were Nicholas Crane, who had apparently been removed from the parish church of Deptford in the purge of 1566, and William Bonham, another deprived minister whose preaching licence Grindal did indeed restore at this point. These two leaders combined their underground ministry with preaching and presiding at Holy Trinity, Minories, so were not fully fledged Separatists. Bonham was then arrested for using the Geneva Prayer Book in a wedding and a baptism. Crane was also arrested.

With these two in prison, their congregation complained to the Privy Council that the bishop had broken his promise of toleration, so the Council demanded an explanation from Grindal. This embarrassment was the final straw for Grindal, who wrote to the Council on 4 January 1570 with his version of events, and this time, far from pleading clemency, added: 'All the heads of this unhappy faction should be with all expedition severely punished, to the example of others, as people fanatical and incurable: which punishment, if it proceed by order from your lordships, shall breed the greater terror.'[4]

In his decency and fellow feeling, Grindal had done everything possible to bring the conventiclers into unity with the established faith with the minimum of coercion, using arguments and urgings and mercy. The result was a resounding demonstration that arguments and urgings and mercy do not produce unity. Happily for Grindal, less happily for the underground church, they then became someone else's problem, as in 1570 the Queen translated him to York.

Divisions

Serious splits appeared in the London Separatist movement. Our information about this is as limited as any other aspect, coming largely from one letter by the Separatist minister John Browne. Writing on 18 March of an unspecified year, he addressed a group who had split away from his own church, reminding them 'you have said you would never join with us again'. Browne lamented, 'The enemies rejoice and say that you have a church alone by yourselves, and Fitz hath another by himself etc. So that they account 4 or 5 churches divided one from another, so that one of them either cannot or will not join one with another.' Before this, Browne says, the underground church had been 'a company ... gathered together out of divers places into one fellowship'.[5]

We gather from this that there had been several splits, with Browne leading one group, and Fitz another, and Browne's correspondent a third. It seems likely that one question that divided them was Separatism: whether they were simply worshipping apart from their sluggish brothers and sisters in the parish church, or had renounced them as a false church and started their own. Robert Harrison in 1582 recalled the different streams of the London movement, 'some only making

51

conscience at the cap and surplice, and therein stood all their religion', while others 'entering into that [Separatist] way, despised all other'.[6] Future generations of Separatists talked of Fitz as the Separatist leader of his day – Bradford in New England traced the pilgrims' movement back to 'a separated church whereof Mr Fitts was pastor'.

However, Browne's letter shows that there was more to their divisions than differing degrees of separation. While Browne seemed to have no clear idea why the people he addressed had separated from his church, he assumed it was 'to forsake the cross', i.e. to avoid persecution. He said that they had previously all suffered together for the gospel and suggested that his readers were now meeting in a small separate group so as to be less noticeable 'for fear of pricking with the thorns'. They had put their hand to the plough and looked back.

In a pattern that was to be repeated throughout the Separatist movement, Browne found himself repeating the same rhetoric to those who split from him as the establishment used about his own Separatism: this

> private assembling of yourselves together … hindereth God's glory … God our master and owner of this building will allow no such private building and builders, which forsaking their place in the public building and edifying of God's house do build alone … And it is not a small matter dear brethren (for so in hope we call you) to divide yourselves from a Christian congregation … except it be a small thing to divide yourselves from salvation which you do in dividing yourselves from the church of God.[7]

Richard Fitz's church left a number of documents, either in the hands of Archbishop Parker or in collections made by sympathetic puritans. One is a short statement by Fitz of 'The order of the privy church in London', making the familiar point that a true church is known by its free preaching, pure sacraments and discipline. Another document is a petition written in 1571 to which we will come later. All the other Fitz documents are versions of one piece of writing, a declaration of Separatism, which seems to have been originally recited in Separatist services, and then adapted more than once as a tract in defence of Separatism. In it, the Separatists declared that 'the church of the traditioners' was compromised by the rags and trash of antichrist, but

I am escaped from the filthiness and pollution of these detestable traditions ... I have joined, in prayer and hearing God's word, with those that
have not yielded to this idolatrous trash, notwithstanding the danger for
not coming to my parish church etc., therefore I come not back again
to the preachings etc. of them that have received these marks of the
Romish Beast.

If, said each speaker, he or she were to come back again, 'I should
forsake the union wherein I am knit to the body of Christ'. After reciting it together in services, Archbishop Parker tells us, members swore
individually, 'and after took the Communion for ratification of their
assent'.[8]

The Separatism of the Fitz church was more strongly worded than
any other we have seen so far, and others may have moved in the
same direction. Yet its attitude to the puritans who remained in parish congregations was subtle. A version of the declaration that was
published as a tract starts by bidding those puritans farewell, but in
the same breath calls them 'my dear brethren' and 'you that believe
in Jesus Christ'. Later Separatists would consider members of the
Church of England antichristian, but this writer, even as he warns
readers that they 'do but mock with God' by attending their parish
church, calls them 'dearly beloved in the Lord'. It is the clergy who
submit to canon law that draw his condemnation: 'you calking cav-
illers, you mongrels, slidebacks, hirelings and timeservers, with your
trifling toys which be but apish'.[9]

That splits should eventually have developed in the London
underground church is entirely concordant with what we know of
every later wave of the movement. Browne's letter tells us that they
happened, and that there were several, even if we know little for sure
about their nature. Before this point, all the information that we have
about the movement suggests a single network with several ministers
meeting in a variety of locations and worshipping together and separately, covertly and at risk of arrest, as spiritual brothers and sisters.

At the more dangerous end of the Elizabethan religious spectrum,
Edmund Bonner died on 5 September 1569 in the Marshalsea prison,
where he had spent the last nine years, and was buried under cover of
darkness. The man who commanded souls with fire had been jailed
after he refused to stop saying Mass, reportedly telling the Council,

'I possess three things: soul, body, and property. Of the two latter, you can dispose at your pleasure, but as to the soul, God alone can command me.' The Separatists, who wore their own sufferings as holy crowns, would undoubtedly have seen in Bonner's imprisonment and death the irresistible judgement of the Lord. Several of them would soon share his fate, though they could not understand it in the same way.

6

Rebellion and discipline

ALTHOUGH ENGLISH PROTESTANTS tended to look to Germany and Switzerland for spiritual direction and theological dialogue, the success of the English Reformation was even more closely connected to the fate of Dutch Protestantism. As the puritan MP Job Throckmorton put it, 'The very finger of God directs us to the Low Countries as though to say, "There only is the means of your safety."'[1]

The Marian exiles, whose reception by Reformed churches had such an impact on English religion, had numbered 800 individuals in total throughout Germany, Switzerland and the Netherlands, but in 1560 there were more English than that in Antwerp alone. Not only did such expats observe and generally admire the Dutch Reformed Church, but they were allowed to imitate it in their own churches in the Netherlands. Grindal, as Bishop of London, had had oversight of English churches overseas, and told the merchants' chaplain in Antwerp that he could dispense with the vestments and be selective in his use of the Prayer Book, out of respect for and solidarity with the Dutch. The Netherlands became a place where some hasty puritan ministers could go to exercise pure religion without the scandal of joining underground churches or the threat of prison.

Being part of the Hapsburg Empire, however, the Netherlands was ruled by Queen Mary's widower Philip II of Spain, who was as keen to extirpate heresy from his dominions as Mary had been from hers. He was urged by some of his allies to lead an international crusade against 'Calvinism' or Reformed Protestantism, and was suspected of wanting to add England to his empire, so events in the Netherlands aroused patriotic fear in English Protestants as well as religious fellow feeling. There was to be considerable contact between English and Dutch Protestants over the coming decades. The extent of Dutch influence on more radical English Protestantism is a matter of debate, but what is sure is that the English watched with trepidation as across the North Sea Reformed Christians were fighting for the survival of their faith against the unrivalled power of the Spanish Empire.

The Dutch revolt

In 1559, as Elizabeth was first imposing her reforms on the Church of England, Philip returned to Spain determined to strengthen and purify the Catholic hegemony of his empire. He renewed the Inquisition, which took an even more bloody form in the Netherlands than in Spain: it was a capital offence to own a Dutch Bible, to discuss Scripture with a layperson or to fail to report a Protestant, and Philip directed the bishops to wipe Protestantism out of the Netherlands. He persuaded the Pope to reorganise the Dutch Catholic Church, increasing the number of bishops and their power over the churches, transferring control of the bishops from the nobles to the king and increasing the revenue he got from them.

Dutch nobles resisted Philip's counter-reformation and on 5 April 1566 delivered a petition of 300 signatures to Philip's regent and half-sister the Duchess of Parma, pleading against the Inquisition as 'surpassing the worst barbarism ever practised by tyrants'.[2] The dismissive attitude of the court to the petitioners gave rise to their nickname *les Gueux* or *Guezen*, 'the Beggars', which the Dutch nobility defiantly appropriated. Reformed field preaching swept the Netherlands, with crowds of thousands gathering in the open air. The Duchess of Parma offered a reward of 700 crowns for each *haagpredikant* ('hedge pastor') delivered dead or alive, so supporters came armed. In August, the *Beeldenstorm* seized the country, traditional images, ornaments, vestments, altars, books and instruments being destroyed – sometimes, as in the cathedral in Antwerp, by the mob; sometimes, as in Delft, by leading citizens with the appropriate paperwork.

Philip responded to the Protestant insurgence in the Netherlands by sending an army of 10,000, soon growing to five times that number, under the Duke of Alba. And so the Dutch Protestant movement became a war of independence, under the leadership of William of Orange, aka William the Silent. Alba established the Council of Troubles to subdue the region and punish heretics and dissidents; over six years, the Council convicted 9,000 people, of whom 1,000 were executed. In 1569, Alba imposed a 10 per cent tax on the Netherlands (including foreign traders) to fund the occupation. Many Dutch people had by this point found asylum in England, 3,000 being settled in Norwich, where the economy had been suffering for the lack of Dutch trade, and they introduced their clothworking skills. Altogether, 100,000 people left the Netherlands to escape Alba, one of the largest displacements of people in the Reformation period.

Some English Protestants urged military intervention to relieve the Dutch. The diplomat Christopher Mont said it was inexcusable to be 'idle spectators and dissemblers in such vast profusion of innocent blood'. For Elizabeth, however, the fact that Dutch subjects were rebelling against their king was a greater offence than the persecution of Protestants, so she was reluctant to get involved. When William of Orange's offensive against Alba's forces in 1568 failed disastrously, Cecil warned Elizabeth that once the Dutch were crushed, the Spanish would be free to turn their attentions to England and that 'her security cannot have continuance if the planets keep their course'. Even then, though the Queen toyed with the idea of intervention, she made no move.[3]

The Northern Rebellion

The danger to England of developments in the Spanish Empire was brought to a head through Scotland. On 10 February 1567, a bomb exploded under the bedroom of the King Consort, Lord Darnley, the estranged husband of Queen Mary of Scotland. His body was found forty feet away under a pear tree, but the doctors who examined it declared that he had already been strangled before the explosion. Suspicions focused on Mary, and she did nothing to allay them by marrying her fellow suspect the Earl of Bothwell a few months later. The Pope broke off relations with Scotland, and rioters demanded Mary's burning. She was forced by the Protestant nobility to abdicate in favour of her one-year-old son, who became James VI, ruling with the advice of those Protestant nobles, which made the Calvinist revolution secure.

For many English Protestants, this was a clear victory for the Lord, who had dethroned a 'parricide and bloodsucking Medea' and strengthened true religion. Elizabeth, however, was horrified by her royal cousin's dethronement. 'We do not think it consonant in nature', she protested with a favourite metaphor, 'the head should be subject to the foot.' She talked unrealistically of invading Scotland to restore Mary, but even when Mary escaped to England, Elizabeth kept her dangerous cousin in custody.[4]

For the Spanish government, this was the perfect opportunity to rouse English Catholics to overthrow Elizabeth, replace her with Mary, restore the Catholic Church and re-establish Spanish influence. Having watched for a decade with growing disquiet as Protestantism bedded down in England, in November 1569, with Spanish support, the Dukes of Northumberland and Westmorland raised an army of 6,000 men for the campaign against Elizabeth. They tore up the English Bibles and Prayer Books in Durham Cathedral. Part of their army went to Hartlepool to join a landing of Spanish liberation forces, another went to Tutbury to release Mary. But the further south they went, the less support they found, and when they discovered that Mary had been moved from Tutbury, the revolt collapsed. Seven hundred commoners were executed, Elizabeth instructing that no village in the region be without a hanging and that the bodies be left till they fall to pieces. Two hundred of the gentry lost property.

This Catholic uprising was alarming for committed Protestants, with their memories of Mary Tudor's regime still warm, and with news of Spanish persecution coming constantly from the Netherlands. English Protestants were, in Cecil's word's, 'keeping from our borders the flame of the fires that are burning so near us'. Their deliverance from invasion was so unexpected, said Bishop Cox, 'it seemed as though the Lord of Hosts and Might had undertaken from his heaven the cause of his Gospel and fought, as it were, with his own hands'.[5]

The Northern Rebellion could hardly have done the puritan cause a greater favour. Puritanism was not only the opposite end of the religious spectrum to Catholicism: it was defined and driven by hatred of it. The uprising had more than ever made Catholicism look alien and dangerous: an invasion, with loyalties to Rome and Spain, not to the Queen of England. Pope Pius V only confirmed this in February 1570 by declaring Elizabeth deposed (the last papal deposition), forbidding Catholics to obey her, and excommunicating all who followed laws she had passed. Puritan intolerance seemed to have been vindicated, and if puritans had appeared rebellious and unruly, next to Catholics they looked rather less dangerous. Though they had the presumption to tell the Queen how to run her church and challenge her religious autocracy, there was little credible risk of their conspiring to overthrow her and no question whose side they would fight on in the event of invasion. The government made little attempt to impose the Prayer Book regulations on any puritans in the north or west of the kingdom, because Protestantism seemed so insecure that any help preaching against Catholicism had to be encouraged.

Cartwright and the Presbyterian movement

Against this background of an international clash between Christ and antichrist, many younger puritans found themselves driven further in their demands for the church. For them, vestments and the like were superficial issues, the fruits of deeper-rooted dysfunction; what was really wrong with the Church of England was its whole shape and organisation, which were still founded on unbiblical Catholic principles. Experience, the Bible and the example of other Reformed churches were in agreement: the men to lead the flock in paths of righteousness were godly ministers, chosen locally; and yet in England everything was controlled by the crown and the bishops, and ministers had too little influence over the parish. The Scots had joined the ranks of nations with a fully Reformed church organisation; so had the Dutch, and they were laying down their lives for it. How could the English, with the armies of antichrist surrounding them, put up with their church being half obedient to Christ? A much deeper reform was needed. In the later words of John Field, a curate of St Giles, Cripplegate, now about twenty-four, who had been helping Foxe with the second edition of the *Book of Martyrs*: puritans 'have made some ado about shells and chippings of popery, but that which beareth up antichrist chiefly, they have said little or nothing about'.[6]

The first star of the presbyterian movement for structural reformation was Thomas Cartwright. As the new Lady Margaret Professor of Divinity at Cambridge, Cartwright gave a series of lectures on the book of Acts in 1570, explaining to his students the differences in organisation between the New Testament church and the Church of England. In the days of the apostles, he said, instead of a hierarchy of bishops and their dependents ruling the nation, appointing ministers and answering to the crown, the church chose their own ministers and elders (*presbyteroi* in Greek), who were free to lead their flock as they saw fit, consulting with each other locally. Each church had ministers to preach and pastor, and a team of lay elders to govern the church and expel incorrigible sinners from the congregation. Deacons were not priests-in-waiting; they organised local poor relief. 'Bishop' (*episcopos*, literally 'overseer') was simply what New Testament writers called any local minister; 'archbishop' they had never heard of. This structure, Cartwright taught, was what the Bible says the church should be, but the authorities of the Church of England 'take away the reins of government out of the apostles' hands and put them in the archbishops' and archdeacons' hands'. This church was condemned by Scripture – by its absence from Scripture – and needed radical reform.[7]

What Cartwright advocated, in his calm, academic tone, was a religious and social revolution, giving local church leaders both far greater powers over local life and far greater freedom from the state, while also making them more accountable to some of their own parishioners. It would change the Church of England from a nation-wide hierarchy of government in the control of the Queen into a network of self-governing congregations.

Cartwright was a brilliant speaker, not excitable, but lucid, authoritative and radical. When he preached at Great St Mary's, it was said, 'grave men ran like boys in the streets to get places in the church' and the sexton removed the windows so the crowds outside could hear.[8] Cambridge University was the heart of puritanism outside London, with its concentration of theological students and anti-establishment academics. The combination of audience, speaker and subject threw Cambridge into uproar.

Cartwright's presbyterian programme was not original – much of its appeal was precisely that it would bring England into line with other Reformed churches. But where Cartwright broke new ground among puritans was in insisting that such reform was not just desirable but essential. A church cannot be truly Christian unless it conforms to the pattern set down in the Bible. The offices that the Church of England had added to the apostolic system were not just superfluous; rather, 'seeing that these functions … are not in the word of God, it followeth that they are of the earth and so can do no good but much harm in the church'. Just as vestments were antichristian because they were a Catholic tradition not sanctioned in Scripture, so archbishops and the like were 'drawn out of the Pope's shop', in the more colourful words of John Field, 'antichristian and devilish, and contrary to the scriptures'.[9]

And so a new kind of radical puritanism was unleashed: presbyterianism. Unlike the underground London church, it was a widespread national movement with influential support, and was driven by the clergy rather than the people. While the underground church was an exodus from the deficient Church of England, the presbyterian movement was a vigorous attempt to change the church's deficiencies. The underground worshippers were naturally sympathetic to the presbyterian programme, having put much of it into practice already – the independence, the lack of hierarchy, the discipline of the flock. A number of them became prominently involved in the presbyterian movement in London. On the other hand, Cartwright was keen to distance the movement from Separatism: 'We make no separation from the church,' he said; 'we go about to separate all those things that offend in the church.'[10]

The appeal of discipline

There is no word more characteristic of the presbyterian movement than 'discipline' – and there are few less likely to endear it to modern readers. The young presbyterian apologist Thomas Wilcox, curate of All Hallows, Honey Lane, said that there are three 'marks whereby a true Christian church is known': pure preaching, purely administered sacraments and 'severe discipline'. William White said that without right discipline, the church is 'disfigured and maimed' and has 'but half a Gospel'.[11] More positively, the later Separatist John Smyth sang of its joys:

> Oh Mr Ber[nard], if you knew but the comfort and power of the L[ord's] ordinances of admonition and excommunication … you would be so wonderfully ravished with the power of God's ordinances, that you would acknowledge the church to be terrible as an army with banners, and yet amiable and lovely, comely and beautiful.[12]

A church with true discipline did not just tell people how to live rightly; it imposed those rules on them, rebuking them when they stepped out of line, and if they continued unrepentant debarring them from Communion until they reformed. It might not be immediately obvious why the prospect of greater interference in the private lives of parishioners would be popular, but it was undoubtedly precious to the more radical puritans, lay people as well as clergy. One reason for this felt need was that Protestantism had raised the standard of active involvement of ordinary believers in their religion: true Christianity was not just about receiving the sacraments, but about reading the Bible, praying, having faith, living a holy life. It was a demanding vocation, and so it helped to be part of a group where people held each other to account, corporate discipline enabling personal self-discipline.

There was a political dimension to the appetite for discipline too. Presbyterianism was a creed of the rising middle classes, its discipline promoting the virtues that led to success in the growing arenas of industry and commerce, rooting out drunkenness, dishonesty, idleness, swearing, waste and luxury. As Robert Browne taught in *A Booke which sheweth the life and manners of all true Christians*, 'Saving goods is a duty of profitableness', while the unrighteous 'waste and lavish them away' by intemperate living. Conversely, Richard Bancroft, the anti-puritan pamphleteer, complained about the convenient selectiveness of puritan morality, which castigated the sins of bishops and the church establishment, overlooking the sins of the burgesses and gentry who represented the puritan cause in local government and in Parliament. Puritans' sermons, he said, never mention 'the gross sins of their good masters, either oppression of the poor, enhancing of rents, enclosing of common grounds, sacrilege, simony, contempt of magistrates, of laws, of ceremonies and orders ecclesiastical, nor any suchlike horrible sins wherewith all the most of our precise gentlemen are infected'.[13]

Discipline promoted solidarity – spiritual, social, political and economic. It would give parishioners independence from the traditional discipline of episcopal institutions such as the Court of Faculties – through which the archbishop controlled church life, that 'filthy quagmire and poisoned plash of all the abominations that do infect the whole realm'. This would allow the church to concentrate on offences such as gambling rather than eating meat during Lent, and, in theory, apply its rules indiscriminately rather than selling exemptions to the rich. It would raise landowners from subjection to the aristocracy, as even Privy Councillors would be answerable to the elders of the parish where they lived, just like everyone else. It would give them greater control over the workers of their parish – would 'help employers in the task of making workers worship God by diligence in their calling', as the historian Christopher Hill put it. While releasing the minister from the control of the diocese on the one hand, it would also give the parish greater influence over him, as his power was shared with elected elders. It would give some men their first experience in local government and local justice. It would decisively change the political structure of England in favour of the middle class.[14]

Opposition to Cartwright's teaching was led by the vice chancellor of Cambridge, John Whitgift, who considered presbyterianism a recipe for 'untolerable contention and extreme confusion'. Whitgift had been something of a puritan in earlier years, trying to stop Parker's *Advertisements* being enforced in the university, but became an ardent convert to the Queen's religion, a change of heart that did his prospects of promotion much good. Whitgift got the university statutes changed in 1570, transferring power from younger masters to the heads of houses. The heads removed Cartwright from his chair, and he, having avoided exile in Mary's time, left England to become a teacher in Geneva, where he could experience presbyterianism in action, in safety.[15]

1571 Parliament

In April 1571, Elizabeth had to summon Parliament to raise funds to cover the cost of mobilising armed forces against the Northern

Rebellion. Parliament responded to the uprising with three anti–Catholic Acts, making it treason to call the Queen a heretic, outlawing the import of Papal bulls, and ruling that anyone in overseas exile for more than six months forfeited all possessions. However, the Queen vetoed a bill increasing penalties for recusancy.

The House of Commons also pressed the puritan case for church reform. MPs, who began each day's business with a forty-five-minute sermon, were not generally interested in the radical new demands of the presbyterians, but they renewed their protests against robes and ritual. Meanwhile, presbyterian preachers congregated in London, hoping to put pressure on Parliament.

This campaign exasperated the bishops, who hoped to get more realistic reforms passed. Bishop Horne reported to Bullinger in Zurich that some puritans were no longer 'content with merely deriding our ministers, but regard the office itself as not worth a straw. And thus, as far as lieth in them, they are too rashly and precipitately accessory to the wretched shipwreck of our church.' Horne and Bishop Jewel of Winchester both preached against the puritans from Paul's Cross, the well-attended open-air pulpit in the grounds of St Paul's Cathedral. Defending the vestments as tolerable, they appealed for unity in the face of the threat of Catholic conquest, and Horne 'wished those cut off that did trouble us'.[16]

William White of the underground church wrote pamphlets in reply to Jewel and Horne, and they were edited by the twenty-two-year-old Thomas Wilcox. White said that the bishops' failure to reform the church arose from their fear of losing pomp and honour, and contrasted them to the dissenters who accepted 'the loss of liberty, living and life' for the sake of seeing the true church in England. It was the bishops who troubled the church, and White prayed that if they did not start doing their duty the Queen would throw them overboard like Jonah, taking back their 'overquiet estates, pompous livings and lordly titles'.[17]

Persecution and its impact

The puritan reforms proposed in the House of Commons were completely quashed by the Queen. The church commissioners then summoned the most prominent puritan ministers, both presbyterians and moderates, from John Field to Thomas Lever the Archdeacon of Coventry, and demanded not only submission to the church order in practice, but a signed statement that the Prayer Book and vestments were acceptable. Field refused and was suspended from preaching and had to become a schoolteacher.

The underground church in London also remained a concern to the bishops, who were painfully conscious of its threat to religious order. Bishop Cox of Ely belatedly informed Geneva in February 1571 that, driven to a 'pitch of frenzy' by puritan preaching,

> they now obstinately refuse to enter our churches, either to baptise their children, or to partake of the Lord's supper, or to hear sermons. They are entirely separated both from us and from those good brethren of ours; they seek bye paths; they establish a private religion, and assemble in private houses, and there perform their sacred rites.[18]

Despite such reports, there is little evidence of new arrests in this period. This may in part be simply because of the general patchiness of our sources. It may also be because Edwin Sandys, the new Bishop of London, was keeping the Separatists in jail, and some had not seen freedom in two years. Perhaps the new presbyterian offensive diverted attention from the underground church. Certainly, the presbyterian second wind of the puritan movement drew some leading London conventiclers back into the Church of England. White stopped going to conventicles and resumed attendance at one of the more acceptable London churches. He and John Browne became influential figures in the presbyterian movement in the church, as did Bonham and Crane. Presbyterianism offered an alternative to Separatism, renewing the movement for reform in the church, and giving it a more radical fringe. The underground church had never wanted merely the freedom to do things in its own way, but was modelling reforms it wanted to see imposed on the whole Church of England. The prospect – however unlikely – of achieving such national reform was worth more to White and others than the experience of imposing it on themselves in a few harassed and struggling London congregations. If Browne, Bonham and Crane were no longer leading conventicles, then the only remaining ministers we know of would be Fitz and Pattenson, both of whom had been kept long in prison. As Harrison put it, looking back a decade later, 'when they were tried and weighed, many were found too light'.[19]

This more moderate path did not avoid all trouble. In January 1572, Archbishop Parker sent to Katherine Bertie, the Duchess of Suffolk, demanding that she hand over Browne, her chaplain. The Duchess refused, and Parker wrote back along with Sandys and others, saying no one had illegally resisted his royal commission before and threatened 'other means' if she continued to protect the dissident. We do not know the outcome of this face-off, but Browne seems to have been free that summer.

Those who stayed the course in the underground, though, found it the harder path. The men and women who languished in jail not only sacrificed their freedom but risked their health and their lives. People died from cold, disease and starvation in London jails. Conditions there varied tremendously, not according to the seriousness of prisoners' offences, but depending on how much they could pay. Ordinary citizens in the Compter prisons were kept in the Hole, where they slept on bare floorboards and, according to a prisoner in 1617, 'A man shall not look about him, but some poor soul or other lies groaning and labouring under the burthen of some dangerous disease … They lie together like so many graves.'[20]

Such experience was reflected in the language of affliction permeating the writings of the Fitz church: tyranny, injustice and persecution, 'wrongs and cruel handling', 'the danger of not coming to my parish church', 'strength to strive in suffering'. Fitz himself, in the single paragraph that survives in his name, talks of 'the true and afflicted church of our Lord and Saviour Jesus Christ', as if to be the true church and to suffer affliction were the same thing. In the same way, Protestant bishops displaced under Mary rejoiced at this proof that the church was restored to truth. Violence, for a group that could withstand it, simply magnified the belief that they were saints in a battle against evil.

Fitz church petition

Eventually jail proved fatal. Mr Pattenson died in prison, as did Richard Fitz, along with three members of his church: his deacon

Thomas Bowland, who had booked Plumbers' Hall, Randall Partridge of Old Fish Street, and Giles Fowler. Their church struggled on without them, further weakened perhaps by the division among the underground congregations, and did not find a replacement for their minister.

In the first half of 1571, that church sent a petition to the Queen, signed by just twenty-seven members, which gives another glimpse into their experience and their radicalised thinking. There is no mistaking their social station: they called themselves 'poor' four times in the one document. They listed the four who had died. They said that the Lord 'hath called us, and still calleth' to separate from the churches of England, and so 'we do serve the Lord every Sabbath day in houses, and on the fourth day in the week we meet … to use prayer and exercise discipline on them which do deserve it'.[21] The phrase 'the fourth day in the week' exemplifies the puritan objection to pagan names for the days and months.

They outlined how they already fulfilled the presbyterian reform programme, exercising independent discipline over the lives of members. The Plumbers' Hall men that Grindal spoke to four years earlier started their own meetings for simpler reasons – to hear good sermons and to avoid the hated vestments. But since then they had developed a way of church life that meant more to them than that: on the one hand, they were answerable to no one, and neither archbishop nor Supreme Governor could tell them what to wear or say; on the other hand, they were answerable to one another, united in a common commitment to holiness and true doctrine. It was what the presbyterians dreamed of, and it had become essential to the Separatists' idea of what a real church is. The petition reiterated two central demands: the old puritan programme – the removal of 'forked caps and tippets, surplices, copes, starch cakes' etc. – and the new presbyterian programme – 'to cut down, root out, and utterly destroy … that wicked canon law, which is the only root out of which these abominable branches do grow'. It took the purification of the state church to new extremes, demanding that all church buildings inherited from the Catholics be destroyed as 'idol temples … builded to the service of their god'.

If Rome is the antichristian beast of Revelation, they said, then the Church of England fulfils the book's prophecy of a second beast, looking like a lamb but with the same evil, bloodthirsty power of the first beast. And yet the Fitz church, now more radically separated from the Elizabethan state church than ever, still had no concept at all that coercive state religion itself was the enemy of their freedom. They told the government, 'Our God hath straitly commanded and charged ... the magistrates of our time, not to use in his service, the manners, fashions or customs of the Papists, but contrarywise utterly to destroy them, to consume them, and abhor them.' They wanted purity of religion for all, and therefore required freedom of religion for themselves alone, as a means to that end.

They lamented their own persecution: 'Though we should cease to groan and cry unto our God to redress such wrongs and cruel handlings of his poor members, the very walls of the prisons about this city, as the Gatehouse, Bridewell, the Counters, the King's Bench, the Marshalsea, the White Lion, would testify God's anger kindled against this land.' And yet their petition was not for themselves, and not for release or toleration, only for the whole church to be reformed. When the government had performed all this, the Separatists would happily return from their London exile to their parish churches. Perhaps the most revealing aspect of the petition is the way that they began by asking the Queen for reformation, but by the end were addressing God instead, asking him to intervene, as if, correctly sensing the Queen's indifference, they appealed over her head to a higher authority.[22]

The petition protested the Separatists' complete obedience to the Queen, as unlikely as it may sound, claiming that it was only the bishops, for motives of 'pomp and covetousness', who impose popish rules on the churches and punish those who refuse to submit. Protestant critics of the Elizabethan Church were generally meticulous in maintaining the fiction that any religious policies they disliked were forced on their godly Queen by wicked bishops. This was partly a matter of diplomacy and self-preservation, bolstered by a desire to believe themselves devoted subjects of the crown. It was also helped by their ignorance about what happened behind the doors of the Privy Council, and by the assumption that if a woman was officially governing men, the men were bound to be calling the shots. It suited Elizabeth to foster the fiction.

After seeing this petition, Bishop Horne wrote in August to Bullinger in Zurich about these 'most absurd ravings of opinion':

> some men of inferior rank and standing, deficient indeed both in sagacity and sense, and entirely ignorant and unknown, who since they do not yet perceive the church to square with their wishes, or rather vanities ... hide themselves in idleness and obscurity; others ... call together conventicles, elect their own bishops, and holding synods one with another, frame and devise their own laws for themselves. They reject preaching, despise communion, would have all churches destroyed, as having been formerly dedicated to popery ... They therefore cut themselves off, as they say, from us.[23]

One leading member of the Fitz church found he could no longer face the ordeal of prison: the elder John Bolton saved his life by finally making his peace with the bishop, reading a public recantation and denunciation of Separatism at Paul's Cross and returning to the Church of England, in return for his release. He was cutting himself off from his family in the Lord, and one can imagine he found it hard to find a new family among 'the papists and neuters, false brethren and domestical enemies', as the petition had put it. Around 1572, he took his own life.

After this, the London underground church disappears from the historical record, and it would be reasonable to assume it had been destroyed by splits and persecution. But out of the blue, nine years later, we find two letters written by continuing members of the Fitz church. One was John Nasshe, a prisoner in the Marshalsea, writing to the Convocation of Canterbury in January 1581. Nasshe complained that he and fellow believers had now been in prison for nine or ten years for their faith. He looked back to the time when their movement had a thousand members, but the bishops had plucked them back, making them dissimulators, neuters and slaves of Satan. He listed some of those who had died in prison: Fitz, Bowland, Partridge and Fowler had now been joined by John King of Islington and John Leonard of Holborn, both of whom had been among the seventy-seven worshippers arrested in James Tynne's house in 1568 and had signed the Fitz petition; a third signatory, Margaret Racye, had also died in prison, as had a Mrs Causlen. Nasshe did not ask for mercy but wrote merely to accuse: their blood shall be required.[24]

The other letter, much shorter, was written by William Dreuit the following month, complaining to an undisclosed recipient about his being imprisoned for nonconformity. The striking thing that the two letters have in common is that both Nasshe and Dreuit conclude with the wording of the Fitz church covenant: 'I have joined myself to the true church of Christ ...'

Then, the following year, 1582, Robert Harrison wrote from the vantage point of his own Norfolk Separatist movement, now in exile in the Netherlands, looking back on the London movement as a failure. Many had joined it, he said, but some failed to see the potential for creating a better kind of church, merely objecting to the vestments, so when they faced persecution they fell away, and 'by their untowardness they caused the savour of the Lord's work to stink in the nostrils of the people'. Even those who persevered were found wanting by Harrison: 'Some entering that way, despised all other, but pitied them not in the bowels of compassion, that they might be brought unto the truth, but were proud in their own conceit.' The fact that there were London Separatists still carrying the flame in such dark times had evaded even Harrison's notice.[25]

7

The charge

ON 29 AUGUST 1571, a Shrewsbury draper by the name of Thomas Browne was paid to take a bag containing some silver from London to the north of England and deliver it to Laurence Bannister, an official working for the Duke of Norfolk. Browne thought the bag was too heavy for its supposed purpose, and knowing that the Catholic Duke's loyalty was suspect, he opened it. He found £600 in gold from the French ambassador to be forwarded to Queen Mary of Scotland, along with letters in code. Browne took the bag to Cecil, now Lord Burghley. The servants of Norfolk's secretaries were tortured for information, or threatened with torture. A search of the duke's house revealed a coded letter from Mary under a doormat, and the key to their code in the tiles of the roof.

The conspiracy Burghley uncovered had been organised by a Florentine banker, Roberto Ridolfi. It had the blessing of Pope Pius, and implicated the Bishop of Ross, the Spanish ambassador and various nobles, as well as Mary and Norfolk. The plan was for a Spanish invasion, which would bring arms and money for the English Catholics, who would join their forces, while Norfolk deposed Elizabeth his cousin, married Mary, claimed the thrones of both England and Scotland for her and restored Catholicism.

The Ridolfi plot made the puritan case for reform, to unite and strengthen the Protestant Church, more persuasive than ever, and necessitated another Parliament, to deal with Queen Mary, which, meeting in May 1572, just one year after the last, gave the puritans an unexpected forum. Cartwright returned from his Genevan exile to add his weight to the lobby. Field, Wilcox and White met with others to discuss tactics and the writing of a radical puritan manifesto. Puritan MPs brought a bill before Parliament that would have authorised ministers to ignore the bits of the Prayer Book they did not like, and it seemed to have considerable support, but the bill was seized by the Queen, who insisted that from then on all religious legislation would have to be vetted by the bishops first.

An Admonition to the Parliament

Parliament had again failed to reform the Church of England, and Field and Wilcox published their manifesto, *An Admonition to the Parliament*, in June. Under the guise of an address to MPs, it was intended to rouse the general population to the cause that Parliament had failed. White wrote a short preface, arguing that if the bishops were keeping popish tradition alive in the church in the hope that they would persuade papists to hear the gospel, the tactic had failed. The preface was never published, however, and the *Admonition* did well enough without it. Field and Wilcox's book was 'a declaration of ecclesiastical war', in the words of the historian of puritanism Patrick Collinson. Wilcox's contribution was a calm exposition of the presbyterian system they wanted. Field's was a shocking satire on the state of the Church of England and a furious denunciation of the imperfections of the Prayer Book that he had lost his job for refusing to overlook. The Prayer Book was 'an unperfect book, culled and picked out of the popish dunghill, the Mass book, full of all abominations'. Non-preaching ministers were 'empty feeders, dark eyes, ill workmen to hasten the Lord's harvest, messengers that cannot call, prophets that cannot declare the will of the Lord, unsavoury salt, blind guides, sleepy watchmen', their craft was 'as evil as playing upon a stage'. 'They profane holy baptism in toying foolishly, for that they ask questions of an infant, which cannot answer … Which is but a mockery of God.' 'They toss the Psalms in most places like tennis balls.' 'When Jesus is named, then off goeth the cap, and down goeth the knees, with such a scraping on the ground that they cannot hear a good while after.' 'The Lord Bishops, their suffragans, archdeacons, chancellors, officials, proctors, doctors, summoners, and such ravening rabblers take upon them, which is most horrible, the rule of God's church – spoiling the pastor of his lawful jurisdiction over his own flock'; they 'tarry in their college and lead the lives of loitering losels as long as they live'.[1]

An Admonition to the Parliament rang with anger at Field's treatment by the Church of England, which fed his presbyterian contempt for the unbiblical and unspiritual offices of its power structure, as well as all the more familiar puritan targets. It sold sensationally well, Whitgift complaining it was 'in every man's hand, and by many thought unanswerable'. It was printed and reprinted anonymously on secret presses. The only printing allowed in England, outside the two universities (which at present did none) and special royal appointments, was by twenty or so London printers recognised by the Company of Stationers. They were inspected weekly for unlicensed work and it was not unknown for amateurs to try to break in to their houses by night and self-publish. Archbishop Parker instructed the Mayor of London to find the printer of the *Admonition*, and, when he failed, suspected he was deliberately hiding the criminal.

Field and Wilcox were arrested on 7 July 1572, and, admitting authorship, were committed to Newgate for a year. They went as celebrities and were visited by many leading puritans, including John Browne of the underground church. Parker sent his chaplain to reason with them, but did not find that prison had cowed them. After discussing church order at length, the chaplain complained that Field's essay had not been written in love or meekness. Field replied, 'We have used gentle words too long, which have done no good; the wound grows desperate and wants a corrosive; 'tis no time to ... sew pill[ow]s under men's elbows.'[2]

White was arrested at about the same time, on an unknown charge. Field and Wilcox were interrogated by the Privy Council in 1573 alongside John Browne and two other members of the underground, Sparrow and King* as well as other puritans. Sparrow, King, Field and Wilcox were returned to prison, while Browne and the others were just told not to preach. Field and Wilcox were not released after their allotted twelve months in prison, until they appealed to the Earl of Leicester to intervene, telling him, 'their poor wives and children

---

* Peel identifies this pair as Harry Sparrowe and John King, whose names appear together on the Fitz church petition of 1571, but there is another pair with the same surnames, Robert Sparrow and Richard Kinge, who appear together on the list of conventiclers released from Bridewell on 22 April 1569.

were utterly impoverished, their health very much impaired by the unwholesome savour of the place and the cold weather, and that they were like to suffer yet greater extremities'. Leicester, the most powerful champion of puritanism among Elizabeth's courtiers, got them freed.[3]

By August 1572, the *Admonition* was in its third edition. The Bishop of Lincoln preached against it at Paul's Cross, and Archbishop Parker commissioned Whitgift to write *An Ansvvere to ... An admonition*. Cartwright responded to Whitgift in *A Replye to an Ansvvere*, published in April 1573 (Field and Wilcox being persuaded it was prudent to leave the dispute to someone who was not already in prison). A man named Lacy was caught operating a secret press in Hempstead in August, and confessed to having printed a thousand copies of a second edition of Cartwright's *A Replye*. Whitgift responded to *A Replye* with *The defense of the aunsvvere* in 1574, which drew from Cartwright *The Second Replie* in 1575, and *The Rest of the Second Replie* in 1577.

Other writers weighed into the controversy too, including the anonymous author of *A Second Admonition*, which Whitgift also replied to. There was clearly a market for the idea of throwing off the power of bishops along with their vestments, and throughout England radical puritan ministers made ad hoc presbyterian reforms. Field, for example, helped devise an unofficial presbyterian council to be set up for the churches around Wandsworth. It was a new kind of underground movement, and though the presbyterians did not see these meetings and arrangements as any kind of separation from the Church of England, they were under no illusion they would be tolerated by the authorities and so kept them completely secret. In 1574, the puritan academic Walter Travers completed *Ecclesiasticae Disciplinae*, a systematic account of how presbyterianism would work in England, writing from exile in Geneva, having been forced out of Cambridge by Whitgift's anti-puritan policies; Cartwright printed it in Heidelberg along with an English translation.

The St Bartholomew's Day massacre

The Northamptonshire MP George Carleton wrote telling Burghley that radical puritanism had seized the whole country, from the nobility to the lowest rank, and the people so disliked 'the Queen's proceedings in religion' that more every day were abandoning the parish church, 'and will practise assemblies of brethren in all parts of the realm, and have their own churches in companies'. The response that Carleton urged on the Queen's minister was far from imprisonment, because he saw them as the most sincerely Protestant subjects of a Protestant queen. They could simply be tolerated, he said, but then there would be no single state religion to hold England together. They could be allowed to go into foreign exile – a suggestion that would have reminded Burghley of the abortive Scottish pilgrimage of 1568 – but that, Carleton reckoned, would deprive the Queen of three thousand of her most devoted subjects. So Carleton's plan was for the Separatists to be sent to an English overseas dominion, which at this point in history meant Ireland, making the island more Protestant, and England more uniform. Meanwhile, non-separating puritans should be armed to create a league for 'the defence of the Gospel and the preservation of the state when the day of sorrow should come'. Carleton's advice did not become Burghley's policy, but the problem remained, as did the possibility of exile.[4]

Those like Carleton who feared the day of sorrow continued to listen with anxiety for news from the Netherlands. In 1571, Dutch leaders in exile at Emden had agreed an emphatically Calvinist settlement for their national church. Elizabeth still did not support their rebellion, and when she refused to open her harbours to the Dutch naval forces known as the Sea Beggars, they were driven by her unwelcome to a desperate attack upon Brielle, the seaport at the mouth of the New Maas, which they had the luck to find undefended and which they conquered on 1 April 1572. This then allowed them to take other strategically important ports in Holland and Zeeland, creating one of the turning points of the war.

In France, a series of religious civil wars throughout the 1560s had ended with Catholicism remaining in power, but the Protestants were allowed a limited number of churches throughout the country, plus four fortified cities, according to the Peace of Saint-Germain. Protestant leaders had considerable influence over King Charles IX, persuading him to send troops to support the Dutch rebels and relieve Mons from Spanish siege. The French Protestants also negotiated a marriage between Charles's sister Marguerite and the Protestant Henry of Navarre, which took place in Paris on 18 August 1572.

Paris, however, was as militantly Catholic as London was militantly Protestant, and after the Queen Mother Catherine de' Medici used the wedding to make an unsuccessful attempt on the life of the leading Protestant Admiral Coligny, the tension exploded in a massacre. On Catherine's instigation, three thousand Protestants, including their assembled leaders, were killed in Paris in the St Bartholomew's Day massacre of 24 August, and perhaps one thousand two hundred more died throughout France. The political power of French Protestantism was destroyed and the country embarked on another decade of civil war. The French forces that had been promised to William of Orange therefore never went. He retreated from Mons, which surrendered to Alba, followed by other nearby cities.

The last archbishop?

In England, although their fear and grief at such news was profound, the puritans found once again that horror stories of Catholic violence enhanced their credibility as the only people unwilling to meet antichrist halfway. The bishops felt themselves losing their battle against presbyterian demands. Sandys, asking the Privy Council for a royal proclamation against Field, Wilcox and Cartwright, said that the presbyterian leaders were, paradoxically, 'honoured for saints'; 'the people resort unto them, as in popery they were wont to run on pilgrimage'. Ministers who had preached acceptable sermons for the bishop at Paul's Cross a year ago now seemed to have nothing to say except to rail against the church and to commend Cartwright. Sandys felt the bishops had lost all authority: 'We are become contemptible in the eyes of the basest sort of people.' Or in Horne's blunter phrase, they were *excrementa mundi*. Archbishop Parker told Burghley he was ready to leave the question with him 'whether her majesty or you will have any archbishops or bishops'. An anonymous biography of Parker was printed in 1574 with the less-than-subtle title, *The life the 70th Archbishopp off Canterbury presentlye sitting ... This numbre off seuenty is so compleat a number as it is a great pitie there should be one more.* The Privy Council was told that, during a sermon in 1572, Edward Dering, the ecclesiastical careerist turned puritan firebrand, solemnly removed his cap and said, 'Now I will prophesy that Matthew Parker shall be the last Archbishop of Canterbury.'[5]

Much of the English religious tumult of the 1570s happened around a kind of indistinct border between mainstream puritanism and Separatism, the grey area between trying to force reforms on the church and leaving the Church of England altogether to found a new church. Back in 1566, hasty puritans had met for underground services in London, then had to work out, with fear and trembling, whether they were merely avoiding the vestments or renouncing the Church of England, or something in between. Now, the illicit presbyterian reform of parishes, with private meetings and secret conferences, created a church within the church, which the church authorities would never allow to remain in it. While Cartwright explicitly rejected Separatism, some presbyterian rhetoric had Separatism as its only logical conclusion. Wilcox, for instance, in the *Admonition* said, 'We in England are so far off from having a church rightly reformed according to the prescript of God's word, that as yet we are not come to the outward face of the same.' If a true church was not yet visible in England, then was the highly visible Church of England a false church? And if so, were true Christians not called to quit the false church and establish a true one as they had done in the case of the Church of Rome? The justice of this logic, and the fact that Field and Wilcox recoiled from it, are demonstrated by the fact that from the second edition 'we are not come' was changed to 'we are scarce come'. Similarly, their planned publication of a joint constitution of the reformed parishes of England would, in effect, arguably have founded a rival church, which may be why they were dissuaded.[6]

Instead, Field and Wilcox were provoked by Whitgift's accusation of heresy to write a confession of their faith. Albert Peel, in publishing the highlights of *The Seconde Parte of a Register* in 1915, described the confession as including 'a strongly worded refutation of the charge of Separatism'.[7] It was indeed strongly worded, as one would expect from anything with John Field's name on it, but it was also slightly slippery in its rejection of Separatism. In it, Field and Wilcox vehemently denied having told anyone to quit the Church of England for an underground congregation and declared it 'utterly unlawful' to quit any church that has sound preaching, pure sacraments and the correct system of discipline. But their *Admonition* had made it extremely clear that the Church of England did not have correct discipline; so they went on to concede that, even without it, it was better to bear with a bad church than for 'private persons of their own authority, without learning or knowledge to establish churches' – adding the qualification that even ordinary, untaught people might set up their own church in time of persecution. Even here, Field and Wilcox had not clearly condemned the underground congregations of their own times, which were led not by uneducated believers but by renegade ministers from the Church of England; and when their leaders died in prison they had a fair claim to be living in times of persecution.

The fact is that when Field and Wilcox denounced 'private conventicles', they had a specific target in mind, and it was not their friends in the underground church, it was the incomprehensibly alien extremism of the European Anabaptists. The Anabaptists, it seemed to puritans, allowed anyone who felt like it to found a church; they were said to denounce all state churches, Catholic, Lutheran and Reformed, and the state itself, and social hierarchies, and private property. They were even said to prefer private revelations by the Spirit to obeying the Bible, which would explain why they had turned bloody revolutionaries in Münster in 1533, imposing the horror of polygamous communism on the population. 'These', Field and Wilcox said, 'we account rather brute beasts than Christians, who are severely to be punished according to their deserts.' They concluded the declaration by saying: 'To knit up our whole faith in one word, we abhor from the bottom of our hearts all those sects called Anabaptists.' The papists finally had company in their abominations.[8]

So while Field and Wilcox did indeed offer a vehement denunciation of 'private conventicles', they did so in a way that avoided the crucial question of what English congregations had been doing in their own day. The idea of private religion and Separatism appalled them, because they identified it completely with the principled separation between church and state that the Anabaptists pursued, which meant the destruction of the state church and the disintegration of the godly realm. Field and Wilcox affirmed that separating from Catholicism was right, and that separating as the Anabaptists did was wrong; but as for separating from the Church of England as London underground congregations had done, to commend it would risk sounding like Anabaptists, and to denounce it would be to betray some of their most valiant fellow soldiers in the war against antichrist. If underground Christianity was the question, they could not bring themselves to give a definite answer.

White's interview

The bishops felt defeated by the puritans, but the Queen led a counterattack. On 11 June 1573, she issued a royal proclamation against the *Admonition*, requiring all copies to be destroyed. The results were limited: in London, the authorities failed to recover a single copy. Then in October, the Queen decreed that anyone who spoke against the Prayer Book would face jail. A commission was set up to investigate irregularities in churches, and a warrant was issued for the arrest of Cartwright, who embarked upon another exile, this time in Heidelberg, where Field may have joined him. In London, ministers had to promise to use the Prayer Book or face prison. The minister of St Clement Danes in Westminster, Robert Johnson, was arrested for marrying a couple without a ring and baptising without the sign of the cross, and died in jail in May 1574.

Lay troublemakers also faced scrutiny. White, having apparently been in prison more than a year, was released on bail under house arrest, at Christmas 1573 — or 'the birthday of our Lord', as White insisted on calling it — and then on 18 January 1574 was brought before an imposing panel of royal commissioners, led by the Lord Chief Justice, to answer accusations about not attending his parish church.

Pointing out reasonably enough that his living arrangements had made church attendance difficult, according to his own record of the interview, White continued in a submissive vein:

> My lord, I did use to frequent my parish church before my troubles, and procured several godly men to preach there, as well as other places of preaching and prayer; and since my troubles, I have not frequented any private assemblies, but, as I have had liberty, have gone to my parish church.

And like Field and Wilcox, White argued that any charge of Separatism against him was malicious slander because he was not an

Anabaptist – and if he had been he would have deserved death: if it 'can be proved against me … that I hold all things in common, your lordship may dismiss me from hence to the gallows'.

As the interview continued, however, White admitted that he had generally avoided his parish church in favour of better ones and that he refused to go to any services that had no sermon. Pressed to say whether he still objected to the Book of Common Prayer and the vestments, he confessed that he did, and the Lord Chief Justice declared: 'Thou art the wickedest and most contemptuous person that has come before me.'

'My conscience doth witness otherwise,' replied White.

For the Lord Chief Justice, religious dissent denied the Queen's right to rule: 'I swear by God thou art a very rebel.' Not so, White replied; but more to the point, 'I heard the name of God taken in vain. If I had done it, it had been a greater offence than that which I stand here for.'

White asked to see a copy of the presentment against him.

'You shall have your head from your shoulders,' was the Lord Chief Justice's only response. 'Have him to the Gatehouse.'

'I pray you to commit me to some prison in London,' said White, the Gatehouse being in Westminster, 'that I may be near my house.'

'No, sir, you shall go thither.'

'I have paid fees and fines in other prisons; send me not where I must pay them again.'

'Yes, marry, shall you; that is your glory.'

'I desire no such glory.'

The Master of Requests reckoned, 'It will cost you £20, I warrant you, before you come out.'

'God's will be done,' said White, and he was taken back to prison. He appealed to Leicester and was moved to the archdeacon's house.[9]

The Undertree conspiracy

'Thou art a very rebel.' Such allegations made no sense to puritans, who considered themselves utterly loyal to the Protestant Queen, and merely wanted her to have better religious advice and to eradicate all remnants of her enemy the Pope from the Church of England. They were defiant but peaceful. But for those who most detested puritans' radical ambitions, the passive persona was unpersuasive. Admittedly, puritan insubordination had so far been a mild threat to the church state compared to Catholic uprisings, but the danger to Elizabeth's rule from the right was so tangible and violent that it was natural to look for it from the left as well.

In June 1574, they finally found what they were looking for. A man calling himself Undertree approached the steward of the Archbishop of Canterbury, told him he was a puritan plotting to kill the archbishop and Lord Burghley, and offered him money for access to his master. Undertree showed the steward bundles of letters proving the seriousness of the plan, implicating as its leaders William Bonham, John Browne and the military chaplain Nicholas Stonden.

The steward said he would help Undertree, but instead informed Parker, who sent a frantic message to Burghley: 'This deep, devilish, traitorous dissimulation,' cried Parker, 'this horrible conspiracy, hath so astonied me, that my wit, my memory, be quite gone.' If the rebellion were not crushed, he warned, not only their own lives and posterity but the Queen's too would be in peril. He hinted that the conspiracy might involve the Earl of Leicester, and said that the plot only confirmed what he had always said about the puritans: 'I have had leisure enough a great while to perpend some men's words and proceedings ... I would I were dead before I see with my corporal eyes that which is now brought to a full ripeness, whereof I gave warning a great while ago, if I had been heard.'[10]

Burghley informed the Queen, and Parker was told to arrest Undertree immediately, but to the archbishop's embarrassment it then took him a week to find him. In the meantime, Stonden was arrested (Bonham already being in prison for the usual reasons and Browne on the Isle of Wight with Cartwright). The authorities made a list of other suspected conspirators to round up, including Field, Wilcox and Cartwright.

Parker faced much greater embarrassment when Undertree was finally arrested, because the whole affair turned out to be a hoax and all his letters forgeries. The Privy Council instructed Parker to release not only Stonden but Bonham as well. Parker replied that he thanked

God 'the realm is not yet corrupted with such sprites as were feared', with masterful use of the passive voice. He insisted that he had 'meant honourably', asked Burghley not to discourage him and his fellow 'searchers', and reported that he was 'so much troubled with the stone' he was sorry to be alive.[11]

8

Relighting the fire

At nine o'clock on Easter morning 1575, a constable surprised eleven men and between fifteen and twenty women worshipping in a house near Aldgate, and arrested them. It would have been a familiar enough occurrence in the story of radical puritanism, but these were not puritans, they were Dutch Anabaptists, refugees from Alba's persecution in Ghent. They had come to London, hoping to live a quiet life amid the thousands of Dutch refugees and migrant workers there. Elizabeth had permitted the stranger churches to return to London so that French and Dutch Protestants could worship in their own style, but this toleration did not extend to Anabaptists: they were seen not simply as a different kind of Christian, but as extremists who perverted Christianity, wanting to destroy what Protestants and Catholics alike meant by church. They were a profound embarrassment to Protestants, confirmation that rejecting the authority of Rome in favour of the Bible led to anarchy, and so had to be decisively restrained. Soon William of Orange would grant toleration to Anabaptists in his Dutch territory, but this would be an unprecedented and controversial development.

Aldgate Anabaptists

The Anabaptists were interrogated by Bishop Sandys, assisted by Dutch and French clergy who interpreted. The prisoners were charged with holding four unacceptable beliefs, and they affirmed them all. First, they believed babies could not be baptised into the church, only true believers could; this meant that church was confined to true believers rather than embracing the entire nation and so they rejected the

83

notion that Sandys put to them, 'There is not an individual in all of England, who is not a member of the church of God.'[1] Second, the Anabaptists believed Christians could not be state officials, because of the violence involved, making the church even more of an enclave within a non-Christian society. Third, they believed Christians could not swear oaths, putting them outside of the justice system and much of civic life. And fourth, they believed that Christ in the womb took all his flesh from God, and none from Mary, a heresy of no very practical significance. Perhaps its function was simply to assert their total independence from all orthodox tradition.

The Aldgate Anabaptists were kept in chains, most of their men in the Marshalsea, the women and the youngest man in Newgate – an arrangement that, Newgate being a capital prison, made them think the latter group would be executed first. They were repeatedly visited, threatened with burning and urged to give up their fanatical beliefs. The Elizabethan authorities could not let such antisocial ideas survive to disintegrate the fabric of the one-church state, nor could they be seen to do so, but they did not want to be re-enacting Mary's persecutions either, and tried hard to get recantations.

After seven weeks in prison, on 25 May, five of the men recanted. Sandys had promised they would walk free, but first he made a show of their capitulation at Paul's Cross before a crowd of thousands. Wearing faggots, they were made to swear that, having been 'seduced by the devil, the spirit of error, and by false teachers', they had fallen into 'damnable and detestable heresies' but would now submit to the state church for ever, 'utterly abandoning and forsaking all and every Anabaptistical error'. They were then released on bail.[2]

The young man who had been kept with the women was put in close confinement, and when that failed to break him was tied to the back of a cart and scourged through the streets. He and the women, though they had been told for a week that they were about to die, were instead forcibly repatriated.

Sandys stepped up the pressure on the remaining men. They were transferred to Newgate on 2 June, where other religious prisoners were kept, and put in 'a deep stenchy hole, filled with unclean reptiles'. They themselves sent petitions to Sandys and the Queen, which they had written with the help of Jacques de Somere, a well-to-do member of the Dutch stranger church who disagreed with their beliefs but opposed their ill treatment. After a week in Newgate, one of the men, Christian Kernels, died. The others were exorcised, tortured according to one account, and then put in close confinement. 'Death was daily announced us,' wrote Gerrit von Byler in a letter from his cell, 'in a terrific voice of thunder, that they would *burn us* – kill us in the most excruciating manner possible. However, the Lord strengthened us.' 'The greatest conflict I had,' he adds, 'was to leave my dear wife and my innocent little children.'[3]

John Foxe, having spent years immersed in stories of the martyrdom of believers by antichrist, wrote to the Queen to plead for the Anabaptists' lives. Even Foxe conceded that they were fanatics guilty of 'monstrous opinions' and wicked, absurd errors, which could not be tolerated in the kingdom, and so he applauded the women's expulsion.

> But to roast alive the bodies of poor wretches, that offend rather through blindness of judgment, than perverseness of will, in fire and flames, raging with pitch and brimstone, is a hard-hearted thing, and more agreeable to the practice of Romanists than the custom of the Gospellers ...
>
> I humbly beg of your royal highness, for the sake of Christ, who was consecrated to suffer for the lives of many, this favour at my request, which even the divine clemency would engage you to, that if it may be, and what cannot your authority do in these cases, these miserable wretches may be spared; at least that a stop may be put to the horror by changing their punishment into some other kind ... This one thing I most earnestly beg, that the piles and flames of Smithfield, so long ago extinguished by your happy government, may not now be again revived.[4]

The letter impressed the prisoners, who wrote to thank Foxe for it and to give him a better understanding of their beliefs; it made no impression on the Queen, who saw the international credibility of her church at stake, as well as relations with Spain. Sandys required all ministers of the stranger churches to declare their support for the burning of heretics, or lose their toleration, and most agreed, though it caused some consternation among members.

In July, the younger two prisoners, von Byler and John van Straten, both under twenty-five, were told they would be burned at Smithfield in three days. Stake and faggots were set in place and an eager crowd gathered, but the men were reprieved. Von Byler realised it 'was all intended for effect', to unnerve them and inspire a last-minute urge to live.

At six in the morning of 22 July, the two others, John Pieters and Hendrick Teerwoort, were taken to Smithfield, and this time not for effect. Pieters was a married man in his fifties, both he and his wife having lost their previous spouses to Alba's flames in Ghent. Teerwoort was a handsome twenty-five-year-old goldsmith who had been married for two months at the time of his arrest. The pair died, according to the chronicler Stow, 'in great horror, with roaring and crying'. Foxe was there to witness the new martyrdom, as was Field. De Somer, the Anabaptists' erstwhile scribe, relayed the news of their 'cruel and unchristian' treatment back home to Ghent, noting that it seemed 'very strange and incredible ... that those who formerly suffered persecution now persecute other people on account of their religion, constraining the consciences of others with fire and sword'.[5]

The last two prisoners tried to escape, but were caught after filing a bar off their window. They were put back in close confinement, and kept under constant threat of death, but they were still alive in September and seem to have been eventually released, presumably into exile.

A rather richer seam of martyrs emerged at the other end of the English religious spectrum. The Catholic exile William Allen founded an English college in Douai in 1568, which became a training ground for missionary priests to be sent back into England in secret. The first to die was Cuthbert Mayne in 1577. Arrested in Cornwall wearing an *agnus dei* (a wax disc depicting a lamb, blessed by the Pope) and carrying an old papal bull, Mayne was technically in breach of the 1571 Treasons Act, but his real offence was his mission. More than a hundred and fifty Douai priests were executed under Elizabeth, along with lay people who helped them. They were hanged, drawn and quartered, to make the point that the state was not persecuting Catholics for heresy but executing traitors for conspiring in a cause devoted to overthrowing the Queen. Any remaining claim over the moral high ground here, however, was seriously damaged when the following year the state started using torture on priests and laity alike to get information about the Catholic underground.

White versus SB

The Aldgate Anabaptists, returning to prison after one of their inter-
rogations by Sandys, had wryly noted the bishop's worry that the
'thieves and malefactors ... might be corrupted by us'. They did
indeed make one convert in Newgate, a London carpenter known to
us only by his initials, SB. Impressed by their Christlike character and
way of life, and assured there was no truth in the rumours that 'they
held women to be in common', SB became a follower. His stay at
Newgate coincided with the latest imprisonment of William White,
who warned SB that he was consorting with a 'divelish sect' of heretics. SB told White, 'I think them worthy of all reverence, yea,
thinking myself happy if I may be but a hewer of wood and drawer
of water among them.'[6]

White and SB were both released from prison and happened to
meet again later that year, 1575, in Letch Lane. They resumed their
theological debate there, and then continued it in a series of letters,
culminating in one from White, written on 11 April 1576, which,
when published in 1920, covered forty-four pages.

The most striking thing about the correspondence is to hear White,
the patiently suffering veteran of the religious underground, suddenly
turn bishop when confronted with someone even more radical. SB's
replies to him were a model of humility, thanking White as a brother in
the Lord 'for your great courtesy you would vouchsafe to take so great
pains to write to me, being so simple and rude in understanding as I
am'.[7] When White denounced SB's opinions as heresy, SB said that he
had learned them from the Bible, and though others might understand
better than him, until they showed him his error so that he could see it
himself he could not change his mind. SB was making the same defence
of his Christian freedom and obligations as every Protestant since Luther
had made when under fire, and White responded with as much vitriol
as any inquisitor, storming that SB, for all his show of humility, was
blinded by malice, maintaining his opinions 'most ignorantly, impru-
dently, and damnably', writing 'to a most divelish purpose', making
'blasphemous and lying' arguments, being 'a very enemy'.

Grindal, examining the Plumbers' Hall dissidents, had argued that
'the learned in Geneva' disapproved of them, and White and his friends

replied that those authorities were fallible and that the only judge was Scripture; now it was White's turn to appeal to the authority of 'that godly father ... Mr Calvin', and SB's turn to say, 'I can lay no better foundation than the holy scriptures.' White was exasperated that SB would not submit to the 'judgment of the Catholic and universal church', and even found himself complaining that if SB had not quit his parish church he would have learned the truth from 'public doctrine and ecclesiastical expositions'. SB's great error, White said, was in 'secluding yourself from ... all public exercises used in Christ's church in England, whereunto ... a prince by her laws ... doth command'.[8]

For all White's insistence on his right to disobey the bishops, he had never extended that to anything like universal freedom of religion. Rather, his right was based on the universal obligation to follow the one true religion, which he and fellow presbyterians had discerned. For all his nonconformity to one particular state church, he never questioned the concept of the state church, united to conformity to one true religion. His conversation with SB gives us a glimpse of the kind of regime he and his friends would have imposed on England given the chance. Any true Christian, White said, who discovered SB's crew at their next meeting, was bound to report them, and, when they were punished, 'should not his light shine and God thereby be glorified?' Heretics 'must be punished, hanged, headed etc. as their demerits deserve by the laws of God and our country; and by keeping counsel with [i.e. failing to report] any such, you are guilty of their sin, and deserve the punishment'.[9]

Archbishop versus Queen

Another drama of conscience and obedience was played out in this period at a rather different level of Elizabethan society. In 1575, the Archbishop of Canterbury, Matthew Parker, died. Grindal was the most eligible successor, but his sympathy towards reform and softness on puritans made him suspect in the Queen's eyes, and it took seven months from Parker's death before Elizabeth agreed to his appointment. It then took just another six months for the conflict to arise that wrecked Grindal's career, over the matter of prophesyings.

Prophesyings were nothing like the wild charismatic events the name might suggest. Inspired by Swiss Protestant practice, they were local preaching workshops run by and for clergy. Typically, they started with a sermon, which was often open to the public, followed by a more private analysis of the sermon and general training and advice in preaching. They were local initiatives without the involvement of the church authorities, but the majority of bishops welcomed them because they educated ministers and trained them to preach. For the most conservative bishops they seemed a little disorderly, and the Queen on the odd occasion when they had come to her attention said they should be stopped, but her orders had had little effect.

So it was that on 12 June 1576, the matter being brought to her attention again, the Queen ordered Grindal to put a stop to all prophesyings. The command showed what a profoundly different sense of religion she had to most of her bishops, certainly to her Archbishop of Canterbury, for whom this was virtually an order to inhibit religion. Instead of suppressing the prophesyings, Grindal gathered information about them from the bishops, on the basis of which he wrote a 6,000-word letter to the Queen defending them. He offered, as a compromise, to ensure they were more orderly, but Elizabeth, appalled by his defiance, only increased her demands, now wanting preaching itself restricted to three or four licences per county.

And so, just as White had exasperated Grindal by saying he would obey royal commands only so far as they honoured God, and just as SB exasperated White by saying he would obey all princes 'their laws not being contrary to God's law' – so now it was Grindal's turn to tell the Queen, 'I choose rather to offend your earthly majesty than to offend the heavenly majesty of God.' He asked her to leave ecclesiastical policy to the bishops and not 'pronounce so resolutely and peremptorily' in religious matters as in secular ones. 'Remember, Madam, that you are a mortal creature.'[10]

Grindal was suspended from duty and placed under house arrest in Lambeth Palace. The Queen was keen to remove him from office, but was dissuaded: when Catholics seemed close to defeating the Dutch rebels, seizing power in Scotland and rising again in England, she could not afford to give their cause such a boost. Still, Grindal's suspension continued for the remaining six years of his life, and the prophesyings for which he sacrificed his career were suppressed nonetheless. Bishop Bentham of Lichfield and Coventry, erstwhile leader of the Marian underground church, wrote to Lever in Coventry, 'to will and require you, and nevertheless in her majesty's name to charge you, to forbear and stay yourselves from that exercise, till it shall please God we may ... obtain the full use thereof, with her good pleasure'. Instead of training ministers to make up the woeful lack of well-informed preaching in the Church of England, the bishops returned, as Wilcox put it, to creating ignorant priests, '60, 80 or 100 at a clap, and send[ing] them abroad into the country like masterless men [i.e. beggars]'.[11]

The kind of church that Grindal hoped to build was, for puritans, a shadow of what they longed for, but his fall demonstrated with brutal clarity that even that shadow was never going to be seen in England. The puritan campaign continued with gusto, and it continued to develop its formidable organisation, but in twenty years it had achieved no change to the worship or structure of the Church of England whatsoever. Once again the most modest measures imaginable to enrich church life had been quashed. If radical puritans concluded that the only way to have a church that was true to the Bible was to create it outside the Church of England, the evidence was on their side. And so the scene was set for the most radical wave of dissent yet.

PART TWO

The willing sort

9

Robert Browne

ROBERT BROWNE'S BACKGROUND was unlike that of any members of the London underground. He was born into the gentry of Rutland, a family of MPs, High Sheriffs and baronets. His grandfather, Francis Browne, had received a charter from Henry VIII allowing him to wear a hat in the royal presence. Robert grew up in Tolethorpe Hall in Rutland and the family was related to Lord Burghley, whose great house was being built a few miles south.

Browne in Cambridge

Browne was also younger than the erstwhile leaders of the London movement, having been a child throughout Mary's reign and probably about eight when Elizabeth came to the throne. He was studying at Corpus Christi, Cambridge, in the early 1570s, when Cartwright thrilled students with his denunciation of the unbiblical episcopacy of the English Church. Browne became an ardent radical puritan – he was 'forward in religion', in his own phrase – and this got him into some trouble at Cambridge, though we do not know the details. Then, graduating in 1572, he became a schoolteacher – a useful career for those who wanted to teach religion without having to submit to the godless laws of the church. Browne made a name for himself locally with his radical ideas, fell out with the local minister and was sacked from the school, but had enough of a following to stay in this unnamed town teaching children privately. He soon became disillusioned with the prospect of changing the world by teaching children, and in 1575 returned to Cambridge.

Browne fell in with Richard Greenham, the puritan minister of a parish five miles outside Cambridge. Greenham preached five sermons a week, so earnestly, it was said, 'that his shirt would usually be as wet with sweating, as if it had been drenched in water, so that he was forced so soon as he came out of the pulpit to shift himself, and this wonderful and excessive pains he took all his time'.[1] Greenham allowed Browne to preach without a licence in his church, and again Browne gained a following, who urged him to be licensed as a preacher in the city. Such lectureships had been the constant recourse of puritans too radical to wear the vestments required of ministers, but Browne's conscience would not even let him take that option. Licences to preach were issued by the bishop, he reasoned, and what possible right did a bishop have to decide who should and should not deliver the message sent to the people by Christ? To accept a bishop's licence would be to accept its authority and to tell those who did not have a licence that they should not preach.

Browne continued his unlicensed preaching around Cambridge, and discussed his objections to the licence with the 'forwardest', but got little support for those views. In 1579, his brother decided to cover Robert's back by applying for the licence on his behalf. Browne was appalled and refused to pay the fee. When his brother paid it for him, Browne burned the licence.

Browne urged the Cambridge churches to throw off the authority of the bishops and reform themselves, but got a cool response. And so an idea started to grow that would redefine the Separatist movement. He concluded that 'the Kingdom of God was not to be begun by whole parishes, but rather of the worthiest, were they never so few'. The difference between Browne and the London Separatists so far was subtle. The London ministers found that the bishops would not let them run their parishes as they saw fit; Browne wanted nothing to do with the bishops or parishes. Both therefore decided to gather congregations of 'the worthiest' only, but for the Londoners this was because they had no control over anyone else; for Browne it was because he was not sure anyone else belonged in the church. For now the difference was academic as well as subtle: Browne spent six months trying to gather an underground congregation in Cambridge, but failed.[2]

Robert Harrison

As Browne was coming to the conclusion that Cambridge was in a hopeless state, addicted to its episcopal bondage, a university friend of his returned to the city, with a view to being ordained – Robert Harrison. Harrison was a published writer, having after graduation translated Ludwig Lavater's *De spectris* into English with an introduction, under the title *Of ghostes and spirites walking by nyght*. It does not seem an obvious subject for a reformer, but ghosts were traditionally seen as the dead visiting from purgatory. Lavater, being a Protestant, denied purgatory and so argued that ghosts are demons masquerading as the dead. *Hamlet* is concerned with the same theological question of whether the ghost is 'a spirit of health or goblin damn'd'.

Harrison had, like Browne, become a schoolteacher, and lasted less than a month as master of Aylsham Grammar School in Norfolk. It had taken six months of negotiations to get the job, because the Bishop of Norwich objected to his puritanism: Harrison had tried to get married in 1573 without the minister using the Prayer Book, and was said to disapprove of children reading non-religious books. The bishop was also worried to hear that Harrison had fits. The mayor and leading citizens of Norfolk had appealed to the bishop on Harrison's behalf, and Harrison apologised for his past behaviour, undertaking to 'have no evil nor strange opinions', to keep no disordered company, to read the required books to the children and to take no part in prophesyings or unlawful games. So he was given the teaching job, and lasted a month. Being godfather at a baptism in his wife's family, he asked the deacon to omit the sign of the cross and to address his questions to all the participants rather than just the baby. As a result, Harrison was dismissed from the school in January 1574. We do not know how he spent the following years, but it seems to have been in 1579 that he met Browne again in Cambridge.[3]

Harrison asked Browne to support his application for ordination. Browne told him what he thought of ordination by bishops, and tried to dissuade him. Harrison's application was rejected, which he took as a sign from God that Browne was right. Instead Harrison became the master of Great Hospital, a poor house and hospice in Norwich.

Browne heard that in and around Norwich, puritanism had become more radical than in Cambridge. In 1575, Edmund Freake had replaced John Parkhurst as Bishop of Norwich, and taken a much stronger Elizabethan line, suppressing the prophesyings, silencing preaching and removing puritan ministers, which had created considerable dissent. It may well even have created an underground church, as in London. Browne wondered if God was calling him there and his time in the wilderness of Cambridge had been a preparation for the real work in Norwich. In Cambridge he had a visit from the thirty-six-year-old Richard Bancroft, the future Archbishop of Canterbury and an arch-villain in the story of the Separatists, but for now an officer of the Bishop of Ely. Bancroft had a message from the Privy Council forbidding Browne to preach. Browne assured Bancroft he would not preach in Cambridge again.

Browne married a woman called Alice, who is said, by the nineteenth-century historian Thomas Blore, to have been from Yorkshire and a member of the Allen family. The Allens of Norfolk were the puritan family that Harrison had married into, so it may perhaps be that Blore confused these two marriages. The Brownes' was a rocky marriage in which religion caused considerable conflict.

In Norwich, Robert Browne seems to have been allowed to preach in a parish church again, and, when he was stopped, preached in the churchyard, before settling for a house adjoining the churchyard. Browne travelled extensively around the region and gained a much more sympathetic hearing for his Separatist message than he had in Cambridge, getting a strong following not just in Norwich but as far afield as Bury St Edmunds, more than forty miles away. According to the former Separatist Henoch Clapham writing twenty years later, Browne drew 'servants from their masters, children from their parents, wives from their husbands'.[4]

To what extent Browne was drawing fresh converts from the Church of England by the power of his own message, or joining in a harvest that others had sowed, is impossible to say. Certainly a local minister, Thomas Wolsey, a man of 'a harsh spirit' who had been ordained in 1568, worked alongside him. Their followers included the tailor Elias Thacker, who had already spent time in jail as a religious dissident, and the shoemaker John Copping, who had been imprisoned in 1578 for saying 'the Queen was sworn to keep God's law, and she is perjured'. Both men lived in Bury St Edmunds. Browne stayed in the house of Edward Tolwine, a man of about fifty, and the pair discussed the question of separation from the Church of England at length. One 1655 source tells us that Browne gained his first followers from the large and ever growing number of Dutch residents of Norwich, but it is not a generally reliable account of Browne's mission.[5]

Early in 1581, Browne published his first known writing, contributing anonymously to a joint publication called *A Viewe of Antichrist*. The main attraction in this tract was the reprinting of a number of short pieces on the state of the church by Anthony Gilby, a father of puritanism, first published in 1570 under the same title. These were followed by another old writing, previously published with Gilby's, by someone identifying himself as TW. Browne's essay was the one new writing, and it was an attack on the bishops, those 'makeshifts and troublers'. It was an unremarkable example of standard radical puritan polemic, and the most extraordinary thing about it was how soon Browne found himself going far beyond it.[6]

Congregational church

As Browne met secretly with his followers for worship and preaching, they abandoned all written liturgy, or 'read and stinted prayers in popish wise' as Harrison put it. Where puritans had protested about this or that objectionable element in the Prayer Book, and the London conventiclers had abandoned it entirely in favour of the Genevan book, the Norwich Separatists found they had no need for a Prayer Book at all. They had freed themselves from the control of the state church to such an extent that they found their own words sufficient to voice their prayers.[7]

The illicit experience of underground Christian community was transforming Browne's idea of what a church is. He had long hated the idea of the church being a national hierarchy under the aristocratic rule of bishops, finding the presbyterian system truer to the simple Christian life of the New Testament. But now, removed from the parish system as a company of the worthiest, he and his flock experienced something simpler and purer still. Without synods and presbyteries, without the validation of a national church, they were a spiritual community answerable to no one but Christ. In truth, Browne reasoned, the church is the people of God, and therefore not ruled by elders or pastors any more than by bishops: what the people of God decide together as a body has greater authority than what any individual Christian, in any role, may decide. As Browne put it in the book he wrote the following year, *A true and short declaration*, 'The meetings together … of every whole church, and of the elders therein, is above the apostle, above the prophet, the evangelist, the pastor, the teacher, and every particular elder.' The community works out its faith by consensus without allowing anyone to impose. Browne conceded that they should take advice from the forwardest but the final authority is in the people as a whole. 'The voice of the whole people, guided by the elders and the forwardest, is said [in Scripture] to be the voice of God.'[8] This is what became known as the congregational, as opposed to presbyterian or episcopal, concept of church.

In a society where the word 'democratic' was only ever used as a pejorative, Browne's new idea was scandalously egalitarian. Excepting the recent emigration of some Dutch Anabaptists, there was nothing like it in English religion or politics. If successful, it would remove the church as an arm of government from the Queen, and hand it to the people. Browne was driven to such extremes, partly by positive experience of Christian community, but also by the failure of every less radical attempt to change what happened in English churches. The approach of respectable Protestants such as Grindal, praying that God would bring the Queen to a better mind, had proved unrealistic. The more radical solution of presbyterianism, giving control of churches to synods of ministers, had failed just as completely, because it depended on the Queen being so minded as to hand her power over to those synods, which was even more unrealistic. If, however, the church is the people, and all decisions about the church are made by the people, then the problem disappears. The only thing one needs in order to have a pure, free and holy church is people who decide to be that church. The will of the Queen, the bishops and the state become irrelevant – apart from the question of the punishment they would inflict on the gathered church.

So one day early in 1581, the Norwich Separatists joined together in a covenant to be a new church. The concept of covenant was central to Browne's thinking. It had been an important idea for many Swiss reformers, Bullinger in Zurich saying, 'Nothing else has been handed down to the saints of all ages, throughout the entire Scripture.'[9] For Bullinger, and for Browne, covenant is the agreement between God and human beings that their relationship is based on, just as the relationship between a husband and wife is based on the covenant of marriage. In Genesis, the Lord makes a covenant with Abraham: he will be the God of Abraham and his descendants, and they will be God's people. Circumcision was a sign and seal of this covenant (comparable, in an analogy puritans would have hated, to the wedding ring), so each new generation was circumcised into the people of God. Later, the Lord gave the law to Moses as the terms and conditions of the covenant. In the New Testament, Browne says, Christ establishes a new covenant ('testament' being synonymous with 'covenant'), where the seal is now baptism, and the terms are the law of Christ, which abrogates the law of Moses.* Browne applied this principle to England: the state church did not obey the terms of the covenant and so its members were not the people of God.

Covenant was Browne's way of understanding church: what it meant to be a church, how the Church of England failed to be a church, and how he and his followers could become a church. The church is not an entire Christian state, but a voluntary Christian community within the state. Browne, Harrison and their congregation entered a covenant with God together in order to become a true church and join the worldwide people of God.

On the day appointed for the making of the covenant, the leaders declared what the congregation were doing and why, the members replying, 'To this we give our consent.' They voted to appoint Browne as pastor and Harrison as teacher, recognising their authority so long as they remained faithful to the conditional covenant, and

---

* Here Browne differed from Bullinger. For Bullinger the so-called new covenant is simply a continuation of the old, modified by the coming of Christ.

prayed for them. They agreed an order for their services: while their ministers were specially appointed to the task, 'all men which had the gift' were allowed to preach; and church members might interrupt the sermon with questions, to clarify what the preacher was trying to explain or even to dispute it, 'in due order'. They also established a regular meeting for disciplining members, as in the presbyterian system, though with less power vested in the ministers. People who had never before had any role in the government of local life decided the terms of their Christian community and drew up the conditions of the covenant that they would arbitrate.[10]

1581 Parliament

While this local drama of ecclesiastical subversion was being played out, events on the national stage served to confirm Browne's thinking that it was necessary. Parliament sat between January and March 1581, for the first time in five years, and once again failed to achieve any church reform at all. Even a bill establishing a public fast was thrown out by the Queen as encroaching on her religious autocracy. Reform was not going to come from above during Elizabeth's reign, and the more forward puritan ministers increasingly started meeting together in formal conferences, creating their own unofficial local presbyterian reformations.

Parliament did, however, pass two Acts that would have an impact on the movement Browne was leading, despite the fact that both were aimed at Roman Catholics. The Lords and Commons agreed a bill stringently punishing recusancy, the non-attendance of Catholics at parish services, which in the historian John Neale's words was a plan 'to eradicate Catholicism from England by making life intolerable even for its peaceful and loyal adherents'. The Queen intervened to drastically tone down the measure but the Act as passed still fined recusants £20 month, with larger fines for hearing or saying Mass. It also declared that if anyone persuaded another to abandon their allegiance to the Queen, both were traitors. The other measure, the sedition bill, was to outlaw anti-Protestant propaganda. This time it was the Commons who toned it down, because, according to Neale, they feared it being used against puritan critics of the church. Both were indeed used against Protestant radicals.[11]

Parliament acted from fear of Catholic mission, which had recently been boosted by the arrival of Jesuits including Edmund Campion, who set up a secret press distributing compelling apologetics. He argued that Catholicism was the heritage of the English and morally and rationally invincible – as proven, he reckoned, by the Queen's resort to violence against it. The missionaries would never 'despair your recovery while we have a man left to enjoy your Tyburn, or to be racked with your torments, or consumed with your prisons'. Campion was found in a priest hole in a Berkshire manor house. His repeated torture, including spikes driven under his fingernails, elicited no evidence of conspiracy, but he was convicted, on false testimony, and hanged, drawn and quartered on 1 December 1581.[12]

Browne's troubles

Early in 1581, the Bishop of Norwich investigated Browne. A number of ministers had complained to Freake about Browne's meetings, so he was arrested, kept in prison for a while and then expelled from the diocese. Browne came straight back and resumed work.

Browne was arrested a second time in April 1581, and this time Bishop Freake wrote to Lord Burghley for advice and support. Browne, reported Freake, had been preaching to audiences of a hundred at a time, to 'the vulgar sort of the people, who greatly depended on him'. Not for the last time, Browne felt the value of his family connections to the most powerful man in England: Burghley told Freake to talk to his kinsman charitably, as one whose wrongdoing 'proceed[s] of zeal rather than malice', and if that did not work, to send him to London where Burghley would talk with him personally.[13]

Browne was indeed taken to London, while Harrison, Wolsey and other Separatists in East Anglia were jailed. 'We were shut up between walls most of us,' said Harrison, 'with our legs chained, all of us put to great expense, and those which were out of prison not able to stir out of the doors, when they were at home, nor able to be at home except it were a little by stealth, for the bursting open of our doors and violent handling.' Freake reported they were 'so greatly dismayed' by the experience that they would be unlikely to disturb the diocese again.[14]

In London, Browne was kept in custody for a while, but still managed to publish two short tracts making the case for separating from the Church of England, *Against disordered preaching at Paules crosse* and *Against parish preachers and hyred lecturers.** In the first, Browne castigated those preachers who submitted to the authorisation of bishops. How can they claim to preach in the name of Christ when they will never say a word unless they have a parchment and 'my Lord's face is in the wax'? Puritans admit that the Church of England does not have the government prescribed by Christ; Browne says that if Christ does not govern it, then it is governed by one who claims the authority of Christ but is not Christ – the bishop sits on antichrist's throne. Their parishes are not free assemblies of Christians but fair cages full of unclean birds.[15]

In *Against parish preachers*, Browne addressed those who felt they were obliged to accept the minister, church order and fellow members imposed on them by the state. Why? he asked. 'Is not every Christian a king and a priest, to rule with Christ by open rebuke?' They have the power and the freedom to keep the church pure, by creating a congregation beyond the power of the bishops. In both tracts, Browne took on the voice of a prophet: 'Therefore thus saith the Lord: I feed not my flock at Paul's Cross in London, or Saint Mary's in Cambridge, or in your English parishes. O ye my sheep, go ye not thither, as though there were my fold.'[16]

---

* The existence of these two tracts seems to have escaped the notice of historians. This has not been a disastrous loss, because Browne incorporated their text into his well-known *A Treatise upon the 23. Of Matthewe*, but it is well worth recognising their separate existence, because they give us Browne's teaching shortly after his conversion to Separatism, rather than a year afterwards when his later works were published. Their existence is demonstrated by Stephen Bredwell, Browne's sparring partner, who quoted from them extensively, under their original names, in his book *The Rasing of the Foundations of Brovvnisme*, 68, 128–30, 136–7. The lapsed Separatist Peter Fairlambe also listed them separately in his Brownist reading list in *The Recantation of a Brownist* (London, 1606), C2 verso–C3 recto.

Harrison versus Fenton

The Separatists came into conflict not only with the church hierarchy but also with radical puritans who would not join their illegal fellowship. Edward Fenton, the Rector of the Norfolk village of Booton and the chaplain of a nobleman, was a puritan ardent enough to have been imprisoned for nonconformity – though as Harrison pointed out, 'in a fair chamber and on a soft featherbed' – and he was still now involved in forbidden prophesyings. Wolsey had hoped that Fenton would join the Separatists, and when he decided against it, Wolsey wrote him a vitriolic letter, saying that Fenton and his 'fellow deceivers' were 'false brethren, men pleasers, blind guides, trees without fruit'.[17]

Fenton wrote back to Wolsey, saying that their disreputable meetings were drawing people away from the public prayers and sacraments of the English Church. Fenton was not the man to make a fierce defence of the Church of England, but, forced to decide, he judged that its faults were matters to complain and pray about, not reasons to abandon it as a false church.

Harrison pointed out that as a presbyterian, Fenton believed the office of bishop was contrary to the gospel; if bishops are against the gospel, said Harrison, they were antichrist, and so ministers in the Church of England are employed by antichrist. 'You have received their waxen seals in your hands, and their handsful of benisons on your heads ... and you do not repent it nor renounce it: therefore you have received the mark of the beast.'[18]

Fenton heard that Harrison had called the preaching of the Elizabethan Church ministers 'prattling', so accused him of blasphemy: he was no longer attacking popish imperfections but the word of the Lord. Harrison replied, as Browne had convinced him, that only messengers employed by God can bring the message of God, so messengers employed by antichrist can prattle but cannot possibly preach.

Fenton accused the Separatists of lurking in corners like sorcerers, running from house to house, persuading the people 'to be rather in houses and in corners than to be where there is the public face of the church'. Harrison pointed out that they first listened to Browne's preaching in a church building; 'from thence we were driven into the

103

churchyard, from thence into a house adjoining upon the church-yard, from whence we [were] had to prison ... Yet now we are charged as people which will not come to the church.'[19]

Fenton even used the Separatists' finances against them: the men let their 'wives and children weep for want', 'going backward with the world and waxing poorer', while the way they helped each other out when in need looked suspiciously like a first step on the road to 'the community of the Anabaptists'. Harrison said some of them are actually richer than they previously were.

> But, Mr F, what if we should lose houses, lands, or all the rest of our goods, wives, children and all (as we durst make none other reckoning; if any better measure come we shall put it among our gains)? ... It is our glory and not our shame, we have received all from the Lord, and we hold all in our hands, even with our lives, to offer to the Lord.[20]

Exile

Life in Norwich was hard for the Separatists though, hard enough for the question of leaving their home country to arise. Some members of the congregation, perhaps remembering Grindal's arrangements with the London underground church, suggested they might move to Scotland. They paid preliminary visits and made provisional arrangements.

Browne, however, sending his advice from prison in London, was dead set against the plan – and not for the most obvious of reasons. As Browne saw it, their group was the body of Christ and it was not up to them simply to relocate if and when they felt like it. God's will for them was to be discerned in the patterns of Scripture, and the pattern that matched their predicament was the exodus story. The land of their birth was a place of cruel, antichristian slavery, the biblical Egypt. The children of Israel did not take themselves into exile – that would be desertion. Instead 'the Lord with strong hand delivered them from thence', and until they saw the same divine intervention, the Separatists should stay and preach in their own country. Those who wanted to leave also investigated the Channel Islands, where the governors had introduced a presbyterian church order created for them by Cartwright in 1576, but Browne again dissuaded them.[21]

Browne returned to East Anglia, and on 2 August 1581 Freake was once more telling Burghley that Browne had troubled the whole diocese. He had such support from influential gentlemen and was leading meetings 'in such close and secret manner' that the bishop was at a loss how to suppress them and feared 'the overthrow of all religion' if Burghley did not intervene.[22]

More prison time and other hardships followed for the Separatists. Harrison told Browne that close confinement was preventing them from teaching their flock or preaching to unbelievers, and eventually even Browne was persuaded that 'the Lord did call them out of England'. Whether Browne had found a burning bush or simply a different way to read the Scripture we do not know, but one way or another he was convinced that God was again leading the children of Israel out of Egypt into the wilderness.[23]

Harrison resigned his post at the hospital on what he certainly did not call Lady Day, 25 March 1582. Wolsey did not accompany them – there is some evidence that he was kept in prison, some evidence that he maintained Browne's former position that it was wrong to flee the country. Copping and Thacker stayed behind too. Tolwine found a buyer for his property, but before the deal was complete the buyer died, so he stayed to find another. But the bulk of Browne's following went together into the unknown, to Middelburg in the Netherlands.

10

Middelburg

REVOLT AGAINST SPAIN had given the Netherlands the most tolerant society in western Europe. It put William of Orange at the head of the Dutch forces, and he was a man deeply committed to toleration. He was personally influenced in this by Dutch thinkers such as Erasmus and Castellio, but it was above all a pragmatic strategy: if Dutch Protestants were to throw off Catholic oppression they could not afford to be fighting religious wars among themselves. Logically enough on that basis, William's toleration did not extend to Catholics, whose churches were seized, but it did include Anabaptists. William had taken over Middelburg, the capital of Zeeland, in 1574, and in 1576 the Calvinist city deputies decreed that no one could pursue a trade there without swearing an oath of loyalty, a decree designed to make life impossible for Anabaptists, who would not swear oaths. The Anabaptists appealed to William, who in January 1577 commanded the deputies not 'to oppress the petitioners contrary to their conscience', having to repeat the instruction in 1578, 1580 and 1582. In this way, the revolutionary Netherlands, starting with Middelburg, became a safer place to be an Anabaptist than elsewhere in Europe.

Middelburg had a double appeal, then, to the English Separatists: the Dutch Reformed Church settlement promised a more congenial environment than episcopal England; and should they fail to see eye to eye with the religious authorities there, the fact that even Anabaptists went unmolested suggested that their own religion would be tolerable. The Netherlands had another recommendation for Browne too: a strong and unrestricted printing industry.

The personal cost of exile was enormous though. Bradford later described the ordeal of these earlier exiles as well as his contemporaries' in going to the Netherlands when he said:

> Being thus constrained to leave their native soil and country, their lands and livings and all their friends, and familiar acquaintance, it was much; and thought marvellous by many: but to go into a country they knew not (but by hearsay) where they must learn a new language, and get their livings they knew not how, it being a dear place, and subject to the miseries of war, it was by many thought an adventure almost desperate, a case intolerable, and a misery worse than death.[1]

An English naval officer, Richard Godard, reported in August 1582 that there were thirty or forty Separatists, 'in poor estate, and for the most part visited by sickness'. They met in Browne's rented accommodation, at first attracting a good number of Dutch worshippers, sympathetic to Reformed refugees, but as their extremism became apparent they lost them and, as Godard put it, Browne exercised 'a ministry in a corner'.[2]

'Reformation without Tarying'

Browne made the most of Dutch printing, publishing no fewer than three books in August 1582, including the most radical work the Separatist movement produced for many years, a ground-breaking declaration of religious freedom called *A Treatise of Reformation without Tarying for Anie*.

The central argument of *Reformation without Tarying* was that local churches who want to start following the pattern of the Bible do not need to – and must not – wait for the monarch to reform the national church. They are directly answerable to Christ, and therefore to no one else. They have a right and a duty to reform their own congregation. If the rulers of the land are genuine Christians, they will 'gladly suffer and submit themselves to the church government'; if they are not, then it is none of their business.

But religious freedom was not for Browne simply a matter of who gets to run the church. In the short period of time he had been leading a church he had come to believe that free choice was at the heart of genuine worship and prayer, and at the heart of believers' relationship with God. A whole parish worshipping in forced obedience to the law of the land is not a church, he said; 'the Lord's people is of the willing sort'. Dipping in and out of the language of Jeremiah, he continued:

> They shall come unto Zion and inquire the way to Jerusalem, not by force nor compulsion, but with their faces thitherward: yea as the he-goats shall they be before the flock, for the haste they have unto Zion, and they themselves shall call for the covenant, saying, 'Come and let us cleave fast unto the Lord in a perpetual covenant that shall never be forgotten.' For it is the conscience and not the power of man that will drive us to seek the Lord's kingdom.

Few later Separatists had quite the same ebullient vision of freedom as Browne expressed here. It was profoundly out of step with the world he lived in, and even he himself failed to hold on to it for long. It clearly reflects a powerful personal inclination, and also the exhilarating experience of being a voluntary church. Browne extended this principle of freedom to their worship: the Separatists were free from set prayers, praying spontaneously, Browne said, as occasion demanded, 'with true feeling and touch of heart', avoiding the 'fond repetitions and vain babblings' of Prayer Books.[3]

Browne found it quite unacceptable for either the church or state 'to compel religion, to plant churches by power and to force a submission to ecclesiastical government by laws and penalties'. He was not a pacifist like the Anabaptists; he was quite happy with the idea that a Christian ruler should execute criminals, but not for crimes of faith. His objection to religious coercion was that true religion is an essentially personal and communal response to God and therefore voluntary, in which case forcing the unwilling to church fails to make them Christians, but makes the church unchristian: 'The Lord's kingdom is not by force.' As Browne said in another book published at the same time, it is antichrist that 'forceth his religion by civil power', while those who make a covenant with the Lord make it 'with all their heart, and with all their soul', driven by 'the conscience and not the power of man'.[4]

Browne concluded from this something like what later generations would call the separation of church and state. The church must direct the lives of Christians spiritually, through preaching, and has no business using state laws or 'civil forcings'; conversely, the state has 'no ecclesiastical authority at all'. Rulers should of course be guided by Scripture but not impose religious observations on people.[5]

One of the most striking aspects of Browne's love of religious freedom is that he took it to lengths that were against his own interests. He championed the freedom and self-sufficiency of the church not only against the authority of the state, but against the authority of the minister. A presbyterian would have said, as Browne himself had said only the previous year, that authority lies with 'the ministers and elders that are chosen out of the congregation to watch over the rest of the flock'. Now though, he demanded, 'Is not every Christian a king and a priest to rule with Christ by open rebuke ...?' It was on this basis that Browne expected the congregation to question the preacher and insisted that church business be decided by the whole church and not just by its leaders.[6]

Where did Browne's extraordinary idea of religious freedom come from? One source was the way the puritan movement in general had developed. As Protestantism had introduced diversity into the European church, so Puritanism had brought diversity into English Protestantism. Puritans opted for their own forms of worship and organisation: they effectively edited the Prayer Book, arranged lectureships, took part in prophesyings and developed secret presbyterian structures. And they claimed the God-given freedom to do so, though the prospect of imposing their choices on the whole country was too beguiling to allow them to extend such freedom to anyone other than themselves.

The Separatist experience was of a great deal more freedom than other puritans enjoyed. This included the choice of congregation and election of pastors and elders, and had developed to the point where lay members could pray in their own words, preach to one another and even create a new church through a communal act of covenant. The first Separatists may have seen themselves as a state church in waiting, but their experience was of being a Christian gathering within an unchristian society – which is what the dreaded Anabaptists believed the church should be. The churches that Separatists read about in the New Testament were the same. And Separatists enjoyed the purity and holiness of church, which puritans talked about so vociferously, in ways a state church never could. As the Queen's intransigence wore down puritan hopes for reform of the state Church, the Separatists' strange experience of voluntary church came to seem like a permanent alternative.

It is a great paradox of the puritan movement that that most illiberal ideal of purity led eventually to the conception of religious freedom. Purity requires compulsion – forcing members of a body to submit to an idea of what is pure or making them leave – and is the opposite of diversity. And yet the English Protestants who most ardently sought the purity of the church ended up with a church so pure it required sincere believers to commit to one another voluntarily, an arrangement that could never be imposed on a whole society. If you want to restrict the church to true believers only, they have to be free to disbelieve and to leave.

Central to Browne's outlook here is the idea of conditional covenant. Browne radicalised the concept of covenant with God by insisting that it was absolutely conditional upon the obedience of the church. God promises to be our God, and the church promises obedience, so when the church disobeys, Browne said, the covenant is annulled and God no longer accepts the church. 'He shall be our God', Browne said, 'so long as we keep under his government and obey his laws, and no longer.' Again, this is an unlovely idea, that Christ is forever ready to divorce his bride for the smallest defiance of his rules, and other writers on the covenant found more room for God's patient grace and abundant mercy. And yet the conditional covenant compelled Browne not only to reject the Church of England as unchurched by disobedience, but also to insist on religious freedom: if the church is ruined when it accepts unchristian members, then forcing the unwilling into church membership is suicidal.[7]

For these reasons, the Separatist movement from Browne onwards believed in freedom for the sake of purity and communal obedience. But Browne was different, writing about freedom with a joy and a fervour, as a positive good and a delightful experience. He embraced – probably designed – a church organisation that gave away his power as pastor in favour of the freedom of the congregation, because freedom was not just a means to an end but a personal passion. And he paid the price.

There is another possible source of Browne's voluntarism too. There were thousands of Dutch refugees in and around Norwich while Browne was there, and a significant proportion were Anabaptists. If it is true that Browne's followers included a number of Dutch people, it would seem more than likely that they were Anabaptists, as they were already Separatists on principle; and even discounting that report, one would still expect some interchange of ideas as Browne travelled the area recruiting members to his radical cause. Moreover, the place where Browne first wrote in this voluntarist vein was Middelburg, the one city in Europe where freedom of religion was most firmly established on principle, and again where Anabaptists were free to meet openly, so there was opportunity to observe, practise and perhaps discuss voluntary Christianity. This is circumstantial evidence and one would not want to claim too much for it, but it raises the possibility that Browne's Separatist experience and personal inclinations may have been helped in the direction of voluntarism by Dutch believers.*

'A Booke which sheweth'

The second book Browne published in 1582 was much longer and rather odder. Entitled *A Booke which sheweth the life and manners of all true Christians*, it was an attempt at a systematic theology of Christianity as Browne saw it, in 185 tables, each dealing with a different theme, from the infinity of God to keeping secrets. Each table was divided into four columns: the state of Christians; the state of heathens; definitions; and divisions. The second two columns merely explained the first two in greater detail, and what those first two did was divide everything in human life into binary

---

* C.N. Kraus published a study of the evidence for Anabaptist influence on Browne in 1960, finding little. On the basis that there are no close parallels between the two, and that Browne's puritan/Separatist experience gave him sufficient reason to embrace voluntarism, Kraus concluded that there was 'a minimum of direct relationship'. This is quite true. If you start with the thesis that Browne's Separatism was entirely dependent and profoundly indebted to Anabaptism, you will find that it was not; but if you start with the assumption that it was independent of Dutch influence, you may find yourself wondering why he went further down this road than other Separatists. (C.N. Kraus, 'Anabaptist Influence on English Separatism as Seen in Robert Browne', *Mennonite Quarterly Review*, 34 (1960), 5.)

opposites of Christ and antichrist: for every aspect of true Christian life and doctrine in the first column, Browne found an opposite in the antichristian church. This was straightforward enough when applied to a subject like heaven/hell or sins/virtues, but Browne fitted every area of life and religion into the antithetic scheme. The believers say prayers, the heathen say false prayers; the believers work hard, the heathen are idle. Browne's dualism even applied to such unpromising ideas as the Trinity, which one might take as a doctrine that united all Protestants and Catholics. According to Browne's scheme, Christians believe in God the Father, Son and Holy Spirit, while antichristians have their Holy Father the Pope, the priests who are his spiritual sons, and seducing and wicked spirits. For Browne, false religion and unbelief did not simply diverge from true Christianity on certain crucial points; they were opposite in every way, perfect inverted replicas.

The book is a graphic illustration of the dualism of puritan extremism. The Elizabethan Church had established itself in the grey areas between Catholicism and the Reformed Christianity of Switzerland, Germany, etc. Puritanism, in contrast, appealed to those who wanted something more uncompromising. The more radical the puritanism, the more it divided those grey areas into black and white. The surplice, the wedding ring, the office of bishop, none of these was negotiable or tolerable; such things are either commanded or forbidden.

Browne and Harrison extended this principle to membership of the Church of England itself. They scorned the 'tolerations, mitigations and other trim distinctions' that even radical puritans had to make in order to justify remaining in the Church of England: it was wicked sophistry, they said, to talk in terms of 'things partly lawful and partly unlawful'. For Browne and Harrison there was Christ and antichrist and nothing else. When people said they had 'the true government in part', the Separatists said that they therefore also had the false government in part, and 'what part hath Christ with Belial?'[8]

The baldest statement of this mindset is in the excoriation of the puritans whom Browne left behind in the church: 'And why halt they between good and evil? For if they do many things well and yet in one thing be open and grievous transgressors, all is made naught. And how should anything be partly good as they say and partly evil? For the evil that is doth make it wholly evil.' The Separatists' willingness to embrace religious radicalism seems to be in direct proportion to their unwillingness to embrace moral complexity.[9]

Browne's third book of 1582 was *A Treatise upon the 23. of Matthewe*. This incorporated the whole of his two Separatist tracts from the previous year, knitted into new material against the dominant style of English preaching, over-reliant on the formal logic and rhetoric taught at the universities and on displays of linguistic learning.

Browne's books were printed by Richard Schilders, a Dutch printer who had learned his trade in London in the 1570s as an exile from Spanish repression and was now printer to the States of Zeeland. (Schilders put his name as 'Richarde Painter' on English books, translating it literally from the Dutch.) Browne's print run had to be abandoned before completion, and although the first two books were finished, *A Treatise upon the 23. of Matthewe* ended mid-sentence and shipped as it was, with a note saying, 'By reason of trouble the print was stayed'. There was no shortage of troubles that might have had this effect, including lack of money, arguments between Browne and Harrison, and political interference, but we do not know which it was. Some copies of the books were sold to English merchants in the Netherlands, but most were smuggled back as loose sheets to Norwich, where they were bound by Thomas Gibson, a remaining member of the Separatist church, and circulated by Copping and Thacker.

Harrison's disappointment

A response to Browne's books was written by Richard Bancroft, now chaplain to the Privy Councillor Sir Christopher Hatton. Bancroft's eight-page tract, *The Most Principall and Chief Heresies in R: Brownes Booke*, lists by name no fewer than thirty-four heresies that Browne is supposed to agree with – or that he 'cometh near to' – in his works, ranging from Anabaptism to Papism, Donatism to Catharism, and Platonism to Judaism, a heady cocktail.[10]

Even Harrison, who by one account paid a considerable part of Browne's printing costs, was not greatly impressed by Browne's books. He had hoped for something to bring comfort and courage to the Separatists back in Norwich who had not been able to come to Middelburg, and he thought Browne 'did but slenderly answer and satisfy the same'. Worse, he thought the voluntary Christianity set out in *Reformation without Tarying* was 'manifold heresy', while *A Treatise upon the 23. of Matthewe*, in teaching that the ministers were subject to the people, was 'a pattern of all lewd frantic disorder'. ('Lewd' here means 'wicked', perhaps with a suggestion of 'ignorant'; 'frantic' means 'insane'.[11])

Harrison decided to write a book himself to make up for the disappointment, but found the business trickier than expected. First he embarked on a lengthy treatise on proper church government, but before it was completed he realised that he could not afford to print it, and he was also incapacitated by illness. Abandoning that book, he tried to write a shorter work, a pastoral exposition of Psalm 122 ('I rejoiced when they said unto me, "We will go into the house of the Lord"'). He wrote 127 pages without getting beyond the first verse and decided to stop there and print it. *A Little Treatise uppon the Firste Verse of the 122nd Psalm* was printed by Schilders and smuggled back to England.

The English Separatists found life in Middelburg increasingly hard. They struggled to make a living and had to pawn cutlery to survive. There was a lot of illness and some of them died. Others talked about returning to England, and Harrison was sympathetic; but Browne, who had so strongly resisted exile in the first place, urged them to remember that the Lord had led them out of Egypt so their present pilgrimage in the wilderness would bring them to the Promised Land. In fact, it was rebellion against God to talk of going back, and Browne reminded them of the punishments faced by Israelites who grumbled against Moses. Browne embarked on a treatise on the book of Revelation 'because men count it so hard, which is so easy and plain'. It would doubtless have outlined how the prophecy of an apocalyptic struggle between Christians and the beast was being fulfilled in their own lives, but Browne was interrupted by a crisis in the church.[12]

Browne versus Harrison

The relationship between the pastor Browne and the teacher Harrison had become seriously strained, and Harrison complained that Browne's 'swerving and leaning to antichristian pride and bitterness' had wounded the church. Their relationship broke down over Browne's pastoral dealings with a woman in the church, a Miss or Mrs Allens, who was Harrison's sister or sister-in-law. Browne's version of events – and the whole story of their quarrels is one of which we only have Browne's version – was that he said to Allens that none of them, including her, 'were sufficiently mortified' for taking part in the abominations of the Church of England in earlier years. The report that reached Harrison, however (Browne tells us), was that Browne had called her a reprobate who had never repented of those abominations and who could not enter the kingdom of heaven until she did. Harrison put this complaint and others against Browne in writing and circulated it among some of the fellowship, refusing to show Browne himself.[13]

At this point they started to discover that the force that created the Separatist movement was also its destruction. They had been driven to quit the Church of England because they found its imperfections simply intolerable. Countless puritans were willing to fight over these things; Browne and Harrison could see no alternative but to split the church and damn those who remained. Such people were unlikely to agree with each other for ever, and once they disagreed it was impossible to live with their differences. So long as they were being constantly arrested and kept in jails, it was relatively easy to be a single movement. Once they were living together in freedom, the cracks started to show, and they could only be fatal. To put it another way, conflict was at the very heart of their religion, and 'if there were no longer any enemies without, it was necessary to reproduce them within'.[14]

Browne's case was brought to a church meeting, where he argued for the biblical principle that no accusation should be upheld against anyone without two or three witnesses. The congregation, guided by Harrison, rejected this argument, but Browne could not consider their voice to be the voice of God on the matter. He told them they were out of order and walked out. He then, he tells us, came back in, pointed out that it was his room, and told them to leave. Browne discovered the cost of his congregational ecclesiology and the renunciation of command over his flock that it entailed, when they sacked him as pastor and started holding their meetings elsewhere.

In October 1582, a familiar face showed up in Middelburg, Thomas Cartwright's. Having left England to avoid arrest in 1573, he had spent four years as an acclaimed academic in Heidelberg before taking work as an agent for the English Merchant Adventurers (i.e. investors) in Antwerp. The Adventurers, enjoying the freedom of expats and driven by 'bravado and a desire for theological excitement' in Keith Sprunger's words, established a presbyterian church in Antwerp in 1578 led by Walter Travers, and when Travers returned to England two years later, Cartwright took over on an enviable salary. At Antwerp, early in 1582, Cartwright had been sent Browne's books and was appalled by his Separatism and his ideas of religious freedom. Cartwright 'doth utterly mislike the epistle touching reformation without attenting the magistrate ...' reported the Adventurers to the Queen's Principal Secretary, Walsingham. 'He saith Mr Browne hath absurdly erred.' For all Cartwright's radical criticism of the state of the church, he was wedded to the state church, and could not believe anyone had the right or ability to form dissident churches. The Adventurers' church faced the grave disapproval of the British government as an affront to the unity and consistency of English religion, but being established in communion with the Dutch Reformed Church it was a very different creature to the Separatist church: one enjoyed freedom through a geographical loophole, the other was sending propaganda back to England fomenting independence. Now, in 1582, the Merchant Adventurers moved their headquarters from Antwerp to Middelburg, and Cartwright moved with them, and so the town gained its second English congregation. Cartwright found himself in the unlikely position of representing the English religious establishment against dissent.[15]

The split between Browne and Harrison was eventually mended and Browne readmitted to the congregation, but problems remained. Harrison's ill health continued and he lost children, which Browne considered the judgement of God on their father's 'malice and troublesome mind' towards Browne. Though Browne still insisted that they would be deserting God's call if they returned to England, he recognised that many of his flock were 'wearied of the hardness of that country'. The example of Cartwright's church reminded them that there were decent reform-minded, preaching ministers in the Church of England and some of the Separatists talked of returning to England, finding such a minister and joining his church, an idea that Harrison said would be permissible, and Browne rejected. Again they quarrelled over the matter, and again they fell out over Allens, this time after Browne rebuked her for unfair criticism of their printer, and for 'want of love and abhorring the pastor'. Again Browne was removed from office, and again he and the others were eventually reconciled.[16]

Browne was sacked a third time, and a third time restored. This controversy seems to have concerned his relationship with his own wife, Alice. Robert never directly mentions her in his memoir – typically of such works – but the later Separatist George Johnson reported that 'the pride of Mr Browne's wife and the other women in the banished English Church at Middelburg [was] a great cause of disagreement between Mr Harrison and Mr Browne'. Browne's guarded report was merely that it concerned 'questions of a husband's authority over his wife'. The evidence points to a serious breach in Robert and Alice's relationship, not least because of religious differences. Johnson talks of Robert's 'miserable and lamentable complaints about his marriage' in this period, and it seems that Alice returned to England before her husband.[17,*]

In 1583, the Separatists were attacked in print when Phillip Stubbes published *The second part of the anatomie of abuses*. Stubbes, a popular puritan pamphleteer, was quick off the mark in what was to become a densely populated field of anti-Separatist writing. Stubbes' polemic was not distinguished by his understanding of

---

* Alice's return without Robert has not been generally recognised, but it seems clear. Parish records place the baptism of the Browne's first child Joan in Stamford on 8 February 1584 (not 1584/5 as Burrage has it, within four months of their second child's). This is sooner than the couple could have got there from Edinburgh, where Robert was in January and February, so Alice must have gone there without him. Robert confirmed that he was still in exile at the child's baptism, saying 'it was baptised in England he being beyond the sea' (Bredwell, *Rasing of the Foundations of Brovvnisme*, 102). Burrage argues, 'Browne could hardly have allowed his wife to return to Stamford alone.' It is unsafe to base any argument on what Robert Browne could not have done, but also unnecessary. The east of England was en route for ships sailing from the Netherlands to Scotland, so Robert could have returned her during his journey to Edinburgh, or a friend or relation could have accompanied Alice either from Middelburg or Edinburgh.

Browne's movement – he thought it was based on the principle 'that those who are lecturers or preach elsewhere than in their own cures are accursed before God' – but he did make the earliest known use of the name by which, from this point onwards, all Separatists were best known to their contemporaries: Brownists. The term made it into Shakespeare, Sir Andrew Aguecheek protesting, 'I had as lief be a Brownist as a politician.' It was a name Separatists absolutely hated, first because they insisted they were the followers of Christ, not of any person, and second because of the particular embarrassment of Browne's later career.

Break-up

The question of the Brownists returning to England did not go away, and it led to a fourth breach between Browne and Harrison, their deepest and final one. Browne said 'that England was as Egypt ... and ... they did sin which had a full purpose to dwell still in England', and Harrison again led disciplinary action against him. But this time, Harrison did not carry the whole church with him and rather than Browne alone being removed the church split, four or five families going with Browne.[18]

The two sides quarrelled over whether it was possible to be a member of the true church and to attend English parish services, but there was another ground of contention between them too, a new and remarkable idea, which Harrison denounced as heresy. Browne said, to quote his own words, 'that all the children must not be counted forthwith to be of the church with the parents believing and received to the church'. Before this point, Browne was already uniquely radical in the Reformed tradition for his teaching that church membership was a voluntary personal commitment, and now it seems that he was driven by the logic of that stance to an even more radical position – the church does not even include the children of believers, until they are ready to make a deliberate personal commitment.[19]

There was enough in Browne's thought to draw him in that direction. He passionately believed church membership was voluntary, individual and a mutual covenant. He defined church as 'a company of believers or Christians, which by a willing covenant made with their God, are under the government of God', committing themselves to God 'with all their heart, and with all their soul', driven by the conscience to seek the kingdom of God. If a voluntary commitment and free choice are essential to church membership, it is fair to conclude that children are not born into the church, but must make a decision to join it.[20]

Harrison's denunciation also had a clear logic to it though, because Browne's new idea was tantamount to Anabaptistry. If children cannot be considered part of the church on the strength of their parents' belief, it follows that they should not be baptised into the church. Browne did not take that next logical step – he was still saying, in the same passage, that children could be committed to God by others – but that left him in what reads as an inconsistent muddle.

According to Browne, Harrison and his supporters denounced their pastor as a heretic, 'worse than the pope and antichrist'. They evicted Browne's followers from their rooms, and persuaded his servant to leave him. They took money from him for debts that he disputed and threatened to burn books he wanted to buy. Browne's version of events is generally followed by historians because he took the trouble to write it down (Harrison excused himself, saying Browne's treacheries were too many to record), but Harrison would undoubtedly have disagreed with Browne's story. In a letter written not long afterwards, he said Browne 'cast us off', and he insisted to his correspondent, 'I am well able to prove that Cain dealt not so ill with his brother Abel as he hath dealt with me.'[21]

It was now that Browne wrote his memoir of their Separatist experiment, to give his side of the story, starting with his time at Cambridge and continuing through their church covenant in Norwich up to their present exile and divisions. The bulk of the tract reconstructed the discussions in which Browne persuaded Harrison that puritan preachers were not Christian ministers so long as they remained in the Church of England. It corrected the claim by Harrison's faction that Browne sometimes permitted followers to worship in English parish churches, and so was inconsistent in condemning them for wanting to return to the Church of England now. His narrative showed that he had consistently held Separatist principles and reviled all unreformed worship since before he came to Norwich.

Browne published his memoir under the title *A true and short declaration both of the gathering and ioyning together of certaine persons: and also of the lamentable breach and division which fell amongst them*. It was printed not by Schilders, but apparently by an amateur in Browne's own church, possibly Browne himself, who did a cheap and hurried job, becoming as Leland Carlson his modern editor puts it, 'increasingly frantic' towards the end, where it is full of random capitals, abbreviations, strange spellings and upside-down letters, and, just like Browne's previous book, ends abruptly.

The permanent breach with Harrison seems to have made life in Middelburg impossible for Browne. And yet his belief in God's call out of Egypt would not allow him to return to England, so instead Browne and his remaining followers extended their pilgrimage to Scotland, arriving in Edinburgh on 9 January 1584.

II

Executions and surrender

THE CHURCH OF St Mary in Bury St Edmunds, like other English parish churches, bore the Queen's arms on the wall, symbolising her supreme governorship of the Church of England. In the spring of 1583, the puritan bookbinder Thomas Gibson arranged to have a Bible verse printed around the arms: 'I know thy works and thy love, and service and faith, and thy patience, and thy works, and that they are more at the last, than at the first.' An uplifting text in its own right, when juxtaposed with the royal arms the words implied – at least to the casual observer – a typically glowing commendation of Her Grace.

Richard Bancroft was not a casual observer, and he saw something different. In addition to his other roles, Bancroft was one of the twelve preachers licensed at Cambridge University and so had been sent to preach at the Bury St Edmunds assizes in 1583. Bancroft noticed that the Bible passage quoted on the wall, from Revelation 2, continues: 'Notwithstanding, I have a few things against thee, that thou sufferest the woman Jezebel which calleth herself a prophetess, to teach and to deceive my servants, to make them commit fornication and to eat meat sacrificed unto idols.' It was a subtle but clear attack on the Queen and her religious policy.

Hangings

Bancroft investigated the offence and struck lucky. He uncovered not only the perpetrator Gibson, but his operations with Thacker and Copping to distribute the books of Browne and Harrison. On interrogation, Gibson saved his life by condemning the Brownists'

121

errors. Thacker and Copping stood firm and defended their teachings, insisting that the Queen had absolute authority in secular rule and none in religion.

Thacker was hanged at Bury's Abbey Gate on Thursday 4 June 1583, Copping the following day, the first actual killings in the history of the Separatist movement, though far from its first martyrdoms. The *Mayflower* pilgrims remembered the pair as heroes, Bradford saying that they told the judge: 'My lord, your face we fear not, and for your threats we care not, and to come to your read service we dare not.'[1] They were hanged, like Catholic missionaries, not burned like Anabaptists, because the idea that ordinary people had the right to establish new churches, organised according to their own beliefs, was an assault on the authority of the Queen to dictate all religion in England, just as Roman Catholicism was.

'They at the very time of their death commended all things in the said books to be good and godly', the Lord Chief Justice Sir Christopher Wray reported to Burghley, apologising for bothering his lordship with such a 'tedious matter'. According to the later Separatist Stephen Ofwod, 'one of them spoke very hardly unto the judge on the gibbet'. Forty volumes by Browne and Harrison were burned at these executions, although Wray's fellow assize judge, Sir Edward Anderson, saved from the flames a copy of Harrison's relatively harmless *Three Formes of Catechismes*, printed earlier that year, and made a gift of it to Bancroft. It is the only copy that survives today.[2]

Wray felt sure there were many people in Suffolk who shared the opinions of Copping and Thacker, but he hoped the spectacle of execution would diminish the number. A man in the crowd was heard to say that if people had known about Thacker's execution 'five hundred good followers more' would have been present. For this, he was arrested, pilloried, and sent to the Bishop of Norwich for further punishment. In the remaining days of those assizes, forty more people, lay and clergy, were tried on counts of attending underground services or leading worship in parish churches without following the Prayer Book. William Dennis of Thetford, Norfolk, was hanged for Separatism that same year.[3]

On 30 June 1583, the Queen issued from Greenwich a general proclamation against Robert Browne and Robert Harrison – though the proclamation was ill enough informed to call the latter 'Rich-ard'. Going somewhat beyond Burghley's verdict of misdirected zeal, the proclamation called them 'lewd and evil disposed persons' who had fled to Zeeland to escape the punishment for sedition, sending 'very false, seditious and schismatical doctrine' back into England to deceive uneducated readers. Any who helped them to publish and distribute the writings would answer for it 'at their uttermost perils'.[4]

Whitgift's three articles

A month after Copping and Thacker were executed in Suffolk, on 6 July 1583, Edmund Grindal died in Croydon. Long deprived of power, frail and almost blind, his final months had been spent in inconclusive negotiations with the Privy Council over retirement. His successor was a man who would have none of Grindal's scruples about imposing conformity to Elizabethan rules, Cartwright's nemesis, John Whitgift. The carrot-and-stick approach of avuncular correction that the state church had tried on the first generation of Separatists had failed, and Whitgift was ready to use all the sticks at his disposal.

Whitgift had become Bishop of Worcester in 1577 and was named Archbishop of Canterbury on 14 August 1583. By the time of his enthronement on 23 October he had prepared an eleven-point pro-gramme for tightening up the discipline of the Church of England, including a comprehensive attack on puritans. Most of this scheme was tolerable to most Protestants, prohibiting preaching in private or by lay people, requiring the vestments, and allowing no Bible translations to be used in church except the Bishop's Bible. One of the eleven points, however, required any person who exercised any ecclesiastical role at all to sign their consent to three articles, the crucial one of which involved declaring that 'the Book of Common Prayer, and of ordering bishops, priests, and deacons, containeth nothing in it contrary to the word of God ... and that he himself will use the form of the said book ... and none other'. This was a demand designed to offend the princi-ples of, and to root out, even the most moderate puritans.[5]

Whitgift launched these reforms in a sermon at Paul's Cross on 17 November, accusing puritans, or 'our wayward and conceited persons' as he called them, of despising and slandering their rulers and bishops. 'These men will obey, but it is what they list, whom they list and wherein they list themselves. And all because they cannot be governors themselves.' However many people might come to their preaching in parish churches, he said, all puritans are effectively Separatists, because if anyone 'break the unity of the church, he is not of the church'. He summoned 'those blasphemous tongues to answer before the judgment seat of God where they shall receive a just reward of their blasphemous speeches'; he beseeched them in the bowels of Christ to give over their contentiousness and advised them, 'Let the plagues and punishments that ensue contention cause you to give it over.'[6]

Whitgift's three anti-puritan articles were first imposed in the diocese of Chichester, where twenty-four ministers were suspended for refusing to subscribe. John Field led a nationwide non-subscription campaign, saying that it made more sense to subscribe to Aesop's fables. In total, an estimated three to four hundred ministers refused to conform. Throughout Norfolk and Suffolk 120 were suspended, though in Leicestershire puritan ministers managed to negotiate a compromise with their bishop and to subscribe to a more limited statement. So many travelled to London to appeal against their suspension that Whitgift talked darkly to the Privy Council of conspiracy.

The Council – though the Queen herself approved of Whitgift's initiative – supported the ministers' appeal. Robert Beale, clerk to the Council, sent Whitgift a tract challenging the legality of the articles. John Foxe, now sixty-six, sent another, suggesting that Whitgift was unwisely dividing Protestants while 'the Roman hawk is hovering around'. Twenty-five leading members of the Kent gentry protested in Lambeth. Eventually Whitgift yielded and allowed the bishops to negotiate subscriptions to more moderate statements, as had happened in Leicestershire, puritan ministers promising to use the Prayer Book but not conceding that it was in no need of reform.[7]

'Our wayward and conceited persons' had by and large evaded Whitgift, but not defeated him, and he now had a better idea who were the most troublesome. He quickly renewed his attack, this time concentrating on the revealed ringleaders, to divide the puritan movement and deprive it of leadership. In May 1584 Whitgift produced a new set of twenty-four anti-puritan articles to be used against specific targets in the Court of High Commission, an instrument of church justice that had grown in size, power and permanence since its processes were improvised under Henry VIII, in which Whitgift sat himself. The accused were to answer his articles under the oath *ex officio mero*, a highly controversial proceeding, before then only used against Catholics, in which the accused had to swear to answer questions before knowing what they were, relinquishing the right to silence, or face prison for refusal.

Few ministers were ultimately removed from their churches in this attack, the only known case being George Gifford of Maldon in Essex. Burghley, who found Whitgift's actions 'too much savouring the Roman Inquisition', tried to intervene on Gifford's behalf, but Whitgift insisted, 'Gifford is a ringleader of the rest.' He was deprived by the court in the summer of 1584, though he continued in Maldon as a lecturer.[8]

As Whitgift led this most concerted national attack yet on individual puritan nonconformity, the undercover Presbyterian movement gathered strength. Field organised local presbyterian conferences of ministers into a national network, a secret presbyterian church within the Church of England. From 1584, he arranged annual presbyterian national assemblies, while Travers drafted a written order for their churches and circulated it in the hope of reaching a consensus on what shape a presbyterian Church of England should take.

Browne in Scotland

Robert Browne and the remnant of his following, which no longer included his wife, arrived in Scotland at the end of 1583. Landing in Dundee, Browne made contact with presbyterian reformers there, who were impressed by his disdain for bishops and the English Church, and gave him a warm welcome. After crossing the Firth of Tay to St Andrews, Browne made contact with Andrew Melville, the principal of St Mary's College and a leading reformer of the Scottish Church. Melville gave Browne a letter of introduction to James Lawson, Knox's successor as Chief Minister in Edinburgh, where the Brownists arrived on 9 January and took lodgings at the top of Canongate, the main road through the city.

The Brownists applied to become members of the Kirk, but when they appeared before its session on Tuesday 14 January, it emerged that Browne's idea of a thoroughly reformed church was even stricter than the Edinburgh elders'. Browne fell out with them over the practice of requiring witnesses at baptisms, which Browne condemned as unbiblical and therefore intolerable and which the elders defended as 'a thing indifferent'. The group's application was rejected but they remained in the city.

The kirk elders told Browne that if he and his friends stayed in Edinburgh they would be subject to their discipline and there was no more question of allowing Separatism here than in England. Browne told them that, thanks to their state church outlook, 'the whole discipline of Scotland was amiss, that he and his company were not subject to it, and therefore he would appeal from the kirk to the magistrate'. Lawson, together with the presbyterian firebrand John Davidson, a friend of John Field's, drew up a list of questionable teachings from Browne's books, and the English were questioned throughout the whole night of 28/29 January.[9]

The Brownists affirmed their contentious opinions, and Browne at least was imprisoned while Lawson and Davidson prepared a detailed report to King James VI, the seventeen-year-old son of Queen Mary. Luckily for Browne, though James was no friend to their radicalism, he had a rocky relationship with the Kirk and had recently been imprisoned for ten months in Ruthven Castle by presbyterian lords. Looking for ways to assert his authority over the church, and on the principle of 'my enemy's enemy', James refused to take action against the Brownists and released Browne from prison. In the words of the Scottish chronicler David Calderwood, 'they were interteaned and fostered to molest the Kirk'. The king still named Browne along with the later John Penry in *Basilikon Doron* as one of the English puritans who had 'come in Scotland, to sow their popple amongst us', popple being a wheatfield weed.[10]

Reporting his impressions of Scotland to his uncle some years later in 1588, Browne said that every elder and preacher there was like another Pope, that they overturned the king's commandments and 'spitefully abused' him in their sermons, and that they controlled the magistrates and enslaved the people. And yet for all the power of the church, Browne said, 'I have seen all manner of wickedness to abound much more in their best places in Scotland than in our worser places here in England.' He left the country, he reckoned, on the point of civil war between church and king. As in Middelburg, Browne had experienced in Scotland some of the toleration that his views had been denied in England, but not the spiritual fellowship he had hoped for, nor solid ground on which he could build his church. His pilgrimage had failed, his dream of leading the chosen people out of their Egyptian captivity, through the wilderness into the Promised Land, had died. In 1584 he returned to England.[11]

Cartwright versus Brownism

Back in Middelburg, the reduced English Separatist church led by Harrison also explored the possibility of joining a more mainstream church: he approached Cartwright and offered to discuss a union of their congregations. With Browne now 600 miles away in Scotland, the way to conciliation seemed more open. When Harrison and Cartwright met for talks, however, it became clear that union was impossible, as Harrison wanted to run their joint congregation as a Separatist church, requiring that anyone who joined them from England publicly repent of having attended their antichristian parish worship.

Cartwright could never agree to such a thing, so he responded to Harrison's demands with a letter arguing that the churches of England, however woeful their condition, were still true churches. Having devoted his career to urging the deficiency of the church, he took up his pen 'not without ... fear and trembling' to defend its adequacy. Cartwright was sufficiently pleased with his anti-Separatist case to send a copy of the letter to England, where it was passed around the radical religious network for five or six weeks before it came into Browne's hands.[12]

Browne settled in London on his return from Scotland. Though his exile had failed, he did not completely despair for the Separatist movement. At least some of his church seem to have stayed with him and they gained new converts in London. A puritan medical student by the name of Stephen Bredwell tried to persuade one of these converts, known only as WF, to come back to their parish church, which led to a skirmish of letters between the three of them.

When Cartwright's letter to Harrison appeared in London, Browne responded with a ninety-six-page book, *An Answere to Master Cartwright His Letter*, which included Cartwright's original letter at the end – in that order, as Browne explained in the foreword, because otherwise the letter might persuade readers before they had the chance to hear why it was wrong. Browne pressed the conditional covenant on his opponent. Cartwright said the English churches were proved true by the sacraments, God's seal of his unconditional covenant; Browne pointed him to the Church of Rome. If Rome's antichristian Mass and baptism did not make it the true church, why should the Church of England's? Cartwright argued that English churches preached the true faith; Browne said that would only prove them true if they lived according to that faith as well as preaching it. If a church contained one real Christian, said Cartwright, that made it a true church; Browne said if it has one bad member and does nothing about it, the whole church breaks the covenant, which is 'the death and perishing of the church and people of God'.[13]

Although *To Master Cartwright* read as a vehement Separatist polemic, not least to the authorities, in a couple of ways Browne's ground was shifting. First, he abandoned his insistence that religion should be entirely voluntary and that it was not up to the state to impose it. He had got no support at all for this extremism, and now he concluded: 'Whereas the law doeth bind us to come to the church it doeth well, for no man ought to refuse the church of God.' He still asserted his right to avoid his parish church because it was antichristian, but said that if it were a true church, the state could compel him to attend. And even though it was not a true church, Browne decided it was acceptable to attend decent preaching there. That second point is conceded only obliquely in the book, but, pressed on it, Browne wrote to his followers in London, allowing them to hear sermons in their parish service, in a spirit of 'trying, looking into and judging'. Browne was wearied by Separatist heroics; any theology that allowed him to blend into the unclean crowd would make life a little more liveable.[14]

Around this time, Robert Harrison died in Middelburg. Leland H. Carlson, in his introduction to *The Writings of Robert Harrison and Robert Browne*, suggests that Browne took it upon himself to respond to Cartwright's letter because Harrison was dead. He would not have to be dead for Browne to write the reply on his behalf – Cartwright himself had written the *Replye* to Whitgift's *Ansvvere* to Field and Wilcox's *Admonition* – and Browne made no reference to Harrison's death in *To Master Cartwright*. However, if Harrison was dead that would cast a light on the strikingly fraternal tones in which Browne wrote about the man who had recently denounced him as a heretic and worse than the Pope and antichrist. Browne defended Harrison on every point at issue and abominated Cartwright for his disagreements with him. Faced with a rebuttal of Separatism from a radical puritan, Browne rediscovered the common ground between himself and Harrison, and set out his own rationale for Separatism, as if he were speaking on behalf of all Separatists – perhaps safe in the knowledge that his erstwhile partner was no longer going to contradict him.

Two Catholic plots

Whitgift's assault on puritans was contentious enough to be high on the agenda when Parliament met in 1584, but the first question was national security, an issue that tended to play well for the puritans. The previous year, Walsingham had uncovered a new Catholic conspiracy to overthrow Elizabeth in favour of Queen Mary of Scotland, who had been in English captivity since 1568. Francis and Thomas Throckmorton had conspired with the Spanish ambassador to gather a party of English Catholics in Arundel, Sussex, allowing an invasion force into the country led by Duke Henry of Guise and co-funded by the King of Spain. On the discovery of their plans, Thomas Throckmorton escaped the country, but his brother was tortured into divulging the full details. He died unrepentant of his crime and refused to ask Elizabeth's forgiveness, but was devastated to have betrayed the confidence of Queen Mary, 'who was the dearest thing to me in the world'. He was hanged, drawn and quartered on 10 July 1584.[15]

The Throckmortons were a religiously divided family. Francis and Thomas were nephews of 'the first true Puritan politician', Nicholas Throckmorton, and of George Throckmorton who administered a fund to pay puritan preachers in Warwickshire. In 1584, George's son Job, another puritan MP, was commissioned by the Privy Council to investigate William Skynner, a supporter of Queen Mary in Warwickshire. Job considered Skynner to be 'a deadly enemy to the Gospel', but failed to gather testimony about any conspiracy thanks to the 'wondrous cunning' of the Catholics.

The gravity of the danger facing the Queen was underlined for English Protestants by devastating news from the Netherlands, where, on the day of Francis Throckmorton's execution, William of Orange became the first head of state to be assassinated by handgun. The course of the war in the Netherlands had already been a source of anxiety for English Protestants in recent years. The Battle of Gembloux in 1578 was a crushing defeat for the rebels, provoking Lawrence Humphrey, President of Magdalen College, Cambridge, to declare, 'Satan is roaring like a lion … It is greatly to be feared that the flames of our neighbour's house may reach us.' The Duke of Parma, now in charge of the Spanish forces in the Netherlands, successively overcame Maastricht, Ghent and Bruges. The Walloon states of the south voted unanimously in 1582 to host his armies, its ruling class hating the unruliness of Calvinism. Emperor Philip now ruled a quarter of the population of western Europe. The following year, William withdrew from Brabant to Delft, and that is where he was shot in his bedchamber by a Catholic freelancer who had bought his pistols with money begged from William.[16]

The English Parliament of 1584–5 took measures to protect its Queen from such a fate. The Safety of the Queen Act established a large tribunal of peers and Privy Councillors to deal with rebellions and attacks. The Jesuits Act expelled all foreign Catholic priests from England and required all English Catholic priests to take the oath of supremacy, returning from overseas if need be, effectively making it treason to be an English Catholic priest.

When it came to religious reform, the Queen once again expressly forbade Parliament to discuss any such matters, and yet, such was their appetite, the Commons debated no fewer than seven ecclesiastical measures. At one end of the scale, Peter Turner's 'bill and book', a proposal for full-scale presbyterian reformation, had little support; at the other, a Commons petition concerning such matters as the lack of competent ministers, backed by a sizeable campaign of petitions from the shires, gained the support of the House of Lords. But once again, the Queen successfully neutralised all attempts at reform, leaving them with nothing but an assurance that genuine shortcomings in the Church of England would be dealt with by the bishops and were none of Parliament's business.

Patrick Collinson has suggested that if the three-articles subscription crisis of 1584 had continued into this parliamentary session, puritan outrage at Whitgift's suspensions would have been sufficiently widespread that 'episcopacy might be unknown in the British Isles today'. As it was, by turning his fire away from the puritan mainstream on to the likes of Gifford, Whitgift ensured that Elizabeth's fifth parliament passed without any change to the religious settlement that was now twenty-six years old.[17]

Thomas Settle

While Browne settled in London, the Separatist movement continued in East Anglia without him. A study by J.S. Craig of wills made in Bury in the 1580s suggests continued support for the cause in the form of provision of the widows of Separatist martyrs. In 1588, for example, Edmund Wyther, a substantial haberdasher, left 6s 8d each to Mrs Copping and Mrs Thacker, as well as to a Mrs Tyler whose husband had died in prison as a Brownist in 1587. On 30 March 1584, five Brownists were arraigned before the Thetford Assizes, including Thomas Wolsey and an Aylsham widow called Emine Okes. All were sentenced to death, though the sentences were commuted. They were held in Thetford prison for a while, but after about a year Wolsey was transferred to Norwich Castle.[18]

Another nonconformist who came to the attention of the authorities was the Rector of St Andrew in Westfield, Norfolk, the twenty-nine-year-old Thomas Settle. Around 1584 he took an additional curacy thirty miles away in Mildenhall, Suffolk, where he also led secret services upstairs at the Barrow Inn. Settle's underground congregation included the tanner John Hargrave, the butchers Adam Daynes and William Poule, and the glover William Johnson, who opened his own home in Bury for similar meetings. Their prayers were so noisy they could be heard across the street and other guests at the inn complained. In April 1585, the bishop investigated Settle, hearing that he considered Whitgift to be 'as evil as Bonner'. On 7 October, Settle quit his post at St Andrew's, perhaps to concentrate on more illicit ministry. Complaints were made about the nonconformity of his Mildenhall parish services, and in May 1586 he was taken to London and interviewed by Whitgift. Settle confirmed that he did not use the ring in weddings or the cross in baptisms, and refused the archbishop's demands to sign the three articles, so he was committed to the Gatehouse.[19]

Browne's London congregation was growing, or so his sparring partner Stephen Bredwell heard, lamenting the success of 'that wretched man'. Who can guess the way or the frame of mind in which Browne continued his underground work. His pioneering recovery of the New Testament church had collapsed and his pilgrimage had failed, and yet in some way he kept going, perhaps under a cloud of disillusion, perhaps finding a way to see the 'strong hand' of God in these events.[20]

He was once again arrested, this time because of his book *To Master Cartwright*, and perhaps this time threatened with a worse punishment than his numerous short spells behind bars. For all his fieriness, he was not the man to languish for ever in jail for a cause the world had forgotten, and this time he capitulated to the state church. On 7 October 1585, under pressure from Burghley, Browne signed a submission to the Archbishop of Canterbury, acknowledging the Church of England to be the church of God, promised to attend church and accept its sacraments, and pledged not to act as a minister.

This capitulation certainly sounds like the end of Browne's Separatist career, and that was how it was taken by Separatists and their opponents alike when they found out about it – the former wanting to forget all about Browne while the latter were keen to keep his name alive. The one person who did not seem to take it that way was Browne himself, who now, with the third and most powerful wave of Separatism close at hand, embarked on the strangest part of his career yet.

12

Reviving the London underground church

WHEN, IN 1582, the sixteen-year-old King James VI of Scotland was kidnapped by presbyterian lords, and held captive in Ruthven Castle, his friend the Earl of Arran rode to his rescue. Arran ended up imprisoned along with him, but James escaped, resumed power, executed Lord Ruthven and made Arran an extraordinary lord of session. In April 1584, the Ruthven lords launched another failed coup. This time Arran became acting Chancellor and under his leadership Parliament passed what became known as the 'Black Acts'.

The Black Acts

The Black Acts denounced presbyterian courts, affirmed the rule of bishops, and asserted the king's supremacy over the Kirk, including his right to summon General Assemblies. On Whitgift's advice, all ministers were required to subscribe to the Black Acts. To avoid this, twenty leading presbyterians went into exile in England with the surviving Ruthven lords. Their number included Melville, Lawson and Davidson, who had dealt with Browne during his attempt to join their church; Melville left the country, fleeing an order of imprisonment in Blackness Castle.

The Scottish ministers spent time at Oxford and Cambridge and conferred with leaders of the presbyterian movement in England, including Field and Wilcox, finding a warm kinship in their ideas and in their trials. They discussed the form of the English presbyterianism that Field was surreptitiously organising, and debated the question of 'the proceeding of the minister in his duty without the assistance or tarrying for the magistrate', the Scots having acted rather more boldly than the English in this area. Davidson preached for a couple of months in London, becoming known as 'a thunderer', until he was silenced by the Bishop of London, John Aylmer.[1]

In 1585, a new favourite of King James, Lord Gray, overthrew Arran's government, and in November most of the exiles returned home. The Scots left behind them an English presbyterian movement more assertive than ever. Cartwright returned from Middelburg, and was promptly arrested by Bishop Aylmer, but was released after Burghley and Leicester intervened on his behalf. Walter Travers was appointed to write an order for undercover English presbyterianism, the Book of Discipline, to be smuggled into the church under the noses of the bishops. The draft Travers produced was circulated among English presbyterian leaders for discussion, but it took them two years to finalise it. It proved easier to agree about the faults of the church than about what to replace them with.

The Babington plot

Across the North Sea, the reconquest of the southern Netherlands by Spanish imperial forces under Parma continued inexorably. Brussels fell in February 1585. Now that the complete capitulation of the Dutch rebels looked likely, Queen Elizabeth, after many years' talk, finally made a commitment, signing the Treaty of Nonsuch on 20 August, which promised 6,000 foot-soldiers and a thousand cavalry. It was far too late to help the southern states; the only remaining question, after Antwerp surrendered to Parma on 17 August, was whether the revolt in the north could be saved. The Queen put the English forces under the charge of the Earl of Leicester, though he had little military experience, and Parma proceeded to take Grave on 28 May 1586 followed by all the other fortresses on the Maas. Then, in December, ill health brought Leicester back to England. He left the important town of Deventer under the command of the English Catholic mercenary Sir William Stanley, supporting the blockade of nearby Zutphen, which was captained by another English Catholic, Rowland Yorke. On 19 January, Stanley surrendered Deventer to Parma, Yorke handed over the siege works without a struggle, and both defected to the Spanish side with many of their soldiers.

During Leicester's absence from England there was yet another attempt on Elizabeth's life: the Babington plot. Anthony Babington had been a page to the Earl of Shrewsbury, in whose household Mary was held captive. On behalf of a group of Catholic gentlemen, Babington wrote to Mary on 6 July offering to assassinate Elizabeth, in preparation for invasion by Spanish forces, and restore Mary to power. The letter was smuggled to Mary in a beer barrel, and she replied committing herself thoroughly to the plan and offering detailed advice. Unfortunately for the conspirators, the messenger who carried Mary's letters hidden in the bungholes of beer barrels was a secret agent of Walsingham. Walsingham let the plot brew in the hope that Mary would incriminate herself, which she did. Babington fled, hid in a wood, shaved, and smeared his face with green walnut husks, but he and the other conspirators were rounded up, tried and executed in September, being hanged, castrated and disembowelled. Their number was brought to fourteen by the inclusion of a friend who had hid some of the fleeing conspirators at his house in Harrow.

In trapping the plotters, Walsingham had ensured that their conviction would depend on information that revealed Mary's role, meaning that Elizabeth could not suppress it to let her fellow sovereign off the hook again. Unaware of how Walsingham had encouraged the scheme through *agents provocateurs*, Elizabeth was finally persuaded to put Mary on trial for conspiring to assassinate her.

Mary was inevitably found guilty, but because of the constitutional complexities of executing the deposed monarch of a foreign state, Elizabeth summoned Parliament in September 1586 to consider the sentence. Parliament pressed for Mary's execution, Job Throckmorton denouncing her as 'the daughter of sedition, the mother of rebellion, the nurse of impiety, the handmaid of iniquity, the sister of unshamefastness' and saying her death would be 'one of the fairest riddances that ever the church of God had'.[2]

After much heart-searching and vacillation, Elizabeth eventually subscribed to the execution in February 1587 and then kept Parliament sitting, needing it to vote finances for her forces in the Netherlands.

Cope's bill and book

The extension gave MPs the opportunity for yet another unlikely attempt to bypass the Queen's religious prerogative. The secret presbyterian national assembly met in London during Parliament, and helped to orchestrate a campaign of petitions for church reform, and on 27 February the presbyterian MP Anthony Cope, George Carleton's stepson, brought before the Commons the most radical bill of any kind that the House had ever seen. The measure simply abolished all existing religious legislation and all church institutions, and replaced the Elizabethan Prayer Book with a revised version of the Genevan Prayer Book that included a presbyterian church order. In the words of John Neale: '*Tabula rasa*; stark revolution. Its like was never seen in English Parliament.'[3]

Supporting Cope's bill, Throckmorton made a powerful speech asserting Parliament's right to deal with religion. The government made a show of MPs' freedom of speech, he said, but if those rights did not extend to religion or royal succession then MPs in fact had no say in 'the very pillars and groundworks of all our bliss and happiness'. The failure of English ministers to preach was a shameful deformity of the church, and yet any attempt to improve it, any appeal to the Queen for reform, was denounced as puritanism. 'I fear me we shall shortly come to this, that to do God and her majesty good service shall be counted puritanism.'[4]

The Commons consented to hear the book read the following day, but overnight the Queen confiscated both bill and book. The presbyterian MP Peter Wentworth gave a list of questions to the Speaker, asserting the House's rights to free speech and not to be reported to the Queen; the Speaker reported the questions to the Queen, and Cope, Wentworth and three other MPs were imprisoned in the Tower of London. On 4 March the Privy Councillor Christopher Hatton revealed to the Commons the contents of Cope's book, demonstrating what a revolutionary scheme they had been incubating. The House abandoned the resolution, and instead pressed on with a proposal to overturn Whitgift's subscription requirement and improve the training of ministers. The Queen stamped on this, telling Parliament, 'you ought not to deal with matters of religion'. For lay people to meddle in her reformed religion, she said, would encourage those who want to overturn the Reformation, would 'breed great lightness in her subjects' and was 'against the prerogative of her crown'.[5]

Throckmorton had got away with his incendiary speech. He was the eldest son of an eminent family, his cousin being a lady-in-waiting to the Queen, and he evidently had some claim on Hatton's protection. But then details emerged of a speech Throckmorton had made earlier in the session on foreign policy: he warned against alliances with Spain, France or Scotland, making scurrilous observations on the private lives of their royal families. James VI of Scotland heard that Throckmorton had called him 'the young imp of Scotland' before making sly allusions to gossip about James's mother. Burghley promised him that Throckmorton would be put in the Tower for his 'lewd and blasphemous' speech, but the MP disappeared, hiding in his sister's house in Hillingdon. From there he wrote a grovelling letter to Burghley saying that parliamentary privilege had brought 'a young head into a distemperature'. Thus Throckmorton avoided prison, but his parliamentary career was over. He looked around for another way to shape English religion.

While Parliament was predictably failing to overthrow the Church of England, a more realistic presbyterian plot was underway. Leaders of the movement gathering in London during the Parliamentary session sent copies of Travers' Book of Discipline – whose prescriptions they had finally agreed upon – throughout the counties of England. They asked ministers to sign a statement approving of the book and committing to use it in their services and to meet together according to its system in regional conferences and an annual national assembly.

In fact the settlement was received fairly coolly by local presbyterian conferences. They had developed their own orders, and though they agreed on the need for one system uniting all English presbyterians, it was less easy to agree what it should be. They discussed the book, but continued to organise in their own ways for now.

Barrow's conversion

Undercover presbyterianism was not enough to satisfy the strongest puritan appetites, and so, in around 1586, Separatism drew in the man who was to become probably its most successful leader, under certainly the most difficult circumstances. Henry Barrow, like Browne, was born into a landed family, of Shipdham in Norfolk, three miles from Settle's parish of Westfield, and he even shared Browne's family connection to Lord Burghley, though Barrow's was more remote. They were a similar age, Barrow graduating from Cambridge a couple of years before Browne, around 1570. While there, he seems to have completely escaped the puritan influence that seized Browne, talking of university life as a riot of 'vanity, folly, idleness'. Seven blank years follow, then in 1577 Barrow started training in the law at Gray's Inn, where he remained some years. There is no record of Barrow practising law, but he became a courtier of Queen Elizabeth, according to his own report and that of William Bradford. Bradford was about six at the time Barrow became a Brownist, and said that his own generation of Brownists learned all about Barrow from 'those who knew him familiarly both before and after his conversion', including a long-standing domestic servant. A later American settler, John Cotton, had heard that 'Mr. Barrow, whilst he lived in court, was wont to be a great gamester, and dicer' and would boast of spending his winnings 'in the bosoms of his courtesans'. Barrow himself admitted 'my former lewd ... conversation', while his enemy Richard Bancroft said, 'Barrow by roisting and gaming had wasted himself, and was run so far into many a man's debt, that he durst not shew his head abroad'.[6]

Then one Sunday early in 1586,[*] Barrow and a friend were walking past a London church, Bradford tells us, when they heard from inside an impassioned, and evidently loud, sermon about God's judgement on sin. Barrow said, 'Let us go in and hear what this man says, that is thus earnest.' His friend replied, 'What! Shall we go to hear a man talk?' So Barrow went alone, was converted and gave up the court, 'and it was quickly bruited about that Barrow was turned Puritan'.[7]

Eighteen months later, in mid-1587, Barrow read one of Browne's books and set about writing a rejoinder to defend the Church of England from Brownism. When it came to it though, he found Browne's arguments unanswerable and concluded he was right. Barrow found himself in an awkward position, becoming a follower of someone who was no longer following the path himself, and does not seem to have sought out Browne. Barrow may or may not have known about Browne's submission to the bishop, but he knew that his movement had failed and he had given up. Instead, Barrow visited Thomas Wolsey, imprisoned in Norwich Castle, twenty miles from Barrow's home town of Shipdham. Wolsey trained Barrow in Separatist thinking, and perhaps put him in touch with the remnant of the London Separatists.

Barrow tried to persuade other puritans to follow his lead out of the church, but generally found them reluctant. He told puritan ministers that they were performing antichristian worship in an antichristian institution. They responded, Barrow says, 'with many slight and lame excuses', saying that, though they disliked the episcopal hierarchy and petitioned the Queen to reform it, until God turned her heart they must wait patiently, realising that no church is perfect. Some ministers told him that the imperfections of the Prayer Book did not pollute their worship because they never used it; others that

---

[*] The dates of Barrow's conversions are based on statements by Gifford and Ofwod. Gifford said in 1591 that Barrow was 'but four or five years from the bowling alleys' (Gifford, A Short Reply, 9), which puts his puritan conversion between early 1586 and late 1587. Ofwod said Barrow had been a puritan 'scarce eighteen months' before he read Browne (Ofwod, *Advertisement*, 40). Since Barrow was an active Separatist in the second half of 1587, the only way these two statements can be true is if Barrow became a puritan early in 1586 and a Separatist in mid-1587.

much of it was good and they used only the good bits. Barrow argued that their very ministry was unlawful because they were not elected by the church after the New Testament pattern, but were imposed on the church by bishops. Their response to this argument was 'railing and blaspheming and persecuting', because it denied the validity of their own work – or threatened 'the foothold of all their tithes, wages and living' as Barrow put it.[8]

Shaking the dust from his shoes, Barrow joined the Separatists in London and worshipped secretly with them. It may be that Barrow helped build a new Separatist church on the ruins of the earlier one, but the evidence suggests that, against all odds, one underground church had struggled on, somehow quietly surviving fifteen years since the movement in general had collapsed. It is true that in 1607 the Separatist leader Henry Ainsworth talked of the Fitz church as an earlier church rather than as an earlier generation of their own, but not in language one would put much weight on.[9]

We have already seen how the church unexpectedly showed its face in 1581 after a decade's silence. Now, from a list of worshippers arrested in 1587, we can see that the church in Barrow's time still included survivors from the earlier movement. The most notable of them was Nicholas Crane, now about sixty-five, who had been minister in the underground from the start in 1566 and spent time in prison; who, along with Bonham, had allegedly been appointed preacher to the conventiclers by Grindal; and who had ended up back on the fringe of the Church of England, preaching in Holy Trinity, Minories. Another name on the list is Edith Burry, an aged widow of Stepney, who Michael Watts suggests plausibly is the same Edye Burre who had signed the petition of Richard Fitz's church in 1571, and the same Edde Burris of More Lane, Cripplegate, who was among those arrested at James Tynne's house in 1568. (Her surname appears on later lists as Barrowe, Burrowghe and Borough.)

The congregation also included a former member of Browne's church, listed as John Chaundler, also living in Stepney, who seems likely to be the John Chandler or Chanler whom Browne mentions as a member of his own church in *A true and short declaration*. Browne names him as one of the three leading supporters of Harrison in his quarrels with Browne.

141

As well as Crane, the church contained a second man who had been ordained as a minister in the Church of England, John Greenwood, also a Norfolk man. The evidence for Greenwood's connection with Norfolk Separatism is tantalisingly circumstantial. Graduating from Cambridge in 1581, he was straightaway ordained by the bishop, and, after serving in Wyam, Lincolnshire, for a couple of years, he seems to have become the Vicar of All Saints, Rackheath, in Norfolk, in 1583. Though Rackheath is just five miles from Norwich, there is no record of any contact between Greenwood and the remains of Browne's church or Wolsey, but around September 1585, Greenwood embraced Separatism, resigned from All Saints, and travelled to London. This gives us an additional reason to think there was still a Separatist congregation meeting there, as the alternative, that Greenwood travelled in the hope of recreating a Separatist church among strangers when there were ones already on his doorstep, seems unlikely. It is a plausible hypothesis, though no more, that Wolsey, as a surviving leader of Norfolk Separatism, was still in contact with Chandler, or recently had been, knew that he was worshipping with fellow Separatists in London, met both with Barrow and with Greenwood, and advised them to seek out Chandler and the London underground church.

We know more about what these Separatists did in their meetings than at earlier points in the movement, thanks to one member, Anne Jackson, bringing her servant, Clement Gamble. Gamble gave a statement to the authorities in March 1589, saying he had been to every Separatist service for eighteen months. In the summer, said Gamble, the church met in the fields a mile outside London and worshipped sitting on a grass bank. In winter, they met in a member's house from five on Sunday morning, where their prayers and preaching lasted all day, or so at least it seemed to Gamble. Men and women mixed together. They had no written prayers or liturgy, not even the Lord's Prayer, dismissing them as 'babbling in the Lord's sight'; in this they were following the practice of Browne's church rather than what we know of the earlier London Separatists. Preaching was not confined to the minister, but was expected of every member – or at least of 'every man'. The phrase is used inclusively, but if women actually preached it seems unlikely that such an irregularity should not have been explicitly mentioned. They ate together, taking a collection to pay for the food, and distributed the surplus to church members in prison.

Gamble never saw Communion celebrated, or a baptism administered, even though the congregation contained two men ordained in the Church of England, Crane and Greenwood. Greenwood had personally renounced that ordination as invalid. As for Crane, the church did not recognise his episcopal ordination, and presumably he agreed, although he had acted as a Separatist minister in 1569. It is possible that he was debarred from office in the Separatist church, having attended parish churches after joining the Separatists, as the church had strict rules about such 'apostasy'. It may seem surprising that, lacking a duly ordained minister, the church did not ordain one, but they did not treat it as a matter of urgency. One leading member, the delightfully named Widow Unyon, had given birth to a daughter in about 1576, and had never had her baptised, saying, 'It was born of faithful parents which was enough for it.' (This is further evidence of the London Separatist church surviving through the 1580s.)[10]

Another witness who gave information to the authorities about the Brownists' services was not a full member but an occasional visitor, John Dove, a university-educated author. Dove recalled emotional displays: 'In their prayer, one speaketh and the rest do groan or sob or sigh, as if they would wring out tears.' Bancroft offered a similar description: 'The chief gentleman of the place beginneth with a groaning, but yet with a loud voice crieth most religiously, "Amen". And then the whole company of that sect follow, "Amen, amen".'[11]

Dove also described the excommunication of a member by the name of Mr Love. Love had been a member of the church until he started to have qualms over their rejection of the Lord's Prayer and the fact that two members were involved in what he considered a financial deception. When the church failed to win him back, one member announced that they were giving him 'over into th'hands of Satan' while the rest kneeled, and they prayed God would ratify their sentence. Though the Brownists treasured excommunication as a way to ensure the purity of the church, so far it seemed to have been used on those who had left of their own accord.

In 1587, Barrow wrote a paper known as *Four Causes of Separation*, directed at puritans who remained in their parish churches, urging them, 'speedily, without any delay, to forsake those disordered and ungodly and unholy synagogues' if they wished to be saved, and castigating those who had argued against his Separatism. Barrow expounded four fatal faults with the parish churches: false worship, non-Christian membership, antichristian ministry and popish government. The first of those was what puritans had been complaining of those thirty years, the imperfections of the Prayer Book. The fourth fault was the focus of the presbyterian movement – the hierarchy and machinery of episcopacy. Barrow's second point was a specifically congregationalist one and shows the influence of reading Browne: the church, Barrow believed, should be a gathering of genuine Christians, not the entire population, but the Church of England expects ministers to give the sacraments to all comers indiscriminately. This became increasingly important to the movement. Barrow's third fault, antichristian ministry, was about ordination: that there could be no true ministers in the Church of England because they were appointed by antichristian bishops, not chosen by Christian congregations.[12]

Puritan ministers defending themselves on this last point told Barrow that, though the appointment processes of the church may be less than perfectly biblical, they personally knew the inner calling of Christ. Barrow replied with the words of Christ, that there is only one true entrance to the sheepfold and 'he that entereth another way [is] a thief, a hireling and a murtherer'. They could hardly claim the inward calling of Christ to preach his word while being outwardly disobedient to his instruction, Barrow argued. The ministers claimed they proved their validity by turning people from their sins, but then so do Catholic priests and secular judges, said Barrow, so they were only dealing with symptoms, not offering souls the true cure of the gospel. 'O cruel mercy! ... Will they pour the sweet oil upon dead flesh, or into stinking and corrupt wounds? ... So shall they lose both their oil and their labour.' Jesus never sent anyone without giving them power to lead people in the right ways; if ministers today lack that power, said Barrow, they are not sent by Jesus.[13]

Barrow echoed Browne's absolutism, answering puritans' claims that they avoid the bad elements of Prayer Book worship. Barrow demanded, 'I would know of them whether the worship of God may be in part true and in part false.' The Prayer Book is utterly compromised by its faults, Barrow said, and 'that best part of it they use is … but a piece of swine's flesh'.[14]

The result of these four great failures of the Church of England are infinite, Barrow said, but as a taster: 'You shall find hereby the last will and testament of our Saviour Christ abrogate, his precious body and blood torn and trodden under feet of dogs and swine, Christ Jesus thrown out of his house, and antichrist his enemy exalted above God and reigning in the temple of God as God.'[15]

The London Brownists had no access to a printer, so *Four Causes of Separation* was copied by hand and passed around as a twelve-page manuscript. Even through this medium the tract circulated widely and caused a stir, making Barrow a wanted man in the sights of the Archbishop of Canterbury.

Probably shortly after Barrow wrote this tract, the London Separatist church produced a shorter paper entitled *A Breefe Sum of Our Profession*. It reads like a statement of faith, for their own use, in ten paragraphs, committing them to fellowship together and living in obedience to Christ. The last four points gave their reasons for separating, and they are Barrow's 'four causes' in different words. Again, though it was not printed, we hear of copies being circulated and one causing controversy in east Essex.

On 8 October 1587, two years and a day after Robert Browne's submission to the bishop, and twenty years after the Plumbers' Hall arrests, an illegal gathering was found at worship in the house of one Henry Martin in the west London parish of St Andrew-by-the Wardrobe. Twenty-one people were arrested, fifteen men and six women, including Crane, Greenwood, Burry, Chandler and Jackson, but not Barrow. They were interviewed by Bishop Aylmer, but kept no record of the conversation. Then they were jailed, separated out around the various prisons of London, punished, as they put it, 'for reading a portion of scripture on the Lord's day in a friend's house'.[16]

As happy as the authorities undoubtedly were to have caught these worshippers, they had missed the main man. Barrow had eluded them and the bishops' officers kept searching. Then, six weeks later, on the morning of Sunday 19 November, between nine and ten, Barrow and a friend by the name of Hul visited Greenwood and others in the Clink prison, Southwark. When the jailer realised whom he had under his roof, he refused to let him leave. Barrow was never released for the rest of his life.

The jailer sent a message to the archbishop at Lambeth Palace and two officers came to collect him. One of them told Barrow, as they were rowed upstream, that he had been looking for him a long time, and showed him an arrest warrant from the Archbishop's Court that Barrow refused to read, it being invalid. Waiting at Lambeth, Barrow took the chance to peruse the extraordinarily grand state in which the archbishop lived, before he was interviewed by Whitgift, who was backed by the Archdeacon of London and the Dean of the Court of Arches.

The tone of the conversation, which Barrow recorded, was a long way from the Plumbers' Hall interview by Grindal of twenty years before. Whitgift's proceedings were more forensic, so Barrow was cagier; and while Barrow repeated the defiant and self-assured indignation of the conventiclers, Grindal's tone of pastoral concern for fellow believers was replaced with the lordly derision of Whitgift towards a religious criminal. The archbishop laughed at Barrow's 'unskillfulness' in challenging the legality of his arrest by a jailer without a warrant, and when Barrow quoted the New Testament, Whitgift asked him to say it in Latin or Greek. Barrow had a very embarrassing moment when he quoted a verse from 1 Corinthians that his opponents did not recognise, and when they fetched a Bible he failed to find it, saying, 'The word of God is not the worse for my ill memory.'

Whitgift accused Barrow of schism, recusancy and sedition. Barrow said he forgave him and Whitgift said he did not care whether he did or not. Barrow refused not only to take the oath *ex officio mero*, but to swear on the Bible at all, 'a needless and wicked ceremony'. Whitgift offered him bail if he could find sufficient surety for his good behaviour, to which Barrow claimed to have 'as sufficient as you can take'.

'What, you cannot have the Queen?' exclaimed Whitgift.

'For my good behaviour I suppose I could get her word,' said Barrow.

'Doth she know you then?'

'I know her.' Perhaps Barrow had expected a rather higher authority than the Queen to vouch for him. Instead they settled on a Mr Lacey – until Barrow realised that failing to attend his parish church would be a breach of bail.

The archbishop sent Barrow back to a different prison, the Gatehouse in Westminster; and, said Barrow, 'I was no sooner out of his house but I remembered the place [i.e. Bible verse] in controversy.'[17]

Whitgift prepared a list of the offensive ideas in Barrow's *Four Causes of Separation*, and brought Barrow back to Lambeth eight days later to answer for them to the Court of High Commission. Whitgift presided 'with a grim and angry countenance', Barrow says, over 'such an appearance of well-fed silken priests as I suppose might well have beseemed the Vatican'. When Barrow again refused to swear without knowing what he was accused of, the beadle read the list of his teachings, but Barrow still refused to swear on the grounds of the disorder of the list.

'You shall not prattle here,' cried Whitgift, according to Barrow's account, 'Away with him! Clap him up close! Close! Let no man come at him! I will make him tell another tale yet I have done with him.'[18]

First though, the archbishop had a rather more dangerous enemy to worry about.

13

The Armada

BY 1587, THE English were expecting a Spanish invasion. England was finally committed to open war against Spain in the Netherlands, Parma's reconquest of the southern Netherlands had given the Spanish a new coastal front against England, and the execution of Mary provided them with all the provocation required for a crusade. Pope Sixtus V agreed to pay Philip a million ducats when the invasion force landed. William Allen, Cardinal of England and founding President of the English seminary in Douai, told Philip that it was the English people's 'hearts' desire to be once more subject to your most clement rule'. Allen called English Catholics to join the invading army, advertising rewards for the capture of Elizabeth and her ministers, and indulgences for their punishment. Francis Drake's 1587 raid on Cadiz and the coast of Portugal cost the emperor thirty ships, but it only postponed the inevitable. A prophecy that the world would end in 1588 become so popular in England that the government banned almanacs from mentioning it.[1]

Defending England

While the Spanish prepared their invasion, Elizabeth set about raising what forces she could through her lords and recalled 4,000 men from the Netherlands, but the accounts of the defensive preparations, for a modern British reader, bring *Dad's Army* irresistibly to mind. Even in the naval town of Portsmouth, half of the gunners manning the defences were 'by age and impotency by no means serviceable'. The crucial Isle of Wight coastline was protected by a four-foot wall of earth and manure, and four mounted guns with a day's supply of powder. Instructions for retreat were circulated through the country, to burn bridges, flood roads and destroy crops. Foundries worked non-stop to cast guns, razing large tracts of forest for charcoal, but the southernmost county of Cornwall with its 300 miles of coastline was defended with 1,500 bows and 2,000 halberds (the Spanish hoped to land 50,000 troops). Residents without such arms were expected to go into battle with pitchforks and scythes.[2]

Whitgift mobilised the church. He called on the bishops to take a lead in the defence of the country, arguing 'our willing readiness herein will be a good means also to stop the mouths of such as do think those temporal blessings, which God hath in mercy bestowed upon us, to be too much'. Whitgift required all clergy to organise and equip local militias, compiling a record of what weapons each minister had provided. He sent them a new prescribed prayer for national deliverance, instructing them to hold services three times a week, accompanied by coordinated fasting – and to permit no unauthorised fasts. Preachers were to tell their congregations to give generously to the poor and to shun Separatist conventicles, and above all were to win the mercy of Christ by sticking faithfully to the Prayer Book. If God were to judge England for its religious sins, to Whitgift's mind they would be sins of diversity. The Bishop of London's Chancellor seized the daughter of the leading Brownist Widow Unyon, who, at twelve, had never been baptised for lack of an acceptable minister, and had her forcibly baptised at St Andrew-by-the-Wardrobe that summer. Barrow and Greenwood, after half a year in prison, were indicted under the 1581 Recusancy Act at Newgate Sessions, fined £260, then moved to the Fleet prison. The Queen decreed that every ship in the English fleet should have a copy of Foxe's *Book of Martyrs* and the crew hear readings from it to illustrate the fate they were defending their people from.[3]

On 5 July 1588, Burghley received intelligence that the Spanish fleet had sailed from Lisbon seven weeks earlier. The consensus in Spain, this informant added, was that 'the Spanish desire but to set foot on land and all shall be theirs'. The Spanish government printed a battle cry of a tract in five languages, English not one of them, itemising 'the most happy Armada', its 130 ships of 57,868 tons, carrying 19,295 soldiers, 180 monks and 2,088 slaves. Cardinal Allen printed a tract denouncing Elizabeth as 'an incestuous bastard', 'an infamous, depraved, accursed, excommunicate heretic' and England's 'poison, calamity and destruction'.[4]

The battle

The Armada was first seen off Cornwall on 19 July by the British pirate Thomas Fleming, who alerted his colleague Francis Drake, who was also Vice Admiral of the British fleet, and so 227 English ships went into battle. After skirmishes on 21 and 23 July, the Spanish failed to gain a base in English waters and so retreated to Calais. Their plan then was to rendezvous with Parma at Dunkirk, twenty-five miles along the coast, and collect a further 30,000 troops from him, including a thousand English Catholics. On arrival though, it turned out that Parma's forces had been halved by disease and desertion, that they were a week away from the rendezvous and the Dutch Sea Beggars were blockading the port.

The decisive engagement between the English and Spanish took place off Gravelines, between Calais and Dunkirk, on 29 July. After the English broke up the Armada's crescent with fireships, the Spanish were devastated by the greater manoeuvrability and longer-range guns of the English ships, with the help of a partisan wind, and only a late change in the weather saved the Armada from annihilation. Five Spanish ships were lost and many more disabled. As the Armada retreated north-eastwards into the North Sea, the English followed, protecting the east coast of England and driving the Spanish into Scottish waters. The English then went home, being out of food. When they heard that reason, the Spanish were amazed at the feeble resources of the enemy; if they had known the English were also almost completely out of ammunition, the story might have ended very differently. Instead, on its long limp home, the Armada came to grief first on the shore of Scotland, then much worse in Irish waters, where those who survived shipwreck and forced landings were executed by the English colonial government. In the end, barely half of the Armada's ships made it home, and a third of its men.

When news of the disaster started to reach Philip, he told his chaplain he was praying to die before hearing the full extent of his disgrace. The Pope observed it was 'curious that the Emperor of half the world should be defied by a woman who was the Queen of half an island'. England held a national day of bonfire celebrations on 19 November. The following Sunday the Queen processed to St Paul's Cathedral in a chariot drawn by four white horses, and knelt on the church steps to pray before the thanksgiving service. A new prayer was sent to parish churches, acknowledging that the invasion would have been God's just punishment on the English, but in his mercy God had turned his wrath instead on those who were 'drowned in idolatry and superstition'. Twenty-four ballads celebrating the victory are extant, and medals were made bearing slogans such as '*Flavit YHWH et Dissipati Sunt*' (The Lord blew and they were scattered). A girl was christened Armada in Barnstaple in 1595. A verse pamphlet, published in 1589, considered the question whether to stop eating fish from the Channel,

> *Because they are fed*
> *With carcasses dead,*
> *Here and there in the rocks,*
> *That were full of the pox.*[5]

The enemy within

For puritans, profoundly relieved as they were not to have fallen under the regime of Philip II for a second time, as the threat of invasion declined over the following years it came to seem as if something had been lost in the victory. For decades the government had needed a united Protestant front against the enemy, and, without conceding any reform of the church, tried to keep as much friendship as possible between puritans and the establishment. As the danger gradually subsided, so did the need for gentleness. More immediately, one person who had most influentially pressed this pan-Protestant policy on the Privy Council, the Earl of Leicester, died in September 1588, followed in 1589 by his ally Mildmay and in 1590 by Walsingham and the Earl of Warwick. John Field himself, the greatest organiser and most popular apologist of the movement, died in 1588. It was the end of an era. In an event full of symbolic as well as other kinds of significance for the future, in 1588 the officers of the Stationers' Company entered the premises where the printer Robert Waldegrave was producing an anonymous presbyterian work by the lecturer John Udall, and destroyed the press.

As for the radicals imprisoned in London for their faith, they had little enough reason to celebrate deliverance from popery, and Whitgift and Aylmer intensified their attack on the Separatist church. Many of those who had been arrested at the 1587 service were still in jail, but others continued to meet together, and the bishops' men, no longer content with trying to catch congregations in the act of worship, started raiding suspects' houses. They entered Roger Jackson's by night, took him from the bed where he lay with his wife, searched the house finding manuscripts in Barrow's hand, and so committed Jackson to close imprisonment in the Poultry Compter. Thomas Legate was arrested in the same way, and without a warrant; Legate's friend William Clarke, a forty-year-old capmaker, complained about this proceeding, and as a result joined him in the Wood Street Compter. Quintin Smythe, a feltmaker in his mid-twenties, was at work when the bishops' men took him and, searching his premises, found Brownist propaganda and a Bible, both of which they confiscated; Smythe was sent to Newgate, where he was kept in irons. John Purdye was imprisoned in Bridewell, where, after refusing to attend sermons by the prison chaplain, he was beaten 'with a great cudgel very extremely', set on the treadmill, and condemned to a stretch in Little Ease, a torture hole where it was impossible to stand, lie or sit.[6]

The death rate was high. Nicholas Crane died in Newgate at the age of sixty-six, and his wife and children wanted to carry his body through the gate into the city for burial but were prevented by the authorities 'lest the people who knew his virtue and godliness should espy and abhor their cruelty', as Barrow put it. John Chandler, late of Browne's church, died in the Poultry Compter, leaving behind a wife Alice, who also spent some time in prison, and their eight children. Two 'aged widows', Margaret Meynard and Alice Roe, died in the same prison as Chandler; as did Richard Jackson, 'that rare young man' in Barrow's estimation. George Bryghte was arrested for 'commending a faithful Christian' who was indicted at the Newgate sessions, and he died in the Wood Street Compter. All these deaths occurred within nineteen months of that first arrest at Henry Martin's house, and no inquests were allowed. Another prisoner, Robert Griffen, being dangerously ill, was bailed on the point of death.[7]

Browne in London

The contrast between the commitment of these Brownists and the slippery continued career of Robert Browne is startling. The submission that Browne made to the archbishop in 1585 made surprisingly little difference to his behaviour in the following years. Immediately, Burghley sent him to live with his father Anthony at Tolethorpe Hall, where he was also reunited with his wife. Anthony had been glad to hear of Robert's promise of compliance, but was disappointed to find that it did not result in his actually going to church; Anthony told Burghley in February 1586 he had 'little or no hopes of [my] son's conformity'. Anthony asked permission for Robert to leave his house and Burghley consented, but Robert went nowhere. The wardens of the parish church reported Robert and Alice to the Bishop of Peterborough for non-attendance, and the case against them came before the Chancellor's Court in April. Robert's lawyer got him a direct hearing with the bishop, which somehow got him off the hook.[8]

Perhaps Browne had promised the bishop he would go to London and attend a tolerable parish church there. That, at least, is what he did. On 21 November 1586 he became a schoolmaster again, at St Olave's in Southwark, and to satisfy the governors he had to sign another declaration of conformity, promising to lead no conventicles, to take his pupils to the parish church and to receive Communion there himself.

So Browne attended St Olave's Church regularly, but he never did take Communion, and when his refusal started to raise questions, he simply moved house to another parish. He also taught his Separatist followers – telling them nothing about his submission to the archbishop – and won new converts, which led to crossing swords with Stephen Bredwell again. Browne persuaded one member of St Olave's to quit her church; after Bredwell failed to win her back she was formally excommunicated, but she publicly scorned the sentence saying that Browne's writings against Bredwell were read 'a hundreth miles' distance from London'. Preaching in a house in Ludgate, near the west end of St Paul's Cathedral, Browne faced the counter-evangelism of one Mr W, who persuaded some Brownists to return to their parish church. There is a story about Browne's preaching in a gravel pit in Islington, and he even appeared in Dartford, fourteen miles east of London, preaching and making converts. This resulted in the parish lecturer in Dartford, Mr Edmondes, preaching against Browne, which in turn led to another pamphlet war. 'Daily', lamented Bredwell, 'such numbers of the younger and weaker sort of Christians are carried out of our assemblies' by Browne's 'violent stream of seducing'.[9]

More incredible still, it seems that while pursuing this undercover Separatism, Browne wrote publicly against the Brownist movement of Barrow and Greenwood. According to a 1589 sermon by Bancroft, Browne wrote *A treatise against one Barowe*. The treatise has not survived, but in the passage Bancroft quoted, Browne spoke on behalf of the Church of England, defending it from Barrow's condemnation and deriding Barrow's insistence on churches having elders. Browne told them, 'indeed you are and will be the aldermen [elders] even to pull the most ancient of all, Christ Jesus himself, by the beard'.[10]

Another anti-Separatist treatise that came into Bancroft's hands, *A Reproofe of Certeine Schismatical Persons*, is a puzzling manuscript. Bancroft believed it was by Browne, as did Bredwell, and it was in Browne's handwriting, so it sounds like an open-and-shut case. The problem is that the tract's defence of the Church of England is so strong in substance and so mild in style, its loyalism so taken for granted, that it is extremely hard to believe it can be by the same person as wrote the earlier works we know are by Browne. Indeed, it is archived at Lambeth Palace with a note by Archbishop Sancroft questioning its attribution, and saying, 'I think rather 'tis T[homas] C[artwright]'s'. Modern scholars have been divided, Burrage publishing the tract as a work of Browne's, Peel republishing it as Cartwright's.

Peel's explanation for the misattribution was that Browne had copied out Cartwright's tract by hand in order to reply to it, as he had before, and his handwriting misled Bancroft.[11]

What neither scholar noticed is that there is a passage in *A Reproofe of Certeine Schismatical Persons*, about three pages long, with remarkably close verbal similarity to a section of a letter Browne wrote to his uncle Mr Flowers on New Year's Eve 1588.* We cannot be dogmatic, but it is hard to explain this replication in any other way than that Browne wrote both works, which would mean that by 1589 he was indeed working as an apologist for the Church of England. If so, he would be by no means the only former Separatist to take that turn.

Bredwell decided to expose Browne to his followers as a hypocrite and published a pamphlet revealing Browne's submission to the archbishop. Browne defended himself against the exposé with a tract known only by the name Bredwell gave it, *The Raging Libel*, presumably not original. The assurances he had given the archbishop, Browne said – with extraordinary interpretive dexterity – did not contradict anything that he had ever taught his followers. He claimed the statement he signed simply acknowledged the bishop's secular rule, accepted that a congregation that had correct preaching and correct sacraments was a true church, and promised that he would not preach unless rightly called to it. He admitted telling Whitgift that his first child had been baptised according to the Prayer Book, but now told his followers that this had happened against his wishes when he was out of the country.

Presumably Browne did not expect Bredwell to have access to the text of his submission to the archbishop, but he did, and he published it in June 1588 in a furious book called *The Rasing of the Foundations*

---

* The passage to Flowers is a list of sins that exclude people from the covenant ('Schism and forsaking the church of God' etc.); the list in *A Reproofe* is phrased in terms of the sinners who commit them ('Schismatics and forsakers of the church of God' etc.). There are changes of order between the two lists, but of the 356 words, excluding Scripture references, in the passage in the letter, 317 (89 per cent) are matched by the same word or a cognate in the equivalent part of the list in *A Reproofe*. The two passages are found in *Browne and Harrison*, 527–8, and *Cartwrightiana*, 243–6.

of Brovvnisme, and 'by this means shewed, that he [Browne] hath not one hair of an honest man about him'. Bredwell insisted – against the protestations of Browne on one side, and Barrow and Greenwood on the other – that Browne was 'the masterworkman of all their mad building' and had never recanted any of his illegal teaching, just learned to speak out of different sides of his mouth as occasion demanded, so that Barrow and Greenwood hated Browne's 'coldness and colourable dealing', while Browne in turn was jealous of their 'running before their old master, and thereby obscuring his light'. 'Full many of his poor disciples lie in prisons, whilest he laugheth at liberty, and, touching that, for which they suffer, addeth affliction to their bands, by all his behaviour.' No reply from Browne is known, and it is hard to imagine what he might have said in his defence.[12]

Gifford, Some and Penry

Another writer who entered the arena against Barrow and Greenwood was George Gifford, the one presbyterian we know of dangerous enough to have been deprived in Whitgift's 1584 subscription campaign. After a failed attempt to regain his living, and being brought before the Court of High Commission on a charge of leading conventicles, Gifford left the country in 1586, as chaplain to Leicester's forces in the Netherlands. He returned in time to petition the 1587 Parliament, asking, with the support of friends, to be restored to the ministry, but the only result of the attempt was that two of his supporters lost their own benefices. Gifford's reputation seemed irreparable, and yet he was also gaining respect and popularity for his writings, which were not puritan polemic, but widely acceptable Protestant spirituality. When the London Separatists' manuscript *A Breefe Sum of Our Profession* and Greenwood's *Reasons against Read Prayer* turned up in Essex, Gifford was persuaded to reply to both, in short manuscripts, defending prescribed prayers and vigorously arguing that the faults of the Church of England were tolerable. Thus another extended pamphlet war broke out. Gifford protested great reluctance to get involved, but it made good sense to do so: as well as protecting his national church from breaking up, he was dissociating the puritan movement from extremism and making a case for his own rehabilitation. In fact Gifford never did win back his pastorate at Maldon, but his reward was negative – the anti-puritan storms of the coming years passed him by.

Robert Some was another pamphleteer who benefited from publicly attacking those more radical than himself. Though he had been an ally of Cartwright at Cambridge in the early 1570s, Some had been promoted out of his radicalism, becoming Vice-President of Queens' College in 1572. He remained in the wider puritan fold, serving as chaplain to Leicester and opposing Whitgift's 1584 subscription campaign. To gain any further promotion in the university, however, Some needed to prove himself safe, and like Gifford did so by writing against those to his left. He published *A Godly Treatise Containing and Deciding Certain Questions* in May 1588, defending the Church of England from the 'anabaptistical recusants' as he called the Brownists, and assuring readers that its sacraments were valid.

A member of the underground church smuggled a copy of Some's book in to Barrow, and he wrote a reply in the margins of Some's book, but before he could pass it back to his friends, the jailer discovered and confiscated it. Robert Some was brought in to debate with Barrow, and the following May Some published another *Godly Treatise*, this one a detailed counterattack to the arguments of Barrow and Greenwood, including Barrow's marginal writings, which got them in print for the first time. 'If they will not be won,' said Some of the Separatists, 'they may and ought to be repressed, lest men's souls be poisoned, and the church rent in pieces and the commonwealth disturbed.' That month, Whitgift awarded Some the mastership of Peterhouse.[13]

One puritan joined the debate on the side of Barrow and Greenwood. John Penry, a twenty-five-year-old from Llangamarch, Brenockshire, had already courted episcopal wrath. Penry was deeply grieved about the lack of preaching ministers (or even resident ones) in Wales: out of 3,400 graduates since Elizabeth's accession, twelve were preaching in Wales. As a result, Protestantism had had very little impact there, even Christianity was patchy, and 'hell is enlarged to receive us', Penry said. He wrote a book asking Parliament to address this failure, and, having obtained an episcopal licence to print it, had the MP for Carmarthen present it to the Commons in February 1587, when Job Throckmorton enthusiastically supported it, before his fall. Whitgift would not tolerate any such interference in the Queen's religious prerogative, and seized 500 copies of the book. Through the Court of High Commission, Whitgift convicted the 'lewd boy' Penry of treason and heresy, for which he spent a month in Gatehouse prison. Penry accused Whitgift of illegally overriding Parliament, who had accepted his book.[14]

Penry published a response to Some's first *Godly Treatise* in August 1588, taking the treatise as a justification of the lack of unpreaching ministers in the Church of England. Penry argued that ministers who did not preach were not ministers at all: communicating God's word was the most essential part of their role, so if they failed to do that they were not ministering. As non-ministers, they could not be relied upon to deliver true sacraments, and it was a sin to receive from them.

The following month, Some replied, warning, with uncanny foresight, that Penry's criticism of the ministry of their church seemed dangerously close to condemning it altogether 'and so to shake hands with the Anabaptistical recusants … If he be thoroughly searched, it is not unlike to fall out so.'[15]

A strange request

Robert Browne put pen to paper again on 31 December 1588, writing for his uncle Mr Flower. Flower had asked his opinion on church government, and so Browne spent the last hours of the year writing a long letter. In this description of how a church should be run, he still maintained his congregational belief that it was the people as a whole who had the authority to make decisions, but he now, following his troubles in Middelburg, said that the state should also be involved, ensuring that the proper procedures are followed so that the voice of the people is clearly heard by the people. His comments on bishops are on a missing page of the letter. In a more profound change to his thinking, and against those on every side of the great contemporary debate, Browne said that the form of office was not so important as the character of the person in it. Whether they were called elders, pastors or even priests, a 'proud popeling may lie hid under the names', and that was what they should be judged on.[16]

Browne ended with a touching note, asking his uncle to return the letter if he did not like it, rather than burning it, as he had not made a copy. 'And if it appear in the light any time, that in no case it be any prejudice or danger to me, seeing I wrote it by your demand. For I am poor enough and broken too, too much with former troubles, and therefore had no need of further affliction.'[17]

The following summer, Browne visited the Bishop of Peterborough bearing a letter from Burghley. In the letter, the Lord Treasurer, admitting it was a 'somewhat strange' request, asked the bishop 'to receive him [Browne] again into the ministry, and to give him your best means and help for some ecclesiastical preferment'.[18]

14

The mystery of Martin Marprelate

T HE PURITAN MOVEMENT took a surprising turn in October 1588. While the last surviving Spanish ships were arriving home in Santander, an extraordinary book started appearing in shadowy corners of England, by an author writing under the pen name of Martin Marprelate.

The epistle and the epitome

The oddity of Martin's book started with the title, the self-referential *Oh read ouer D[r] Iohn Bridges, for it is a worthy worke*. Its title page called the work an 'epitome', or summary, of a lengthy anti-puritan work by Bridges, the Dean of Salisbury, before admitting that the summary was not ready yet, and that this was an 'epistle' to hold the place for it. Bridges' book, *A Defence of the Gouernment Established in the Church of Englande*, was a thoroughly unremarkable one, except perhaps in its length – Martin says it is so portable 'a horse may carry it if he be not too weak'.[1] Martin's reply proved much more memorable than Bridges' original, not because of any theological innovation, but in its tone and style.

Where Cartwright was scholarly, Field outraged and Barrow vituperative, Martin's writing is a heady mixture of nonsense, satire, protest, irony and gossip. Calling Bridges' book a worshipful volume by a worshipful priest and 'Doctor of Divility', Martin rejoices that Bridges has done the cause of sincere religion so much good by attacking it with such confused arguments, and he chastises the bishops for allowing the puritans' case to go effectively unchallenged. Where other writers quoted scriptures against the bishops, Martin tells stories. The Bishop of London plays bowls on the Sabbath and swears 'like a lewd swag'. The Bishop of Gloucester went beyond the law by imprisoning a layman for refusing to subscribe to the Prayer Book, despite himself being a closet papist. The Bishop of Rochester, having a benefice at his disposal, 'presented himself thereunto, even of mere goodwill'. Whitgift, says Martin with strong innuendo, used to be 'Doctor Perne's boy and carried his cloakbag after him'. A dog ran off with an unnamed bishop's cap, perhaps thinking it was a cheesecake.[2]

Simply the terms in which Martin addressed the bishops were remarkable. He was hardly the first to call them antichrists, 'proud popes and petty prelates', but he was the first to have such fun disrespecting them. Whitgift he calls 'his Canterburiness', 'his Gracelessness of Canterbury', the 'Pope of Lambeth', 'John of Canterbury', 'Brother Canterbury'; and, using abbreviations that were fairly standard but gained a double meaning in Martin's hands, 'my Lord of Cant.' and 'John Canter.' Aylmer is 'Lord Dumb John', 'Don John of London' and 'dumb dunstical John'.

The tract was full of the language of the street that had rarely made it on to the pages of religious tracts before: 'Wohoho, brother London!' In the margin, beside a particularly convoluted sentence quoted from Bridges, Martin says, 'Whoa, whoa! Dean, take your breath and then to it again.' Where other writers used marginal notes for additional information such as Bible verses, Martin played with them, and even argued with himself. He ended by dating the book, 'within a year of midsummer, between twelve and twelve of the clock'.

The appalled bishops scrambled into action, sending all their forces of investigation and enforcement to find the perpetrators. They were spurred on by the Queen, who told Whitgift that not only was the content of the book seditious but its covert printing and distribution set 'a dangerous example to encourage private men in this covert manner to subvert all other kinds of government'.[3] Martin was also attacked from the other side: Puritan ministers were embarrassed by his scurrilous support for their cause, and preached sermons against him. Those who did want to read the book did not know where to find it. The Bishop of Winchester, Thomas Cooper, was given the job of replying to Martin and refuting his accusations.

Before Cooper had the chance to complete his reply, or Whitgift's agents had a chance to find out anything, Martin's sequel appeared, a month after the first book. Under precisely the same title, this second version of *Oh read ouer* actually contained the promised epitome, as well as plenty more episcopal ridicule. Martin made fun of the bishops' scouring the country for him in response to his friendly letter. 'I thank you brethren, I can be well, though you do not send to know how I do.' He also defended himself from the disapproval of puritans, who blamed him 'for telling the truth openly'.[4]

The response

The bishops' first investigations pointed towards the preacher and author John Udall, who they heard had recently been dictating a book to a scribe, which perhaps suggested he wanted to hide his handwriting from the printer. That trail soon ran cold though. In December, the Court of High Commission authorised its men to search persons, houses and shops in pursuit of Martin and his accomplices, and to question suspects under the oath *ex officio*. John Penry's house in Northampton was raided in his absence, the archbishop's agent ransacking his study, seizing books and papers, and threatening to break down doors and pull apart the roof. The most incriminating thing he found there – according to Penry's formal complaint to Parliament – was his latest reply to Robert Some.

In January 1589, Bishop Cooper's reply to Martin, *An Admonition to the People of England*, was published. It was a commendably rapid response at 180 pages long, but thoroughly misguided. Cooper solemnly engaged with Martin's satirical criticism, giving weight to innuendo and gossip, excusing or denying stories of questionable episcopal behaviour in a way that only served to underline the allegations. Worse still, it only encouraged the pseudonymous writer, who straightaway responded with a broadsheet under the whimsical title *Certaine Minerall, and Metaphysicall Schoolpoints*, listing thirty-seven questionable claims made by members of the church hierarchy, largely from Cooper's book. Martin, pretending to believe these claims, said that if any person dared dispute them and 'defend Christ Jesus', he would send a pursuivant for them.

A more successful attack on Martin Marprelate came from Richard Bancroft, who on 9 February preached a long sermon that he then printed. The Apostle Paul, he said, had prophesied that in their time there would be many false prophets, and sure enough true Christians were besieged by papists on the one side and puritans on the other. The heresy of the papists, Bancroft argued, was to forbid people to read the scriptures and to search out the truth for themselves; the heresy of the puritans was to urge people never to stop reading and searching. The happy medium was for a person to investigate so far as necessary in order to choose between the Churches of Rome and of England, join the right one, 'then content yourselves and seek no farther'. He spoke of Martin as the puritan par excellence – rash, disrespectful, unreasonable, unlearned, divisive and determined to have everything his own way. 'He wisheth that our Parliament, which is now assembled, would put down Lord Bishops, and bring in the reformation which they look for, whether her Majesty will or no ... I fear he will be found a traitor.'[5]

Instead of the defensive tone of Bishop Cooper, this was a robust counter-offensive presenting Martin and his fellow presbyterians as the enemies of the people. Bancroft pointed to James VI's treatment by the insubordinate Ruthven presbyterians as evidence that those who rebel against episcopacy end up rebelling against monarchy. In a mark of how the times had changed, Bancroft, who shored up his case with apt quotations from church authorities from Justin Martyr to John Calvin, also took delight in quoting Robert Browne against presbyterianism, both from his treatise against Barrow and his private letter to his uncle, which Bancroft's secret police had given him access to. 'I think he hath bin of another judgement,' Bancroft said, but experience 'is no foolish master'.[6]

During the investigation, the MP George Carleton was examined by the Privy Council, as was Thomas Settle, the nonconformist minister, who since his release from prison had become Carleton's protégé and preached for him in Northamptonshire. Carleton was not able to convince the Council that he knew nothing about the tracts, but it was Settle who went back to the Gatehouse.

The search for Martin Marprelate made some progress when Richard Cosin, a lawyer in the Court of Chancery, interviewed

Nicholas Tomkins, a servant of the puritan lady of the manor in East Moseley in Surrey by the name of Elizabeth Crane (no relation of Nicholas Crane). Tomkins reported that the printer Robert Waldegrave had spent some weeks in Crane's house shortly before the first tract appeared. With Waldegrave in the house were John Penry, and Giles Wigginton a radical puritan minister who had been removed from his Yorkshire parish in 1585. Waldegrave offered Tomkins the entire print run of *Oh read ouer* to sell, Tomkins said, but he declined. As for the identity of the author, Tomkins could only repeat rumour: some said it was a posthumous work of John Field's; others, seeing that it championed Wigginton's cause, suspected him; still others Penry. The fact that East Moseley was only three miles from Udall's parish in Kingston might put him back in the frame too. But by 1589, Udall had moved to Newcastle, Wigginton was in jail in London, and Field was dead, and still the tracts kept coming. Waldegrave and Penry, however, were still at large.

Certaine Minerall, and Metaphysicall Schoolpoints turned out to have been a placeholder, buying time for the writing of a much more substantial Marprelate tract, which appeared in March, called *Hay Any Work for Cooper* after the marketing cry of London barrelmakers. In it, Martin teased Bishop Cooper – or 'Tom Tubtrimmer of Winchester' – for giving Martin's stories of episcopal misdemeanors greater circulation. He pointed out that Cooper seemed to have confirmed some of the allegations, such as the Bishop of St David's bigamy, by failing to deny them. Martin had considerable fun with some of Cooper's less convincing defences: Cooper had argued that the Bishop of London's habit of swearing 'by my faith' was the same as saying 'Amen'; Martin pointed out that, as Jesus uses the word 'amen' frequently in the Gospels (often translated 'verily'), Cooper was offering a rather surprising translation of Jesus' turn of phrase.

The tone of this book seemed rather different than the first two though. Martin offered much more solemn debate about the rights and wrongs of church government, while also feeling the need to earnestly justify his riotous tone. 'The Lord being the author both of mirth and gravity,' he said, 'is it not lawful in itself for the truth to use either of these ways when the circumstances do make it lawful?' There were also marked changes of style and subject within the one text, perhaps suggesting more than one author – something that Martin plays up: 'Whau, whau! but where have I been all this while? Ten to one among some of these puritans. Why Martin? Why Martin, I say, have you forgotten yourself?'[7]

Barrow before the Privy Council

In 1589 there were about twenty Separatists imprisoned in London, spread across Newgate, Bridewell, the Fleet and the Wood Street Compter. Seven of them had been there for a year and a half, and in March they sent a petition protesting against their treatment to the Queen. They complained that they were being held by the Bishop of London and the Archbishop of Canterbury under the 1581 Recusancy Act, which they said was only aimed at Catholics, while many of them had never even been told what crime they were accused of. The bishops had made false accusations about them to the Queen and to their congregations, that they would never make to their faces. For their loyalty to the gospel, the believers faced 'daily spoiling, vexing, molesting, hurting, pursuing, imprisoning, yea, barring and locking them up close prisoners in the most unwholesome and vile prisons, and there detaining them without bringing them to their answers, until the Lord by death put an end to their miseries'.[8] They appealed for an audience with the Privy Council.

Twelve members of the church managed to get face to face with the Queen and presented the petition to her directly. For this effrontery, three of them were arrested and imprisoned by order of the Privy Council: John Sparrow, a fishmonger, went to the White Lion in Southwark; John Nicholas, a thirty-two-year-old glover, to the Gatehouse; and Christopher Bowman, a twenty-nine-year-old goldsmith from Smithfield, to the Wood Street Compter. Bowman had married a fellow Brownist, Ellyn, the previous year (illegally, as no minister officiated, because the Brownists did not consider marriage a religious ceremony), at a meeting of the underground church in the Fleet, and left her now expecting her second child.

Despite this retribution, the Brownists were granted the audience they requested with the Privy Council. Five days after they sent the petition, on 18 March, Barrow was brought before the Council in the Lord Chancellor's office in Whitehall. Spotting other members of his church who had also been brought there from their prisons, but unable to talk to them, he was led into the chamber and required to kneel before the assembled lords, who included the Lord Chancellor Christopher Hatton, the Lord Treasurer Burghley, the Archbishop of Canterbury, the Bishop of London, and the Privy Councillor Baron Buckhurst, as well as a host of attendants including Robert Some. It was the most powerful panel that any of the Separatists ever faced, but if viewed as a test of Barrow's refusal to be a 'respecter of persons', it was one he passed with distinction.

Burghley, according to the account Barrow wrote on his return to his cell, began by asking him, 'Why will you come not to church?'

'My whole desire is to come to the church of God,' said Barrow.

Straightaway Burghley concluded, 'Thou art a fantastical fellow I see; but why not our churches?'

Barrow summarised his four causes of separation, and was asked to elaborate on the point about idolatrous worship. His answer was considerably more extreme than earlier Separatists, who called the Prayer Book idolatrous because preachers were made to choose between obeying either it or God: Barrow argued that every instruction in the book was idolatrous because it added to God's instructions in the Bible. This even included the book's readings from the Bible, because the state was presuming to tell Christians which parts of the Bible to read when.

The Council discussed with Barrow his objections to saints' days and tithes, Lord Buckhurst concluding that he was out of his wits, Burghley that he had a hot brain. The general impression was that he was proud and presumptuous.

Questioned on his petition protesting against false imprisonment, Barrow made the point that the law keeping him in prison had been intended for Catholics. Burghley and Hatton both replied, that being the case, 'There must be straiter laws made for you.'

Barrow argued at length, and heat, with the two bishops, who assured the Council that he had no learning. Barrow conceded this, but told the bishops, 'You are void of all true learning and good lives.' The manner in which he addressed them shocked the Council, and Hatton asked him if he realised whom he was talking to.

'Yes, my Lord,' said Barrow, 'I have cause to know them.'

'But what?' said Hatton. 'Is this not the Bishop of London?'

'I know him for no Bishop, my Lord.'

'What is he then?'

'His name is Elmar, my Lord.'

Hatton pointed to Whitgift, asking, 'What is this man?'

'The Lord,' Barrow tells readers, 'gave me a spirit of boldness.' He told Hatton, 'He is a monster, a miserable compound, I know not what to make him. He is neither ecclesiastical nor civil, even that second beast spoken of in Revelation.'

Burghley calmly asked Barrow for chapter and verse. Whitgift was less calm: 'The beast arose in anger', said Barrow, 'gnashing his teeth, and said, "Will you suffer him, my lords?" So I was plucked up by the warden's man from my knees and carried away.' Back in his cell, Barrow repented his 'unsanctified heart and mouth, which can bring no glory to God or benefit to his church, but rather reproach to one and affliction to the other'. But the error he regretted was not his outburst against Whitgift; it was his timidity in calling Aylmer by his surname, when he had been given the opportunity to lay him open 'as a wolf, a bloody persecutor and apostate'.[9]

Barrow had twice during his interview asked the Council for a public debate with an apologist for the state church. Each time, Whitgift angrily refused, saying Barrow had made his opinions public enough already in writing. Instead, said the archbishop, Barrow would be interviewed about his beliefs on suspicion of heresy.

Barrow, Greenwood and others were interrogated separately on 24 March before a large court led by Whitgift, Aylmer and Cooper, and senior judges including two Lord Chief Justices. The defendants refused the oath *ex officio* but the proceedings continued without it, and Barrow and Greenwood were required to answer a list of questions formulated by Some in an attempt to distil the most dangerous aspects of their teachings.

The questions started in the shallow end of sedition, asking whether it was permissible to recite the Lord's Prayer and other scripted prayers. This led the defendants on to whether the Prayer Book was idolatrous, whether the laws for worship established by the Queen and Parliament were antichristian, whether the Queen was Supreme

Governor of the Church of England, whether ordinary people could reform the church without her permission and whether she could be excommunicated. Greenwood pleaded with the court not to force him to incriminate himself in his answers, but when the bishops quoted his own words from his writings there was no escape and he accepted all the propositions put in his mouth; Barrow showed no such anxiety and told them his opinions without reservation.

The bishops told Barrow and Greenwood in conclusion that they had proved they had no greater allegiance to the Queen than any Catholic. Both denied this, saying that Catholics' allegiance was to the Pope who claimed to be a higher authority than the Queen. The bishops had them in a corner though. The Separatists affirmed that they could only obey the Queen so far as she obeyed Scripture – their own higher authority. Where the Pope had excommunicated the Queen, the Separatists claimed the right to do so themselves. In fact, by the logic of their position – although the question did not arise in their interviews – the Queen was already excluded from communion in the true church because she had never been a member of it in the first place. Barrow was sent back to his cell 'with more commandments yet to keep me more straitly'.[10]

Anti-Martinists

The spring of 1589 saw a lull in the output of Martin Marprelate, but his name and the controversy around it were everywhere. Verse pamphlets appeared mocking Martin's campaign and using his satirical style against him. A poet calling himself Mar-Martin criticised Martin in generally excruciating doggerel, and in a relatively tolerable moment warned his readers:

> *Martin the merry, who now is Mar-prelate,*
> *Will prove mad Martin, and Martin Mar-the-state.*

Mar-Martin lumped Martin together with Browne and Barrow as the three men spreading theological poison around England.[11]

In reply, another poet, by the pen name of, inevitably, Mar-Mar-Martin, protested that Martin and Mar-Martin were as bad as each other, arguing and calling each other names. Calling the pair of them 'wanton calves' in reference to Aesop's fable about the dangers of giddiness, he argued that such division would delight England's Catholic enemies, and that

> Martin, Mar-Martin, Barrow, Browne,
> All help to pull religion down.

The playwright John Lyly joined in with a poem called 'A Whip for an Ape', pointing out that, as a martin was a kind of ape, Martin could not have chosen a more appropriate name for himself: 'Wise men regard not what mad monkeys patters [sic].'[12]

Martin was satirised on the stage as well. Four theatre troupes are known to have included him that summer as a character in their plays, wearing an ape mask. In one play, the monster tried to force himself on Dame Divinity, who escaped with a scratched face, vomiting. Collinson believed that Bancroft orchestrated both the search for Martin and this slew of counter-satire, but the Privy Council disapproved of the unseemly theatrics and instructed the archbishop, the Lord Mayor and the Master of Revels to form the first theatre censorship committee.

After four months of silence, a fifth Martin Marprelate tract appeared in July 1589, *Theses Martinianae*. The theses purported to be written by Martin but published by 'Martin Junior, son unto the renowned and worthy Martin Marprelate the Great'. Martin Junior said his father had gone missing and the theses were among a bunch of his father's papers found beside a bush. 'Many flim-flam tales go abroad of him,' says the youth: that he has been arrested, was killed fighting the Spanish or injured 'at the Groine', or is busy about the bishops' business, having been 'choked with a fat prebend or two'.[13]

Martin Junior's introduction and conclusion, which form more than half the tract, sound a lot like the Martin of earlier tracts. Paradoxically, the 110 theses themselves of Martin the Great take the more serious tone, offering a straightforward argument against episcopacy, at least at first. They become slightly more playful when they attempt the rather outrageous argument that, because John Foxe published the complete works of the martyrs William Tyndal, John

Frith and Robert Barnes in 1573, bearing a stamp indicating state approval, and because those works condemned episcopacy, therefore episcopacy was condemned by the English state and 'by the doctrine of the Church of England'.[14]

Later the same month, another Marprelate tract appeared, this time in the name of Martin Junior's elder brother, confusingly called Martin Senior. Entitled *The Just Reproof and Censure of Martin Junior*, it purported to join the anti-Martinist diatribes, rebuking Martin Junior for printing their father's writing and thus turning the bishops' attention back to him in earnest, when the 'rhymers and stage-players' had been drawing all the attention and turning the business into a joke.

Martin Senior recites a long speech by Archbishop Whitgift, as a warning to his younger brother of how 'the Canterbury Caiaphas' will respond. This was an audacious act by the anonymous writer. Not only does the imagined Whitgift set out his strategy in detail – telling his agents to look for Martinists in the congregation at Bishop Cooper's sermons, to befriend booksellers, watch London inns for deliveries of paper and intercept puritans' mail – but he repeatedly names his suspects: 'Have you diligently sought me out Waldegrave the printer, Newman the cobbler, Sharpe the book binder of Northampton, and that seditious Welshman Penry, who you shall see will prove the author of all these libels?'[15] It seemed like the brazen recklessness of someone who either had nothing left to lose or felt themself invincible.

Arrests

Then, on 4 August, a cart loaded with boxes arrived in Warrington, Lancashire, outside the house of John Hodgkins, a trader in saltpetre and gunpowder. The sight was interesting enough for passers-by to stop and watch, and, as Hodgkins and his men unloaded the cart, they mishandled one of the boxes and spilled its contents – lots of small pieces of metal. Hodgkins explained to the watching townspeople that they were shot for guns, but the witnesses were sufficiently suspicious to report the incident to local authorities, with the result that agents of the Earl of Derby started shadowing Hodgkins.

On 14 August, the earl's men raided a house rented by Hodgkins thirty miles away on Newton Lane, near Manchester. They found a printing press there, on which Hodgkins, and his assistants, Valentine Simmes and Arthur Thomlyn, were printing the first page of the next Marprelate tract, *More Work for Cooper*. As they were led away, Hodgkins reminded the other two that they had sworn not to divulge their contacts, assuring them they would only be in prison for a short while, on full pay, and provided with food and drink, then given work in Ireland on their release. They were interviewed by the earl, who got nothing from them, then sent to London to face the Privy Council. The Council also got nothing and in September sent them to the Tower of London with instructions to their keepers to use torture if necessary.

Meanwhile evidence found in Hodgkins' papers led the church authorities to the man Martin Senior had named as a suspect, 'Sharpe the book binder of Northampton'. Henry Sharpe was arrested in September and eventually gave the authorities a good deal of information. On the all-important question of the writer of the tracts though, neither Sharpe nor any other witness so far admitted any knowledge, but the investigator who wrote an anonymous report on 21 September was pretty confident. The circumstantial evidence put one man in the frame; and one piece of direct evidence confirmed it: the manuscript Hodgkins had been working from when arrested contained Penry's handwriting. Admittedly it was one of two different hands seen in the script, but the other (writing twice as many words) was presumably Penry's servant taking dictation, so the investigator concluded the tracts had been uniformly 'contrived by Penry'. He was mistaken.[16]

15

Round-up

B ANCROFT'S SEARCH FOR Martin Marprelate found more than he was looking for. Raiding the studies of puritan ministers in the English Midlands who were suspected of having connections with the underground press, he came for the first time across evidence of an unofficial presbyterian church network. The documents of illicit synods and conferences came to light, along with the Book of Discipline, the proposed order for English presbyterianism, and the names of those who had subscribed to it. On the strength of this, the officers started arresting those involved in presbyterian leadership as well as the Martinists. The presbyterian association that had met in Dedham in Essex eighty times since 1582 held its last meeting on 2 June 1589, recording in the minutes that their work had been 'ended by the malice of Satan'.

As for the Marprelate project, even though many of the conspirators were in prison, and the net was closing around the others, and they had lost their press, a seventh tract appeared in late September 1589, *The Protestatyon of Martin Marprelat*. Reflecting on the August raid, Martin assured readers that he would never give up the campaign, that he was at peace with God should he be killed for it, and that setbacks in the cause of reformation did not make it a bad cause. He asked the reader to pass a message to the bishops, that 'the last year of *Martinism* ... shall not be till full two years after the last year of *Lambethism*'. And because they were so keen to know his identity, he offered to take part in a public debate with the defenders of episcopacy, on the condition if he should win the system would be dismantled.[1]

Martin added Some to his rogues' gallery, as a controversialist 'whose bald writings without sap or edge, unworthy of a boy of

172

twelve year old, have (I am persuaded) made and will make (if it be not looked unto) more Brownists in our church, than all that ever they have hitherto published themselves'. The tone of the tract was defiant and surprisingly self-assured, but there is not a great deal of Martin's patented merriment, though he does slip some gossip about the Dean of Lichfield into the note of printing errors on the last page.[2]

Martin revealed

On 15 October, the jailed bookbinder Henry Sharpe was interviewed under oath about his role in the Marprelate operation. He confirmed that the first four tracts had been printed by Waldegrave, who had salvaged enough letters from the destruction of his press in 1588 to set up the operation in Elizabeth Crane's house. Moving to avoid detection, Waldegrave printed the second tract at the house of Sir Richard Knightley in Northamptonshire, and the following two tracts at the house of Knightley's nephew John Hales of Coventry. Then Waldegrave quit, and after a hiatus Hodgkins became the printer, producing the next two tracts in Wolston, near Coventry, at the house of Mr and Mrs Wigston, before carting the press on its fateful journey to Warrington. In each case, after Sharpe had stitched the pages together, the tracts were distributed by the London cobbler Humphrey Newman, who would receive 600 or 700 copies at once.

As for the principal organiser of the operation, Sharpe told the authorities that John Penry had been present at several of the printing locations, that it was he who recruited Hodgkins as printer, and that he helped Newman with distribution. Finally the government had the evidence they needed to arrest Penry, and the Privy Council declared him an enemy of the state, but he had already left the country, escaping a couple of weeks earlier to Scotland. He was followed there by Waldegrave and by his wife of one year, Helen, who left their daughter Deliverance with her family.

Burghley urged James VI to banish Penry from Scotland, but the king was reluctant to antagonise Scottish presbyterians, and even when he did issue the ban, the Kirk refused to proclaim it. Waldegrave

173

got work as the king's printer, and in 1590 published a book by Penry defending Scottish presbyterians from Bancroft's sermon of February 1589, which had said 'they trod upon [the king's] sceptre, and laboured to establish an ecclesiastical tyranny of an infinite jurisdiction'. Penry also noted Bancroft's appeal to Browne, who he said was the perfect witness for the Church of England – a 'proud, ungodly man' and a 'noted schismatic'.[3]

Those Martinist collaborators who did not go into exile went to jail: Elizabeth Crane, Richard Knightley, John Hales and Mr and Mrs Wigston were all arrested for housing the press at various stages in its travels, and held in the Fleet.

The same fate befell the Midlands presbyterian leaders whose activities were discovered in the search for the Marprelate press: eight ministers were imprisoned in the Fleet. They were all examined by the Court of High Commission and all refused to take the oath. Whitgift's eyes, however, were on a bigger prize: Cartwright was his nemesis of thirty years, publicly defying his authority, contradicting him in print and leading the movement for his abolition. Cartwright had powerful friends on the Privy Council, including Burghley, and the case against him was not yet as strong as for the other nine ministers, but he had lived near them in Warwick, and Whitgift meant to include him in his haul.

After three months under the ministrations of the Church of England's torturers, the assistant Martinist printers Simmes and Thomlyn were brought before Hatton on 10 December. Finally willing to talk, they gave the Lord Chancellor detailed information about the operation during the time they were involved, including the first mention the authorities heard of the man they eventually realised was Martin Marprelate: Martin was the fallen MP Job Throckmorton.

The identity of Martin intrigued historians for centuries, and as recently as 1969 Patrick Collinson, in his magisterial account of Elizabethan puritanism, wrote of it as a mystery that might never be solved. Candidates have included Henry Barrow, George Carleton, Giles Wigginton, John Udall, and the late John Field. It was Leland H. Carlson who first (among modern scholars) uncovered Job Throckmorton in 1981, citing stylistic evidence, Throckmorton's character, contemporary accusations and the lack of solid evidence for any other contender. This identification has gained consensus, and since then Joseph Black has brought in a wealth of solid evidence from state papers relating to the investigation, confirming that Throckmorton was the main writer and the one who gave Martin his characteristic voice, but that Penry also supplied much of the text. The testimony of Simmes and Thomlyn is key to the case for (or against) Throckmorton: Simmes told Hatton that it was Throckmorton who had given him the manuscripts for each of the three tracts he worked on, and that Throckmorton had interpreted any handwriting that Simmes found illegible.

A True Description

Barrow had his own rather more modest secret writing operation, and though he faced greater restrictions than ever after the questioning in March 1589, he wrote, concealed and smuggled out of the cell the first of his works to be printed, an eight-page tract called *A True Description Out of the Worde of God, of the Visible Church*. As the title suggested, it set out how the church should be organised, hoping to prove the point with a barrage of Scripture references, 113 in the first two paragraphs alone.

Barrow started with a point all Reformed Christians could agree on: there are a visible and an invisible church. The invisible church is all the elect throughout the world and throughout time, whom God has decided to give true faith to. Humans cannot see God's election though, so the church they organise on earth is the visible one, those who look like Christians now. For it to be visible, Barrow said, it has to be a group of 'faithful and holy people gathered together' and not a whole parish or nation. It cannot have ministers foisted on it from outside the church, so they must be appointed 'by the holy and free election of the Lord's holy and free people'.[4]

The freedom of the church was vitally important for Barrow, but not religious freedom itself. If the church was controlled by the state it could be forced into unchristian practices; if membership was not voluntary, the church would be destroyed by having non-Christian members. Barrow did not share Browne's visceral love of freedom, only his motivation of purity, so there were much greater limits on the freedom that Barrow believed in. Church membership should be voluntary, but not attendance. As he wrote later, 'the profane may be compelled to the hearing of the word, and prayer'. And he saw no point sharing the freedom of the true church with anyone else: the Queen ought 'to forbid and exterminate all other religions, worship and ministries within her dominions'. Barrow was totally committed to the idea that true religion is free, the true church a voluntary gathering and the state having no business controlling it or enforcing it, and this commitment had profound influence over the future of the movement. And yet, because he demanded the state leave true religion alone while destroying false religion, he needed the state to determine which religion was true – a serious logical flaw at the heart of his understanding of freedom and coercion.[5]

A *True Description* was printed in the Netherlands at the expense of a wealthy gentleman in the congregation, Robert Stokes, and smuggled back. Twenty-four years later, the former Separatist Christopher Lawne said he had heard many Separatists say 'that this book of their *Description* hath been the only cause that brought them unto Brownism'.[6]

Udall and the Martinists on trial

Towards the end of 1589, the Privy Council summoned John Udall from his new parish in Newcastle to answer questions about his writings. Udall was no longer suspected of being Martin, but the investigations had found evidence connecting him with two other controversial anonymous books printed by Waldegrave at Crane's house in 1588.

Udall had indeed written both. One, *A demonstration of the trueth of that discipline which Christe hath prescribed*, was a hundred-page argument against episcopacy; the other, known as *Diotrephes* after a character in it, was a dialogue between a puritan, a bishop and other unsavoury characters, making the same point in a more popular style. Udall had none of Martin's frivolous tone, but was extremely outspoken in his condemnation of the bishops. They had sold their souls to Satan for worldly pomp, he said. 'You are in league with hell,' he said, '… you do persuade yourselves that there is no God, neither shall there be any … day of account.' The most hair-raising part of all in the book was Udall's choice of Bible verse for the title page: 'Those mine enemies which would not that I should reign over them, bring hither, and slay them before me.'[7]

Interviewed before the Privy Council on 13 January, Udall admitted that he had been at Crane's house while Waldegrave was printing there, but refused to say whether he had written *Diotrephes* or the *Demonstration of the trueth*. He was committed to close imprisonment in the Gatehouse.

The inconclusive prison spells that nonconformists had endured throughout the last twenty years were the only punishments Whitgift had at his disposal through the Court of High Commission, so from February 1590 the cases of the Martinists were referred to the Star Chamber. This court, named after the gilt stars that spangled its ceiling in the Palace of Westminster, had been developed by Henry VII to impose the rule of law on the aristocracy, with greater powers of summary justice than other courts. It could not impose the death penalty, but in addition to imprisonment, it could inflict fines, the pillory, whipping, branding and mutilation. Crane, Knightley, Hales and the Wigstons were all brought to the Star Chamber in February, accused of abetting seditious printing. Except for Mrs Wigston, all claimed to have had no idea what the printers were printing and her husband said he only agreed to the crime because she insisted; she however explained she was driven by 'the zeal of reformation in the church' and saw no harm in the books. Elizabeth Crane was eventually fined £500 for her crime, plus a thousand marks (£666) for contempt of court in refusing to swear, and returned to the Fleet. Richard Knightley was fined £2,000, Hales a thousand marks, Mrs Wigston a thousand pounds, and Mr Wigston 500 marks 'for obeying his wife'.[8]

16

Debate in prison

THE LONDON UNDERGROUND church was as active as ever despite its leaders being in prison, and members continued to be arrested. Between May 1589 and February 1590 the number of Separatists in London prisons doubled to fifty-two across six prisons. Ten Separatists had now died in prison. Edith Burry in Newgate was the only woman remaining among the prisoners, Meynard and Roe having died and Alice Chandler having been bailed. In February Burry was listed as a widow for the first time. The authorities were seeing the wisdom of Simon Renard's rejected advice to Mary: why risk martyring your enemies when you can let them die quietly in jail?

That list of prisoners was made because of Bishop Aylmer's new initiative to dissuade the Brownists from their schism: he assembled a team of forty-two ministers and academics and briefed them on Brownist teaching, instructing them to visit twice a week and engage in theological debate in order to win them back to the church. The team included Richard Bancroft, and Lancelot Andrewes, the minister of St Giles Cripplegate, who would become Bishop of Winchester under James I and oversee the translation of the King James Bible. Aylmer had less than total confidence in his men achieving their stated objective of conversion, telling them to keep records of their conversations that could be used against the Separatists in court.

Barrow and Greenwood, as ever, took notes on their conversations, and wrote them up afterwards. The two of them, usually separately but sometimes together, were visited by several of the Church of England's evangelists, including Andrewes, William Hutchinson the minister of St Botolph's Bishopsgate, and Thomas Sperin the puritan minister of St Mary Magdalen, Milk Street. The battleground that Barrow and Greenwood consistently chose was the contention that was coming to seem their most fundamental: the Church of England could not be a Christian church because it included the entire population regardless of belief or behaviour.

Against this, Hutchinson appealed to the biblical precedent of John the Baptist, who baptised all comers, even Pharisees, without examining their beliefs or behaviour. Greenwood replied that John castigated the Pharisees who came for baptism as a brood of vipers, so it was safe to say that he did not in fact baptise them. The rest of their debates then circled around that verse without ever getting anywhere.

When Hutchinson and Andrewes visited Barrow, the latter complained of his two years' close imprisonment, on which Andrewes congratulated him: 'For close imprisonment, you are most happy. The solitary and contemplative life I hold the most blessed life. It is the life I would choose.'

'You speak philosophically, but not Christianly,' replied Barrow. 'So sweet is the harmony of God's grace unto me in the congregation and the conversation of the saints at all times, as I think myself as a sparrow on the house top when I am exiled from them.' At which the cunning Andrewes asked where these alleged saints met, but Barrow declined to say.[1]

When Barrow argued that the Christian church is a holy people gathered out of the world, while the Church of England *is* the world, Hutchinson and Andrewes argued that the whole land had been gathered to Christ. Barrow said this was nonsense; gathering the church means separating it from the wicked. Barrow had his visitors in a bind, because they all agreed that the church described in the New Testament was a Christian community, while the Church of England being a national state church was a lot less picky about its membership. Andrewes, on the defensive, claimed that the church had exercised just such separation as Barrow described when two Londoners were excommunicated the previous Saturday. Were there, asked Barrow, only two wicked people in all England? 'We know no more,' said Hutchinson and Andrewes. 'That is well!' cried Barrow. 'I report me to all your jails.'[2]

If Barrow held his own against Andrewes and Hutchinson, he ran rings around Sperin. (That is assuming his own account can be trusted, but he did not spare his feelings when conversations went badly for him.) Homing in on the awkward question of membership, he quickly drew from Sperin a similarly implausible claim to Andrewes and Hutchinson's: the reason Sperin as a minister did not exclude anyone from Communion in his church, he said, was not so much that he was not allowed to, but rather 'I know none wicked in all my parish.' This claim was all the more awkward coming from someone with puritan standards, and Barrow pressed his advantage. Does the same go for all the parishes of England? he asked.

Sperin, as a puritan, believed many ministers were woefully failing to convert their parishioners because they never preached, and could not overlook this. 'I will justify all those parishes that have preaching ministers,' he said.

'And what think you of those that have unpreaching ministers?'

'I think not such to be true churches.'[3]

Delighted, Barrow asked Sperin to put that in writing, but he declined. Even without such self-incrimination, Barrow had Sperin on the back foot. What incredible preachers the Church of England has, Barrow said, with greater powers than Christ: their preaching makes the parishioners Christians without them having to obey it or even listen to it. Sperin backtracked. It was not preaching that made parishes true, and non-preaching ones were true churches because they confessed the Reformed faith. So Sperin admitted every sinner in England was in the church, and no discipline happened there after all.

Flushed with this success, Barrow demanded to know how Sperin's appointment as a minister compared to the biblical pattern. Again, Sperin tried to bridge – or fudge – the gap between his puritan ideals and Elizabethan reality, saying, 'My ministry is from God, with the approbation of the assembly of the church where I am.'

Surely, Barrow said, in truth, Sperin and his colleagues were ordained by bishops and appointed by patrons, and the people had no say. Sperin insisted his ministry did not depend on the ordination of bishops; he was called by God and accepted by the flock, therefore 'I have a better calling than the calling of bishops.' If so, Barrow asked, where does that leave the calling of bishops?

'I confess it to be unlawful,' said Sperin.

'Set down that under your hand,' said Barrow again.

'To what end? That were to bring myself unto danger.' It was not an impressive answer to give a man who had spent two years in prison for his faith.

Barrow asked Sperin why he had received unlawful ordination, and Sperin explained, 'I did it in ignorance, I have since repented of it.'

In that case, said Barrow, why was he still licensed by and subject to a bishop? Sperin said that was because of his great respect for the Queen and Parliament who authorised episcopacy. Barrow warned him against obeying the state rather than Christ.

At last Sperin saw a chance to turn the tables on Barrow. 'Why,' he cried, 'then you affirm that the Queen and the Parliament do evil in giving this power and authority unto the bishops. Will you write that?'

If Sperin thought he could win an argument that way, he had seriously misjudged his opponent. 'Yea,' cried Barrow, 'that I will by the grace of God whilst I have breath, and seal it with my blood also (if so God will), it being directly contrary to the testament of Christ, as yourself confesseth and yet continue to do contrary to your own conscience.' If, however, Sperin wanted to provoke Barrow into saying something that could be taken down and used in evidence against him, he had struck gold.[4]

Books and trials

Barrow and Greenwood were so pleased with how these debates had gone they decided to publish them. They had long demanded a public dispute to establish whether their God or the bishops' was true, and were never going to be granted it, but now had the chance to create it themselves in print. They obtained Aylmer's original letter of instruction, including his twelve-point briefing on their false teachings (which they now annotated) and a list of the forty-two preachers and their fifty-two captive charges. Barrow and Greenwood added the records of their seven debates with five London preachers plus the friends they brought with them, as well as letters the two sides then exchanged. Mrs Greenwood smuggled the pages out of the Fleet, then Robert Bowle, a twenty-year-old fishmonger, took them to Dort. There they were printed by a man known only as Hans, in two volumes, 500 copies of each, the first volume in May, the second a couple of months later. The proofs were read by Arthur Bellot, a twenty-two-year-old Cornish gentleman who had joined the underground church, and were smuggled back to London by Robert Stokes, who also financed the printing, and by Bowle. Both men later told the authorities that 200 of the books were carried in Stokes's cloakbag. Some of the books were then smuggled back into the prison by the Greenwoods' maid Cycely, others were sold secretly by Nicholas Lee for 8d each. The first of the two books was called, referring to Aylmer's briefing document, *A Collection of Certaine Sclaunderous Articles Gyven Out by the Bisshops*, though in fact the Separatists' annotations could find few points to correct in the largely accurate summary of their teachings; the second took the milder title *A Collection of Certain Letters and Conferences*. The books were an impressive display of confidence from the Brownists: the Church of England, refusing to debate with them in public, had sent a taskforce to talk to them behind locked doors; it was the Brownists who were enthusiastically making both sides of the conversation public, at their own risk and expense, and against the will of the church. Which church seemed more sure of having the truth on its side? The bishop quickly abandoned the prison-visiting scheme.

The Separatist Christopher Bowman sent a petition to Burghley in March 1590. He had become seriously ill after a year in the Wood Street Compter's Hole, and begged to be released in order to be with his wife and young children, who were in great poverty. Having originally been imprisoned for the presumptuous petition to the Queen on behalf of the whole church, now his more humbly worded plea for himself was also rejected.

A month or so later, the Separatist prisoners en masse petitioned Burghley. Already the signatories included eleven new prisoners taken since Aylmer made his list in February, while three or four had been freed in that time. The petition warned the Lord Treasurer that the blood of innocent victims was pleading to God against England, so when the wrath of God fell on the land no prayers would save them. The Brownists asked for a disputation in public or before the Privy Council to establish whether their gospel was true. Failing that, they requested bail; failing that, that they might all be in the same prison; and failing that, that Burghley would at least let the Privy Council know how much they were suffering.

In the same month, Burghley received a delivery from Robert Browne, a treatise that the former Separatist had written on educational reform, arguing for a thorough overhaul of university teaching, based on scriptural principles. Dealing with logic, grammar, rhetoric, arithmetic, geometry, music, metaphysics, ethics, economics and politics, Browne told Burghley, 'I have justly altered the arts.' He assured him that he could defend his biblical system 'against the multitude of philosophers, doctors and writers heretofore' and suggested that Stamford could become a centre of learning to eclipse Oxford. Browne said that he had sent the book to 'some learned and reverend fathers the bishops', but they had all been too busy to reply.[5]

Burghley was the dedicatee of two books written against the Separatists in 1590 by George Gifford, *A Short Treatise Against the Donatists of England* and *A Plaine Declaration that our Brownists be Full Donatists*. Gifford's point about Donatism was that the Separatists were not just criminals offending against the imperfect religious laws of Elizabethan England, but heretics offending against the canons of historical Christianity. The Donatists had been one side of a split in fourth-century Christianity. Living through imperial persecution, they believed that Christians who once denied their faith could not be readmitted to the church. They also held that any priests who were thus readmitted could not deliver valid sacraments, and those baptised by them needed rebaptism. Their position was denounced as heresy by the mainstream church and that judgement had been accepted down through the ages. Gifford argued that English Separatists held the same heresy: they believed the church is perfect and so they had split from a true church because of mere imperfections; they held that any sinner admitted to Communion would pollute the whole church; and they said sacraments delivered by unpreaching ministers were invalid. Gifford's own puritan nonconformity came up repeatedly in the Star Chamber's hearings on puritan sedition, but his anti-Brownist

183

writings tipped the balance to keep him on the comfortable side of the law.

Udall, after six months' close imprisonment was brought before the assizes at Croydon on 23 July 1590, charged under the Seditious Words and Rumours Act of 1580 with attacking the Queen's religious policy in *A demonstration of the trueth*. It was a capital crime and Udall was found guilty. He was offered a pardon if he would confess that he was the author and that the book was seditious. Unwilling to declare that presbyterianism was sedition, Udall offered to confess instead that the style of the book was offensive. His offer was refused and the case referred to the Lent assizes of 1591 for sentencing.

In October 1590, Job Throckmorton appeared before a grand jury at the Warwick Assizes, charged with authorship of the Marprelate tracts – with 'disgracing her majesty's government and making certain scornful and satirical libels under the name of Martin'. The jury agreed that there was a criminal charge to answer, and the case was referred to Westminster. Throckmorton appealed to Hatton to intervene on his behalf, giving the Lord Chancellor an impressively favourable account of his situation: he had been accused of a few 'slips and infirmities', though he had never had so much as a criminal thought against her majesty, but to be on the safe side he had already signed a submission to the assize judges and the archbishop, and as ever submitted to the Lord Chancellor himself. The case continued.

Cartwright versus the Separatists

While Whitgift's net was tightening around Cartwright, the presbyterian leader resumed his efforts to reclaim Separatists to his flawed but valid church, though without the self-promotional flair of Gifford's work. In the summer of 1590, Cartwright was persuaded by Sperin to visit Barrow in the Fleet. No record of their conversation survives, but Cartwright evidently found it disheartening, because when two years later he was invited to renew the discussion he absolutely refused.

Cartwright faced the Separatist challenge closer to home from his sister-in-law Anne Stubbe, who was a part of the Norfolk Separatist network. Cartwright had entered the Stubbe family in 1578, marrying Alice Stubbe whose brother John was a well-known puritan lawyer and writer. John was suspected of being one of the anonymous authors of *The Life of the 70th Archbishop of Canterbury*, and in 1579 he had his hand cut off for writing (openly) *The Discoverie of a Gaping Gulf*, which vehemently criticised the Queen's prospective marriage to the Duke of Anjou, arguing that it cast suspicion on her commitment to Protestantism. It was said that, immediately after the punishment, he doffed his hat with his left hand and cried, 'God save the Queen!' The Separatist Anne was married either to John or to his brother Francis.

Anne Stubbe lived in Buxton, Norfolk, four miles from Aylsham and ten from Norwich, and Cartwright visited the family there in January 1590. The pair argued about the church, Stubbe saying that it was 'a peculiar people' distinct from the non-Christian world, a definition that the Church of England did not fulfil. She said that Christ gave his church the power and authority to exclude non-Christians from their membership, but instead of doing this the Church of England punished people through the popish bishops' courts; so the Separatist church operated by the power of Christ and the Church of England by the power of antichrist. Similarly, she said that Christ gave his church the freedom to elect its own ministers, and the Church of England has no such freedom.

Stubbe sent a record of their conversation to Cartwright, and he eventually replied with a long letter on 30 August, saying that, with 'the day of my trouble approaching', if he did not write now he might not have another chance. Cartwright argued that, while the Church of England fell far short of presbyterian discipline, it contained ministers who exercised the power and authority to exclude sinners from Communion – and who got into trouble for it – while others did something similar through private admonition, through public preaching and through reciting the liturgy, which proclaimed God's judgement on sinners. And even if the church failed to exercise Christ's authority, he said, that did not mean that it does not have Christ's authority, and it is the having not the exercising that makes a true church. As for the free election of ministers, he said, that point would count just as much against Stubbe's church, because they have no minister at all.

Cartwright was right about his day of trouble. Two days after he wrote to Stubbe, Whitgift made a list of thirty-one accusations against Cartwright, including that he had gone overseas without permission and been elected minister to churches there; that he omitted parts of the Prayer Book when leading worship; that he practised excommunication, organised public fasting and imposed penance; that he took part in Presbyterian synods; that he co-authored the Book of Discipline; and that he had known the identity of Martin Marprelate and about Udall's anonymous books, but had kept quiet.

Cartwright came down to London to face the Court of High Commission, and wrote to Burghley entreating him to intervene as he had before. Sadly, Burghley's power to help him was slipping away. Since the Armada, Burghley's policy of an alliance between puritans and the establishment against Catholicism had suffered defeat, and the government supported Whitgift's campaign to crush puritanism. Burghley asked Whitgift to confine his case against Cartwright to recent nonconformity, arguing that whatever he had got up to in the 1570s, if he had behaved himself since, that deserved to be recognised. Whitgift ignored the request; the only suggestion of Burghley's that the archbishop followed was that he should not be personally present at Cartwright's trial to avoid it looking like the personal vendetta it was. Cartwright was interviewed by Aylmer in St Paul's Cathedral, around October 1590, and, after he refused to swear, the case was transferred to the Star Chamber and Cartwright was kept in the Fleet.

Penry, from his Scottish exile, published a book in April 1590 usually known as *Reformation no enemie*, again printed by Waldegrave. As well as the usual arguments for presbyterian reform, he said that the case had become increasingly urgent because popery was on the ascendant in the Church of England, and if its course was not reversed the English could see in the next reign the complete restoration of Catholicism, as under Mary. Again Penry defended the Kirk from the aspersions of Bancroft, the 'most shameless and most impudent slanderer'. But the most controversial passage was where Penry talked about England in anthropomorphic terms: 'Surely with an impudent forehead she hath said, "I will not come near the holy one, and as for the building of this house, I will not so much as lift up a finger towards that work, nay I will continue the desolations thereof."[6] If England was a person, she sounded very much like the Queen. Penry became an even more wanted man.

17

A Brief Discoverie

HAVING ALREADY PROVED that close imprisonment and being forbidden pen and paper were not going to stop him publishing books, late in 1590 Barrow excelled himself, writing a huge book, 264 pages long when printed, which he saw fit to call *A Brief Discoverie of the False Church*. He passed each page as he wrote it to Daniel Studley, a Separatist girdler who had permission to visit, and Studley took them to the physician James Forrester, who was paid to make fair copies for the printer – perhaps Barrow's excuse for the title is that by the time he finished the book it was too late to change it. Forrester was dismayed by the 'sharp style' of the book, quit the church and became a vociferous opponent of Brownism. The manuscript was smuggled to Dort, perhaps by Scipio Bellot, the brother of Arthur, and it was printed there from December to February 1591.

A Brief Discoverie starts with a survey of church history. All Protestants agreed that the church had gone wrong at some point, in order to require reformation, and the more radical their reformation the further back they had to trace the fall of the church. Barrow, like the Anabaptists, went all the way back to the first generation after the apostles, as soon as the Bible was complete. Believers started venerating their leaders, he said, abdicating their freedom and responsibility to understand and teach and organise for themselves. The leaders succumbed to pomp, power and superstition; 'then were these called bishops'. Hierarchy developed as they took more and more power, until the diocese of Rome went from being supported by the Roman Empire, to being 'mixed with the Empire, and in the end swallowing it up'. Thus Rome 'became the very throne of antichrist ... to whom the key of the bottomless pit was given'. Throughout the centuries there was always a tiny remnant of true believers who 'had the light in the midst of these hellish fogs'. The scriptures were clear, Barrow said, that, in his own day, the judgement of God was about to fall on the false church; God was waiting only 'till his ark be built' – which is the true, separated church – and till the full number of his chosen ones had entered it.[1]

This took Barrow on to the question of how to tell the true church from the false, much of his answer reiterating the arguments that had been the focus of his writing to date. But he went beyond into new ground, opposing and correcting Calvin's understanding of the church.

The Separatists had always until now presented themselves as the true upholders of Reformed Christianity in England. On questions from vestments to episcopacy, the Church of England was out of line with its foreign brethren, embracing corruptions that other churches rejected. The problem with this stance was that Barrow, like Browne before him, had come to understand the church in a radically new way: not as a whole nation that imposed a religious identity on all citizens, but as a gathering of believers called to live differently from the nominal Christians in the world around them. Barrow's opponents pointed out that in this it was Barrow who was out of line with Reformed thinking and practice, not the Church of England, and they appealed to Calvin as an authoritative yet progressive voice of Reformed theology. Gifford, for example, cited Calvin's condemnation of extremists who do not understand that the church will be 'weighed down with the mixture of the wicked – until the Day of Judgment'. 'Because they think no church exists where there are not perfect purity and integrity of life,' Calvin said, 'they depart out of hatred of wickedness from the lawful church, while they fancy themselves turning aside from the faction of the wicked.'[2]

This censure by Calvin, intended for Anabaptists, was an uncomfortably accurate description of the Brownists, so Barrow had a case to answer. At first he protested his respect for Calvin as a reformer of the previous generation. Being 'so newly escaped out of the smoky furnace of popery', it was hardly surprising that Calvin did not immediately see the true shape of the church, and God will doubtless have pardoned his errors. But, Barrow said, Calvin was wrong about what the church is, and his ignorance should now be improved upon, not made a precedent.[3]

However, Barrow soon got drawn beyond this respectful divergence from Calvin. What was at stake was the soul of the church and the meaning of Christianity. Is Christianity a matter of national allegiance or personal faith? Must the church consist of real Christians or should it open 'her knees to every passenger'? In such questions, Barrow believed his opponents were dangerously, wickedly wrong and in attacking them he unleashed a sustained philippic against Calvin. Calvin 'hath insufferably perverted' the Bible texts he appealed to 'and drawn very foul and corrupt doctrine from them'. 'Nothing can be devised more unclean and corrupt, or more unworthy the church of Christ, as breaking all the ordinances and laws of God at once, and utterly subverting and defiling all Christian communion.' 'What fleshly libertine hath or can breathe forth more poisoned doctrines than these?' Barrow condemned Calvin's 'rash and disorderly proceedings at Geneva', which this 'detestable stuff' was designed to defend. 'These smokey errors of Mr Calvin ... [have] darkened the sun.' They are 'pestilent errors and unsufferable blasphemy'. This was an astonishing outburst against a father of Reformed Christianity that the Separatists would not be allowed to forget.[4]

Barrow also used *A Brief Discoverie* to weigh into a controversy between Penry, Some, and an author known only as JG but who seems to have been Job Throckmorton. Their dispute concerned whether the Queen of England needed to be rebaptised – an oddly specific question, but one with far-reaching consequences.

When Penry argued that baptism does not work without preaching, Some had pointed out that the Queen was one of the many English people baptised by non-preaching priests. If the Supreme Governor of the Church of England had received counterfeit baptism, she must now be rebaptised. Imagine the scandal! In fact, all baptism in the Churches of England and Rome was fine, said Some, because they are true churches, however faulty, baptising in the name of the Trinity. He found it hard to explain why it was right to separate from Rome for its faults, and wrong to separate from the Church of England for its faults; Penry found it hard to explain why the

Queen did not need rebaptism. Throckmorton came to Penry's aid, agreeing that the Queen had received invalid baptism, but saying she experiences God's love, which proves 'she hath the inward baptism'.[5]

Barrow's assessment of this debate was that all three authors were disastrously wrong. Dr Some's conclusion that Catholics' baptism and church were valid offered an open goal to Catholic apologists and it made his Protestantism logically unsustainable. 'Upon further advice,' said Barrow, 'the wind may blow in such a quarter, as he will be ready (together with his Lord's Grace), to go back again.' So much for Some's 'deep divinity derived from Mr Calvin'.[6]

On the other hand, Barrow rejected Throckmorton's answer as absurdly subjective. If it feels good, God must be all right with it? That, Barrow said, was advice worthy of the godforsaken Anabaptists.

As for Penry, the only problem Barrow found was that Penry's arguments had demolished the sacraments of the Church of England, so he had no business staying there. 'If Mr Penry provide not better stuff for his own defence, than his friend of Oxenford [Throckmorton] hath as yet brought, I can tell you this, that both he and his companions must become Brownists.'[7]

Having shot some sizeable holes in the ships of his opponents, Barrow then hoped to provide an answer of his own. If only people would read the Bible, he assured them, they would 'safely sail through these difficulties ... neither striking against the rocks of popery, nor falling up on the shelves and quicksands of Anabaptistry'. What they would find in the Bible is as follows. The people of Israel under the old covenant had circumcision as their equivalent to baptism and Passover as their equivalent to Communion. (This notion of equivalence was accepted on all sides.) But when Israelites turned away from God, then repented, they 'were received and admitted to the Passover, without ... repeating the circumcision they had received in the time of this their schism and apostasy'. So the Queen does not need rebaptism because the people of Israel did not need to be recircumcised in comparable circumstances.[8]

'Thus', Barrow concluded somewhat optimistically, 'methinks this hard difficult knot is (even with a trice) undone.' There were two huge problems with his solution though. One was that the Israelites could not be asked to repeat their circumcision because that would be physically impossible, while it was perfectly possible to repeat the rite of baptism. Barrow and Greenwood both contended that these Israelites could if necessary have reattached their foreskins, then removed them again, which must be one of the most spectacularly silly arguments of the Reformation period. The second problem was that Barrow had only proved, if anything, that baptism was not to be repeated, which all his opponents agreed with already. He had failed to explain why it should not be repeated, leaving the reader to turn to either Some's or Throckmorton's explanations.

And so the problem remained hanging. It was difficult for Protestants like Some to explain why they separated from the Church of Rome when it was a true church; it was even more difficult for a Separatist like Barrow to explain where, if he rejected both the Churches of Rome and England as utter shams, he had received his baptism into the true church. It was a question that would cause later Separatists a great deal of grief.

Browne the rector

Separatism continued in East Anglia, and as Wolsey approached ten years behind bars he still did a remarkable job of promoting the movement. Twenty years later, with Wolsey still in jail, the former Separatist Stephen Ofwod reckoned that he himself had known twenty of Wolsey's converts personally.

In 1589, the Vicar of Chattisham, near Ipswich, William Hunt, was removed for 'Brownism', and became a pastor of the Norwich church. In 1590 he was jailed in the Guildhall. John Debenham, a man old enough to be known as 'Father' and who had a role in the Norfolk church, visited the London church, was arrested there and joined the Londoners in prison. The London church sent a delegation to 'their elder sister' in Norwich, to encourage them and strengthen links, led by Daniel Studley. It seems the Londoners were invited to lead worship, taking over from the elder Thomas Ensner, who had been in charge while Hunt was in prison. The Londoners were then themselves arrested, and rather than letting Ensner return to duty, Studley arranged for his friend Bradshaw to take over. Hunt complained that Bradshaw was 'openly and manifestly known of evil behaviour' and not even a member of their church, so he called on Studley to repent. Studley, on his release, returned to London saying the Norwich church were 'a simple people' who had disapproved of him because of his clothing.[9]

In September 1591, Robert Browne completed his reconciliation to the Church of England, being ordained as the Rector of Thorpe Achurch in Northamptonshire. This reconciliation seems to have brought another too. Early in the first decade of Robert and Alice's marriage, while Robert had been one kind of Separatist or another, they had had two children; in the following eleven years they had six more. Their father baptised them all in the parish church following the liturgy of the Prayer Book. He 'returned back into Egypt ...', so the later Brownist John Robinson quoted Browne as saying, 'to live off the spoils of it'.[10]

Barrow versus Gifford

While *A Brief Discoverie* was being printed in the Netherlands, Barrow continued his remarkable illicit output. Despite repeatedly being subjected to surprise searches, by February 1591 he had smuggled another book, this time of 165 pages, out of his cell. This one, *A Plaine Refutation of Mr George Giffarde's Reprocheful Booke*, offered a reply to Gifford's 1590 attack on Separatism in *A Short Treatise Against the Donatists of England*.

Barrow debated with Gifford the nature of the covenant with God that makes the church – which Browne had always insisted was conditional on people's continued obedience, and which Gifford said was unconditional, depending only on God. Gifford pointed out that when God made a covenant with his people in the Old Testament – with Abraham and with the Exodus generation – he mentioned no conditions but promised 'I will be thy God and the God of thy seed', and extended the promise for a thousand generations. So English people can be thoroughly wicked but their children are still born into the church, inheriting membership from 'the ancient Christians their forefathers', which remains valid to a thousand generations. Barrow applied to this a successful *reductio ad absurdum*: if membership of the covenant is passed from parents to children ad infinitum, irrespective of obedience, then 'you make the Jews at this present also the visible church'. This was a conclusion that Gifford certainly would not want to draw. Moreover, continued Barrow, God also made a covenant with Noah, which means, on Gifford's logic, that 'the whole world [is] within the covenant, of the church [and] holy, all being sprung within far less than a thousand generations ... from the patriarch Noah'. Gifford's generosity, argued Barrow, if he could be consistent in it, would give such a broad definition to the church as to make it meaningless.[11]

Barrow addressed *A Plaine Refutation* to Lord Burghley, following the lead of Gifford and Some, asking the treasurer to lead the government in a proper debate of the matters he raised. The book was bundled up with another by Barrow, much shorter, continuing the same conversation with Gifford; with two writings of Greenwood's, one defending the church from Gifford's accusation of Donatism and the other continuing their debate over read prayers; and with an earlier summary of their reasons for Separatism. One of their church, Arthur Bellot, took the collection to Dordrecht in the Netherlands to be printed as a 257-page book, at the expense of Robert Stokes, who had now spent £40 on printing Barrow and Greenwood's books.

The printer still had to complete work on Barrow's *A Brief Discoverie* before he could move on to *A Plaine Refutation*. Some copies of the former had already made it back to England, but Bellot had to get the bulk of the two-thousand-strong print run home, as well as a thousand copies of the second book. It was an extremely expensive illegal cargo, as well as a bulky one.

Bellot successfully conveyed the books seventy miles to the port of Flushing, but there he ran into trouble. The chaplain of the Merchant Adventurers at nearby Middelburg, Francis Johnson, heard what he was up to. Johnson, fitting the mould of his predecessor Cartwright, was a puritan radical enough to have been ousted from Cambridge, and had done prison time for his presbyterianism, but he was no friend to Brownism. Johnson passed his information to the English governor of Flushing, Sir Robert Sidney, on 20 April

1591, and Sidney arrested Bellot. According to Sidney, Bellot confessed 'without any force in the world' where the books were, and
they were seized, along with a soldier called Bonnington from the
English garrison, who had helped Bellot transport them. Sidney
sent six copies of each book to Lord Burghley, asking what he
should do with them. Burghley wanted them burned, and Francis
Johnson was given the job. Johnson supervised the bonfire, ensuring every page was destroyed, except that he kept a copy of each
book 'that he might see their errors', as Governor Bradford later
recorded.

'But mark the sequel,' Bradford continues. 'When he had done
his work, he went home, and being set down in his study, he began
to turn over some pages of this book, and superficially to read some
things here and there, as his fancy led him.' And thus, in Francis
Johnson, Brownism won its latest convert.[12]

18

The new Messiah

JOHN UDALL WAS sentenced to death at the Lent assizes of 1591 for his attack on bishops in *A demonstration of the trueth*. His execution was delayed while he appealed to the Queen, and Lancelot Andrewes urged him to sign a submission to her religion. Instead, Udall attached a presbyterian statement of faith to his letter. The large fines imposed on Mrs Crane and the other hosts of the Marprelate press had all been cancelled, so Udall had some hope of reprieve. From his Scottish exile, Penry persuaded the leaders of the Kirk to take Udall's case to King James, who wrote asking Elizabeth to spare his life. For now, the Queen was content to let him stew in prison.

Throckmorton was brought to court in Westminster to face charges relating to Martinism – slandering the Queen and the House of Lords, 'declaiming the laws', libelling clergy. The case was deferred to June.

The group of presbyterian leaders who were in prison in London for underground organising – nine men now that Cartwright had joined them – had been repeatedly brought to the Court of High Commission for questioning, and had repeatedly refused the oath. They successfully exhausted the patience and powers of that court, and in May 1591 their cases were transferred to the Star Chamber. There the prosecution aimed to prove revolutionary sedition – that they aimed to overthrow the episcopal government of the Church of England.

This case of the presbyterian nine was a *cause célèbre*. The whole puritan movement was in the dock, as those who had always seen it as a threat to the Queen's government had the chance to prove that it was, and after thirty years of opposition its leaders were in the clutches of the resurgent leadership of the church. It was an hour of crisis for puritanism, and it was unspeakably unfortunate that for some supporters that translated into apocalyptic terms.

Hacket's strange calling

William Hacket had been a Catholic household servant in Northamptonshire, notorious in his circle for his violent temper. It was said he bit off a schoolmaster's nose in a fight and 'did in a most spiteful and divelish outrage eat it up'. In the habit of hearing puritan preachers so that he could mimic then in the alehouse afterwards, he heard one too many and was converted to radical puritanism. He became a disciple and business partner of the sacked minister Giles Wigginton, with whom he produced malt and led a secret presbyterian group. He was censured for pinching his parish minister's surplice and sitting on it through the service, and got into the habit of waiting outside church until the sermon started. Hacket started travelling around the north and Midlands, prophesying and exorcising, and people were impressed with his unscripted prayers, 'as it were speaking to God face to face'. It seems he also used this opportunity to take sexual advantage of women – or fell foul of his enemies' plan 'to entrap him with women', as he saw it. He was punished by local authorities for making seditious speeches, which in good Protestant tradition confirmed his conviction that he was doing the work of God, and during one spell in custody it was rumoured the guard saw a bright light coming from his room in the night, as if he were visited by an angel.[1]

Hacket came to London in 1591, where he later claimed to have wrestled the lions in the Tower of London without being hurt, though his main purpose was to follow the trials of Throckmorton, Udall, Cartwright and the other jailed presbyterians. Wigginton, who was now himself in prison for his puritan writings, introduced Hacket to Edmund Coppinger, a puritan gentleman, who in turn introduced him to Henry Arthington. Hacket's new friends were impressed by the way he cried to God to strike him down instantly if his prophecies were untrue, and by his claims to be tormented by devils ever since a Catholic whom he defeated in debate paid sorcerers and witches to punish him. ('I know and can name [them]', he said, 'and mind one day, to help burn them.')[2]

Coppinger and Arthington started to develop their own visionary powers and the trio discussed God's plans to free the imprisoned presbyterians and purify the church. They repeatedly failed to gain an audience with the Queen, but befriended Job Throckmorton, to the extent that he believed Coppinger's overlong prayers made him ill. They showed Throckmorton their petitions to the authorities and introduced him to Hacket. They also contacted John Penry, who returned from Edinburgh to confer with them. However, when Throckmorton tried to introduce them to Cartwright, Cartwright refused, saying Coppinger sounded as if he had 'some crazing of the brain'.[3]

In May 1591, Throckmorton heard some startling rumours: that the plans of Coppinger and friends for godly reformation had gone rather further than petitioning. How much he heard, we do not know, but if he knew the truth his response was remarkably mild. He wrote to Coppinger saying he had heard he was taking a 'singular course' and urged him, 'be sure of your ground and warrant, before you strive to put in execution'.[4]

Before they could fulfil their plans, Throckmorton's case came to trial again. His connections pressed Hatton to help him, and the case was dismissed on a technicality. Throckmorton walked free. What happened behind the scenes we can only speculate, but if the case had dragged on a month longer it might have ended very differently.

The plan that Coppinger, Arthington and Hacket had been cooking up was a revolution. They would release all the imprisoned presbyterians, overthrow the bishops, depose the Queen and cast all non-preaching ministers out of the church. Hacket would succeed to the throne and become King of Europe. They do not seem to have drawn any presbyterian leaders into this conspiracy, and perhaps this is what made them conclude that they themselves must be more key apocalyptic figures than they had hitherto realised: Coppinger was the last prophet of mercy before the coming of Christ and Arthington the last prophet of judgement, from which the unavoidable conclusion was that Hacket was Christ himself.

Coppinger produced hundreds of pamphlets and distributed them to Londoners throughout the night of Thursday 18 July, promising tremendous events the following day. On Friday morning, Coppinger and Arthington went through the streets gathering a crowd while Hacket had a lie-in, then the pair of them mounted a cart outside the Mermaid Tavern, Cheapside, and proclaimed Hacket as king and Messiah. They escaped the constables, but the three of them were arrested later the same day.

All three maintained their minority beliefs in prison and Coppinger fasted and prayed continuously. Hacket was tried on 26 July, his counsel pleading insanity, and he was condemned to be hanged, drawn and quartered. He was taken out for execution two days later, denouncing the Queen, proclaiming himself Jehovah and calling on God to 'send some miracle out of a cloud', but was killed anyway. Faced with this substantial counter-evidence to Hacket's claims, Arthington recanted and repented, which, perhaps with the support of some influential friend, saved his life, although he remained in prison. Coppinger starved himself to death.[5]

Whitgift and his allies could hardly have hoped for better evidence that the presbyterian nine were leading a seditious movement, and they capitalised on it immediately by arresting one of their lawyers, Nicholas Fuller. Then, from July through to October, the prosecution brought in a series of witnesses who had also been thoroughly involved in covert presbyterianism. They included two Northamptonshire ministers: Thomas Stone, who believed it was his duty to cooperate with the authorities as the presbyterians had nothing to be ashamed of; and John Johnson, who bore a bitter grudge after having been on the sharp end of some presbyterian discipline. They and others gave the Star Chamber a great deal of information about local meetings and national synods, including the names of others involved.

And yet the prosecution did not manage to present a consistent story concerning the crucial points of the case, and the defending lawyers, who still had some powerful support, exposed contradictions in the witnesses' stories. The defence's tactic was to concede the fact of presbyterian organisation but contest its interpretation: it was not a Separatist church, or a plot to overthrow the bishops by force, but an attempt to model the church structure that they were asking the Queen and Parliament to introduce; neither schism nor sedition but merely an ecclesiastical illustration. That interpretation may have been stretching a point, but the prosecution had a hard time refuting it and the case continued for months. On 20 November 1591 Hatton died, and the attempt to convict the ministers through the Star Chamber seems to have been abandoned. They remained in prison though, discredited and demoralised by Hacket's stunt and awaiting Whitgift's next move.

In December, the nine ministers, several of them now seriously unwell after two years in prison, petitioned Burghley for release, but he was unable to help now, except that they were allowed out on Sundays for church. They were granted an audience with the Privy Council in January, with whom they agreed a statement of capitulation: that their presbyterian meetings had had no sinister purpose, but had offended the Queen, so they would give them up. Even with this submission, however, Whitgift still refused to release them until they signed a renunciation of presbyterianism itself, which they all refused.

Barrow versus Gifford again

Gifford published the latest instalment in his pamphlet war with the Separatists in December 1591, *A Short Reply unto the Last Printed Books of Henry Barrow and John Greenwood*, which had the distinction, thanks to the seizure of their books at Flushing, of being a public reply to arguments the public had not seen. Gifford was eager though to publicise Barrow's attack on Calvin, which he presented as the Brownists' most discreditable performance yet. Gifford argued that when the Brownists had parted from the Church of England, they also left the international Reformed community to which it belonged. The parting had grown wider, he said, when the Brownists condemned read prayers and the inclusion of all citizens in the church, because these were practised throughout the Reformed community. In their assault on Calvin himself, he said, the Brownists made it graphically explicit that they are a tiny extremist sect with a religion of their own invention and no connection to international Protestantism.

Barrow responded to Gifford, both in a manuscript entitled *A Few Observations*, and also by writing in a minuscule hand in the margins of Gifford's book. Across ninety-two pages, Barrow wrote as many words as Gifford, effectively managing to write an entire book in the margin of someone else's. Barrow explained, rather awkwardly, that he had nothing against Calvin and that it was the strain of 'being pressed by the adversaries with the writings and practice of Mr Calvin' that had provoked his exasperated comments. He had not condemned Calvin, he said, merely treated his writings just as Calvin demanded – reverently following them 'no further than they are found consonant to the word of God'.[6]

Gifford had Barrow on the run here though, because as scandalous as his censure of Calvin was, it was the only logical conclusion of his congregational beliefs. Barrow condemned the Church of England for being a state church not a gathered church; the Church of Geneva was also a non-gathered church; therefore the Church of Geneva was condemned too. The only way out that Barrow could find was through an ecclesiastical fiction: Calvin had written in the early days of the Reformation, when Christians were still learning to tell the difference between popish tradition and biblical Christianity. Now, more than thirty years later, Geneva would have learned and embraced the full truth, as Barrow had, so his criticisms were 'to be understood of their first coming out of popery, and not of the present estate of these foreign churches'. In fact neither Geneva nor any other Reformed church had advanced that far, neither did Barrow have any reason to suppose they had, other than that he believed it was the right thing for them to have done. Only the unmentionable Anabaptists had gone down the same road to a gathered church, so the Separatists really were on their own. When Gifford called the Separatists Anabaptists, this was not literally accurate, but he did have a point.[7]

Barrow was on firmer ground when Gifford called his church Donatists, and he successfully turned that argument against him. Gifford argued that it was heresy for the Brownists to condemn the Church of England for mere imperfections, and it was damnable to separate from their true church. Barrow reminded Gifford that the Church of England separated from Rome because of its imperfections. Gifford pointed to the due process by which the English Church convicted Rome of its faults before purging them, unlike the rash, unauthorised actions of the Separatists, but, as Barrow said, that defence hardly applied to Luther's first separation from Rome. So Gifford cited Calvin's rather convoluted argument that Protestants only separated from Rome's corruptions, not from its true teachings or Christian practices. Barrow simply told Gifford: however you have separated from Rome, so we have separated from you.

With this, Barrow nailed a fatal crack in the Protestant state church. The Church of England was founded on the right to judge its mother church, condemn its failings, and, if it would not rectify them, to separate. In establishing that that right exists, it unintentionally gave permission for its subjects to form their own separate churches, whenever it would not reform itself according to their expectations. Protestantism was fundamentally the right and responsibility of Bible readers to judge the church, so a government that established a church on those principles and then told every citizen to submit to it, was going to face difficulties. The notion of imposing one form of Protestantism on the whole population was not about to go away, but its ultimate unsustainability had been exposed.

Around April 1592, attempts were made to arrange a meeting between Cartwright and Barrow to discuss the Church of England. This time, the initiative came from Whitgift of all people, who, despite his animosity towards Cartwright, thought that so long as he had him in custody he would use him to reclaim the even more radical extremist. Cartwright refused the offer, to Barrow's disappointment. According to George Paule, the registrar of the Court of High Commission, writing twenty years later, when Barrow heard about Cartwright's refusal, he sighed, 'And will he not? Hath he brought me into this brake, and will he now leave me? For from him I received my grounds, and, out of his premises, did I infer, and make the conclusion of the positions, which I now hold, and for which I suffer bands.'[8] The quotation is included in the works of

Barrow and Greenwood edited masterfully by Leland H. Carlson, but Barrow never said any such words. The uncharacteristic flow-eriness could simply be Paule's rephrasing, but the sentiment itself is entirely alien to Barrow. Barrow never considered Cartwright a fellow traveller, still less his mentor; rather, an unrepentant servant of the antichristian state church. He said countless times that he took his 'positions' from no person, but only from his own reading of Scripture, and that if he were a follower of 'the learned' instead of Christ, he would not be in prison. The true source of the alleged quotation is simply Paule's desire to show, as he put it himself, 'that Master Cartwright was the fountain and principal author' of the 'stirs and seditious attempts of sundry persons' during Whitgift's rule. Cartwright was released to house arrest in Hackney, and by the end of the year most of the nine ministers were out of prison, though not off the hook.[9]

In the summer of 1592 an anonymous tract appeared, printed in Middelburg, called *A Petition Directed to Her Most Excellent Majestie*. It defended the presbyterian movement from accusations of sedition, particularly defending Udall's writings and the Marprelate tracts. The Dean of Exeter, Matthew Sutcliffe, printed a reply in December, publicly connecting Job Throckmorton with the Martinist operation and Hacket's insurrection. Entitled *An Answere to a Certaine Libel Supplicatorie, or Rather Diffamatory*, Sutcliffe's tract suggested that Throckmorton was 'abettor and counsellor of [the conspirators'] treacherous practices' and asked whether 'his libels and scoffs published under the name of Martin ... did not tend wholly to an insurrection'. Sutcliffe was aware that Throckmorton had not written the Marprelate tracts alone, claiming that 'J Penry, J Ud[all], J F[ield], all Johns, and J Thr.' all 'concurred in making of Martin'. Throckmorton tried to clear his name two years later in an outraged but slippery tract, *The defence of Job Throkmorton against the slaunders of maister Sutcliffe*. After some rather vague protestations of acquittal in high places – 'I hope those that are in authority and Mr Sutcliffe's betters are sufficiently persuaded of mine innocency' – Throckmorton concluded with an oath that he said ought to settle the matter. He swore, 'I am not Martin, I knew not Martin.' But Sutcliffe was not impressed: 'As if any did say that his name is Martin.'[10]

Udall was still in prison in 1592, but a group of merchants offered to employ him as chaplain in Syria or Guinea if the Queen would agree to his being released into banishment. The Earl of Essex drafted such a pardon for her majesty to consider, but she had not yet signed it when, around the end of the year, Udall died in prison. Once again the Church of England had allowed prison conditions to kill its critics, without having to decide between toleration and hanging. The same, however, did not apply to Barrow and Greenwood.

On trial

IN MIDDELBURG, FRANCIS Johnson, inspired by Barrow's writing, told his Merchant Adventurers congregation that they needed to have a church covenant, like the Brownist churches in England. This would mean that their church was founded not on the author- ity of bishops but on their own commitment 'to live as the church of Christ'. To be part of the church, every member would have to sign the covenant, swearing to uphold their faith 'against men and angels unto the death'. There was strong resistance to Johnson's proposals, led by the deputy governor of the Merchant Adventurers Thomas Ferrers, who sent a copy of the putative covenant to the English authorities. The church was split, the Dutch authorities sus- pended its services, and around April 1592 Johnson was removed. He returned to England, visited Barrow and Greenwood in prison, and joined the covenant of their church instead. Thomas Settle, the Norfolk minister who was now living in Stepney with his wife, also joined the Brownists in 1592.[1]

Free to worship

Then, unexpectedly, Whitgift seems to have taken a leaf out of Grindal's book, and experimented with arbitrarily allowing one of his most notorious troublemakers out of prison. Greenwood and a number of other Separatists, though not Barrow, were released in July 1592, after four years in the Fleet, in Greenwood's case, follow- ing seven months in the Clink. Whatever the authorities intended by this move, for the Separatists it was a God-given opportunity to organise their church as they had always believed it should be.

That September, a congregation of sixty met in Mr Fox's house in St Nicholas Lane not far from London Bridge, and after prayer they elected Francis Johnson to be their pastor and John Greenwood to be their teacher. They chose as deacons Nicholas Lee and Christopher Bowman, and as elders Daniel Studley and George Knifton. Three of those we have met before, while Knifton was a twenty-four-year-old apothecary living at Newgate Market. He was one of the Londoners whom Robert Browne, in his erratic evangelistic efforts, had persuaded to stop receiving parish Communion without embracing full Separatism, around 1588. Later he talked to Greenwood, Barrow and Penry before quitting the Church of England.

Rejoicing to have their first ordained ministers since the inception of the church five years earlier, they celebrated with their first baptisms. Francis Johnson baptised seven children, applying water to their faces and saying, 'I do baptise thee in the name of the Father, of the Son, and of the Holy Ghost.' These words they believed essential to real baptism, but they used no other liturgy.

In the months after this joyful occasion, they met twice a week from four or five in the morning, ending each meeting by agreeing the place of the next. Their most frequent haunt was the schoolhouse where Francis Johnson's brother George taught in St Nicholas Lane. They also moved between the houses of various members and met in the fields or woods around Islington and Deptford, and in St John's Wood, an eight-mile range. Sometimes they numbered as many as a hundred. According to Robert Abraham, a twenty-six-year-old leather dresser and regular attender, they celebrated Communion once in that time, Johnson breaking five white loaves, passing them around, and reciting the Bible verse: 'And when he had given thanks, he brake it, and said, Take, eat: this is my body, which is broken for you: this do ye in remembrance of me.'

Less joyfully, the church for the second time lost a member of its printing operation. Robert Stokes, who had bankrolled the work and smuggled books, had second thoughts about the message he had been broadcasting, returned to the Church of England and was excommunicated by the Brownists.

Penry the Brownist

In October 1592, the Separatist church gained a celebrity convert, when the most wanted puritan in England, John Penry, joined them. Returning to Scotland after the failure of Hacket's apocalyptic insurrection, Penry had embarked on a book called *The Historie of Corah, Dathan and Abiram*, arguing that loyalty to the Queen did not entail belonging to her church, and before he had finished it he left for England. He travelled to London overland with his friend John Edwardes, while his wife and daughters went by sea, meeting him in the Cross Keys, Bow, to the east of London. They straightaway joined the Separatist church, where John sometimes preached, and they hosted services in their lodgings. Christopher Bowman got remarried there, Ellyn having died, with Settle leading prayers. Penry wrote more than once about their meetings being 'in woods, in caves, in mountains', something he found demeaning, but better than not meeting at all.

Francis Johnson lasted about a month as the pastor of the London church before he was arrested in October at Fox's house. In another throwback to the gentle days of Bishop Grindal, Johnson was only held a short while and led services again in November. Then, in the early hours of 6 December, the constables raided the house of Edward and Thomasine Boyes in Fleet Street. If a service was in progress, it was a very late one, but they found both Greenwood and Johnson there. After ransacking the place, they took the two ministers to the Wood Street Compter and stopped Edward Boyes leaving his house. The next day they were all placed in close imprisonment, Boyes and Johnson in the Clink, Greenwood returning to the Fleet. Settle and Studley were arrested when a service in George Johnson's schoolroom was raided in December. Penry still somehow managed to evade arrest.

In January 1593, Barrow wrote an appeal to the Privy Council, outlining the peaceable activity of their church and the violence they had suffered for it. The petition was received by a clerk in February but never presented to the Council.

Frustrated by the fact that members were dying away from the public gaze, that month the Brownists performed perhaps their single most provocative act other than simply existing as a Separatist church. On Friday 16 February, Roger Rippon, a Southwark Brownist, died in Newgate jail. The church bought a coffin and the next day they carried Rippon's body a third of a mile to the house of Justice Richard Young, an officer in the Court of High Commission, and left the coffin at his door. It bore the following inscription:

> This is the corpse of Roger Rippon, a servant of Christ and her Majesty's faithful subject, who is the last of sixteen or seventeen which that great enemy of God the Archbishop of Canterbury with his high commissioners have murdered in Newgate within these five years, for the testimony of Jesus Christ.
>
> His soul is now with the Lord and his blood crieth for speedy vengeance against that great enemy of the saints and against Mr Richard Young who in this and many the like points hath abused his power for the upholding of the Romish antichrist prelacy and priesthood.[2]

An urgent search for the offenders followed. Bowman, who had paid for the coffin, was arrested at the end of February, and on Sunday 4 March the constables found the congregation worshipping in St John's Wood, in exactly the place where the Protestant underground had worshipped in Mary's time. About fifty-six people were arrested, more than quadrupling the number of Brownists currently in prison, and they were interrogated by Young about the coffin inscription. One of them, the twenty-five-year-old pursemaker Abraham Pulbery, confessed to taking part in the procession, but no one admitted to any other responsibility.

The prisoners were also grilled about their most-wanted fellow member, John Penry – where they had seen him, and when, and how well they knew him. In fact, the constable had let the prize slip through his fingers. Penry was among those arrested on 4 March, but gave his name to the constable as John Harries. This was not exactly untrue. The name Penry was a contraction of the Welsh Ap Henry, or son of Henry, so the slippery suspect was translating his name into English, a common enough practice in the period. The constable missed the significance, however, and while he was holding them overnight in his house the prisoners allowed Penry to escape.

1593 Parliament

Intelligence from Spain confirmed English suspicions that King Philip was planning another invasion attempt. He was rebuilding the Armada with more modern ships, learning from the manoeuvrability and firepower of the English vessels that defeated the Spanish in 1588. Though he could not bear to say Elizabeth's name, he vowed, according to one report, 'that he would spend his candle to the socket, but he would be revenged and have his will of her'.[3]

However, Philip's military resources were also drawn to other trouble spots for Catholic hegemony. The bloody course of French royal succession fell to the Protestant Henry of Navarre on 2 August 1589. In theory, Henry of Navarre became King Henry IV, but the Catholic League (French forces supported by Philip and the Pope) stood between him and the throne. Elizabeth sent forces to support Henry, and when Henry defeated the League at Ivry in March 1590, Philip ordered Parma to divert his forces from the Netherlands to save Paris. The capital fell to Henry that same year and Rouen followed in 1592. Philip dismissed Parma and sent invasion forces to Languedoc in the south of France and to Brittany in the north-west – the latter base also providing a coastal station a hundred miles across the Channel from England. By 1593, Henry IV was in power in France, but over a bitterly divided nation that was likely to resume battle at the drop of a hat. So, in a move that somehow seems at once both cynical and humane, Henry converted to Catholicism. Allegedly saying 'Paris is worth a Mass', Henry was received into the Catholic Church on 27 July 1593, and started to reconcile his Catholic and Protestant subjects after three decades of religious bloodshed. Though Parma's presence in France had failed to stop Henry, his absence from the Netherlands had allowed the Dutch rebels, now led by William of Orange's son Maurice, to secure permanent control of the northern states.

Elizabeth was forced to call her eighth Parliament to finance war in the Netherlands and France; it assembled on 19 February 1593. Once again she told MPs that they had liberty within limits: they were free 'to say yea or no to bills', but not 'to frame a form of religion or state of government, as to their idle brains shall seem meetest'.

Peter Wentworth responded with a bill to decide the royal succession, for which he was again sent to the Tower, and James Morice, MP for Colchester, brought two bills designed to hamper Whitgift's attacks on puritans, restricting the use of oaths and imprisonment, for which insubordination Morice was kept under house arrest for the remainder of the parliamentary session.[4]

There was no attempt at puritan reformation. No presbyterian synod met in London to lobby MPs and orchestrate their work. Whitgift had at last dealt a debilitating blow to the puritan movement, presbyterian leaders having promised to stop practising their faith. But the archbishop did not feel he had won the total victory he aimed for and did not have any heads on plates. He also had the side effects of radical puritanism to deal with, in the form of the Separatist movement, while the greatest religious source of anxiety for the government was, as ever, Catholicism. The 1593 Parliament attempted to deal with all these.

On 26 February, the government brought to the House of Commons a bill imposing brutal penalties on Catholics: their children were to be seized; recusants forfeited all personal possessions and two-thirds of any income from land; they could not buy, sell or lease land; their dowries belonged to the crown; householders with wives, guests or servants who failed to go to church were fined £10 a month. The Commons seemed to have lost some of its appetite for Catholic persecution and drastically tamed the bill, removing the forfeiture of possessions and reducing the fines, though the only change to the seizing of children was to raise the age from seven to eight.

But the Commons also discerned a second, clandestine purpose to the bill. Though it was framed as an anti-Catholic measure, a number of the bill's provisions – as in the 1581 Act – were phrased vaguely enough to apply to anyone who did not go to their parish church. As Barrow and Greenwood had found, the church authorities were quite prepared to apply such laws to Protestant nonconformists as well as Catholics, so MPs suspected they might even be applied to puritans who attended a neighbouring parish because there was no preacher in their own. To prevent this, the Commons added the word 'popish' throughout the bill. The government abandoned it, and set to work on some alternative religious legislation that it hoped to squeeze in before the end of the session.

Brownists on trial

Separatism was increasingly in the public eye. After the arrests of 4 March, John Penry had written an anonymous petition to Parliament on behalf of those in prison. Not only were they being kept indefinitely in close confinement, he protested, but 'these bloody men will allow them neither meat, drink, fire, lodging, nor suffer any whose hearts the Lord would stir up for their relief to have any access unto them, purposing belike to imprison them unto death'. Wife and husband were kept in separate prisons, while their children were left to fend for themselves. Their houses were broken into, he said, their families treated barbarously and their possessions stolen. 'Bishop Bonner ... dealt not after this sort.' Penry argued that they had been found guilty of no errors or crimes, adding, 'We have as good warrant to reject the ordinances of antichrist ... as our fathers and brethren in Queen Mary's time days had to do the like.' He ended by offering the authorities a pretty reasonable choice: 'We crave for all of us but the liberty either to die openly or to live openly in the land of our nativity. If we deserve death, it beseemeth the majesty of justice not to see us closely murthered, yea, starved to death with hunger and cold, and stifled in loathsome dungeons.' It was a point well made, and did not it seems fall entirely on deaf ears.[5]

Two copies of John Penry's petition were delivered to Parliament, one for each house, by Helen Penry, Katherine Unyen and Mrs Lee, Nicholas's wife. As a result, the three of them were arrested. Lee and Penry, it seems, had the money for bail, but Unyen was kept in prison.

Unable to find John Penry, the government decided that the next best thing was to deal with Barrow and Greenwood. Since the pair had been indicted five years previously and examined by the Privy Council a year later, they had committed a great deal of radical teaching to print, increasing both their offence and the evidence for it. Their case would be rather easier to prosecute than Cartwright's.

A member of the prosecution team went through Barrow and Greenwood's books compiling passages illustrating their belief that the membership of the Church of England was unchristian and its episcopacy antichristian. They included Barrow's acknowledgment to Sperin that it was wicked of Queen and Parliament to give power to the bishops, and his willingness to 'seal it with my blood'. Then, on Sunday 11 March, Barrow and Greenwood each received visits from the two Lord Chief Justices. They showed the prisoners three printed books and asked them about their authorship. These were the two reports Barrow and Greenwood had compiled of their debates with Sperin and other members of Aylmer's team, plus a book by Greenwood debating read prayers with Gifford. They had printed their books anonymously, so the prosecution needed to establish authorship, but the writers had never attempted to conceal their identity and made no attempt to do so now. In contrast with this openness about their own crimes, both claimed to have no recollection of anyone else who was involved in the printing and distribution of the books. 'His memory is so decayed', said the notes of Barrow's interview. The only other person Barrow remembered handling a copy of any of the three books was Ellyn Bowman, wife of Christopher, who had since died. The only collaborator Greenwood named was Stokes, who had by now renounced his Separatism and safely rejoined the Church of England.[6]

It took longer for the prosecution's reader to plough through *A Brief Discoverie*, but on 20 March Barrow and Greenwood were questioned on it by the same people, plus the Attorney General and others. Both men readily admitted that Barrow had written it, and took the opportunity to outline Stokes's involvement again. Barrow, however, also named two other collaborators this time: Studley, who smuggled the pages out of the prison, and Forrester, who copied them out. Forrester, like Stokes, had now given up Brownism, but Studley was still an active member of the church. Forrester and Stokes were interviewed by the authorities, but since they had seen the light of conformity no action was taken. Studley, however, had to stand trial alongside Barrow and Greenwood. Two others joined them: Bowle, who had taken *A Collection of Certaine Sclaunderous Articles* to be printed in the Netherlands, and Scipio Bellot, who did the same with *A Brief Discoverie*.

The trial of the five Separatists began in the Sessions Hall of the Old Bailey on 21 March 1593. They were charged under the Seditious Words and Rumours Act of 1581 and tried before nine judges, including two members of the Privy Council. The prosecuting counsel were the Attorney General Thomas Egerton and the Queen's Sergeant Thomas Owen. Others present included the Mayor of London and the Chancellor of the Exchequer.

The centrepiece of the trial was Barrow's *A Brief Discoverie*. He was accused of denying the Queen's baptism and her authority to govern the church, and of calling the Church of England unchristian and its members unbaptised infidels. Bellot and Studley were charged with publishing the book. Greenwood's alleged offences were to do with *A Collection of Certaine Sclaunderous Articles*, produced by him and Barrow, which denied the validity of the Church of England and condemned episcopacy, and in which Barrow had criticised the Queen for accepting the system. Bowle was charged with publishing that book.

The prosecution argued that if her majesty was not baptised, then the whole of the Church of England and every part and office of it were invalid, as was its authority over the people, and as were the authority of Queen and Parliament that had established the church. This, they said, proved that Barrow was guilty of sedition. But, for a conviction, the law required that malicious intent be proven. This was less easy, but the prosecution were content with the assertion that in making his allegation about the Queen and church, 'he did it maliciously in that it is false'.[7]

Barrow pointed out indignantly that they had rather missed the subtleties of his argument about the Queen's baptism. But he was not there to minimise the offence of Separatism. Finally having his day in court, Barrow insisted that the Church of England was not true because it was not free. Elizabethan clergy 'were not of the church [of Christ] in that they are prescribed their time, their form of prayer, their place to preach in, to wit a tub in which they bellow and belch out'.[8] The bishops were the beast of Revelation, he said, and 'limbs of the devil'. More calmly, says the report, Barrow accepted the

Queen's supremacy – presumably according to his own definition – and detested Spanish invasion.

Greenwood was examined by Egerton, who asked his opinion of the Church of England. Greenwood said that the parishes 'are gathered together in the name of Antichrist by a bell, that they be in bondage to the Egyptians'.[9] Egerton pointed out that this made the Queen equivalent to Pharaoh, the enemy of God's people. Asked about their excommunication of Stokes and what authority they had for such an act, Greenwood said Christ gave authority directly to the whole congregation of the church to do such things where they have consensus.

The other three defendants were dealt with swiftly. Bellot pleaded guilty, repenting and asking for mercy. Bowles and Studley stood firm. All five were found guilty of felony. They were sentenced to die the following day, 24 March, and were placed in 'the Limbo', the dungeon of Newgate prison.

20

The scaffold

WHILE THE BROWNISTS' trial was in progress, the Vicar of Stepney made a thrilling discovery. His name was Anthony Anderson, he had livings in Essex and Leicestershire as well as Stepney, and he was Subdean of the Chapel Royal. He had, incidentally, secured a place in the history of the bizarre by investigating the case of Agnes Bowker, who in 1569 claimed to have given birth to a monstrous cat. He concluded that the birth was a hoax, the monster being an ordinary cat boiled, and his drawing of it is in the British Library.

As a rising establishment figure, Anderson had in 1589 come to the attention of Martin Marprelate. In *The Just Censure and Reproof*, Martin Senior mocked Whitgift for employing a jester, argued that Dr Bridges should have the job, and went on to suggest similar roles that notable churchmen could play at Lambeth Palace. 'Anderson, parson of Stepney,' Martin suggested, 'should make room before him with his two-hand staff, as he did once before the morris dance.' The marginal note went rather further: 'This chaplain robbed the poor men's box at Northampton, played the Potter's part in the morris dance, and begot his maid with child in Leicestershire: and these things he did since he was first priest.'[1]

For some years, Anderson had had the worry of a family of Brownists living in his parish. Thomas Settle had been in and out of prison, while Mrs Settle offered her house to the underground church for their illicit goings-on.

One can imagine the relish Anderson felt when he realised in March 1593 that the family who had been lodging with Mrs Settle for some months was none other than the Penrys, and he notified his superiors. On 22 March, the constables arrested Penry in Ratcliffe, a hamlet in Stepney parish, in the house of Mr Lowes, along with

Knifton the Brownist elder, Edward Grave and Arthur Bellot, whose brother was on trial. They were taken to various prisons, Penry to the Poultry Compter, and the interviews started.

Tyburn

Early on the morning of Saturday 24 March, Barrow, Greenwood, Studley, Bellot and Bowles were brought out of the Newgate Limbo and their shackles were cut off. Before they could be taken to Tyburn, however, a message arrived that the Queen had granted a temporary stay of execution.

They were returned to Limbo, whence Barrow wrote twice to the Attorney General Egerton, appealing once again for a debate with representatives of the Church of England. He said he did not want to go to his death stubbornly upholding error, and wanted to heal the divisions between his congregation and the state church, whether he lived or died. It was a hard request to refuse. Egerton himself visited Barrow on 26 March and spent the whole afternoon in what he called 'a fruitless, idle conference', afterwards returning to parliamentary business 'both weary and weak'. Barrow was then visited by a number of ministers, including Andrewes. There is no reliable record of their conversation. Paule reports some nonsense in which Barrow tells them his Separatism is all Cartwright's fault. Barrow's own version is that the ministers arrived uncalled for, so he told them the time for conference was over and he wanted to be left alone to prepare for his death, a claim that is very hard to reconcile with the contents of his letters to Egerton.

On Saturday 31 March, even earlier in the morning than the previous time, Barrow and Greenwood were again taken from the dungeon, this time without the other three, and in darkness. They were tied to a cart, driven to Tyburn and put on the scaffold. Although they were taken there in secrecy, a supportive crowd gathered. Once the nooses were around their necks, Barrow and Greenwood were allowed to speak publicly. They insisted that they had no malice towards the Queen or anyone else, asked forgiveness for any offence caused by the tone of their writings, and urged their readers to follow them no further than they followed Scripture. They exhorted the people of England to live in peace, defend the realm with their lives, and humbly submit to any punishment the government might inflict. They prayed for the Queen and forgave their enemies.[2]

They spoke at some length and were eventually reaching their conclusion when a messenger arrived from Burghley with a second stay of execution. It was greeted, Barrow said, 'with exceeding rejoicing and applause of all the people, both at the place of execution, and in the ways, streets and houses as we returned'.[3]

A second chance

Later that day, the House of Commons received another bill from the government to deal with religious nonconformists. This bill declared that it was treason to dissuade anyone from obedience to the Queen, or to be so dissuaded, making it clear that this applied to Protestant dissidents as well as Catholics. It would become a felony to attend conventicles oneself, or, from seditious motives, to persuade others to attend them, or to miss church. The penalty was three months' imprisonment, followed, if they persisted, with banishment from the realm; if they returned or failed to leave, they would be killed. There was also a £10 a month fine for those who sheltered such sectaries.

The second reading of the bill on 4 April provoked fierce debate. One opposing voice was Sir Walter Raleigh's, who was happy for Brownists to be banished for their rebellious actions, but thought it dangerous to ask a jury to judge defendants' motives. He reckoned there were between ten and twelve thousand Brownists in England, so he worried about the practicalities of banishment: 'at whose charge shall they be transported, or whither will you send them? ... When they be gone, who shall maintain their wives and children?' Others protested that again the bill was phrased loosely enough to apply to non-Separatist puritans: meeting privately for prayer, attending a neighbouring parish church or speaking against any abuse in the church would all become punishable. The Commons sent the bill to be amended by committee the following day.[4]

At the same time, Barrow was writing to an aristocratic relative (Carlson reckons the Countess of Warwick) asking her to appeal to the Queen for his life before she left town at the close of Parliament. Barrow gave her a brief account of his opposition to the abuses in the church, of his trial – in which his malicious enemies in the church hierarchy conspired to convict him despite his innocence of all charges – and of his two recent miraculous escapes from execution. In the Limbo he was no longer sure what day it was – though his ability to write and get his writings out was undiminished – and he signed off:

> This 4th or 5th of the 4th month 1593
> Your honour's humbly at commandment during life,
> condemned of men but received of God
> Henry Barrow[5]

On Thursday 5th, the committee of the House of Commons sat from 2 p.m. till eight. They revised the bill, ensuring that it applied only to those who held 'that we had no church, that we had no true sacraments, nor no true ministry'. Mainstream puritans had been protected, but Separatists had finally been hit harder even than Catholic recusants, and would now find life in England impossible.[6]

What happened next is a mixture of fact and rumour. The rumour is that Whitgift was enraged by another defeat. He had twice applied to Parliament for legal powers to inflict a reign of terror on puritans, and twice in five weeks been thwarted by the Commons. So, it was said, he vented his passion on the men he had in his power, 'to spite the nether house'.

The fact is that, early on the morning of 6 April, Barrow and Greenwood were again taken out to Tyburn. They again offered long prayers, but were not this time interrupted. They said that they thirsted, and drink was fetched. Then they were hanged.*

---

* According to Ofwod, the Sheriff persuaded Barrow to recite the Lord's Prayer on the scaffold, 'that we may testify you hold not that error which it is said ye do hold'. Barrow supposedly replied: 'M[aster] Shref, my time is at an end, therefore why should I now pray for daily bread; notwithstanding if you will pray it, I will pray with you' (Ofwod *Advertisement*, 41–2). The story cannot be discounted out of hand, but Ofwod wrote forty years after the event, at which he was not present.

PART THREE

New Jordans

21

Amsterdam

PENRY HAD LITTLE hope of earthly life after the executions of Barrow and Greenwood, and prepared for death, while preparing his church for exile. His first priority was a statement of faith, clearing him of Whitgift's accusation of heresy, in which he concluded, 'Imprisonments, indictments, arraignments, yea, death itself are no weapons to convince the conscience grounded upon the word of the Lord.'[1]

Penry's farewell

Penry then wrote to his wife, to his four daughters, and to his church. He told Helen that he loved her, and acknowledged that life with him had not been easy, but exhorted her to continue on the same path, bringing their children up in the church. He wanted the girls to learn to read and write, as Helen never had, and to stay with their mother if possible, and to gain a new father quickly. He warned her to tell no one she had received a letter from him, except whoever read it to her, and asked her to pray and petition for his release. 'I know, my good Helen,' he assured her, 'that the burden I leave upon thee, of four infants, whereof the eldest is not four years old, will not seem burdensome unto thee. Yea, thou shalt find that our God will [be] a father to the fatherless and a stay unto the widow.'[2]

To his daughters, Deliverance, Comfort, Safety and Sure Hope, John wrote 'with many tears', instructing them to have nothing to do with the Church of England, but to follow in the footsteps of their parents and be willing to suffer for the true faith. They should remain Separatists no matter how poor it made them and, he said, if they did have money, should give to needy members of the persecuted church, to strangers remembering the kindness their family had received from strangers, to Scots for similar reasons, and to people from the land of their father.

In his epistle to the church of London, Penry assured the believers that he was utterly certain of the truth for which they suffered together, and was ready, even eager, to join the saints who had gone before, from Jeremiah and Paul to Henry Barrow and John Greenwood. He recognised that the new law against nonconformists would mean exile from England, in which case, he urged them to live as a selfless community and provide for one another, and not leave behind 'my poor and desolate widow and my mess of fatherless and friendless orphans'. He suggested that they send a scout to any proposed destination before the whole church left the country, and join with other Separatist congregations going into exile from other parts of England to become one holy people in the wilderness.[3]

Penry was brought for trial before the King's Bench, in Westminster, on 21 May 1593. Attorney General Egerton drew up a sizeable dossier of evidence linking Penry to the Marprelate tracts, but it was apparently deemed too circumstantial to bring to court. Instead the prosecution accused Penry of sedition and rebellion on the basis of quotations from *Reformation no enemie* and from private notes found in his Edinburgh lodgings, which were first drafts of other writings. Returning to the Compter that night, Penry wrote to Burghley protesting against this line of prosecution. Penry argued that it was scandalous to use notes he had never shown another soul to accuse him of sedition. Burghley intervened and the trial was suspended.

A retrial was arranged quickly, beginning and ending on 25 May, rushed to its conclusion before any more interference. Penry was not even allowed to defend himself; 'the jury', he said, 'were sent away before I could have time so to do'. There was confusion about which law he was being tried under. Members of the Privy Council were involved, ensuring, Penry said, the 'misunderstanding' of the law, and it was obvious to him that they themselves were overseen by a more senior enemy of the puritans. Clearly a quick guilty verdict and sentence of death were required from the court, and that is what they delivered.[4]

Penry was taken to the King's Bench prison, where he prepared for death. Finding himself unexpectedly still alive on 28 May, however, he got hold of a scrap of paper and a little watery ink and wrote again to Burghley. He reported the continued irregularities of his trial and asked Burghley to do what he could to prevent a miscarriage of justice. Penry's biographer William Pierce describes the note as 'badly written for him, his manacled wrists perhaps at fault, with many broken sentences, and penned in a small hand, for his paper was scanty, and with an ill-cut quill'.[5]

Burghley received the letter and the Privy Council met the following morning, Tuesday 29 May. Whatever debate may have ensued, the meeting ended with Whitgift signing a warrant for Penry's immediate death. At eleven that morning, before his wife or friends could be informed, Penry was taken from the prison, mid-meal, carted to St Thomas-a-Watering on the Old Kent Road, and hanged before a small group of strangers. He was thirty years old. Vengeance was the Lord Bishop's and Pierce notes that before bed that night Whitgift would have had the satisfaction of hearing the evening's Psalm, which concluded: 'And for thy mercy slay mine enemies, and destroy all them that oppress my soul: for I am thy servant.'

Exile in Amsterdam

The Separatists had lost three leaders in two months, others were in prison, and the law of England now offered none of the survivors anything better than prison followed by banishment. There was little alternative for those believers who were free but to bypass prison and take themselves into exile like the Norwich Separatists had eleven years before.

While they discussed the practicalities, Francis Johnson wrote on 2 and 12 June to Burghley, suggesting he also be allowed to leave the country in preference to staying in jail. He assured Burghley that the only reason the Brownists were punished was that the bishops misrepresented their devotion to the scriptures and the Reformed faith. Johnson sent with the second letter two works by Penry, saying they spoke for the whole Separatist fellowship. He also sent a petition for radical reform, asking Burghley to pass it on to the Queen, after Johnson had left the country, without telling her whom it was from.

Burghley ignored Johnson's appeal for himself, but the ordinary members of the church were another matter. Clearing London's jails of dozens of religious prisoners, and the city itself of many more dissidents, was an alluring prospect. Since Carleton had first suggested that Burghley allow the Separatists to go into exile, twenty years of repression had achieved nothing: their numbers had grown, their writings proliferated and their nonconformity increased. Now that their leaders had been executed, Burghley did not want that to set a precedent for culling radical Protestants. The Seditious Sectaries Act provided banishment as a punishment for Separatists, and this seemed to offer the best solution. The more influential Brownists were kept in prison, including the Johnson brothers, Daniel Studley and Thomas Settle, but others were released on the understanding that they would leave the country. Fifty or sixty sailed to Amsterdam in June 1593, rented accommodation and set about making their livings by their various trades, or trying to learn new ones.

Amsterdam was a growing, prospering and thoroughly cosmopolitan city of trade where Jews, Anabaptists, Lutherans and Catholics coexisted with the Reformed majority. An English travel writer forty years later was struck by the 'infinite number of ships', the wealth, the 'corrupt and unwholesome' air, the utter lack of fresh water and firewood, and 'the most impudent whores I have heard of'. Migrants were welcomed with open arms, and could buy citizenship for eight guilders, though they were not required to. When the Brownists arrived, they were welcomed by some of the English merchants there, one of whom, Israel Johnson, let them worship on his property. But while the city fathers were happy for all faiths to gather freely, the Dutch Reformed Church was not, and in their third week in town the Separatists received a visit.[6]

The two men sent by the Amsterdam Consistory were Jacobus Arminius and Jean de Taffin. The first of these was destined to make a major contribution to Protestant theology, one directly connected to the Separatists' story. Arminius had lost most of his family in the Spanish massacre of Oudewater in 1575 when he was fifteen. At sixteen he enrolled at Leiden University, newly founded as a symbol of Dutch Protestant hope and defiance, and he emerged as a bright star of the Dutch Church. The question that made Arminius's name concerned the doctrine of election – the idea that God had decided beforehand which individuals will be saved and which damned, humans having no free will in the matter. This, though it is now called 'Calvinism', was originally the standard Protestant doctrine, the creed of Luther and the English Prayer Book. As in so much, it was the Anabaptists who first broke ranks, saying, 'God does not want to harden, darken, or eternally condemn anyone except those who, out of their own wickedness and freedom of the will, want to be hardened, darkened, and eternally condemned.' The first crack in the Reformed consensus came when the Dutch philosopher Dirck Coornhert wrote denying predestination, and the Consistory sent two ministers to combat his errors. In an unusual case of theological debate changing someone's mind, both delegates were converted. So Arminius was sent to pick up the pieces, and in the process he too lost faith in predestination. Freedom of the will seemed to be an idea whose time had come. Arminius was painfully aware that his conversion seemed like a betrayal of the creed of the Dutch republic, and he revealed his opinions so cautiously that they only fully emerged after his death, but his lukewarm Calvinism had already sparked controversy.[7]

Meeting now with Israel Johnson and the Brownists, Arminius warned the merchant that his guests were disreputable, and told him he should not allow unlicensed worship on his premises. Arminius informed the city fathers about the arrival of the Brownists, and told the English government too – the Brownists believed Whitgift had written to warn the Dutch about them. But the Brownists told Arminius they did not plan to stay in Amsterdam anyway and were heading to Kampen, fifty miles along the coast, a city that was positively advertising for immigrants and offered citizenship for free. So Arminius wrote to warn the Kampen church authorities about them, hearing back from them on 2 September that the Separatists had arrived and been allowed to settle.

Francis and Thomasine

In London, the authorities deliberated over what to do with their remaining Brownist prisoners. Two of them, we do not know which, were indicted under the Seditious Sectaries Act at the Newgate Sessions at the start of December, and William Smithe was interviewed by the MP for Middlesex, Robert Wroth.

On 8 January 1594, Francis Johnson wrote to Burghley from the Clink warning him that the persecution of the saints would bring God's judgement on England, starting with the present plague that was claiming a thousand lives a month in London as a punishment for the deaths of Barrow, Greenwood and Penry. The letter was taken to Burghley by Johnson's father. John Johnson, a former mayor of Richmond, Yorkshire, who had nearly ended up in prison himself in 1593 when he applied to the Dean of Westminster for his sons to be allowed the freedom of their prisons. (This was the same Dean of Westminster, Gabriel Goodman, who had assisted Grindal in the Plumbers' Hall interview twenty-six years before.)

Francis's letter had complained about the restrictions he and his brother suffered for their faithfulness to the gospel: Goodman had confiscated Francis's writings and some of his books, George was kept in a stinking part of the Fleet, and both were in close imprisonment. And yet that did not stop Francis marrying a glamorous twenty-five-year-old woman. Thomasine Boyes was a widow whose husband Edward had been a successful Fleet Street haberdasher and he had left her well off. Edward had been a member of the Separatists since at least 1587 and the couple opened their house to the church. It was there that Edward was arrested when the meeting was raided in December 1592. He lived long enough to be questioned in April 1593 and died in the following twelve months.

Once Francis and Thomasine had made their feelings known to each other, in the summer of 1594, Francis asked his brother for his opinion. George was appalled. He thought the way Mrs Boyes dressed utterly inappropriate for the wife of a minister: a long busk with a low-cut top, the 'abominable and loathsome' fashion known to the worldly as 'codpiece breasts', a 'painted hypocritical breast ... in truth nothing but a shadow'. She also wore lots of lace and several gold rings, ornamented and whaleboned skirts, elaborate sleeves and a feathered hat. Francis should call off the engagement, said George.[8]

Francis had asked his brother's opinion, but had no intention of following his advice. Boyes passed a series of letters between them. George said he spoke on behalf of others who had also commented on the unsuitability of the match. Francis managed to arrange a visit to the Fleet to discuss the matter with George face to face. It was an angry encounter. George tells us that Francis was a proud man with a ferocious temper and that he had always treated his younger brother as a servant; on the first point, many others agreed. The meeting ended with Francis saying he would do as he pleased and George replying that he 'would pray God to pass over the offences'. Francis and Thomasine married secretly in his cell around September 1594, without a minister.[9]

After the marriage, the rift between the brothers widened. George believed Thomasine had promised to dress more plainly once she was a pastor's wife, but she seemed to do the opposite. She denied making any such promise, and, when the complaints continued, she started – put up to it by Francis, George reckoned – to challenge George's theology. Did the Bible really prohibit feathered hats? Surely all things made by God 'were lawful to the children of God'.[10]

For George the Bible was as clear about busks and ruffs as it was about the alb and surplice, and he listed the unbiblical faults in Thomasine's apparel, with chapter and verse for each one. He sent a strongly worded letter to Francis and Thomasine concluding that she should be given a new wardrobe, which he itemised, telling Francis that if the late Mr Boyes' legacy was not enough to pay for it, 'let it be done upon your credit and I doubt not the LORD will provide'.[11]

Francis was furious. 'He returned taunts and reviling,' said George, 'calling his brother fantastical, fond, ignorant and anabaptistical.' Francis felt George was making ungenerous criticisms of his new sister-in-law; George felt Francis was making unjust exceptions for her. Francis was accused of bringing the church into disrepute; George of dividing it and undermining its leader. George wrote to Studley and

Settle and initially gained their support, but Francis was able to visit them in person in Newgate and the Gatehouse respectively, and won them round. Settle told George the clothes 'were things indifferent'. The Separatists' own vestiarian controversy continued as long as the brothers were in prison.[12]

The combination of persecution and self-inflicted woes that faced the Brownists became too much for Settle and he made his peace with the Church of England. Released from prison, he returned to Norfolk where he was relicensed as a minister on 10 March 1596. He was awarded the neighbouring parishes of St Peter's, Barningham Winter, and St Mary the Virgin, Matlaske, in May 1601.

A True Confession

Francis kept up the Brownist tradition of writing books in the Clink. The first, *A Treatise of the Ministery of the Church of England*, printed in 1595, was a reply to Arthur Hildersham, a puritan so radical that when he preached for the Leicester assizes the judge threatened to put him on trial himself. Hildersham had written to a jailed Separatist known only as Mrs N, a woman of gentle birth, arguing that though the Church of England's structures are abominable, it is only false doctrine that makes a church antichristian, and the Church of England's doctrine was fine. Johnson replied, at Mrs N's request, in one of the better-natured exchanges in the history of the Separatist movement, talking of Hildersham as an errant brother and saying, 'I do and shall alway love him in the Lord.' Johnson's book argued that the New Testament depicts antichrist as ruling in the church, making antichristianity a matter of structure as well as teaching, and he was easily able to show that this is how puritans had understood it, applying it to the Church of England in, for example, *An Admonition to the Parliament*.[13]

More importantly, the following year, Johnson wrote *A Trve Confession of the Faith … vvhich vve hir Majesties Subjects, falsely called Brovvnists, doo hould tovvards God*. Clearly intended as a foundational document, it was a forty-two-point statement of faith, more comprehensive than the church's *A Breefe Sum of Our Profession* and more

comprehensible than Browne's *A Booke which sheweth*. The first eighteen points or so set out fundamental theology about God, redemp-
tion, etc., calculated to place the Separatists squarely in the Reformed
consensus. When Johnson got on to ecclesiology, however, he gradually separated his movement from his opponents'. The organisation of the true church, he said, is exactly described in Scripture, so
any deviation is a violation of Christ's law. Every congregation 'hath
power and commandment' to shape itself to that model, electing its
own officers and excommunicating the ungodly. Every office of the
Church of England is 'strange and antichristian', from archbishop to
church warden, including parson and vicar, and even those heroes
of the puritan movement, unbeneficed lecturers, or 'hireling roving
preachers' as Johnson called them.[14]

Johnson's idea of the congregational church as set out here was
less radical than Browne's, though he affirmed the church's right to
remove their pastor. Where Browne expected all those who had the
gift to preach, Johnson allowed laymen to preach 'by the appointment of the congregation' only until a pastor or teacher be elected.
Membership of the church has to be voluntary – forcing unwilling
sinners into membership would defeat the whole object – but religious freedom in general meant nothing to Johnson at all. It is the
God-given duty of the state, he said, 'to suppress and root out by
their authority all false ministries, voluntary religions and counterfeit
worship of God … yea to enforce all their subjects, whether ecclesiastical or civil, to do their duties to God'. In the unlikely event
that the state should choose the right religion to enforce, Christians
should give thanks for this 'happy blessing'; if not, they have the freedom to disobey, and may petition the authorities, but otherwise must
simply stay faithful to God in the face of affliction.[15]

Excommunications

The pilgrims from Johnson's church were unsettled in the Netherlands.
Having moved from Amsterdam to Kampen in 1593, in 1595 they
moved to Naarden, back twelve miles south-east of Amsterdam.
There they won a convert from the French Reformed Church, Jean

de l'Ecluse, who became a frequent preacher in the Separatist church, but they lost members to the Anabaptists.

The church struggled enough to be given poor relief by the town, and this became a source of conflict when a widow, Mrs Colgate, accused Bowman the deacon of failing to distribute half of the money. The congregation reported all such things to Johnson, who investigated as well as he could from the Clink, and he decided that Bowman was in the right.

In 1596, the congregation moved again, back to Amsterdam, and met in L'Ecluse's house in an alley on Lange Houtstraat, Vloomburg. Vloomburg was an artificial island created in the docklands of the Amstel in the previous decade for the purpose of storing wood, a cheap area outside the walls, and home to Jews, Anabaptists and warehouses. The Amsterdam Consistory reprimanded L'Ecluse for housing the Brownists, as they had Israel Johnson, and urged the city to take action, but nothing happened.

If excommunication of errant members had often seemed a power that the Brownist church treasured in theory rather than exercising in practice, in the Netherlands that changed dramatically. Like Browne's church, they quickly found that once the oppression and enmity of the state church were gone, they had too little to unite and were a less homogeneous group than they had seemed. After they had formally excommunicated the Anabaptist converts, a new dispute arose that may also have involved Anabaptist teachings. It led to about twenty-seven members, nearly half the church, being summarily excommunicated. A number repented and were allowed back, after which a church meeting decided the excommunication had been overhasty, and revoked it. Unfortunately, other members vehemently disagreed with the revocation and quit the church, so now they also had to be excommunicated. Then a letter arrived from Johnson, who had been notified about the crisis, in which he said that the original excommunication was valid, however it was done, so the revocation was revoked.

22

Newfoundland

O N 11 JUNE 1578 Queen Elizabeth had given letters patent to the soldier Sir Humphrey Gilbert, half-brother of Walter Raleigh, for a six-year commission to find 'remote, heathen and barbarous lands' and claim them for England. Gilbert had enough barbarity of his own to spare, having gained his knighthood in a vicious campaign of colonial subjugation in Ireland, in which those who submitted to him had to walk down a lane lined with severed heads. The kind of people likely to share his interest in colonialism were adventurers for whom life at home was sufficiently difficult to make the other side of the world attractive, and so Gilbert negotiated a 13,000-square-mile settlement in North America with a group of English Catholics. This scheme, however, fell through when the Privy Council demanded the settlers pay their recusancy fines before leaving.

Gilbert went on a scouting expedition without them, arriving with four ships, including the *Golden Hind*, in St John's Harbour, Newfoundland, on 3 August 1583, where he claimed all land within 700 miles as a crown colony. He was opposed by the English fishermen who used St John's as a seasonal base for cod fishing and harvesting walrus oil, but he subdued them. One of his ships abandoned the expedition and another sank, but Gilbert headed homewards confident of raising funds for a permanent colony. His own ship was lost in a storm in the Azores, and he was last seen by the *Golden Hind*, standing on deck with a book in his hand, shouting, 'We are as near to heaven by sea as by land.'

Colonial proposal

For the time being, the plan to colonise North America had sunk with Gilbert, but then in March 1597 the imprisoned leaders of the

London Separatist church revived the idea, petitioning the Privy Council for release into another colonial expedition to Canada. They argued that it would not only be economically advantageous, but would 'in time also greatly annoy that bloody and persecuting Spaniard'. This was not just a nationalistic point scoring, but an apocalyptic hope. The army of antichrist had spread out from Europe to seize a 6,000-mile strip of the Americas, so if Brownist foot-soldiers could do anything to sabotage it, they would be fighting Christ's battle.[1]

The colony was a good strategy for the Brownists. If successful, it would transform them from outlaws to state-sanctioned pioneers, and gain their church a measure of authorisation by the English government for the first time. Four leading prisoners would sail first, and, if they found a viable site, other Brownists from London and the Netherlands would join them. The several hard years in a succession of Dutch towns would prove to be the wilderness period between the Egypt and the Promised Land – although Newfoundland also had enough wilderness to keep them going for a while.

Burghley warmed to the proposal, which revived Carleton's idea of turning England's nonconformist problem into a colonial opportunity, and an ideal candidate to captain the expedition presented himself. Thomasine's cousin Charles Leigh was a successful foreign merchant known at court, and knew the Johnsons well enough to have visited George in prison, trying to reconcile him and Thomasine. Two ships were fitted out for the expedition, the dubiously named *Hopewell* and *Chancewell*, and the brothers Johnson along with Daniel Studley and John Clarke were released with instructions to colonise the Magdalen Islands, a small archipelago to the west of Newfoundland in the Gulf of St Lawrence, establishing a walrus-fishing monopoly.

Between release and departure, Francis had a short while with Thomasine before leaving her behind. He wanted some resolution of the conflict with George over Thomasine's dress so that the first church in North America would be founded on good terms. Francis and his elder, Studley, called a church meeting. George professed astonishment that Francis would publicise criticism that he had made only in private, but the church heard it all. Francis and Studley also quoted George's claims that Thomasine stood around exhibiting her glamour in doorways or window shopping, that she drank enough to make Catholics comment, that she stayed long enough in bed on Sundays to delay worship and that she was reluctant to visit the poor. Most controversially of all, the meeting heard that George had quoted Jeremiah 3:3 at her, 'And thou haddest a whore's forehead: thou wouldest not be ashamed.' George reckoned Francis and Studley were using tactics against him they had learned from the Church of England's lawyers, broadening out the terms of questioning to move the focus from George's original accusation and undermine his character.

George tells us that in the meeting they treated him roughly to begin with, but, after a woman in the church supported his criticism, Thomasine was persuaded to apologise and promise to change. However it was achieved, the meeting ended in reconciliation between George and his brother and sister-in-law. The church joined together in a final service at Francis's house, before the four men left London in April.

Bishop Bancroft

John Aylmer turned seventy in 1591 and was keen to escape the draining, conflict-ridden post of Bishop of London. As he had been a valuable ally to Whitgift in the anti-puritan campaign, Whitgift was keen to ensure that Aylmer was replaced by someone equally useful – specifically, Richard Bancroft. Aylmer offered to resign in Bancroft's favour, his price being a good pension and the bishopric of Oxford, but Bancroft repeatedly refused such an expensive arrangement.

Aylmer died on 3 June 1594, leaving a £1,500-a-year legacy to his children. He had personally made £6,000 from selling timber from episcopal lands, for which reason Martin Marprelate had called him Mar-elm among his other nicknames, and the Privy Council had questioned Aylmer on the matter, to his fury. To Whitgift's disappointment, Bancroft did not get the job, Richard Fletcher being moved from Worcester to London instead, but Fletcher only lasted eighteen months before dying in 1596. Bancroft was elected Bishop of London on 21 April 1597. He wrote a damning report on Aylmer's nepotistic looting of the bishopric and sued Aylmer's son Samuel to recover some of it, putting him in a debtors' prison.

Journey to North America

The four released Separatists boarded their ships at Gravesend on 8 April 1597. Francis Johnson and Daniel Studley travelled on the larger ship, the 120-ton *Hopewell*, captained by Leigh. George Johnson and John Clarke were on the 70-ton *Chancewell* under Stephen van Herwick, whose brother Abraham was Leigh's commercial partner in the venture. George did not understand why Francis would choose to sail with his elder rather than his own brother, but decided not to mar the historic occasion by fighting over it. Still, the pilgrimage got off to a bad start when Captain van Herwick found George showing his sailors *A Trve Confession of the Faith*, but Francis smoothed over the ruction. Half of their six-week journey time was spent navigating the English south coast before a quick Atlantic crossing, and they reached Canada on 18 May. Skirting Newfoundland waters towards the Gulf of St Lawrence, the two ships lost each other in fog, and the *Hopewell* reached the Magdalen Islands alone on 14 June, enjoying a visit to the spectacular bird colonies of Bird Rocks.

Leigh was thrilled with the fishing there, the cod coming as quick as the sailors could reel them in. Off Brion Island, to the north of the archipelago, they caught 250 cod in a hour with four lines, and a four-foot turbot got away. They were less successful with the walruses, which they knew as morses or sea oxen: they found a herd sleeping on Bird Rocks, 'but', said Leigh, 'when we approached near unto them with our boat they cast themselves into the sea and pursued us with such fury as that we were glad to flee from them'. Brion seemed to have good land for wheat and grazing, they thought, as well as plenty of woodland, but no spring.[2]

On 18 June, the *Hopewell*, still alone, reached Basque Harbour, the main haven of the Magdalen Islands, but found it rather less uninhabited than expected. Four European ships were anchored there, with more in the other Magdalen harbour. There were huts on the shore, and hundreds of indigenous Canadians had come from the mainland to fish and hunt. Though the four ships all claimed to be French, Leigh accused two of them of being Spanish and therefore hostile. He commandeered their ammunition and his sailors talked of making off with one of the ships, but they woke the next morning to find three cannons on the shore trained on the *Hopewell*, with 200 armed men, both French and English, and 300 Canadians. After a skirmish, Leigh returned the ammunition and the *Hopewell* escaped.

The Magdalen Islands did not seem to be a promising place for a colony, so Leigh revised his plan and announced they were heading for a place he called Grande Coste, perhaps the north coast of the gulf, to attempt their colony there. His crew announced they were going home and turned the ship back eastwards, a mutiny that turned out to be extraordinarily lucky, or providential, for their separated brethren, George Johnson and John Clarke.

After their separation in June, the *Chancewell* had failed to find the Magdalen Islands. The ship eventually ended up at Cape Breton Island, Nova Scotia, where, on the same day as the *Hopewell* turned home, the *Chancewell* was wrecked. A mile from the Cape Breton shore, the ship was, according to George, 'through the headiness of the master, in a fair, sunshine day, run upon the rocks'. The crew managed to get the *Chancewell* into a sandy bay, but it was raided by Frenchmen, who emptied it of everything, including all the settlers' possessions with which they planned to establish their new home. To replace their ship, the crew spent four days preparing boats in which they planned to sneak up on a Spanish ship and seize it. Captain Herwick told Johnson and Clarke that the pair had three options: to stay on Cape Breton where they would be 'devoured by the wild'; to surrender themselves to a French ship where 'they should be urged to hear Mass'; or to join the shipless crew in their adventure. Johnson and Clarke were too frightened to choose and asked Herwick to choose for them, but he refused.[3]

While Herwick was talking to Johnson he saw a distant ship and sent a boat to beg its help. To their overwhelming relief it turned out to be the *Hopewell*. After their reunion, Leigh went to find the French crew who had stolen their things and negotiated the return of some of them. A few weeks later, they seized the opportunity of surprising a French 200-ton man-of-war in a harbour on Cape St Mary's. They crept up on it in the night, boarded it in the morning, and 'through the help of God we caused them to yield unto our mercy', reported Leigh. Thanks to this intervention he at least ended the expedition with as many ships as he started with, but he had given up on it, and on 5 August 1597 they left Newfoundland for England.[4]

Had the colony been established and survived, doubtless someone would have fulfilled the chronicling role Governor Bradford took upon himself in Plymouth. As it is, we have frustratingly little information about the Separatists' thoughts on their first attempt to become the Pilgrim Fathers. Francis, in his eight or so books, wrote not a word about it. George's narrative of the expedition is a very small detour in the much longer account he wrote six years later of his quarrels with his brother, containing more than enough information about George's clashes with Studley on the way home, almost nothing about the colonial purpose of the journey. As for Leigh, his log makes no mention of the Brownist settlers at all, doubtless preferring his name to be connected to higher pursuits than the transportation of felons. For an interpretation of the expedition, we have to read between the lines, but it seems that their motivation was the hope of finding in the perilous wilderness a measure of state toleration as well as de facto freedom, and that the expedition failed because of a combination of the hostility and prior occupation of the territory, the loss of their belongings and the non-cooperation of the crew. Whether the Separatists returned feeling disappointed by the failure or, having seen the realities of Newfoundland, relieved by the escape, we can only guess.

The four Brownists now had a chance to join their brothers and sisters in the Netherlands, taking with them others who had remained free in London. This involved a furtive visit to the city where their return from banishment was a capital offence, staying in separate houses to avoid detection. Francis was worried that George's indiscretion would give them away, and Studley talked of locking him in the ship, but in the end George came with them on the assurance that once in London he would stay indoors. Sure enough, George saw people he knew on the road to London, and when Francis would not let him do any more than wave, complained about the subterfuge.

In London, Francis and Thomasine were reunited and they prepared to travel to Amsterdam. George received a message from them telling him it was time to go to Gravesend and meet the ship, which he did, but when the others did not get there for three days he realised they had simply wanted him out of the city. His feelings were hurt, and he had to borrow money for food in Gravesend, having only pennies to his name.

Henry Ainsworth and Matthew Slade

By the time the Johnsons and others arrived in Amsterdam in late September 1597, the church, with pastor Johnson's approval, had elected a teacher who would now serve alongside him, the twenty-seven-year-old Henry Ainsworth. Born in Norfolk, Ainsworth had studied at Cambridge, but though in later life he would be a considerable scholar, he left without a degree. He had worshipped with the Separatist congregation in London in the early 1590s, where he was arrested and agreed to attend his parish church. He rejoined the Separatists, was arrested again in Ireland, and submitted again.

Ainsworth had a facility with languages and seems to have come to Amsterdam alone and worked as a porter for a Dutch bookseller before joining the Brownist church when they returned to the city from Naarden. Bradford says that he lived in severe poverty, 'for he was a very modest and bashful man and concealed his wants from others' and 'being a single young man and very studious was content with a little'. He had learned to read biblical Hebrew, which doubtless helped to commend him to the struggling Separatist church as the man to replace Greenwood as their teacher.[5]

The newcomers found that they were not the only English Separatist church in Amsterdam, as a rival had been set up by Henoch Clapham. Clapham was ordained in the diocese of Lincoln in 1591, then became an itinerant presbyterian preacher, and was in the

Clink at the same time as Francis Johnson. By his own account, he drifted from one group to another, back and forth between Scotland and the Netherlands. In the eyes of English and Scottish authorities, Clapham was simply a Brownist, but in his own there was a world of difference. He criticised the democratic extremism of the Johnsons' church, and their tendency to split over trifling disagreements: 'They, upon every sly and unstayed crochet buzzing in their itching ears … do fly the congregation grinning and barking like dogs of the evening against all such as will not presently conform to their opinion.' The Brownists replied 'that neither Clapham nor England teach the Gospel of Jesus'.[6]

Clapham's Separatist church lasted until 1598, when he quit to become a lecturer in Southwark, and condemned Separatism – 'the evomitings of the Brownist' – in a series of nine sermons and then a book called *Antidoton*. He argued at length against the congregational version of church, one of its problems being that 'the Brownists of common inferior lot' take upon themselves the ordination of their superiors. He was jailed in the plague year of 1603 for encouraging people to illegally attend funerals if they had the faith to resist infection.[7]

Francis and Thomasine Johnson and Daniel Studley rented a large house together in Reguuierspoort, half a mile from L'Ecluse's, and made it available for church meetings. George was again offended by his brother's failure to invite him to lodge with them despite having rooms to spare. When the church decided to elect a third elder to work with Studley and Knifton, George, according to his own account, was favourite, but Francis and Studley threatened to prevent his election because he was still criticising Thomasine. Unless George repented his worst offences – particularly the 'whore's forehead' comment – Francis said he would resign rather than accept him as an elder. George appealed to Ainsworth, who apparently supported George until Francis rebuked him, after which Ainsworth, a milder character than Francis, threw his weight behind the pastor. On 15 January 1598, Ainsworth chaired a church meeting which considered George's behaviour towards Thomasine and censured him. It did not go any further though, and that kept him quiet for the time being.

The man elected as elder instead of George was Matthew Slade, a twenty-eight-year-old from Dorset. Despite a university degree and having been a teacher in Devon, Slade is said to have worked as a mason in Amsterdam. If so, he was not the only one going below his accustomed station. George said there were graduates in the church who 'were content to card and spin or to learn trades, thereby to maintain themselves'. Roger Williams, the New England Baptist, reported that Ainsworth 'lived on 9d a week with roots boiled', much less than unskilled labourers in England earned. George said he himself relied on charity from the church and often had still less than Ainsworth.[8]

Slade was offered a job as assistant master in the Latin school in Koestraat, which he started on 1 July. This congenial post required him to attend the Dutch state church, which brought up the tricky question of Separatists' attitudes to that church. They were very keen to call the Dutch their brothers – if the continental Reformed churches were not their family then they were alone in all the world. The Dutch Church did not return the fraternal sentiment though; and, while it was not nearly so conservative as the Church of England, it retained some of the practices that Brownists condemned, such as read prayers and baptising the children of non-members. Slade considered these to be acceptable differences, so he had attended Dutch services when working outside Amsterdam. Johnson and Ainsworth disagreed. They argued that the Dutch had not progressed so far down the path of true Christianity as the Brownists had, so it was right to bear with them until they did, but that for someone like Slade, who had known the full glories of pure worship, to join the Dutch would be turning back and falling away. Johnson and Ainsworth spent months talking this through with their elder, but he persisted and was excommunicated. Slade joined the Dutch Reformed Church, was appointed head of his school in 1602, and became the municipal librarian of Amsterdam in 1603.

This was not the kind of tone that the Separatists wanted their relationship with the Dutch Church to take; they needed them as allies in their stand against the Church of England. So in 1598 they translated Johnson's *Trve Confession* into Latin and sent it to the Reformed universities of Europe, asking for their opinions and for biblical proof of any errors they saw in it. The response was demoralising. Most recipients merely turned their noses up at the document. The only one who replied, Francis Junius of Leiden, though he called the Brownists 'his beloved in Christ', refused to take sides, simply advising them not to draw attention to the divisions between them and the Church of England.

The Brownist leaders wrote back to Junius, complaining that he had not engaged with their confession and offering a lengthy justification of their enmity with the church. Junius replied that the only reason they could have for publicising this enmity was to justify their separation in the eyes of the Reformed churches, which was quite unnecessary as no one had heard of the Brownists before they sent their confession. The Separatists responded with what Junius described as 'an huge bundle of letters' to which he replied with one short note saying, 'I gave you counsel to rest from questions; you command me to enter into questions. I continue still in my purpose, for I esteem more of peace in the church than of the seeds of strife.' The conversation ended.[9]

In 1598, Thomasine Johnson bought a new velvet hood and George's campaign against her reared back into life. Francis threatened George with excommunication. George suggested asking the Norwich church led by William Hunt to arbitrate between them, but Francis refused. The balance of power in the Brownist church between the minister and the people had always been ambiguous, and Johnson, by the force of his formidable personality, had shifted it more towards the minister than previous leaders. He was not about to submit himself to an external authority he could not control. Studley also refused to submit himself to a minister who had called him an unrepentant sinner.

The Johnsons' father John wrote repeatedly, urging the brothers to be at peace with each other, but to no avail. In the winter of 1598–9, Francis led a church meeting, which consented to George's excommunication, but Francis could not persuade anyone to pronounce the penalty. After an hour's debate, George said, Francis, 'in his fury and rage', pronounced his brother's excommunication himself. George remained in Amsterdam. Francis might be forgiven for thinking that, after this painful decision and a display of strong leadership, things would go more smoothly and happily for the fellowship, but that would have been a mistake.[10]

In 1599, the Synod of North Holland issued warnings about the Brownists, saying that their disorders should be referred to the civil authorities. The Brownist leaders visited the Amsterdam Consistory to complain that the Dutch Church was receiving into membership people the Brownists had expelled, like Slade, as if they did not consider the excommunication valid. The meeting began with the secretary noting the visit from the delegation from 'the English church living here', but once the Brownists had their say he crossed out the word 'church'. 'We do not acknowledge their gathering as being a church,' declared the Consistory, and when Johnson wrote, trying to continue the debate, they responded witheringly that he would receive a reply 'if they found anything that was worthy of answer'.[11]

Against Henry Jacob and John Johnson

Johnson had to defend Separatism from a more familiar enemy when Henry Jacob took on Johnson's old job as minister of the Merchant Adventurers in Middelburg. The puritan and the Separatist had argued in a series of letters while Johnson was in the Clink. Now that Jacob had a position in the Netherlands, in 1599 he let a friend publish his final letter (incorporating the earlier ones in its text), printed by Schilders. Johnson responded, advised by Ainsworth and Studley, with *An answer to Maister H. Jacob his Defence of the Churches and Ministery of England,* printed in 1600.

Jacob got into difficulties defending his church from the accusation of unbiblical worship. He argued that Christ asks for two different kinds of obedience from his followers: what they believe and what they do. Requisite beliefs are written in the Bible; requisite activities are unwritten and so are 'at the arbitrary appointment of the church and magistrate'. Whatever the Supreme Governor decides worship should be like, that becomes the decree of Christ. This was an extraordinary argument for a puritan, indicating just how defeated puritanism now was. Jacob was repeating – actually in stronger terms – what the bishops had told puritan campaigners in the 1560s: that they should stop looking in the Bible for instructions about church life, forget reform and accept the Queen's church. Johnson made short work of it: Jacob was admitting that his own church government was arbitrary; this was a Catholic argument for accepting Latin, the seven sacraments and the Pope; and it is preposterous to say that the Bible contains no instructions for worship. Jacob was not even consistent with the principle himself, but the fact that he propounded it shows that the choice before puritans at the turn of the seventeenth century seemed to be between quietism and Separatism.[12]

And so the Amsterdam Brownist church grew. Around 1601, a group including Stephen and Frances Ofwod came from London. Stephen owned farmland in Suffolk, but had faced attempts to seize it and imprison him when he avoided his parish church for more than a year. After their son died, 'whether it was by witchery or by the falling sickness no learned man could determine', Stephen had persuaded Frances that God's 'grievous punishment upon our child' was a message that they should join a separating church. Coming to London, they did not join the remnant of Johnson's church, but made a new church covenant with other radicals, saying, 'We do covenant to walk obediently unto the word of God in all things the Lord hath revealed or shall reveal unto us.' Driven out of the country by persecution, some of them joined the Amsterdam church, being accepted as true Christians 'by the Minister and most of the people'.[13]

The Brownists' relationship with the Dutch Reformed Church grew worse and worse. In 1601, they sent the Dutch a list of ten faults needing remedy, such as set prayers, holy days, worshipping in former Catholic buildings and holding weddings in church. The Dutch responded, accusing the Brownists of 'great calumnies', calling them schismatics and 'holders of conventicles'.[14]

The Amsterdam Brownists also quarrelled with the Norwich Brownists. Pastor Hunt wrote to Francis Johnson in March 1601 outlining the offence Studley had caused there in 1591 and requiring Johnson to discipline him. The time lapse of a decade and the fact that George had a copy of Hunt's letter suggests that George may have asked Hunt to intervene. Wolsey also wrote to Johnson's church, in July 1602, drawing their attention to a difference between them he thought essential: Wolsey obeyed the instruction of the

Jerusalem council in Acts to follow a condensed version of the Torah, abstaining from blood, strangled animals, meat sacrificed to idols and unchastity, and he urged others to do the same. Barrow had condemned Wolsey's 'judaising' tendencies, though despite this, according to Stephen Ofwod, Barrow was the only one of Wolsey's twenty-plus converts he never excommunicated. Johnson's church wrote to Wolsey denouncing his innovation and Ofwod delivered the letter. He found Wolsey still in jail after twenty years, but on surprisingly trusting terms: 'He had a key for to let in unto him whom he would, and to go out as he pleased at a back gate.'[15]

Johnson had a better relationship with the remnant of his church that had stayed in London, but even that was difficult. The only officer the Londoners had left was the deacon Nicholas Lee, so they wanted a 'Mr Cr' as their teacher. Johnson and Studley feared that if the London church was too well provided for, there would be less incentive for people to join them in Amsterdam, so they 'made a jar between the people and him', according to George, and Mr Cr quit the church.[16]

John Johnson, father of Francis and George, came to Amsterdam in 1602, hoping to reconcile his sons. He lodged with Francis, but only lasted a week there. Francis 'was so far from peace', John told him, 'and so unkindly used me, that you made me weary before the week was ended'. So John went to stay with George, thereby breaking the church's rules about contact with the excommunicated. John found Francis determined to reject all conciliation, wanting to force his father to choose between his sons. When he continued with his peace mission, John felt that Francis turned the church against him, until everyone was watching for evidence to use against him. In the end, John had to answer to a church meeting chaired by Francis, standing through a two-hour interrogation. He was excommunicated, whereupon Francis and the rest of his church ended all contact with him. Even the ungodly, said John, would not treat their own fathers so; such unnaturalness had never before been heard of.[17]

The departure of George and John Johnson did not bring an end to controversy in the Brownist church. A member by the name of Mr Castle was accused of cheating people out of money, and when the elders confronted him he quit the church. In 1601, the teacher of the church, Ainsworth, was himself touched by scandal when the story emerged that he had twice submitted under pressure to the Church of England before coming to Amsterdam. These lapses were the more damaging because it had, when Ainsworth first joined, been Johnson's policy that no one who fell away could ever be read-mitted to the church, so Ainsworth had kept quiet about his past, but, since then, experience had made Johnson more understand-ing. When they elected Stanley Mercer as elder that year to replace Slade, Mercer felt compelled to confess that since his conversion in 1593 he had once been persuaded to attend a parish sermon; his lapse was forgiven.

Studley's scandal

If Johnson's church seemed to lose its way somewhat after emerging from the underground into the freedom of exile, worse scandal came the following year when a member visited Johnson to tell him of a rumour that Studley had sex with his stepdaughter. Johnson inves-tigated, tracing the story through a number of tellers to a member called Rose Philips. According to Johnson, she could not say whom she had heard it from, 'but confessed it was her own addition, and then shewed great sorrow and repentance for her so doing'. Never-theless, a number of people confronted Studley directly. By his own account, if they were reproachful, he ignored them or invited them to sue him; so long as they spoke to him in an appropriate manner, he 'answered them to their full satisfaction'. His account made much of the lack of proof against him, without making a direct denial. According to Johnson, Studley took Philips to court and she was not able to prove her allegation.[18]

Philips got into further trouble with the church when she refused to have her child baptised there and entertained Slade in her house. She told Johnson that in both cases her husband insisted, and Johnson respected her obedience; the church tried to excommunicate her, but Johnson intervened. Then, however, she accompanied her husband to the Dutch Reformed Church and started defending their cor-ruptions, so Johnson pronounced her excommunication. Both Rose

Philips' accusations and her excommunication would come back and bite the church.

On 26 June 1603, John and George Johnson made a formal enquiry about joining the Dutch Reformed Church, but instead they decided to return to England. As a parting shot, George published an unfinished memoir of his mistreatment by Francis and Studley. Saving money by using a minuscule typeface, he offered the public a painstaking though not entirely clear record of his complaints. Despite his expulsion, George still believed in the Separatist cause and argued that his brother's wrongdoing did not discredit the church, any more than the disagreement between the Marian exiles had disgraced the Church of England. In fact he modelled his book on the account of that conflict, *A brieff discours off the troubles begonne at Franckford in Germany*, and called it *A Discourse of some Troubles and Excommunications in the Banished English Church at Amsterdam*. George was arrested in Durham for preaching Brownism, finished his book in jail, and around 1605, after 'very heavy and great exclamations about his sins' according to an eyewitness, died there. Thomasine seems to have been left in peace then, and when Bradford got to know her a few years later it was as 'a grave matron and very modest both in her apparel and all her demeanour ... and an ornament to [her husband's] calling'.[19]

23

A new hope

THE TWENTY-THIRD OF March 1603 was the last full day of the Queen's life. Ill and depressed, she had refused treatment or food, and now lost her voice. The Privy Council gathered and asked her to name her successor. King James of Scotland had become their firm favourite and Robert Cecil, who had taken over from his father Burghley as Secretary of State, had carried on a secret correspondence with him. When James was mentioned, the Queen put her hand to her head, which the Council were content to take as a nomination.

By another sign, she called for the Archbishop of Canterbury, who knelt to question her on her faith, answered by more signs. Then, according to the courtier Robert Cary, 'the good man told her plainly what she was, and what she was to come to; and though she had long been a queen here upon earth, yet shortly she was to yield an accompt of her stewardship to the King of Kings'. Whitgift then recited long prayers, with the attendants joining in the responses, until his seventy-year-old knees started to trouble him, but when he tried to rise the Queen motioned for him to continue. He gave her a good half-hour more, but the same thing happened again. Finally she allowed the court and council to leave her with her ladies-in-waiting and she died in the early hours of the morning.[1]

The Millenary Petition

Cary, hoping to transfer his lucrative standing in court from one monarch to the next, had promised James that he would be the first to tell him the news of his accession. Slipping out of

Richmond Palace, he rode to Edinburgh in an astonishing three days, having arranged for fresh horses to be ready for him at inns along the road.

The king's journey to London was rather more leisurely, taking a month, as he met his new subjects, presided over feasts, attended services, gave out knighthoods and broke his collarbone hunting. He emptied jails of all but traitors, murderers and Catholics, and summarily hung a cutpurse. Streets were swept, houses painted and weapons collected in by mayors. By the time James left the first English city on this route, Berwick, he had 500 attendants.

The journey allowed time for petitioners to reach the king before he reached his Council. Because each of the last three royal successions had brought religious change, puritans and Catholics rushed to put their case to James. Catholics told themselves that, out of respect for his dear mother, the Catholic martyr, he would relieve the burden of persecution on them; puritans told themselves that he had spent his life in a properly reformed church and would want to bring England more in line with Scotland. James had encouraged the ambiguity, wanting all the support he could get for his claim to the English throne.

The king received a number of mildly worded petitions for Catholic toleration en route, but one petition, from the priest Thomas Hill in York, suggested that those who suffered religious tyranny had 'just occasion to leave their due obedience'. Hill soon found himself in the Westminster Gatehouse.[2]

On 17 April, King James reached Huntingdon where he stayed at the house of the puritan Oliver Cromwell, uncle of his more radical namesake. James was treated to his most lavish welcome yet, an extravagant banquet supplemented with generous gifts, and Cromwell allowed the Millenary Petition to be delivered to the king.

The Millenary Petition, for reform of the church, had been organised by puritans including Arthur Hildersham, Johnson's sparring partner, and Stephen Egerton, one of the team sent to debate the Separatists in 1590. The petition got its name from its claim to have the explicit backing of a thousand ministers, though it bore no actual signatures. The petition's demands covered all the familiar puritan concerns – objectionable elements in the Prayer Book service, non-preaching and ill-educated ministers, pluralism, and the reform of church courts. Evidently, although the puritan movement had been dormant and defeated for a decade, it was not dead, and a glint of opportunity revived its hopes. Yet although the petition was extensive, it was also restrained. On vestments it only asked for toleration of nonconformity, not for their abolition. The same went for saints' days. The request that no court be allowed to excommunicate anyone without their minister's consent would have had major consequences, but fell far short of a demand for presbyterianism.

James's response was a world away from Elizabeth's. Although the Catholics got nothing at all from their petitions, James invited the puritans to a debate with the bishops, chaired by him. He loved theology, and experience had taught him it is easier to rule your councillors if they have opposition.

The result was the Hampton Court Conference of January 1604, which involved bishops, other senior clergy and a panel of moderate puritan academics selected by the Privy Council. Cartwright was invited, but died eighteen days before the conference started. In the months before it met, the machinery of puritan agitation creaked back into action. Egerton worked with Johnson's other antagonist Henry Jacob on a strategy document, *Advice tending to Reformation*. They called for a campaign of many small petitions, all differently worded, covering different points of reform, including discipline, but never mentioning the abolition of bishops. A puritan summit met in London in July to coordinate these efforts. This campaign was counterproductive: James received so many far-reaching demands that in October he pre-empted the conference by issuing a condemnation of seditious campaigns for reformation and assuring the public that the existing constitution of the Church of England was in accord with the Bible.

In the first session of the conference, on Saturday 14 January, the king met only with the bishops and deans, reminding the puritans of their status. And yet he brushed aside the pleas of Whitgift and Bancroft to ignore the puritans' complaints, and when they said it would damage the Protestant cause to change the church after forty years' stability, he answered, 'It [is] no reason that because a man had been sick of the pox forty years, therefore he should not be cured at length.'[3]

And yet, when it came to hearing the puritans' arguments for reform on 16 January, James found little good in them. Dismissing one after another of their biblical proofs, he said that if one of their own students had offered such poor reasoning 'they would have fetched him up in place of a reply and so should the rod have played upon the poor boy's buttocks'. James still kept silencing Bancroft's angry interruptions, but when the puritans suggested moderating the power of bishops by requiring them to work with the 'presbytery', James rebuked them as if they had advocated wholesale presbyterianism, with his famous outburst: 'No bishop, no king.'[4]

James agreed to a set of moderate reforms: there would be slight changes in the Prayer Book, mainly to clarify the wording, and its orders would be less strictly enforced; the Apocrypha would not be read in church; bishops would lose the power to singlehand-edly remove ministers and their employees would lose the power to excommunicate; new schools and greater funding would reduce the numbers of ill-educated and non-preaching ministers; and a new translation of the Bible would replace the Bishops' Bible. It was far from radical, but neither was it the status quo that Whitgift and Ban-croft argued for. Puritans were disappointed but could console them-selves that it was a significant step in the right direction, such a step as they had not seen in forty years.

The problem was that James was more interested in making the right decision than in making anything happen about it. Commis-sions consisting of bishops and Privy Councillors were appointed to put the king's decisions into practice, and generally, with the excep-tion of the Bible translation, that was the last that was heard of them.

The following month Whitgift caught a cold while being punted to Bancroft's palace in Fulham, then suffered a stroke. He died at Lambeth on 29 February. At his funeral in Croydon, the puritan courtier Lewis Pickering pinned a poem to the hearse, calling the deceased 'Reformer's hinderer, true pastor's slanderer, the papist's broker, the atheist's cloaker'. The poem imagined Richard Bancroft as chief mourner singing, 'Jocky is gone, and Dicky hopes to play Jocky alone'. Pickering was convicted of seditious libel and Bancroft was appointed Archbishop of Canterbury.[5]

Johnson and Ainsworth's petitions

From Amsterdam, Francis Johnson proclaimed that the death of the archbishop so soon after the conference was God's way of telling the king 'what he would have him to do with the rest of the bishops'. In the meantime, where the new regime had raised puritans' hopes for reform, Separatists hoped they might be allowed home. They wrote their own petition, saying that they held the same doctrines as the Church of England, while renouncing its 'antichristian hierarchy, form of worship and confusion of all sorts of people in the body of that church'. They attached the Latin version of Johnson's *Trve Confession* to confirm this, and asked, not for any reformation, but for the king to call off his bishops and let the Brownists worship in their home country in peace.[6]

Johnson and Ainsworth went to England to deliver the petition to the palace. James took no notice of it, and weeks passed, but the men could not bear the thought of going back with nothing to show for their journey. Wondering if perhaps the nineteen-point *Trve Confession* had been too comprehensive for the purpose, they wrote a second petition, this time attaching only what the king needed to know to decide their case, a fourteen-point exposition of the differences between them and the Church of England. Again they got no response, and they now feared that by merely outlining the differences they had failed to show that they were in the right, so they rewrote it with lengthy notes proving each of the fourteen points, expanding it to many times the size.

This third petition finally got a response. Someone with access to the king told Johnson and Ainsworth to condense their petition into something short and pertinent, and he would show it to him. Their fourth draft simply asked for permission to return to England, and offered to take part in a second Hampton Court Conference with the bishops, should the king wish. The king did not wish, and the Separatists returned to Amsterdam with nothing to show for their expedition but a pile of their own papers, which they printed in a compendium called *An Apologie or Defence of svch trve Christians as are commonly (vnjustly) called Brovvnists.*

Bancroft's 141 canons

Bancroft was determined to use his archbishopric to renew the assault on puritanism as well as Catholicism, and he started before he even took office. James's first Parliament met in March 1604, and with no archbishop to preside over the simultaneous Convocation of Canterbury the king appointed Bancroft, being dean of the province, to do it. Bancroft presented his colleagues with 141 proposed canons for the church. These brought together acts and decrees made since the Reformation, including Whitgift's fearful three articles of 1583, along with new contributions by Bancroft himself. The canons reaffirmed all the aspects of Elizabethan worship that had offended puritans, from the cope and surplice to the sign of the cross, holy days and baptism by midwives. They reaffirmed episcopacy and the church court system, forbidding prophesyings and private meetings. They limited preaching, requiring all preachers to administer Communion by the book twice a year and giving bishops power to silence unruly preachers. Above all, the canons declared the excommunication of anyone who affirmed that the Prayer Book contained 'corrupt, superstitious or unlawful worship' or that episcopacy was unbiblical. Anyone who attended conventicles was also automatically excommunicated.

Convocation passed the canons. The Commons tried to hold up the proceedings by charging Bancroft with treason, and passed two reform bills, one against pluralism (one area in which the canons had agreed with puritans) and the other promoting the education of ministers. Both bills were rejected by the Lords, and Convocation passed a resolution to the effect that the Commons should mind their own business.

James issued a proclamation on 16 July 1604 saying he had heard all the arguments for reform at Hampton Court and at Parliament, and decided against them, and that those who made the arguments were content with his verdict. All subjects had until 30 November to conform 'or else dispose of themselves and their families some other ways'.[7]

Four days after that deadline passed, Bancroft was enthroned as Archbishop of Canterbury. On 22 December he issued instructions for all ministers and preachers to subscribe to the 141 canons or be deprived. The crisis had begun.

24

A rough crossing

JOHN ROBINSON WAS a gifted and passionate preacher, in his late twenties, and a fellow of Corpus Christi, Cambridge, when he preached at St Andrew's Church in Norwich, in August 1604, hoping for a curacy. St Andrew's, like Holy Trinity, Minories, was able to elect its own ministers and had chosen a succession of ardent puritans, becoming a centre of prophesyings in the 1570s and repeatedly getting into trouble for nonconformity. Robinson's sermon vehemently denounced the episcopal courts, which impressed the congregation and its minister Thomas Newhouse, and worried the Bishop of Norwich, who took several months to issue his preaching licence. The joint ministry of Newhouse and Robinson was so popular that St Andrew's added extra seating, but it was not to last.

The royal decree demanding conformity came during Robinson's first year at Norwich. When the bishop started to enforce Bancroft's canons in 1605, Robinson, like many ardent puritans, vacillated – he had married the previous year and had a child, as well as securing a well-suited post. Newhouse conformed, finding this an acceptable price to pay in order to keep preaching the gospel in the Church of England. Robinson, though, stood firm long enough to be suspended from office.

In Nottinghamshire, the Vicar of Worksop Priory, Richard Bernard, toured the region preaching defiant sermons to packed churches on the text from Daniel, 'Be it known to you, O king, that we will not serve your gods'. Bernard likened Bancroft's articles to the golden idol that King Nebuchadnezzar ordered the Jews to worship, saying that the godly would need the same courage as Shadrach, Meshach and Abednego, whom Nebuchadnezzar sentenced to be burned for their faith.

Perhaps as many as three hundred minsters were suspended, but, as in 1566, the majority of them capitulated. Even so, that left at least eighty minsters to be sacked, and though seven later recanted and were reinstated, it was still by far the greatest cull of puritans to date. Robinson and Bernard were among the deprived ministers, as was Arthur Hildersham.

The middle way

While a new generation of puritans faced the old choice of conforming or separating, this time there was a new option under discussion, known today by the unwieldy names of semi-separatism or non-separating congregationalism. This involved creating new congregations, much as Brownists had, or stripping parish churches of offensive rituals, and giving the congregation power to appoint its own ministers, but not separating from unreformed churches or condemning them as false churches.

One of the leaders of this movement was Henry Jacob, who six months after the Hampton Court Conference published in Middelburg *Reasons taken ovt of Gods Word and the best hvmane Testimonies proving a necessitie of reforming ovr Chvrches in England*. This book argued that each congregation should be autonomous and have authority over its officers. Another leader was William Bradshaw, who joined Jacob in the agitation of 1603 after being removed from his preaching post in Chatham, Kent. In *English Puritanisme*, published in 1605, Bradshaw argued that the congregational system would be more loyal to the crown than episcopacy or presbyterianism, as each congregation was directly answerable to the king, without bishops or synods perverting his will. Bradshaw vociferously opposed Separatism, as Jacob had, but the churches they described could be created or reformed without tarrying for national reformation.

Neither man as yet founded a new church himself, but Bradshaw argued that ministers who did reform their churches should not be punished. He urged ministers not to subscribe to Bancroft's articles, though Jacob, being arrested for his book, subscribed in order to get

out of prison, but like Browne, Jacob had his own personal interpretation of what the subscription meant. In 1605, Jacob and friends
petitioned the king for permission to found a congregational church
in England in 'brotherly communion with the rest of our English
Churches'. Inevitably this was unsuccessful, James having no greater
inclination to surrender his church to the people than to the presbytery. But finally, puritans had a new plan to put their hope in after the
collapse of presbyterianism.[1]

Robinson felt torn by arguments such as Jacob's. He searched the
scriptures with a growing sense that they described an entirely different church than the Church of England, and that he was called into
it. Could it be created within the Church of England? Could it be
created overseas without quitting the Church of England? Robinson
read the Brownists' books, finding their uncompromising arguments
for total separation 'sweet as honey unto my mouth', but then was
held back by the thought of heroes of the faith, such as Cartwright
and Perkins, who had disagreed and disapproved. Robinson applied
for the job Robert Harrison had held twenty-five years before at the
hospital in Norwich, but without success.[2]

Robinson travelled extensively and consulted widely, hoping 'to
find satisfaction to my troubled heart'. When Lawrence Chaderton
preached in Cambridge about church government being more open,
Robinson heard that as a call for congregational church. After hearing
Paul Baynes, Perkins' successor at St Andrew's the Great, preach on
the need for the godly to shun the wicked, Robinson put it to him
that this was an argument for abandoning the Church of England.
The fact that such godly men had no sympathy for Separatism of
any kind continue to restrain Robinson, and yet he felt the call 'as a
burning fire shut up in my bones'.[3]

Coventry summit

Bernard was going through similar turmoil, 'tossed by the present
tempest', in his own words, 'sometime to a favouring [of Brown-
ism] but otherwise to a great dislike'. He talked through the questions with a friend, his fellow minister John Smyth, who no longer

had any official position in the Church of England but preached at Gainsborough, fifteen miles to the north-west of Worksop.[4]

Originally from Sturton-le-Steeple, Nottinghamshire, Smyth had been taught at Christ's College, Cambridge, by Francis Johnson. He was ordained and made a fellow of the college himself, but lost the fellowship for criticising church ceremonies. He spent two years as lecturer for the town of Lincoln until he was sacked in 1602 for preaching 'enormous doctrine'. He got into trouble for preaching while suspended in Gainsborough and (like Bredwell) for practising medicine without a licence.

Smyth had more radical instincts than Bernard and had toyed with Separatism even before the present crisis. According to Bernard, Smyth 'disclaimed episcopal authority utterly and fell in love with the doctrine of the separation, but warily and secretly at the first'. Smyth's views got him into trouble, and he was persuaded to sign a statement forswearing Separatism. He published two books of standard puritan theology, including one commending the Lord's Prayer, which he admitted himself had nothing original to say but was intended to distance him from the Brownists.[5]

In the summer of 1606, Smyth considered separation more seriously than ever. He and Bernard both felt they had disciples who would follow wherever they went, and they talked of taking them to the Netherlands, where they could either join the Brownists or establish a church like Jacob and Bradshaw wrote about – free, pure and directed by the people, but without condemning the godly of the Church of England.

A summit meeting of radical puritans was held later that year in Coventry, to discuss their response to the subscription crisis. Smyth, Bernard, Robinson and Hildersham met at the mansion of the wealthy puritan Isabel Bowes, whose brother Sir William Wray had been a patron of Smyth's. Other participants included John Dod, who had preached Cartwright's funeral sermon and been deprived of his Oxfordshire living, and Richard Clifton, the deprived minister of Babworth. Clifton, being about the age of Robert Browne, was described by Bradford at this point as 'a grave and fatherly old man ... having a great white beard'. Bradford said Clifton's preaching had converted many people, including Bradford himself. One lay participant in the conference was Thomas Helwys, the master of Broxtowe Hall, near Nottingham.[6]

The Coventry summit was an important moment in radical puritanism, but our information about it is contradictory. Smyth later swore that the question under discussion was not whether to renounce the Church of England, but whether to form new congregations professing friendship with the Church. 'I did not confer with them about the separation ...' he said, 'but about withdrawing from true churches, ministers, and worship, corrupted.' This was clearly not the whole story though, as Smyth talked elsewhere about full-scale Separatism being 'opposed by some adversaries' at the meeting.[7]

So far as Bernard was concerned, the conference was about quitting the Church of England. He said that Smyth had arrived in Coventry convinced that God called them into Separatism, but that during the debate his opponents showed him he was misreading Scripture and convinced him he was wrong. At this, said Bernard, Smyth fell to his knees, praised God for saving him from the error of Brownism, and said he would go to Amsterdam 'to dissuade his tutor Mr Johnson from the same'. Smyth's explanation for this display was that he knelt to pray, as requested by his fellow participants, merely in thanks for 'the quiet and peaceable conference', that he had never made a commitment to Brownism nor abjured it, and that it was he who had corrected the others when they made the case for a middle way between Separatism and conformity. This was an important point for Smyth, because Separatists taught that once a definite commitment had been made, any turning back constituted the serious, perhaps unforgiveable, sin of apostasy.[8]

By the close of the conference, Bernard had decided to return to his unbeneficed ministry in the impure Church of England. He told Hildersham and Robinson: 'Well, I will return home, and preach as I have done, and I must say as Naaman did, [when bowing unwillingly in an idol temple,] "The Lord be merciful unto me in this thing."' According to Robinson, Bernard assured them that despite rejecting Separatism he would never preach against it or dissuade anyone whose conscience drove them to it, and yet 'the very next Lord's day, or next but one, [he] taught publicly against it'.[9]

Smyth continued what he called 'the time of my doubting', but pressed arguments for Separatism on the others. He exchanged letters with Clifton, who argued for remaining, though Bernard criticised Smyth for picking a weak opponent. Robinson's tussles with 'those bonds of flesh and blood' persisted. Hildersham continued his precarious ministry in the Church of England, allowed to lecture in one diocese despite his deprivation in another, and supported by an aristocratic relative.[10]

Separation

Smyth defied his preaching ban from the pulpit of Basford, near Nottingham, on 19 February 1607, and doubtless other places, before returning to his followers in Gainsborough. Clifton, impressed by Smyth's example, occupied the church in the village of Bawtry twelve miles west of Gainsborough, and was excommunicated on 20 March. By April, Smyth had led his followers in founding a Separatist church in Gainsborough. As one of them, John Murton, described it, 'First one stood up and made a covenant, and then another, and these two joined together, and so a third, and these became a church.' Or as Bernard put it, Smyth 'was made minister by tradesmen'.[11]

Robinson finally submitted to 'the light of God' and to Smyth's arguments for Separatism, but was still impressed enough by the middle way that he insisted it must be acceptable to pray with godly people who remained in the Church of England, though not to join their services. Smyth preferred the all-or-nothing separation of Barrow and Johnson, and this was a big enough difference to stop Robinson joining Smyth's church, but small enough that they still called one another brothers. They made the Brownist covenant with God 'to walk in all his ways made known, or to be made known, unto them, according to their best endeavours, whatsoever it should cost them, the Lord assisting them'.[12]

Clifton and his followers also decided to separate, and at first planned to join Smyth's church, but they disagreed over some element of the church constitution. Clifton said Smyth broached 'opinions both erroneous and offensive'; Smyth said he had shown Clifton his faults and he had refused to reform, so he avoided that group as a corrupt, though true, church. Instead, Clifton joined Robinson in leading a Separatist church in Scrooby, a stop on the Great North Road neighbouring Bawtry.[13]

Bernard attempted the middle way. He led a hundred people in making a covenant, thirty of them from his own former parish of Worksop, eight miles south of Gainsborough. This covenant was not to be a Separatist church, it was to live holy lives, watch over one another, admonish each other and avoid unpreaching and sinful ministers. According to Robinson, Bernard later said that the purpose of the covenant was merely 'to keep [his] people from Mr Smyth'.[14]

The various London Separatist groups also gained recruits from the crisis. About thirty-six worshippers were arrested on 22 October 1608 in Finsbury, with their preacher Mr Trundle. This group quarrelled with other London Separatists, according to Christopher Lawne, who reported 'the manifold curses which the Brownists remaining in London have oft laid upon one another'.[15]

The Scrooby group following Clifton and Robinson met in the palatial manor house of William and Mary Brewster – which was owned by William's employer the Archbishop of York. William had been at Peterhouse, Cambridge, with Penry, then worked for the English ambassador to the Netherlands for twelve years. In 1590, he took over his father's job in Scrooby as the archbishop's bailiff-receiver and postmaster, and the house came with it. William and Mary underwent puritan conversions in the later 1590s, judging by the names of their children, their earlier son Jonathan being followed by Patience, Fear, Love and Wrestling.

This Scrooby conventicle was believed by Joseph Hall, chaplain to the Prince of Wales, to have 'made a secession, rather than a separation from our church', meeting separately rather than renouncing all connection. This, combined with the fact that Clifton had recently stood against Smyth's arguments for full-blooded Separatism, suggests that this group as well as Bernard's may perhaps have been attempting the middle way between Brownism and conformity. If so, neither sustained it.[16]

The Separatists, whatever the nuance of their position, were arrested and their houses raided. The Archbishop of York, Tobias

Matthew, started his visitation in July 1607 and imprisoned Joan Helwys, Thomas's wife, in York Castle. The couple had joined Smyth's church, and tended him at Broxtowe Hall through a bout of consumption. Thomas Helwys was also summoned to court, but evaded capture. On 10 September, the archbishop visited Bawtry, to preach against the Separatists and encourage coercive action. On 10 November, Gervase Nevill, another local gentleman, joined Joan Helwys in York Castle prison, having been convicted by Matthew as 'a very dangerous schismatical Separatist, Brownist and irreligious subject'.[17]

Conversely, the archbishop made an effort to woo Bernard, and persuaded him to submit. Bernard subscribed to Bancroft's articles and returned to his post and house in Worksop. Smyth was devastated and wrote Bernard a 14,000-word letter that worked through the theological reasons Bernard gave for his decision, before ending with a personal appeal to his friend:

> It grieveth my soul for you, to see you so strangely seduced by Satan ... I beseech you in the name of the Lord, look to yourself and search into this truth. I wonder you should not see it, it is clearer to me than noonday ... Consider that this truth prevaileth daily, and shall prevail ... God hath no need of you, you see he can work his work without you ... I write ... out of compassion and love to you, unto whom I wish so well.[18]

Sailing to the Netherlands

There was another way to escape from persecution, one which Bernard had himself been considering before he made his peace with the Church of England: to follow the footsteps of earlier Separatists into exile. 'Seeing themselves thus molested,' says Bradford, 'and that there was no hope of their continuance there, by a joint consent they resolved to go into the Low Countries, where they heard was freedom of religion for all men.'[19] Thomas Helwys was the main organiser and funder for the emigration of Smyth's Gainsborough group. According to Robinson, 'If any brought oars, he brought sails.' William Brewster did the same for the Scrooby church.[20]

The would-be exiles faced far greater difficulties than earlier Separatist migrants, however. The English establishment, by allowing Johnson's church to decamp to Amsterdam, had given it a vantage point from which to fire propaganda into England unmolested, and every year brought a new publication. So the authorities would not cooperate with the Separatists' plan, and from 1607 no traveller was supposed to leave the country without a licence; as Bradford put it, 'though they could not stay, yet were they not suffered to go'.[21]

All their preparations had to be kept secret. Clandestine arrangements were made to hire a large ship from the Lincolnshire port of Boston, for a hundred members of the Scrooby church. They had to pay over the odds and take their belongings on board under cover of darkness. The captain, having taken their money, then informed the constables, who arrested them, ransacked their cargo and searched their persons, confiscating books, money and other possessions. The migrants were imprisoned in Boston while the magistrates reported to the Privy Council and awaited instructions. They were released after a month, apart from seven of them, including Brewster, who were kept and eventually bound over to the assizes.

These events in Boston were cited by Bradford as one example of many betrayals in their attempts to leave. The future chronicler was now a seventeen-year-old member of the Scrooby congregation. Brought up by uncles after the death of his parents and grandparents, he shone at school but had to work on the family farm. He had been converted by Clifton at the age of twelve, but was the only member of his family to join the Brownist church, so he was leaving them behind to go to the Netherlands, or trying to.

William Brewster and Richard Jackson, also of Scrooby, failed to attend court on 1 December. The court issued a warrant for their arrest, but heard a fortnight later that the constable 'cannot find them, nor understand where they are'.[22]

In the spring of 1608, the Scrooby pilgrims tried again to make the crossing. Thinking they could expect more understanding from a Dutch captain, they found one in Hull who arranged to pick them up on the far side of the Humber estuary. The men travelled from Scrooby by land, the women and children by water with the luggage. The women arrived early and feeling seasick, so took their boat into a quiet creek to wait, where it got stuck in the mud. When the ship arrived, the captain sent a boat for the men and waited for the tide to free the women. While they were still stuck, a large crowd appeared on the shore in pursuit, armed with guns and halberds, on foot and horseback. The captain, Bradford remembered, 'swore his country's oath, "Sacrament"', and sailed away. The men left for the Netherlands without their families, possessions, or even a change of clothes.[23]

A violent, protracted storm took them way off course. For seven days, 'they saw neither sun, moon nor stars, and were driven near the coast of Norway'. At the worst point, according to Bradford, the sailors shrieked, 'We sink', while the Separatists, 'when the water ran into their mouth and ears', cried 'Yet Lord thou canst save', and indeed the ship survived the storm to arrive at Amsterdam.[24]

The women and children meanwhile had been arrested, but it was not practical to keep them all in prison. Even sending them home was a problem, as many had sold their houses. Eventually they were allowed to go and join the men. The Gainsborough church, including Thomas Helwys and Nevill, emigrated in the summer of 1608, though Joan Helwys stayed, and Smyth seems to have gone earlier.

On his arrival in Amsterdam, Bradford was arrested, after a fellow passenger reported him to the authorities as a fugitive from English justice. He explained the religious reasons for his flight, and the enlightened authorities released him.

Thomas White

While the Brownists in England faced such troubles from the religious establishment, those in the Netherlands created their own. In 1604, a Separatist group had come to Amsterdam from Slaughterford, Wiltshire, giving us one of those glimpses of English Separatist churches about which we otherwise know little. The twenty-five-year-old Vicar of St Nicholas, Slaughterford, Thomas White, had quit his post to lead the Separatist church there early in 1603, but the congregation was at least fifteen years old by then – Bredwell mentioned it in his attack on Browne, and Penry had asked the London church to write to them in one of his last letters. Johnson himself had visited and preached there in the house of Thomas and Ann Cullimer. White's successor at St Nicholas's, Thomas Powell, also joined the Separatists in February 1604. Members were arrested, including the weavers Silvester Butler and John Harford, who were interrogated by the Bishop of Salisbury. Twelve or thirteen Separatists escaped to Amsterdam, including White and Powell.

The newcomers joined Johnson's congregation, and White lodged at the Johnsons' house, but there was friction. It was not easy for leaders like White and Powell to become ordinary church members again, and Johnson did not make it any easier. White used a church meeting to accuse a fellow member, Robert Jackson, of sin, but Johnson and Studley told White that this was a private matter which he should have brought to the elders first, so he himself was guilty of 'evil walking'. Another controversy involved White tangentially: the member Robert Bayly had an affair with a married woman, and the church – urged on by White – ruled that adultery automatically ended a marriage so the spouses had to separate. Afterwards, three husbands and one wife, according to White, 'accused themselves of adultery, that so they might be rid of their spouses'. The farce made Johnson rethink his theology, but White opposed him.[25]

The newcomers decided to form a second church, in communion with Johnson's, led by White and Powell. Johnson was unhappy, arguing that true churches should not sit side by side in the same location. White and Powell said that two churches were better than one, and that they knew each other better than Johnson did. They also suggested that critics of the movement were saying Johnson had set himself up as a new bishop, and that separate churches would help counter that accusation. And so White and Johnson, like Smyth and Robinson, discovered that rare phenomenon: a difference between churches small enough that Brownists could live with it.

White married an excommunicated member of Johnson's church, the widow Rose Philips, in April 1604. Relations between the churches deteriorated and the Whites abandoned Separatism to rejoin the Church of England. Thomas's round trip – from Wiltshire vicar, to Separatist leader in England then Amsterdam, and back to the Church of England – had taken little more than a year. In 1605, he published a book called *A discoverie of Brownisme* in which he and Rose tried to dissuade people from joining the Brownists by cataloguing every story and allegation they could think of that discredited them: Bowman's embezzlement, Studley's incest, the apostasies of Ainsworth and Mercer and how the church changed its theology to accommodate them, adulteries, quarrels, excommunications, the Johnson family's strife, Francis's impatience and malice, and much more. They mentioned 'their savage and cruel dealing to fatherless children', including the children of 'Master P', possibly Penry. Just as the book was about to go to press, White heard that Thomas Canady, one of those who confessed adultery to be rid of his wife, 'hath lived in sodometry with his boy', and squeezed the news in.[26]

The book presented quite a catalogue of sin for a church that defined itself by its purity. Several Separatists, men and women, sued White for slander, and Johnson published *An Inqvirie and Ansvver of Thomas VVhite his Discoverie of Brovvnisme*, replying point to point to the allegations. He made quite a convincing case that White had misrepresented numerous incidents and had repeated rumours that the elders had investigated and found no truth in. Some cases that White reported, argued Johnson, were misdemeanours that the elders had dealt with rightly – either the sinner had repented or had been excommunicated and returned unrepentant to the indulgent bosom of White's Church of England. In one instance, White accused the Brownists of heresy for a teaching they no longer held and of which White himself had been a leading proponent. Often though, Johnson was content to point out White's failure to prove accusations against the church, an attitude that fell short of convincing readers there was no substance to the claims. White was arrested in Amsterdam, on the initiative of Johnson and Ainsworth, but brought witnesses to the burgomasters to support his accusations and was discharged on 24 February 1506. According to one disputed report, Johnson and Ainsworth had to pay costs.

The Slaughterford church continued for a while, and more weavers and wives were interrogated by the archdeacon in October 1605. In 1609, White became Rector of St Mary Woolnoth in London (which 170 years later would become John Newton's church) and died two years later.

The Ancient Church

On the arrival of the churches from Gainsborough and Scrooby, Johnson's church became known as the Ancient Church, being able to trace its history twenty years back to Barrow and Greenwood's day. One member more ancient than most, unnamed, had a Separatist history of more than thirty years, having belonged to the Fitz church in the 1570s and seen Bolton's dead body. They were also joined by Edward Tolwine, who had been prevented from joining Browne in exile fifteen years before, and finally fulfilled his ambition.

Despite its strife, the Ancient Church had grown to about 300 members, with four elders besides its two ministers, three deacons and an elderly deaconess who sat 'with a little birchen rod in her hand and kept little children in great awe from disturbing the congregation'. The new arrivals numbered about 150 and the question arose of whether they should all merge into a superchurch. Johnson had argued for it in White's day, but perhaps the experience of having insubordinate former ministers in his church had made him wiser. Robinson also felt, despite 'their beauty and order', his disagreement with the Ancient Church and Smyth over private prayer with non-Separatists should keep them apart.[27]

Smyth then came up with a more far-reaching disagreement with the Ancient Church. Having a number of former ministers in his church, it had never seemed right to him that they should forsake their gifts to become ordinary members and backseat drivers. Rather than fighting them for power like Johnson, Smyth wanted to share it. He argued, convincingly, that when the New Testament referred to ministers, pastors, teachers, elders, bishops, etc., it was using different names for the same job, so the presbyterian tradition of having one pastor, one teacher and a plurality of lay elders was unbiblical. Instead, Smyth's church had several ministers and no lay elders. Smyth also took a leaf out of Browne's book in recognising the church body as the ultimate decision maker, relinquishing the power of the elders over the people. He urged these patterns on the Ancient Church, who disagreed. Under Johnson and Studley, the church had become less democratic in practice than in Browne and Barrow's

265

days, though retaining the same structure, so they were not about to embrace democratic reform. Johnson's church then found themselves in the novel position of being accused of refusing biblical reformation in favour of popish traditions.

Individually, members of the Ancient Church were still struggling for money, but as a congregation they amassed the funds to start constructing their own building on Lange Houtstraat early in 1607. The Dutch Consistory complained to the town authorities about this, to no avail. Then on 16 March a storm destroyed the unfinished building – leaving every other building in the area untouched, according to the gleeful description of the puritan John Paget.

Like so many migrants before and since, the newcomers found themselves surrounded by eye-popping wealth while having to work desperately hard learning new skills just to put food on the table. Bradford, who himself became a clothmaker, said, 'It was not long before they saw the grim and grisly face of poverty coming upon them like an armed man.' Eventually, he says, most earned a reasonable living, 'but with hard and continual labour'.[28]

Ainsworth's books

Vloomburg, where the Separatists lived and worshipped, was a cheap part of Amsterdam outside the walls, an artificial island created in the docklands of the Amstel in the previous decade for the purpose of storing wood. It had become home to Anabaptists, and to the city's 500 Jews, the Beth Jacob synagogue being founded there in 1602 by those driven out of Portugal by the Inquisition. This gave the English a rare opportunity, for those who would take it, to consult Jews about the Hebrew language in order to better understand the Old Testament, Jews being banned from England. Ainsworth and Slade both became experts in Hebrew, but for now the man who made the most of the opportunity was Hugh Broughton, the minister of the Merchant Adventurers, who often came from Middelburg to Amsterdam for the purpose. Broughton was an ardent evangelist to Jews and used his conversations to debate with them as well as to learn.

Broughton had written a book in 1604 to persuade King James that the Bishops' Bible needed revision because of inaccuracies in the Old Testament, and when James commissioned the Authorised Version, Broughton was bitterly disappointed not to join the translators. Ainsworth wrote to Broughton disputing one of the inaccuracies that Broughton had alleged, a question of whether Aaron's ephod contained wool or silk. Broughton replied with a bad-tempered series of letters, mocking Ainsworth's lack of learning and the fact that he wrote by hand instead of paying a printer.

Happily for Ainsworth, a member of the Ancient Church, Giles Thorp, then set up his own press and successfully produced a stream of books for the Separatists. In 1607 he printed Ainsworth's first solo work, *The communion of saincts*, which argued that the true church is a holy community while a church that incorporates the entire population is neither holy nor a community. That same year, on 29 April, Ainsworth married Marjory Appelbey, a widow from Ipswich with one daughter.

Another new English church opened in Amsterdam on 2 February 1607. This was an English-language branch of the Dutch Reformed Church, planted on the recommendation of Matthew Slade, in deliberate competition with the burgeoning Brownist congregations. Allis Slade, Matthew's wife, became a member, though Matthew himself never did. Thomas White hoped to become the minister, but Slade blocked the appointment; Broughton was approached but declined. The minister appointed was John Paget, who had been ejected from St Mary's, Nantwich, for nonconformity in 1604, and was another keen Hebraist.

A book arrived in Amsterdam from England in 1607 that gave Ainsworth and Thorp another chance to hone their skills. It was written by John Sprint, the puritan minister of Thornbury, in Gloucestershire, who had been persuaded to subscribe to Bancroft's articles. Ainsworth considered Sprint's argument 'the sum and weight of that which may be said for that church', and responded to it in a book called *Covnterpoyson*.[29]

Covnterpoyson contained perhaps the most compelling apologia that the Separatist movement ever produced. Sprint argued that he and his fellow puritans rejected and avoided the faults of the Church of

England as well as any Brownist, so Brownism was a dangerous over-reaction. Puritans had achieved the middle way between conformity and Separatism, removing themselves from the evils of the church without quitting it, and this made Separatism unnecessary. 'A separation we deny not', said Sprint, 'from the corruptions of the church wherein we live ... But the difference is, we suffer for separating in the church: you, out of the church.'[30]

Ainsworth told Sprint that this was the supreme example of puritans accepting the logic of Separatism but baulking at the action. The four great faults that made the Separatists quit the Church of England had all first been identified by puritans – non-Christian membership, antichristian worship, popish ministry and unbiblical hierarchy. Ainsworth quoted violent condemnation of these things from classic puritan texts such as *An Admonition to the Parliament*, which said 'there can be no right religion' while they continue. 'Thus have we been taught by yourselves ... and now you have added unto all the former to teach us a separation from your corruptions.' But what separation from episcopacy is there among those ordained by bishops? What separation from the faults of the Prayer Book among those who signed Bancroft's articles? And, if Sprint and friends had separated from the membership, worship, ministry and hierarchy of the Church of England, Ainsworth asked, what would that leave for them to join with? Separatists practised consistently what the puritans preached, he said, and yet Sprint called them 'the seduced brethren': 'Are not you then the seducers?' Their middle way was to know the truth but not to do it.[31]

Sprint also walked into difficulty using the troubled history of Separatism to discredit it. First, Bolton hanged himself. 'And so did Judas,' replied Ainsworth, 'one of the first and principal publishers of Christ's Gospel. Will you therefore call Christianity into question for it?' Second, said Sprint, Browne apostatised; Ainsworth had plenty of parallels to that story too. Then Sprint lumped together with such losses the Brownists' sufferings for their faith: Barrow, Greenwood and Penry were hanged; 'And', said Ainsworth, 'so was Christ himself.' Fourth, Johnson et al. were banished; so was the apostle John. Expecting some such defence of their losses, Sprint noted that the Brownists were sentenced and punished not by antichristians but by a Reformed Christian government. Ainsworth retorted that Christ was executed

> not by heathen tyrants (for Pilate washed his hands of his blood), but by priests, scribes, and Pharisees, professing and maintaining the religion of God, as your church now doeth. And you that allege the hanging of these men to reproach our faith: it is probable that if you had then lived, you would have reproached Christ himself.[32]

The area where Sprint did hurt Ainsworth was the Brownists' relationship with other Reformed churches. When Sprint argued that the Church of England was accepted by other Reformed churches, Ainsworth replied robustly: churches can err, only God's approval counts; Sprint's argument was the same one Catholics used against Protestants; 'the Jews objected as weighty an argument against Christ himself, when they said, "Doth any of the rulers or of the Pharisees believe in him[?]"' But all of his arguments accepted the premise, unavoidable since the Junius affair, that the Brownists had been cut adrift by the international Reformed communion. However confident they were in their rightness, they were uncomfortably alone in it.[33]

Similarly, Sprint cited against the Separatists Barrow's railing at Calvin. Ainsworth's reply to this was revealing. He cautiously defended the bitter tone of the great martyr, and found no fault in the content of Barrow's attack: he was making 'severe speeches in a good cause', the sharpness his but the truth God's. And yet Ainsworth had the discretion not to directly mention Calvin at all or to repeat Barrow's denunciation. This was the bind that the Brownists found themselves in with respect to Calvinism: they could not face the thought that they were Separatists from the international Reformed communion, but they could not deny that that communion was guilty of faults that they abhorred in the Church of England.[34]

Just as Ainsworth thought he was at the end of his book, in 1608, another anti-Separatist tract arrived, this from none other than Richard Bernard, erstwhile fellow traveller of Smyth and Robinson. Ainsworth, Smyth and Robinson all wrote replies, Ainsworth extending *Covnterpoyson* for the purpose.

Bernard set out seven 'probabilities' that Brownism was a false path, such as 'the novelty of it' and 'the ill success it hath had'. He then offered three more solid 'reasons': the evil of shunning godly ministers in the Church of England; the sins of the Brownists, including their ingratitude to the church that bore them and the harshness of Barrow's polemic; and their errors, including their condemnation of the church's constitution and their own 'democratical and popular' structure.

Ainsworth answered Bernard's writing point by point, while dismissing it as lacking 'weight of reason'. Smyth and Robinson felt Bernard's attack more personally and both responded with their own books. Smyth's *Paralleles, Censures, Observations* took him a year to finish, and though it focused on Bernard's arguments, Smyth allowed himself one personal explosion:

> The Prelate of York hath so bewitched you with his flattery, eloquence and angels [gold coins], that your covenant is profaned and cast in the dust … I do therefore proclaim you unto the whole land to be one of the most fearful apostates of the whole nation, that excepting Whyte and Clapham, you have no superior nor equal … You are as changeable as the moon, as mutable as Proteus, as variable as the chameleon.[35]

Robinson's book took even longer, weighing in at almost 500 pages when it finally came out in 1610. Even by the time of Smyth's book though, the argument was already out of date as Smyth had, with one action, completely changed the landscape of Separatism.

25

'The quicksands of Anabaptistry'

DISAGREEMENTS STARTED TO break out between the three Amsterdam Brownist churches as soon as they were sharing a city. The first argument was over the different leadership structure of Smyth's church, but he soon provided a much stranger one: his church banned the Bible from worship. Smyth argued that the Brownists had long ago excluded written prayers, because true worship was 'pouring forth our heart'. In the same way, he said, if a preacher reads from the Bible, he quenches the spirit – the spontaneity and emotional engagement of worship – with words on a page. And because the words are in translation, the preacher is bringing human invention between worshippers and God. The proper time to read from Scripture, Smyth said, is in church business meetings and in one's own studies. In worship and preaching, we should draw on it spontaneously from memory.[1]

Smyth argued for this new idea in *The Differences of the Churches of the Separation*, which he published in 1608. Reading during worship, he said, whether for liturgy, preaching or hymn-singing, was 'the invention of the man of sin'. He also set out his different understanding of the structure of the church: lay elders were anti-christian, 'the presbytery of the church is uniform'. He reiterated the democratic principle of Brownism, which the Ancient Church had somewhat cooled towards: 'The Presbytery has no power, but what the church hath and giveth unto it: which the church upon just cause can take away.' Smyth found another difference too: the financial giving of church members should be separate from the money of unbelievers, just like other parts of the church are separate from the world. This does not mean, as Thomas Helwys took care to clarify in a letter home, that they refused donations

271

from puritan wellwishers, but they 'do not sanctify their alms with prayer'.[2]

Ainsworth responded to Smyth's book, defending the authority of the elders. Smyth replied combatively that the hierarchy of the Ancient Church usurped the power Christ gave to the whole body; it was an inheritance from Rome and 'one part of the Antichristianism in your church'.[3]

There was plenty to fight over in Smyth's innovations, especially for people as theologically trigger-happy as the Separatists, but the greatest significance, in retrospect, was not in Smyth's ideas but in how he justified them. One argument against book worship that Smyth came up with in writing *The Differences of the Churches* had tremendous resonance for him, became central to his thinking, and had a huge influence on the future of the movement. Book worship belonged to the Old Testament, he said, because the old covenant between God and Israel was essentially physical, consisting of ceremonies; the new covenant is spiritual, so its worship is quite different. Smyth was putting a gulf between the Old and New Testaments. The point of the old covenant was to foreshadow, in concrete symbols, the more spiritual religion of the new covenant. Now that spiritual religion has come, to maintain the old ways is to worship an idol, to 'make the New Testament, the Old Testament: and abolish Christ, and set up Judaism again'.[4]

It is a general pattern in the Reformation that the further left one looks, the greater priority was given to the New Testament over the Old. Zwingli, for example, argued against priesthood, telling Catholics that the Old Testament priesthood is only a shadow of the spiritual work of Christ. And then when Zwingli was faced with the even greater radicalism of the Anabaptists, who argued that the Old Testament state church was only a shadow of the gathered church of Christ, he reverted to more conservative thought, rediscovering the unity of the covenants: 'We are in the one covenant that God made with Abraham.'[5]

As the radicals of the English Reformation, Browne and Barrow argued against following the Old Testament literally. The gulf they saw between the two covenants was not between law and grace – they were too legalistic themselves to think like that and, indeed, saw Christ as a lawmaker. Rather, the dichotomy was between ceremony and spirit, driven by their hatred of ritual. This allowed them to discount many inconvenient precedents of Old Testament religion: reforming kings, altars, holy days, tithes, and, of course, priestly vest-ments. All these, they said, had spiritual not literal equivalents in Christianity. Smyth followed their line but took it further. He was about to take it much further still.

The first Baptist

In January 1509, Smyth and his followers, about forty in number, came to the conclusion that babies should not and could not be baptised into the church. All infant baptism was counterfeit, an antichristian initiation rite into a false church. Any church that practised it, from the second generation of Christians in ancient Rome to the Ancient Church of Amsterdam and London, was a non-church. Anyone who had received it was an unbaptised non-Christian who needed to be baptised properly if they were to be saved.

This new conclusion presented Smyth and his church with a big problem. They needed to be baptised into the true church, but where was there a church to be baptised into, or a person able to baptise them into it? The only people in the world who practised believers' baptism were the Anabaptists. Smyth could no longer see them as the alien monsters he had been brought up to hate and fear, and there were Anabaptists on hand in the neighbourhood; but though they were right about baptism, Anabaptists were wrong about other things: that the state was unchristian, for example, or that Christ got his flesh from heaven not Mary. Smyth had no one to baptise him.

When the first Anabaptists had faced the same predicament in January 1525, they baptised one another. Smyth's answer was dif-ferent: he baptised himself. In January 1609, the Smyth church met and dissolved itself as having been an antichristian false church. They did not open with prayer, as no unbaptised person had a right to lead public prayers. As Robinson heard it, there was 'some straining of courtesy who should begin', then Smyth baptised himself. He baptised Helwys next, and then the rest of the group.[6]

Other Separatists were horrified. Johnson said it was 'a case woeful and lamentable', while Ainsworth called Smyth a heretic and antichrist, who had gone 'from error to error, and now at last to the abomination of Anabaptism', which 'in him was the worship ... of the devil'. Clifton said, 'he hath destroyed the faith, is become an enemy to the covenant of grace and a perverter of the right ways of the Lord'. Robinson was less ferocious, but considered the innovation a dangerous error which 'cannot but gender many monsters'.[7]

Robinson had no taste for the ensuing fight. His hundred-strong congregation had been disheartened by the churches' internecine conflicts since their arrival, and were now dismayed by this escalation. Robinson wanted to stay on friendly terms with fellow radicals so far as possible, and decided the best way to do that was not to be around them. In April 1609, his church extended its pilgrimage to Leiden, to escape 'the flames of contention ...', as Bradford put it, 'though they well knew it would be much to the prejudice of their outward estates'.[8]

Leiden was an industrial town built on fulling English wool, with bleaching clay smuggled from England, and producing cloth, and many members learned those skills. William Brewster had struggled for money in Amsterdam – Bradford explains that his upbringing had made him unfit for manual labour – but now that they were in a university town, he made a decent living teaching English to students. Brewster was appointed elder to the church. Clifton did not make the journey, but joined the Ancient Church instead. Robinson took out a mortgage on a large house called Groene Poort (Green Gate) in Kloksteeg, near St Peter's Church, where he built houses in the garden for church members.

Where had Smyth's new extreme of Separatist radicalism come from? It is possible that in embracing believers' baptism he was influenced in some degree by local Anabaptists, but there is no positive evidence for this and even in 1609 Smyth still considered them 'false churches' and 'heretics or antichristians'. This question was widely debated by twentieth-century writers, but B.R. White in 1971 showed that the garbled account of Anabaptist beliefs Smyth wrote after his baptism ruled out close contact with their ideas.[9]

In fact, there were, as White recognised, such strong implications of believers' baptism in Separatist thinking that no Anabaptist influence was necessary in order for Smyth to take Brownism to its logical conclusion. The question of infant baptism was essentially about whom to let into church – the question that had become the fundamental point of the Brownists' separation. The true church for them was voluntary, requiring choice and commitment, faith and Christian life from every member. If entry to the church requires all this, it is not obvious how babies qualify.

So, for example, Barrow said it was 'confirmed through the whole Bible from the beginning to the end ... [that] none [enter] into Christ's church but by a voluntary profession of their true faith and obedience'. Taken at face value, this only applies to adults and so is pure Anabaptistry.[10]

What the Separatists actually meant by such apparently Anabaptist statements is that membership and baptism belong only to obedient believers and their children. The coda 'and their seed' was a refrain throughout their writings as a guard against Anabaptism – though Barrow omitted it in the quotation above, so the guard could slip. Even when they explicitly stated it though, one can still see a drift towards believers' baptism. Barrow said:

> We hold that only such as voluntarily make a true profession of faith, and vow of their obedience, and as in the same faith and obedience seek the communion and fellowship of the faithful, are to be received as members into the church. And that only children of such by one parent are to be baptised.

The second sentence reads like an afterthought, Barrow first insisting on membership criteria that only adults fulfil, before adding that their children are also included. It separates 'receiving as members' from baptism, despite the fact that in theory they are the same thing. It raises the question: why not restrict membership to those who actually fulfil the criteria, only extending it to their seed when they come to fulfil the criteria themselves?[11]

This is a question worth answering. If believers' baptism is such a logical corollary of Separatists' vision of the church, why did most Separatists other than Smyth and Helwys recoil so violently from it?

One answer is simply the horror of the word 'Anabaptist', which evoked not merely a heresy but an incomprehensible world of destructive insanity, comparable to 'Islamic fundamentalist' and 'communist' in other times and places. It required serious intellectual courage for Smyth to leap into those icy waters.

A more positive reason for rejecting believers' baptism was that it clashed with Brownists' experience of church community. Brownists were driven by what M.M. Knappen called, paradoxically, 'collectivist individualism': because they required each church member to qualify individually, they enjoyed a powerful sense of like-minded community that the all-inclusive parish could not offer. It would seem strange, impoverishing and unnatural for those same rules to exclude their children from their community.[12]

A third reason is that the Brownists desperately wanted to see themselves as the purest and most advanced wing of the international fellowship of Reformed churches, not as separate from it or shunned by it. The Anabaptists were unambiguously beyond that pale, and now, having rejected the baptism performed by all Reformed churches, so were Smyth's Baptists.

Defending believers' baptism

The first person to cross swords with Smyth over his Baptist teaching was Richard Clifton. Smyth sent Clifton a one-page summary of his new position, arguing first that baptism in the New Testament is only of believers, and second that those baptised as babies must be properly baptised now. The pair of them then exchanged letters, circling around the inconclusive biblical evidence for and against infant baptism.

At the heart of the argument were their ideas of covenant: Israelite children, said Clifton, were circumcised into the old covenant; Christian children are baptised into the new. Why would the covenant of Christ be meaner? Smyth replied that the New Testament is better by being spiritual, and spiritual babies – born-again believers – are to be baptised into it.

Smyth published these letters in April 1609 under the title *The Character of the Beast*, with an introduction defending himself from the charge of inconstancy. It was only slowly, as Smyth prepared the correspondence for publication, that he realised that he had a more devastating argument against his former friends' position.

Smyth's new argument was that when someone is purportedly baptised, there are two possibilities: they receive Christian baptism into the church of Christ, or they receive antichristian baptism into the church of antichrist. In the latter case, if they realise their mistake and come to Christian faith, it follows that they must now, like the Baptists, enter the church through baptism. The Brownists, he pointed out, had renounced the Church of England as a false church that practised antichristian baptism. They quit it, but never reattempted baptism, which, he said, left them in a completely inconsistent position. Either they must accept that they are unbaptised and undergo rebaptism; or they must accept that they were baptised truly at birth into a Christian church, in which case they had made a terrible mistake in leaving it. 'The separation must either go back to England, or go forward to true baptism.'[13]

Smyth set this argument out in the introduction he added to *The Character of the Beast* before publishing it. In it he also defended himself from the charge of having become an Anabaptist, setting out the ways in which he disagreed with what he thought they taught.

The argument from rebaptism would in time prove to be a body blow to Brownism, but historians have also attributed to it an influence it never had. B.R. White, and others following him, argued that doubting the validity of baptism received in 'the apostate Church of England' was the main factor that led Smyth to conclude that 'baptism should be for believers only'. There are two problems with this. The first is that it is a *non sequitur*: there is no logical link from doubting the baptism of an apostate church to embracing believers' baptism. If Smyth's starting point was that all antichristian baptism needed to be repeated, then his church could have rebaptised themselves and then carried on baptising babies; there was no reason for them to become Baptists. The second problem with the theory is that it does not follow the order of Smyth's writing. Immediately after his conversion, the arguments Smyth put to Clifton were all against baptising babies, not against baptism in apostasy; even his argument for rebaptism is based on the premise that infant baptism is invalid. Smyth was first converted to believers' baptism, and only later, in writing the introduction to the letters, did he develop the argument that the Brownists' baptisms were invalid by their own logic.[14]

Francis Johnson published a reply to Smyth's Baptist arguments in *A brief Treatise Containing Some Grounds and Reasons against two Errours of the Anabaptists,* a genuinely brief book. He explained, easily enough, the reasons why Separatists baptised their infants, the key being continuity between circumcision and baptism. The newer question of rebaptism though, Johnson found seriously disconcerting. He and Ainsworth had set out in their 1604 petition to the king their justification for denouncing the church's false baptism without having a second washing. Their argument followed Barrow's in *A Brief Discoverie* and was unconvincing and inconsistent (explicitly both affirming and denying that the Church of England's baptism left one with 'a true outward sacrament'). Now Johnson abandoned that line and simply argued that God's covenant with the church is not conditional on obedience: 'The covenant of God's grace in Christ is an everlasting covenant' continuing to apostate churches, so their baptism is from the Lord.[15]

The conditional covenant, so vital to the Separatist thinking of Browne and Barrow, had never been quite as important to Johnson or Ainsworth, but now Johnson was urgently retreating from it, and in so doing caused further problems for the Separatist movement. Readers of Johnson's latest book had good reason to ask, if apostate churches remain within God's covenant, then on what basis does anyone separate from them?

26

Against Calvin

IN 1610 JOHN Robinson at last completed his rejoinder to Richard Bernard's anti-Separatist book, two years after Ainsworth's and a year after Smyth's. *A Justification of Separation* was intended to offer a more exhaustive refutation of Bernard's arguments than Smyth and Ainsworth had provided, while picking his fellow Separatists up on a couple of points. Robinson's book was finally at the printer's when a second book by Bernard arrived, so Robinson stopped the press to expand his book in response, finally reaching 483 pages.

However much Robinson may once have been drawn to the idea of a middle way between Separatism and conformity, he was now a thoroughly convinced Separatist, repeating their many familiar arguments. Robinson also vigorously defended freedom of religion against Bernard's conformist polemic, with compelling echoes of Robert Browne. Bernard had condemned 'the silly Brownists' for advocating voluntary religion. Robinson pointed out that the apostles founded churches not by passing laws but by persuading people to join. Anyone who professes a religion, said Robinson, does so either willingly or against their will. If the profession is forced, it is insincere and untrue; so all true and sincere religion is voluntary. Would Bernard really 'have men involuntary professors against their wills'? Nicely, Robinson asked Bernard whether he had signed his submission to the bishop voluntarily. If not, he must have 'a treacherous disposition'; if he did, then what was wrong with the Brownists saying true religion is voluntary? 'The nature of religion is not to be constrained, but persuaded.'[1]

In a striking example of Robinson's irenic nature, he constantly referred to Smyth as a friend and fellow believer. Robinson took Smyth's side against Bernard, defending most of his arguments, even rebuking Bernard for censuring Smyth's 'unstableness'. Uniquely among the Brownists, Robinson's fraternal attitude had survived Smyth's Baptist conversion. Robinson preferred to minimise the differences of the churches of the separation, defending the sound arguments of the former Brownist without demonising him for his more recent errors.

Arminiamism

The Brownists had come to a country at war, and though they were far from the fighting, still they were impressed by the sight of soldiers and armaments around Amsterdam and Leiden. But on 9 April 1609, Spain and the Netherlands agreed the twelve-year Truce of Antwerp. Then, within a year, the Netherlands was split by bitter theological conflict.

Leiden, where the Robinson church had gone to escape the flames of contention, was the centre of the controversy seizing the Dutch Church. The death of Arminius in October 1609 intensified the disputes around his teaching on predestination, and he was succeeded as Professor of Theology by Conrad Vorstius – a man so outspoken on the subject that King James burned his books at St Paul's and pressurised the Dutch into firing him.

The Arminians had the support of the Land's Advocate of Holland, Johan van Oldenbarnevelt, and in 1610 wrote a 'remonstrance' stating their position in five articles and asking the government to resolve the question. The government of Holland declared Arminianism orthodox, but traditionalists insisted that the church, not the state, should decide theological questions. The traditionalists delivered their counter-remonstrance – the original of what became 'the five points of Calvinism' – to a conference organised by the States General of the Netherlands. Agreement proved impossible between the two sides, the remonstrants and contraremonstrants; both documents were published, and debate split the country. To its opponents Arminianism seemed like a compromise with Catholicism, one year into the Spanish truce. As a theological question, today the predestination dispute sounds as esoteric as they come, but it had resonance with burning questions of self-determination and rights, as well as church and state, and became one of the most divisive faultlines in Protestantism for many generations to come.

The Waterlanders

The Baptist church moved into a new building in 1609 or early 1610. This was hardly a purpose-built meeting house such as the Ancient Church enjoyed; it was a former biscuit factory. The twelve-chimneyed Grote Backhuys (Great Bakehouse), just across the river from Vloomburg, had supplied trading ships bound for India, but production ceased in 1603 and it served as an arsenal before it was bought by the wealthy Anabaptist merchant Jan Munter. The factory area was divided into three halls, with a dozen cottages behind it originally built for apprentices. Munter offered the cottages to Anabaptists in need and to the English Baptists.

Smyth's group were granted church premises by Anabaptists because they had become friendly since their conversion to believers' baptism. Like the majority of Amsterdam Anabaptists, these were Waterlanders, a Mennonite grouping named after the Waterland area of Holland, to the north of Amsterdam. After the catastrophe of Münster, Menno Simons had emerged as the leader of Anabaptist renewal, insisting on peaceful separation from the world. In the 1550s, the Mennonites divided over the question of relations with outsiders and the excommunicated, the Waterlanders taking the most moderate position, allowing marriage to unbelievers, and broke with more stringent Mennonite churches.

Though there were still differences between the Baptists and the Mennonites, the common ground they now shared allowed the English to cut through the mythology and horror stories to find rational people rather than monsters. Language remained a barrier – a meeting between Helwys and the Anabaptists was abandoned when neither side could make itself understood – but with the help of Latin the two churches managed a fair amount of communication.

In fact, their communication seems to have been sophisticated enough to propel Smyth's church into their second radical change of theology in a year, as the Baptists abandoned the doctrine of pre-destination. The Baptists came to the conclusion that, in Helwys's words, 'God hath [not] predestinated men to be wicked, and so to be damned ... for God would have all men saved ... and wills not the death of him that dies.'[2]

As this affirmation of free will was also a teaching of the Ana-baptists, the timing of the change suggests Anabaptist influence, and Helwys confirmed this in thanking the Waterlanders for 'discovering divers of our errors unto us'. The prominence of the remonstrant controversy also helped to draw their attention to the question. But the way had been prepared by the Brownists' insistence that Christi-anity is essentially voluntary: if earthly justice must observe freedom of religion, it seems more likely that divine justice also observes it. Their conversion was also made easier by their alienation from the Reformed tradition – in their arguments about the gathered church, in Barrow's attack on Calvin, in their unhappy experiences with the Dutch Reformed Church and in the Junius affair. Smyth, before his Baptist conversion, was particularly forthright in accepting the Separatists' isolation: 'From some (such as are the English churches) we separate for the falsehood of them ... from other (such as are the Reformed churches) we separate not for that they are false, but for that being true they are corrupt ... if they repent not we leave them to the Lord.'[3] Later, the church's rebaptisms put them com-pletely beyond the Calvinist pale, giving them less reason than ever to respect the Reformed consensus on controversial matters. In the Dutch debate, opponents of Arminius framed their position as stand-ing 'with the Reformed churches' or against them, and the Baptists found themselves free to stand against.

Some of the Baptists embraced the Mennonite teaching that Christ grew in Mary's womb without taking her flesh. Smyth and Helwys rejected this idea, and, according to Clifton, those who accepted it quit the church, forming the second English Baptist church.

The Baptists' sense of disinheritance from the Reformed family made them keener to accept Anabaptist ideas, so that they could join a new family. It came as a profound relief to the Baptists to discover they had spiritual kin after all. Despite their confidence in their ability to mine the truth from Scripture that had eluded everyone but their own little band for one and a half thousand years, it was easier when they met fellow travellers.

Helwys versus Smyth

Unfortunately, finding fellowship with the Anabaptists also raised a new problem for the Baptists. Smyth had baptised himself believing that such an extraordinary measure was necessary because there was no one else to do it. But if the Anabaptists were true Christians, had he rejected a true church by failing to ask them for baptism? Was his self-baptism unnecessary and therefore illegitimate? Smyth had told the Brownists that true baptism makes a true church, so if even the Church of Rome had kept believers' baptism it would have been wrong to split from it. But in that case, how could the Baptists justify spurning the Mennonites? Smyth concluded that in trying to baptise himself, when he could have walked half a mile for true baptism, he had made another serious mistake. He decided to join the Water-lander church and, presumably, to be re-rebaptised.

This was the issue on which Helwys drew the line and refused to follow Smyth. He accused Smyth of resurrecting the Catholic notion of succession, according to which priests can administer valid sacraments because their ordination goes back in an unbroken institutional line to the apostles. That, said Helwys, was how priesthood worked in the Old Testament, but, as Smyth had taught him, the New Testament was different. Believers today receive their validation directly from Christ. John the Baptist baptised believers, argued Helwys, without having been baptised himself, 'and whosoever shall now be stirred up by the same Spirit' may do the same.[4]

Helwys failed to dissuade Smyth from his course, and so excommunicated him as an impenitent sinner, along with everyone who stayed with him. It was a bold move, because Smyth's group was the large majority. About ten people stayed with Helwys.

Smyth's group applied to join the Waterlanders early in 1610, while Helwys urged the Waterlanders to refuse them. Just as Johnson had appealed to the Dutch Reformed Church, in would-be fraternal tones, not to welcome people the Brownists excluded from communion, Helwys warned the Waterlanders, as 'dearest brothers', 'do not receive such things by which you may be defiled'. Writing them one letter in Latin in order to be understood, and one in English in order to say what he meant, Helwys argued that to receive Smyth would be to accept his error that succession made it necessary. It would mean claiming a better right to baptise than their fellow Christians, ascribing powers to their ministers that ordinary Christians do not share: 'How dare any man or men challenge [i.e. claim for] themselves a pre-eminence therein, as if the Spirit of God was only in their hearts and the word of God only to be fetched at their mouths and the ordinances of God only to be had from their hands.'[5]

In these two letters, Helwys emerges in his own voice for the first time. He proved himself an even more radical thinker than Smyth, with his contention that Christ gives the right to baptise believers to all Christians equally. Where Smyth had revived the egalitarian spirit of Browne with a vengeance, Helwys was taking it even further.

On the Waterlanders' request, Smyth wrote a statement of faith in Latin to support his application. He clearly wanted to show that the Baptists were a good match for the Mennonites, agreeing with them on virtually all their distinctive teachings. The confession focused mainly on denying Calvinist predestination, then considered Anabaptist thinking on justification by faith. The Mennonites accepted this Protestant doctrine but thought the magisterial reformers had overplayed it, so they tried to restore works to the equation too. In the words of Smyth's confession, 'faith, destitute of good works, is vain'. Smyth said that the sacraments are symbolic and that baptism is not for children, and affirmed the Waterlanders' milder understanding of Mennonite excommunication.[6]

There were areas of theology in which Smyth's group were perhaps not prepared to go all the way with the Mennonites. The confession made no mention of pacifism or working for the state, and it fudged the question of whether Christ grew in Mary's womb without taking her flesh. As Smyth said later, 'the scriptures do not lead us (as far as I can conceive) to the searching of that point'. There were members of Smyth's group though who disagreed even with this equivocation, and left to form a third Baptist church led by Leonard Busher, a former London grocer. In 1612, Christopher Lawne mentioned a fourth Baptist church, which failed the 'where two or three are gathered together' bar, in that John Hancock had 'a separation by himself'.[7]

Helwys presented his own statement of faith to the Waterlanders, showing that his church was a true one with the authority to excommunicate Smyth's group, and challenging Smyth's teaching. Helwys highlighted their common ground on baptism and free will, but affirmed justification by faith alone and that Christ took his flesh from his mother. The confession said that the church delegates its power and authority to elders, whom it appoints and removes.

The Waterlander church warmed to Smyth's application, but decided to consult the wider Mennonite fellowship before admitting his group. The Waterlanders were part of the Bevredigde Broederschap (Conciliated Brotherhood), a union of Dutch Mennonites including High Germans and Frisians. It was a diverse and somewhat unstable union of autonomous congregations in which the Waterlanders were the most liberal, and they did not want to do anything to cause a rupture with stricter churches. So a Waterlander minister, Lubbert Gerritsz, wrote around the other ministers, inviting them to a meeting with the Smyth group on 23 May 1610. Most were unenthusiastic. With their history of divergence, their many conferences for union had generally proved frustrating and futile.

In the end, only two representatives agreed to attend the meeting. The result was inconclusive, the visitors reluctant to make a controversial decision without wider consent. Having begun the consultation though, the Amsterdam Waterlanders were now stuck. If they unilaterally accepted the Smyth group, after making it a matter of consultation and debate, there would be an even greater danger of breaking the Broederschap. So they wrote urging the others to engage with the question or give them leave to make their own decision, but the ministers of Leeuwarden replied warning that union with the English might cause the 'ruin, harm, hurt and perdition' of the Broederschap. Helwys, at least, was happy to see his former friends' application fail, which he said would have 'strengthened them in their evil'.[8]

Smyth's group continued to worship with the Waterlanders, but as outsiders, condemned to wander in a churchless wilderness, having escaped the Egypt of the English false churches – including their own – but found no entry into the Promised Land. Even in the Waterlander services they were lost, said Helwys, and 'gaze at [those] who speak to them in a strange tongue'.[9]

27

'Tell the church'

CLIFTON PUBLISHED HIS reply to Smyth's *The Character of the Beast* in 1610, but it was a less-than-compelling case. Clifton made the most of Smyth's isolation, pointing out that what Smyth called a dispute between the Baptists and Brownists was in fact between the Baptists 'and all Christian churches that have been and are to this day'. To be fair though, much the same could be said about the Brownists' position. And the same goes for the capital Clifton made out of the divisions between the Baptists, which he thought discredited both Smyth and Helwys: that was an argument no Brownist could afford to make.[1]

On the question of infant baptism, Clifton argued that the Baptists were foolish to make the sacrament dependent upon a person's confession of faith, 'which oftentimes is hypocritical'. This rather overlooked the fact that all Separatists made adult membership dependent on confession of faith, an unfortunate foundation if it was as unreliable as Clifton suggested. As for rebaptism, Clifton just repeated Barrow's argument that apostate Israelites did not have to be recircumcised when they repented, so apostate baptism follows the same pattern. This overlooked the long-standing problem that Smyth's conversion had now floodlit: if the sacrament of the apostate church remains valid, how can it be right to separate from it?[2]

This point was pressed on the Brownists from both sides. While Smyth made the most of it, Joseph Hall wrote to them from the diocese of London:

> There is no remedy: either you must go forward to Anabaptism, or come back to us. All your Rabbis cannot answer that charge of your rebaptised brother: if we be a true church, you must return; if we be not

(as a false church is no church of God) you must rebaptise. If our baptism
is good, then is our constitution good.[3]

Johnson's conversion

Members of the Ancient Church, troubled by the controversy, discussed whether infant baptism was biblical and whether separation
without rebaptism made sense. For Johnson, years of disputes in the
church came to a head – the endless arguments over clothing and
doctrine, discipline and membership, money, sex and worship. He
surveyed his two decades as a leader of the Separatist movement with
despondency and fear. It looked like anarchy. Its democratic ethos
had been the begetter

> of strange opinions and aberrations, of lamentable contentions and divi-
> sions, of opposing and despising the elders' government, of emulation
> and debate among people, with sundry other evils arising and spreading
> themselves daily to the great dishonour of God and our own continual
> grief, and trouble and much reproach from others abroad.

The Baptist movement was only the latest and worst so far. What
monstrosities would Brownists spawn next?[4]

Johnson might have considered returning to the Church of
England, but he had too much invested in Separatism. Instead, his
answer was a coup. He abandoned the democratic church government of congregationalism, in which all Separatists had agreed, from
Browne, through Barrow, and Johnson himself, to the newer congregations, including the Baptists. They had held with Browne, 'the
voice of the people is ... the voice of God'; Johnson concluded that
this authority belongs to the elders. He had always by nature been
more authoritarian than other Separatist pastors, and now he wanted
the constitution of the Ancient Church to reflect that.

Ainsworth was shocked and led the opposition to Johnson.
Though Ainsworth had always believed church members needed
to be governed, he held on to the idea that the final authority is
in the congregation as a whole. He reminded Johnson how their

own petition to the king had expounded congregational government as the biblical model, as had the writings of Barrow before them. But no human authority could settle the matter for Brownists, so their argument circled around the shortest proof text of all: 'Tell the church'. This comes from instructions in Matthew's Gospel about how to deal with a Christian who hurts you: first, you talk to the person directly; then, if that fails, you involve one or two others; finally, you 'tell the church'. If the offender refuses to hear the church, he or she is to be shunned. Congregationalists had always quoted this verse to Presbyterians to show that the government of the church does not belong just to elders. This suddenly seemed absurdly literal to Johnson, and he argued that telling the church did not mean addressing the entire membership but talking to the relevant officers. Henoch Clapham had ridiculed the democracy of Brownism where 'Tell the church' meant 'Tell Tom Tinker, tell Dick Collier, tell Joan the Oyster Wench', and now Johnson could relieve the sting of that mockery.[5]

This dispute between Johnson and Ainsworth continued throughout the whole year of 1610. Their differences were irreconcilable, but they tried to find ways to remain together. Ainsworth's group offered to overlook Johnson's wrong teaching if they could continue to be a congregational church in practice, which was obviously impossible. Johnson's group offered to overlook the others' refusal to accept the truth if they would only submit to Johnson's rule, which was also obviously impossible. Ainsworth then suggested 'a peaceable parting', living as 'two distinct congregations, each practising as they were persuaded, yet nourishing brotherly love and unity', much like Robinson and Smyth had. This proposal, however, ran into Johnson's old objection to having two true churches in the same place, so he wanted Ainsworth's group to leave town. And yet, according to Ainsworth, when some of them suggested moving to Robinson's church in Leiden, Johnson disagreed with that too.[6]

Ainsworth asked the Leiden church to mediate. At first they were loath to interfere, but eventually they sent Robinson and Brewster. The conciliators criticised both sides, but eventually concluded it was Johnson's 'extreme straitness' that prevented peaceful resolution.[7]

By 15 December 1610, the dispute was a year old, and they were further from resolution than ever. That night, Ainsworth and his followers split from Johnson to found their own church. Johnson's party – nicknamed by their enemies 'Franciscans' – had thus, in Robinson's verdict, 'made their brethren their adversaries, and themselves, yea and us all, a byword to the whole world'. Clifton took Ainsworth's place as teacher in Johnson's church, while Ainsworth's church appointed Jean de l'Ecluse as elder and Giles Thorp as deacon. Ainsworth laid out the points where Johnson disagreed with him – and with his own former opinion – in a document called 'Articles of Difference'.[8]

One member who went with Ainsworth, the former vicar William Gilgate, complained that he had only just joined the Separatists and now 'I was constrained to make a new separation again'. He had once thought Johnson and Ainsworth might be the two witnesses foreseen in the book of Revelation, but was so disillusioned by their fight for members following the split that he returned to the Church of England.[9]

The printer Giles Thorp produced a tract of his own for the first time, *The Hunting of the Fox*, though paradoxically it seems only to have been passed around as a manuscript. It was said to contain damning information about Johnson, Studley and others, but it has not survived intact. Johnson did not reply, but did set out his reasons for rethinking the management of the church in *A short Treatise concerning the Exposition of those Words of Christ, Tell the Church*.*

Puritan exiles

A trio of puritan exiles gathered in Leiden between 1610 and 1611. Henry Jacob was one, and the others were two men who had caught his vision of a congregational middle way between Separatism and

---

* Burrage argued that it was only a manuscript on the basis of the way Paget referred to it (*Early English Dissenters*, I, 169). He might also have mentioned that *A Prophane Schisme*, by Lawne et al., tells readers 'ask Master Thorpe … and desire to see' the tract, suggesting that he had the only copy.

conformity: William Ames, a preacher who had been forced out of Cambridge because of his puritan rigour and denied a preaching licence by the Bishop of London; and Robert Parker, a minister who had signed Bancroft's articles but was suspended anyway for writing a book against the sign of the cross.

It was probably the hope of discussing their ideas with Dutch academics that brought Jacob, Ames and Parker to Leiden. They lodged with Robinson's church and respectful debate ensued. Neither side convinced the other on the question of separation from the Church of England, but Robinson treasured their brotherhood and seems to have been persuaded to return to his old belief that it is permissible to pray privately with godly members of the false church.

Helwys, Baptist leader

Helwys, now finding himself the lone defender of the ground he once occupied alongside Smyth, published three books in 1611, one positively setting out the beliefs of his Baptist church, the second confronting the errors of the Waterlanders, and the third confronting the errors of the English, especially the Brownists.

The first book was called *A Declaration of Faith of English People remaining at Amsterdam in Holland*. Having written a confession of faith for the Waterlanders, Helwys now wanted to define his position for a wider public. In the preface, he mourned, in moving tones, the loss of Smyth to their great cause. It was some consolation, Helwys said, that people could no longer say the Baptists held their opinions because they were seduced by Smyth, but they would have preferred to endure the calumny and keep the man. Indeed, they would have laid down their lives for him, just as they had already 'neglected our wives, our children and all we had' to follow him.[10]

Writing, second, to the Waterlanders, Helwys did not sustain quite the fraternal tone that he had used with them when trying to come between them and Smyth. Instead, he addressed them as people guilty of damnable errors, while pointing out that in correcting them he was repaying the debt he owed them for correcting him about predestination. The four errors he confronted were their rejection

291

of sabbath rest, their refusal to work for the state, and their beliefs in Christ's celestial flesh and in succession.

Finally, for the English, Helwys wrote *A short and plaine proofe by the word, and workes off God, that Gods decree is not the cause off anye mans sinne or condemnation*, which he dedicated to Lady Bowes. Seeing that Smyth had already published a formidable attack on infant baptism, Helwys restricted himself to attacking predestination.

Arguments about baptism continued between the Baptists and Brownists, and though Ainsworth held his position confidently, Johnson felt increasingly cornered. He had already ditched the foundational Brownist belief in the conditional covenant in order to explain why baptism received in an apostate church did not need to be repeated. Now, the Baptists turned the screws. What, they asked him, was your ordination in the Separatist church for? If the apostate churches have the authority to perform valid baptism, then their ordination must be valid too. Either Johnson was wrong in being reordained, or wrong to refuse rebaptism.

Again, Johnson could not resist the Baptists' logic. He conceded that his reordination by the Brownists had been unnecessary, because the Church of England made him a real minister. Rome and England had true baptism, true ordination and true ministers.

It became harder than ever for Johnson to explain why he was a Separatist. Ainsworth and the Baptists asked him: in what sense is the Church of England, or even Rome, a false church, if it has true baptism and ministry? Johnson tried to argue that it was all relative. If you compare Catholics with Jews, Turks and Pagans, they are Christians and their church is the church of God; if you compare Catholicism to Johnson's own pure church, it is a false church and 'the great whore'.[11]

The Baptists laughed at Johnson's sophistry. If Rome is in some respects a true church and in some a false church, then 'in one respect they shall be saved, in another respect they shall be damned'.[12] Ainsworth's conclusion was that Johnson and his followers had 'returned into the communion and body of Antichrist's synagogue ... and are bound to communicate even with friars and Jesuits'. The Franciscans, he said, 'acknowledge the whore of Rome to be their mother ... let them return and cherish her also'.[13]

Lawne's attack

Johnson and Studley, for all their insistence on the power of the church eldership, found themselves weaker after the split with Ainsworth. Some members took advantage of this, pressing Johnson to sack the unpopular Studley. Fifteen of them met to draw up a list of fourteen occasions when Studley had been prejudiced in his rulings as elder, but Johnson rejected the charges. Then Christopher Lawne, a buttonmaker from Blandford in Dorset, and his friends, drew up a wider-ranging list of complaints against Studley. As well as the prejudice, these included the allegation of incest from a decade ago, and a more recent charge of 'many lascivious attempts' on Henry Ainsworth's stepdaughter, Marjory's daughter by her first marriage, a charge that four additional members of the church signed. Other accusations included Studley's writing a 'most ungodly' letter, teaching inappropriate songs to children, leaking elders' secrets to a church member, Marie May, and telling her to lie with her husband before marriage, and committing 'known evil' with Judith Holder.[14]

Studley responded in a tone of outraged innocence, but without denying wrongdoing. His behaviour towards his stepdaughter, he admitted, had been 'sinful and unseemly' but had not involved 'carnal copulation' in the strictest sense. Similarly with Miss Ainsworth, his actions had been foolish and wicked once or twice, he said, but he had merely 'clapped' her, never intending full copulation nor saying a single unchaste word to her. In modern terms, Studley protected himself from allegations of extramarital sex by confessing to sexual assault. He also conceded the accusation of including 'unsavoury words' in a letter, but rejected all the other charges against him.[15]

Again Johnson stood by Studley. He told the church that Studley had confessed and repented, and that sexual matters were personal, not 'sins of his administration', so his eldership was not affected. As strict as Separatists had always been about church membership, their theology never told them that falling into sin meant expulsion; it was persisting in sin in the face of admonition that could not be tolerated. Johnson and Clifton had the right to remove Studley, but under their new constitution the rest of the church had no say in the matter. Studley had been Johnson's closest ally since their days in prison two decades previously, and the pastor could not see his way clear to sacking his elder. Instead, Johnson reminded the complainants of how Noah was found drunk and naked by his son Ham, and it was Ham who was therefore cursed; they 'uncover the nakedness of [their] father, and therefore are in danger of the curse', he warned.[16]

Lawne broadened his attack and argued that the congregation, having proved itself no better than its mother church, should make its peace with the Church of England. This, according to Lawne, threw Johnson into an impotent fury. He gave Lawne and the other complainants a long lecture on church history, the moral of which was that only the Ancient Church had fully escaped from antichristian corruption, so it would imperil their souls to quit it. Or as Lawne put it, that Johnson himself was 'the brightest star in the firmament, above Hus, Luther, Calvin and the martyrs of England'. Lawne left them for the English-language Dutch Reformed Church and was excommunicated by the Franciscans on 19 July 1611. Several others followed.[17]

In Lawne's excommunication, the elders cited an additional offence: that he had sent a letter to England containing 'divers slanders of the elders and brethren'. In 1612, Lawne expanded the letter into a book, collaborating with three other ex-members, John Fowler, Clement Sanders and Robert Bulward. (Robinson claimed that the book, though in their names, was 'certainly penned by some other persons [with] greater knowledge', but it was obviously a compilation from a wide range of sources anyway.) *The Prophane Schisme of the Brownists* followed in Thomas White's footsteps, except that, rather than shaming as many members of the church as possible, its fire was concentrated on the leaders, especially Studley, concluding: 'We are fully persuaded that he is unworthy to bear office and dignity.' The book included accounts by former members, letters, legal documents and excommunication decrees, along with original writings, and it drew heavily on Thorp's *The Hunting of the Fox*. The writers devoted much of the book to contending, as so many had before, that the Separatists were schismatics from the true church, but interspersed the argument with much more salacious stories too.[18]

Lawne took the manuscript to London to ask permission from the archbishop's office to print it. Richard Bancroft had died in 1610, having spent his later years, following his success against the puritans, trying to reconcile the Church of Scotland to episcopacy and to suppress a Catholic revival. The new archbishop was George Abbot, and Lawne left the book for Abbot's chaplain Dr Nidd to examine, while he travelled on other business. Nidd seems to have judged the book in need of considerable censorship or at least judicious editing. Lawne returned to London to find the book already printed and on sale, with three-quarters of its content removed, and additions and amendments to the remaining text. The writers disowned the book, while also assuring readers that everything left in it was true.

Considering what stayed in the book, the mind boggles to think what was in the parts Nidd considered unfit for publication. Lawne's reports ranged from farcical vignettes to much grimmer stuff. There were comic scenes, such as Studley's being found hidden behind a basket in Judith Holder's bedroom and explaining that he was hoping 'to see the behaviour of G.P. who came thither after him'. Studley accepted equally poor excuses from his friends: when Geoffrey Whitaker was found in Holder's busy bed 'and the action being naughty', Whitaker explained 'he did it not to satisfy his lust but to comfort Jud[ith] Holder, being sick, to keep her warm'; and Studley believed him despite making harsh judgements against many others. Holder, Lawne says, was eventually expelled from the church, unlike any of the men linked to her. The book included an account, translated from Dutch, of Studley being found with his stepdaughter. As well as details about 'his breathlessness ... his daughter's colour', this account also said that Studley beat his wife when she complained about this behaviour, and that when she told a non-member of the true church, she was disciplined. There was more general talk of his 'haunting women'. The darkest material in the book was not actually about Studley but about a Separatist on Ainsworth's side of the split, Richard Mansfield, though the writer tried to argue, point by point, that Studley was guilty of the same things, if only metaphorically. The passage was a detailed account of sexual abuse inflicted on a female servant, including hanging her naked by the hands to be whipped, among grosser episodes – an account which, for all its moral indignation, seems to have wandered into a new genre of puritan pornography.[19]

Clifton was given the job of replying to Lawne's accusations and arguments, and he published *An Advertisement concerning a book lately published by Christopher Lawne and others* in 1612. Clifton's first concern was to address the perennial accusation of schism, which he did as inconclusively as ever. His second was to answer Lawne's complaints about their singing. Using new hymns – that is, anything other than the biblical text – would have been unthinkable to the Separatists, but Ainsworth had translated biblical psalms into English verse and the Ancient Church had set them to music. Lawne's book reckoned that 'by the uncouth and strange translation and metre used in them, the congregation was made a laughing stock', while also complaining that the elders kept them secret so that no one else could sing them. Clifton assured readers that the Psalms would be published.[20]

Clifton gave a little less than three pages of his lengthy book to the sexual scandal, although he also reproduced Studley's answer to the eight articles against him towards the end. Clifton admitted that his church had had its 'transgressions and infirmities like as in the churches of Corinth, Galatia and others ... for which we are much grieved'. Some of Lawne's stories, he said, were 'very false and untrue'; of those that were true, it was impious and immodest to make them public. All sins of church members had been repented of, the church was therefore in the right: that was the end of it. Clifton then went on to deal in great depth with the arguments between the Franciscans and Ainsworthians.[21]

Ainsworth replied the following year with an equally long book concerned entirely with the dispute between their two churches and the fact that in addressing it Clifton had reproduced private correspondence between Ainsworth and Robinson. The accusations against his follower Mansfield, and other offences alleged during Ainsworth's leadership, got no mention.

Impossible though it is to adjudicate at this distance between all the accusations and counter-accusations, certain things are clear. Studley, by his own account, was guilty of repeated sexual assaults on young women. Though he denied numerous other charges, he was not the kind of man to confess to anything more than was absolutely necessary, as his response to White's book had shown. Numerous accounts, from George Johnson's onward, agree that Studley was a man who loved power, and that being an elder of the Ancient Church in Amsterdam gave him the opportunity to cultivate it and to abuse it.

The response of other Separatist leaders was to close ranks against the accusers. Robinson talked of Lawne and his collaborators as 'brethren in evil' motivated by 'cruel hatred'. His evidence for their bad faith was that they are 'enemies to our profession' having been excommunicated, and 'no person running away from his master will easily speak well of him'.[22]

An answer came to one of Lawne's complaints, however: Ainsworth published the psalms Separatists sang in 1612. This was much more than a hymnbook. *The Booke of Psalmes, englished both in Prose and Metre; with Annotations opening the words and sentences by conference with other Scriptures*, as the title might suggest, contained Ainsworth's prose translation of the book of Psalms, with a full commentary, plus metrical versions with tunes. The tunes, still extant, give us a dimension of Brownist worship that nothing else can, being sober, pretty and surprisingly complex. Regarding the metrical words, the 1885 *Dictionary of National Biography* noted that Ainsworth 'had not the faintest breath of poetical inspiration', but they were used by churches beyond his own, including the pilgrims in Plymouth. His translation and commentary established him as a leading Hebrew scholar (as late as 1866, W.S. Plumer's commentary on Psalms cited Ainsworth as an authority more than a hundred times and the 1885 Revised Version of the Bible drew on his work), and the book was reprinted four times in the thirty-two years following. In the wake of its success, Ainsworth applied himself to annotated translations of the rest of the Hebrew scriptures, his Genesis being printed in 1616 and reprinted in 1621.

Ainsworth kept up the theological pressure on Johnson. Noting how Johnson had defended himself from the Baptists by accepting the baptism of England and Rome as true, and then their ordination and ministry too, Ainsworth pushed him further. If Rome has the true sacrament of baptism, then presumably it has the other sacrament

297

too and 'the cursed Mass' is 'the blessed supper of our Lord'. And what about excommunication? Johnson had argued that popish ordination was true because it was done by true ministers in the name of the Lord. Ainsworth pointed out that a popish minster – the Pope – had excommunicated all Protestants in the name of the Lord. Was that valid on the same grounds? The Franciscans had saved their baptism from the attack of the Baptists, but 'what are they the better for being baptised in their infancy, now that they are excommunicated in their man's age?'[23]

The final straw came when the Franciscans lost their building to the Ainsworthians. According to Ainsworth, the chief owners of the building from the start had been two men and a woman who were now in his church, and who tried to resolve the property question with Johnson, resorting to the law when he persistently refused. The Franciscans lost the lawsuit and were forced to sell their share for 5,530 guilders and vacate the building. Drawing a firm line under their humiliation, they moved all the way to Emden, 150 miles to the north-east.

Smyth's last thoughts

Smyth's branch of Separatism was also in desperate straits. By the summer of 1612, its humblest of missions, to be absorbed into the Waterlander church, had dragged on without resolution for two years, and their existential crisis – having renounced their own foundation without being able to join anyone else's church – continued with it. Smyth himself now became seriously ill.

Looking back on his career, he was overcome with regret. He could not repent his separation from the Church of England, or his Baptist conversion, or any of the other new opinions that divided him from others. Neither could he lament his notorious changeability, as that had been his journey towards truth and he was ready to continue wherever it led. What troubled Smyth was the attitude in which he had disputed and disagreed. His words had been 'biting and bitter', 'stout and mingled with gall', where he 'should have, with the spirit of meekness, instructed them'. In defence of God's law, he said in a handwritten paper, he had 'broken the rules of love and charity, which is the superior law'.[24]

Smyth withdrew his condemnation of puritans who remained in the Church of England. They were not in real churches, but that did not make them wicked people or antichristians, as he had believed 'in the days of my blind zeal and preposterous imitation of Christ'. Instead, Smyth offered a short, uncontroversial summary of the Christian faith and said, 'Whosoever walketh according to this rule, I must needs acknowledge him my brother.' Penitence and faith were all, he said; ceremonies were not worth arguing about.[25]

Smyth still had some theological arguments to make, but only on the defensive. Helwys had accused him of the unforgiveable sin of blasphemy against the Holy Spirit, in that Smyth had once renounced the false teaching of baptismal succession, only to return to it to join the Waterlanders. Smyth said that he never accepted succession, and even if he had, can it really be the unforgiveable sin to be wrong, or even to forsake a known truth? Surely anyone who does so 'may repent and receive mercies'. At this point Smyth could not resist a sharp censure of Helwys, who 'breaketh the bond of charity above all men I ever read or heard in uttering so sharp a censure on so weak a ground'. Beyond that though, Smyth said that he would not satisfy readers who wanted him to respond to attacks on his teachings – mainly because it would be a waste of time and 'breed further strife among Christians', but also because he could no longer afford a printer. 'And so I rest, having peace at home on this point.'[26]

Smyth began a new paragraph, 'Concerning the …', but wrote no more. After a seven-week illness, 'examining his life, confessing his sins, praying for patience, always having confidence in the mercy and favour of the Lord', as his follower Thomas Pigott reported, Smyth died at the end of August 1612.

28

Home to die

WHILE SMYTH TOOK his own personal journey of toleration, Helwys's thinking was leading him in a very different direction, but one that would make him the most radical prophet for religious toleration that the Separatist movement produced.

Though Separatists had always rejected the idea of an all-inclusive state church, they varied in how far they pursued the logical conclusion that the state should not exercise religious compulsion. Browne's intuitive love of freedom was extreme but unsystematic and, in its most radical version, short-lived. Barrow was more consistent, but unwilling to surrender all vestiges of power over the population. Johnson and Ainsworth had less interest in freedom and urged the king to attack false religion. Robinson vigorously defended freedom, though it was not a major focus; and the question did not come up much for Smyth at all.

As Helwys came to see it, the Brownists had only ever half left the state church, having held on to its baptism. The Baptists, in renouncing their baptisms, and all baptism without consent, separated church and state further. The Baptists' rejection of predestination had taken them even further in this direction, drawing a starker line between the church and the world, and denying that even God used compulsion. Helwys's own yet further radicalism produced the harshest, most austere version of Separatism yet: believers baptised into his true church were saved; Brownists, state church puritans, Smyth's Baptists, Catholics – all alike had no faith, no baptism, no salvation. 'A hard doctrine will this seem to the most,' admitted Helwys, realising that he was damning where no English person had damned before. 'But the mouth of the Lord hath spoken it.' To the Brownists, who claimed 'there are thousands in England's apostasy

300

in as holy and blessed estate as any people of God can be', Helwys demanded to know why they then 'deny all spiritual communion with any one of them'.[1]

And yet the other side of Helwys's position was the most far-reaching declaration of universal religious freedom yet seen in English: 'Men's religion to God is betwixt God and themselves; the king shall not answer for it, neither may the king be judge between God and man. Let them be heretics, Turks, Jews or whatsoever, it appertains not to the earthly power to punish them in the least measure.' From this extreme position, Helwys looked back throughout 1,600 years of history and saw that no state church had ever done any spiritual good at all, no power that any government had ever claimed in order to compel its subjects to religious observance had saved a single soul, because real Christianity was freely choosing to join a church of free believers. He ridded himself of the Brownists' last hankering for power over non-believers.[2]

The mystery of iniquity

Helwys set out his new ideas in *A short declaration of the mistery of iniquity*, not only the most radical but the most outspoken book produced by the Separatist movement. His central argument was that all alleged churches, from Rome to the Ancient Church, were antichristian and worthless, the Church of Rome being the first beast of Revelation, the Church of England being the second beast, which copies the first, the puritans submitting to its rule and the Brownists united to it by baptism. More remarkable than the argument though was the fact that Helwys repeatedly addressed King James, not humbly asking the godly monarch for reformation as earlier Separatists had, but warning him that he was a non-Christian 'who should be saved and come to the knowledge of the truth'. Those who believe the King of England has a right to punish subjects who dissent from his religion, Helwys said, ought logically to say that the King of Spain has the same right, as did Queen Mary of England. If Philip and Mary had no power over their subjects'

301

consciences, then neither does any king, 'for all earthly powers are one and the same'.[3]

'Men should choose their religion themselves,' Helwys told the king, 'seeing they only must stand before the judgement seat of God to answer for themselves.' If the king forces subjects' religion in the wrong direction, then he has damned them; if he forces them in the right direction, he has not saved them, because he has not converted their hearts. The king, said Helwys – asking him not to be angry – is 'but a subject of Christ's kingdom'. James should not let anyone take away his rightful power, but if he dictates to the church then he takes away Christ's rightful power. Those who dissent from the religion of their homeland should not be punished as seditious, said Helwys, unless Jesus and the apostles were seditious.[4]

Helwys's argument for religious freedom was not just an academic exercise, it was a matter of life and death, because he had made the momentous decision to return to England. The Separatists, Helwys thought, had saved their lives by leaving home, but had not advanced the gospel. They had come to a land where their preaching could not be understood, and left behind their own children and parents to do so when they should have led them in the truth. They had been driven by fear of men, not of God. 'The disciples of Christ cannot glorify God and advance his truth better than by suffering all manner of persecution for it.'[5]

One Bible verse that had convinced Brownists to leave their home was Jesus' instruction to the disciples, 'And when they persecute you in this city, flee into another.' But Helwys noticed that Jesus was telling them to travel around their homeland preaching, moving on when they faced hostility. It was not permission to hide or run away, but an injunction to keep moving. The God of the Bible might impose exile on his people as a punishment, but never called them into self-imposed exile. His call was to pilgrimage, which for the children of Israel had meant a journey to their ancestral home to face hostile armies.

Helwys presented this case for going to preach in England, whatever the cost, in an appendix to *The mistery of iniquity*, with an argument as ungracious as it was courageous. In following Smyth out of England, he said, they had been 'drawn by ... seducers', 'misled by deceitful hearted leaders who have and do seek to save their own lives'. To justify this 'doctrine of devils', 'these men of corrupt minds, lovers of themselves, utterly pervert the meaning of our Saviour', to their own damnation. It is a pity that this most ground-breaking treatise of the Separatist movement should also be its most mean-spirited, but then it was the same overwhelming compulsion to follow his antipathy for the state church wherever it led that drove Helwys's vision of universal religious freedom and his damnation-happy denunciations.[6]

Early in 1613, Helwys and his handful of followers packed what little was left of the belongings they had brought with them to Amsterdam, and the pages of *The mistery of iniquity*, and sailed for England. They had not expected exile to be easy, nor had it been, but they returned from it to face the full force of antichrist's wrath against the saints.

Within months of their arrival, the last two burnings for heresy in English history took place. Unconnected with each other, Bartholomew Legate and Edward Wightman were both Anabaptists accused of denying the Trinity. Legate was executed in March in Smithfield, Wightman in April in Lichfield.

In London, Helwys selected one copy of his book to deliver, so far as possible, to the king. He wrote in the flyleaf:

Hear, O king, and despise not the counsel of the poor, and let their complaints come before thee.

The king is a mortal man, and not God, therefore hath no power over the immortal souls of his subjects, to make laws and ordinances for them, and to set spiritual laws over them.

If the king hath the authority to make spiritual lords and laws, then he is an immortal god, not a mortal man.

O king, be not seduced by deceivers to sin so against God whom thou oughtest to obey, nor against thy poor subjects who ought and will obey thee in all things, with body, life and goods, or else let their lives be taken away from the earth.

God save the king.

Spitalfield, near London

Tho. Helwys[7]

The first Virginia expedition

Another, less dangerous nonconformist returned from the Nether-lands – Henry Jacob – who decided the time had come to found the non-separating congregational church he and friends had talked about for a decade. He gathered a congregation in Southwark, and following the pattern of more radical predecessors, they made a cov-enant. Standing in a ring and holding hands, they went round the circle declaring their faith, in their own words. Then, together, they vowed 'to walk in all Gods ways as he had revealed or should make known to them' – which is close enough to the wording of the Brownists' covenant to suggest it was based on it. They notified the Brownist congregation remaining in London of their formation, and then elected Jacob as pastor.[8]

So far as the English authorities were concerned, such a con-venticle was just as illegal as any Brownist gathering, but there was a crucial practical difference: Jacob allowed his followers to attend their parish church as well as their underground congre-gation, making their movement much less visible. This attracted puritans who were not prepared for the danger of Brownism; it also brought in some Brownists who shunned parish churches but could worship with those who did not. Later it became large enough to plant a second congregation in west London. Jacob wrote about his approach to reformation without tarrying for the magistrate and it appealed to many who despaired of the defeated presbyterian movement. Parish congregations who followed his example of covenanting to keep their worship pure included John Cotton's in Boston, Lincolnshire.

Jacob's friend William Ames remained in Leiden and continued his discussions with Robinson. Now that Robinson had changed his mind about praying with puritans, they spent more time together, and Ames tried to persuade him to join him in public worship too. Robinson refused, and wrote *Of religious communion private, & pub-lique* to explain his reasons. Those reasons were familiar enough, but what was remarkable was the cordial tones in which Robinson was now talking of the Church of England and its members. It was an antichristian institution and he would never join its worship or structures, but still it taught 'many excellent truths' fostering the 'knowledge, zeal and other personal graces of many'. It was a church of heroes martyred by Rome and was recognised by other Reformed churches. Robinson rebutted the Brownist teaching that non-Separatists were not 'our brethren, or Gods children, or that there is no bond of faith and the Spirit between their and our persons'. They were wrong not to separate, he said, but, when one considered the affliction suffered by Separatists, the opprobrium in which they were held and the self-inflicted scandals that followed them, it was understandable.[9]

Robinson's was now the largest Separatist church, growing to 300 members, three times the number that had first moved from Amsterdam. Their friendliness to outsiders was mirrored by their friendliness to one another, and uniquely among Brownist churches in the Netherlands they never suffered splits. It 'was a crown unto them,' Bradford said, '[that] they lived together in love and peace all their days'. Bradford and Winslow agreed in crediting this to Robinson, 'for his study was peace and union'. Watts notes that Robinson was an excellent pastor though 'he had neither the originality of mind of Smyth nor the reckless bravery of Helwys'; surely the strength was connected to the weakness. Robinson defended divorces between Brownist factions from critics who remained shackled to the state church – 'they only, who enjoy liberty, know how hard a thing it is to use it aright'. It would perhaps be fair to say that he alone among them all, though he was not an intellectual pioneer of freedom, did know how to use it right.[10]

Nevertheless, Robinson could fight when needed, and so took on Helwys's writings. As well as tackling his Baptist teaching – 'a kingdom of heaven ... out of which we should throw our children' – Robinson answered Helwys's insistence that it was wrong to flee persecution. Helwys condemned cowardly false teachers who led the people out of England, but it was as much the people, Robinson said, who had led the teachers, not least Helwys himself. And if things had gone better for him in Amsterdam, he would never have worried about the question, but the wreck of his church drove him into a desperate course to prove himself. It is 'a bold spirit and haughty stomach' that challenge the king to his face; the humility of Christ runs away.[11]

Johnson's congregation were on the move again too. From Emden, they made their second attempt to relocate to America, this time with the aim of joining the existing, though struggling, colony of Virginia, which on paper stretched from modern-day North Carolina to Maine, but on the ground was a hamlet of 400 people. A settlement had been established at Jamestown in 1607, supported by a joint stock company in London, at the same time as another at Popham in what is now Maine. Popham was abandoned in 1608, while Jamestown was reduced to starvation and cannibalism by the failure of supply expeditions, until the fourth supply ship arrived in 1610. The settlers then engaged in four years of war with the indigenous Americans. Contemporary accounts of the colony, however, made it sound more like a dangerous adventure than a desolate horror, and the prospect of joining the Virginia settlement was less suicidal than being dropped alone in Newfoundland. The Franciscans were desperate enough to try it.

Their expedition was managed by their elder, Francis Blackwell, who back in 1605, before they had Thorp's press, had published the correspondence between Ainsworth and Broughton disputing points of Hebrew translation and been attacked in print by Broughton as a result. The expedition was not a success, and perhaps never departed. We know about it purely because of a vague reference in a letter by Robert Cushman of Robinson's church, who blamed Blackwell for a fiasco, saying his plan caused the 'subversion' of Johnson and the Emden church. Cushman suggested that Blackwell could have died or even been executed as a result, but 'cleanlily, yet unhonestly, plucked his neck out of the collar'.[12]

Baptists for freedom

Helwys's Baptists landed more or less straight in jail on their return to England. In 1614, a year after their arrival, they petitioned Parliament for release, having, they said, been imprisoned 'not for any other cause but only for conscience towards God, to the utter undoing of us, our wives and children'. The Baptists argued that the Recusants Act of 1606, responding to the Gunpowder Plot, had required Catholics to take an oath of allegiance, which they could be jailed for refusing and freed for taking. It was only fair, they said, that Protestant nonconformists should also be freed upon taking the oath, which they were more than willing to do. The petition was rejected.[13]

The third Baptist church in Amsterdam had survived, and its leader Leonard Busher published another compelling polemic for religious freedom. The superb pamphlet *Religions peace* offered a relentless stream of arguments against coercion. Like Helwys, Busher directly addressed King James, warning him against violently upholding the religion he had been born into: Christ said, 'Except a man be born again, he cannot see the kingdom of God', so anything one is originally born into is not the kingdom of God; James used godless weapons to drive people into a non-Christian church.

Persecution cannot promote Christianity, argued Busher: it makes people sin against their consciences, but does not change their beliefs. Execution is the worst possible answer to heresy, as it removes any possibility of changing the heretic's mind. Molesting or banning Jews as unbelievers only drives them further away from becoming believers. Persecution promotes dishonesty and hypocrisy and invites counter-persecution. 'The burning, banishing, hanging and imprisoning of men and women, by Protestants, for difference of religion, do justify the burning, banishing and imprisoning of men and women, by the Papists, for difference of religion, even as the Papists do justify the Turks and pagans in suchlike cruelty and tyranny.' And those who take comfort in the *Book of Martyrs*, condemning antichrist's persecution, 'do therein condemn themselves'. In sum: 'The believing do not persecute the unbelieving, nor the true church the false.' Busher wrote two other books, but could not afford to print them and they have disappeared without trace.[14]

Religious freedom became a central theme for the Baptists. In 1616, the Baptists in Newgate prison managed to write, smuggle out and print *Persecution for Religion Judg'd and Condemn'd*, which has been variously attributed to Helwys and his follower John Murton.

Murton had gone to Amsterdam with the Smyth church from Gains-borough, marrying there and working as a furrier, before coming to London with Helwys. If Murton wrote the book, he had taken on Helwys's ideas perfectly.

The book took the form of a dialogue between Christian and Antichristian, with the twist of Antichristian fading out of the story, replaced by Indifferent, when the author apparently found his own fictional character too hard to win round. Antichristian makes the reasonable argument that God commands religious violence in the Old Testament, but Brownist hermeneutics have prepared that ground for Christian: the old covenant was physical, with physical punishments; in the new covenant, souls who fall into Christ's hands 'must die by the spiritual sword'. The new covenant is not nicer – all those not baptised by consent are 'without exception ... to be cast into the lake that burneth with fire and brimstone' – but earthly violence is forbidden.[15]

Christian and Indifferent agree with Helwys in lamenting the Brownists' flight from persecution: it 'hath been the overthrow of religion in this land, the best able and greater part being gone'. Indifferent makes the intriguing statement that many Brownists, though they still reject believers' baptism, now accept 'that antichristians coming to the truth may be baptised'. There is no evidence for this in their own writings.[16]

Christian pityingly described the Baptists' three years so far in Newgate. They lived in foul-smelling filth, among blasphemers, far from their families and any means to make a living. This exhausted their families' means and left 'them and their wives to horrible temptations of adultery'.[17]

One authority cited in *Persecution for Religion Judg'd and Condemn'd* was James himself. The king had told Parliament in 1610 that theology and politics agree: 'God never loves to plant his church by violence and bloodshed', and 'when men are severely persecuted for religion, the gallantness of many men's spirits ... makes them take a pride boldly to endure any torments', even if they are wrong. Despite this inclination though, James had to concede that persecution is sometimes necessary, having himself allowed Wightman and Legate to be killed for their opinions, and the Baptists to be kept in prison. He saw the uselessness of religious violence to achieve any positive good, and how badly it sat with the faith of the New Testament, but he was inescapably wedded to the idea that the church is a whole Christian society, which was impossible to maintain without coercion. As the Supreme Governor of a state church, he could only ever argue for moderation in religious bloodshed.[18]

In Amsterdam, the remnant of Smyth's Baptist church applied again to join the Waterlanders. Smyth's death had left them more alone than ever and the Broederschap of Dutch Mennonites had dissolved since they first applied (a split that James Coggins argues was a direct result of their application), so the impediment was removed. The Waterlanders considered each of the thirty-six or so Baptists individually, rejecting four, requiring four to be baptised and accepting the others into membership on 21 January 1615.

Robinson champions Calvinism

On 5 September 1615, Robinson enrolled as a student at Leiden University, evidently believing his Cambridge degrees could be improved upon. Another member of his church, the wealthy merchant William Brewer, had enrolled earlier that year. Robinson's decision suggests a humility towards Dutch Reformed scholarship of which no other Brownist leader would have been capable; it also allowed him to engage in the Arminian dispute that had divided the Netherlands. In 1614, the Holland government had forbidden preaching about predestination, but in the university debate continued at full heat. Oldenbarnevelt had appointed two professors to replace the sacked Vortius – the ardent Arminian Simon Episcopius and the mild Calvinist Johannes Polyander – who gave rival lectures to their respective followers. Robinson, a passionate Calvinist, was unusual in attending both sets of lectures, and he made such an impression that Polyander persuaded him to go head to head with Episcopius in debates. This, according to Bradford, 'caused many to praise God that the truth had so famous a victory'.[19]

One new member who joined Robinson's church from England during this period was the printer Edward Winslow. Winslow had grown up in Droitwich, Worcestershire, the son of a prosperous saltmaker, studied at King's School in Worcester, and at seventeen entered an eight-year apprenticeship to the London printer John Beale. Halfway through his term, Winslow ran away to join the Separatists in the Netherlands.

The Separatism of Robinson's church, as Winslow found it, had mellowed further than ever. Robinson, said Winslow, so admired puritans such as Ames that, as well as private prayer meetings, he now allowed his people to attend their church services. He was also, unlike other Brownists, happy for them to attend Dutch services. Winslow – writing thirty years after the event in a conservative polemic – went so far as to claim that when new members applied to join and protested

> separation from the Church of England, I have divers times … heard either Mr Robinson our Pastor, or Mr Brewster our elder stop them forthwith, shewing them that we required no such things at their hands, but only to hold forth faith in Christ Jesus, holiness in the fear of God, and submission to every ordinance and appointment of God, leaving the Church of England to themselves.

It seems that Robinson's physical distance from other Brownists had given him space to maintain friendship while developing a moderation they would not have tolerated. In 1617, Robinson had talks with the Anabaptist Pieter Jansz Twisck, who like Helwys argued for universal freedom of religion, and some scholars have detected his influence on Robinson's thinking.[20]

It may have been Winslow's arrival that inspired a new venture for the Leiden church: they set up a printing press, managed by Brewster, and financed by William Brewer, a wealthy gentleman who had come over from Kent with his wife Anne. They set up shop in Koorsteeg (Choir Alley), off the enticingly named Stinksteeg, close by St Peter's Church. Brewer's mission was to make available any books 'that have been published against the bishops and are forbidden by them', so they printed works by more mainstream puritans, including Ames and John Dod, as well as Brownists, with reprints of Cartwright, Travers, Field and Wilcox. Brewer also sold existing books as well as printing. It was a missionary enterprise rather than a profitable business, and within a few years Brewer was said to have mortgaged half his estate.[21]

The first new writing published by Brewster was by Francis Johnson. His church had not thrived as an isolated outpost in Emden, Clifton had died, and, failing to emigrate, in 1617 they retreated to Amsterdam. Johnson had arguments to continue with the late John Smyth about baptism, and with Ainsworth about the covenant. He could hardly ask Thorp to print this, and, anyway, his press was constantly busy with Ainsworth's biblical works, so Johnson took it to Leiden.

In *A Christian Plea* Johnson was still trying to defend his baptism in the apostate church from Baptist condemnation. To do so, he conceded that the Church of Rome was simply an entirely true church: 'The baptism had in the church of Rome, is the Lord's baptism, the sign and seal of his covenant ... Therefore the church of Rome, is the church of God, and under his covenant.' The covenant is entirely unconditional, continuing 'even in the times of apostasy'. Johnson now saw his church as being in one saving brotherhood with the Church of England. He avoided its services because of the sins committed there, but separated only from those antichristian elements, not from the Christian ones.[22]

The slipperiness of Johnson's position led him finally, like Smyth, to consider the possibility of toleration, raising the question 'whether that Christians and churches may not and ought not to bear one with another, in their differences'. These two thinkers had been driven through so many theological transitions that eventually a kind of ideological travel sickness made them less certain that their own path along the narrow road was the only one that did not lead to destruction. Johnson had not yet come so far as Smyth. His answer to the question of whether to tolerate differences was a firm yes, but only when the churches in question have the true faith and no bishops, and when all members are free to avoid every sin, do not obstinately refuse the truth and in turn tolerate people like Johnson. It was a toleration that would not travel far from the doors of his own church. And yet Johnson was recognising for the first time that there was room for different interpretations in the one faith, and said he was offering this as a humble and tentative approach to an answer, calling for further discussion on whether degenerate churches are to be separated from or not.[23]

In 1617 the Ainsworth church excommunicated Stephen Ofwod after a fellow member, Thomas Stafford, came round to court his daughter Susanna and Stephen chased him out of the house with a weapon. When Frances joined in excommunicating her husband, he told her, 'You have received the poison of scorpions.' He joined the English Reformed church.[24]

By 1617, the Separatist movement was not what it had been. The Smyth church was absorbed into the Anabaptists; Helwys's tiny faction would, one would have thought, never be heard of again. The Ancient Church was split in two, discredited by scandal, and struggling. The flow of newcomers, never mighty, had diminished.

Their very Separatism was not what it had been. The scandal of the Baptist movement, so firmly building upon the logic of Separatism, had profoundly shocked Brownist leaders, with Johnson in particular driven to a far more forgiving relationship with the Church of England. Robinson took a more positive route to the same place, persuaded by friendship, and both seemed likely to continue further in the same direction. Smyth had sounded the same note in his swan-song. With Jacob founding a nonconformist church in London, there now seemed to be a convergence on the middle way. Brownism had never become the mass movement its proponents expected, and it was not clear it had a future. If their story was to end in success and justify their belief that they were the Lord's chosen, a mighty intervention was needed. It was against this background that Johnson's church once again, and Robinson's for the first time, set their sights on America.

29

The Promised Land

THERE WERE A number of considerations that made the Separatists look to America in 1617, but the most commonly cited motive for the sailing of the *Mayflower* – to escape persecution and worship freely – was not one of them. Persecution had driven them out of England to the Netherlands, but they had not suffered persecution in the Netherlands and the Leiden church had especially good relations with the Dutch. Persecution prevented them from going home, but not from staying where they were.

Reasons for going

The key consideration, according to the Separatists themselves, was that life in Dutch cities seemed just too grim for their church to have any future. They were losing the older generation, Bradford said, who seemed to be dying prematurely after years of unskilled urban labour, or, having used up their savings, returned to England to lodge with family. And they were losing the younger generation, who were fed up with godly poverty and surrounded by worldliness they would never have encountered in an English village. 'Getting the reins off their necks', Bradford said, some young people joined the army, some went off to sea and others took 'worse courses'. Those young people who remained in the faith, he said, joined in their parents' labours and were incapacitated by them. The leaders feared that within years their church would collapse. America, they imagined, would allow them to create an English village 3,000 miles from the nearest bishop, returning to the agricultural life they yearned for, and escaping the fleshpots of Leiden and Amsterdam.[1]

A sense of failure in their mission added to the Brownists' discontent, according to Winslow, who lamented 'how little good we did, or were like to do'. He had hoped that the purity of their church would inspire the Dutch to a new reformation, but they ignored them. The English paid more attention, and many were impressed by the Brownists' example, but too few were willing to join them in the Netherlands, and fewer stayed. Admittedly, America would offer still fewer opportunities to convert the English, but perhaps, Bradford said, they would be God's instrument for converting the Americans.[2]

On top of all the difficulties of life in the Netherlands, the English feared that it was about to get worse. The Spanish truce expired in 1621, and it seemed likely that the war would resume. This was a serious consideration, though war with Spain had not stopped the church coming to the Netherlands in the first place.

Another motive Winslow mentioned for going to America was, paradoxically, to stay English. The younger generation had gradually integrated with Dutch society, and it was clear, as Winslow put it, 'how like we were to lose our language and our name of English'. This undermined their mission to model reform to the English churches. If the Brownists did survive in the Netherlands, becoming just another Dutch denomination would defeat their object in being there.[3]

There is, however, something intriguingly inconsistent and incoherent about the reasons the colonists gave for their decision. Although Bradford's main explanation was that they were driven to America by the grimness and poverty of life in Leiden, which lay behind all their other problems too, yet he says elsewhere: 'At length they came to raise a competent and comfortable living'; and though it was not easy at first, he adds, '(after many difficulties) they continued many years, in a comfortable condition'. He describes their departure from 'that goodly and pleasant city'. Above all, he says they looked to America as a 'place of better advantage and less danger' than Holland, but also says that they were aware of its 'inconceivable perils'. 'The miseries of the land ... would be too hard to be borne.' It would be likely 'to consume and utterly to ruinate them'. They feared famine and nakedness, 'sore sicknesses, and grievous diseases'. They had heard terrifying accounts of the indigenous Americans torturing people to death. They were aware of how many settlements had failed and how many lives had been lost. Add to all this the perils of the journey itself, and the frailty of the travellers, and one has to wonder in what sense exactly Bradford was using the phrase 'less danger'.[4]

When members voiced their serious doubts about the expedition Robinson and Brewster proposed, the reply, as Bradford has it, is fascinating: 'All great and honourable actions are accompanied with great difficulties; and must be both enterprised, and overcome with answerable courages.' The reason they needed to leave Leiden, supposedly, was to escape its hardships; and when critics of the plan worried that America would have great hardships, they were told that this great enterprise was worth great hardships. So what was the enterprise, if not to escape hardships?[5]

The colonists seemed to have difficulty articulating exactly what compelled them to leave the Netherlands for America. They had a sense of an important enterprise, which, though they might rationalise it in terms of escaping the difficulties of life in Holland, did not meet that objective terribly well. Their calculation of the risks and imperatives does not add up unless we remember how ingrained it was for the Separatists to see their story in biblical terms, as following biblical patterns. They saw their reflection in countless scriptural parallels, but above all in the exodus – God leading the new children of Israel out of the bloody and antichristian land of their birth, to a place he had prepared for them. From Browne's first writing, to Helwys's last, the Separatist equation was repeated (critically in Helwys's case): 'England was as Egypt'. They had been delivered and there could be no going back. The Netherlands, however, had not felt at all like the Promised Land, which meant that instead they were in the wilderness, the stretch of wandering and learning that occupied Israel before reaching Canaan. They were God's 'little church, fled into the wilderness', in Ainsworth's words, or, as Johnson put it, they had followed Moses' path, rejecting the treasures of Egypt 'to suffer adversity with the people of God'; they were 'but strangers and pilgrims'.[6]

The Separatists were prime examples of the fundamentally forward-looking nature of Protestantism – 'a religion of *progress*', as Alec

315

Ryrie puts it, 'of restless, relentless advance toward holiness, not of stagnation'. Each stream saw itself as the culmination in a century of progress towards truth and obedience, while still challenging its own orthodoxies, their church covenants explicitly committing them to embrace God's future revelations, to be ready to take the next step. Individual members had once walked miles to acceptable churches, then moved to London maybe, then sailed for Amsterdam, then moved again to Leiden or Emden. If their dreams had failed to come true and no simple way forward presented itself, then their whole religious experience and outlook told them God would reveal a new path ahead. Satan called them back, the Lord called them on. And if the way forward involved a terrifying leap of faith, 'yet might they have comfort in the same'. Whatever America might entail, it was not retreat; it was not going back to Egypt.[7]

The opportunities for such an emigration were more plentiful than might be supposed, and the Brownists were far from lone American pioneers. According to the records of the Virginia Company, 1,291 people went in 1619 alone, hoping to make their fortune in the New World, about two-thirds by official arrangement with the company, and the rest to private plantations. As a proportion of the population of the kingdom, this would equate to 20,000 a year today.

The church of Johnson and Clifton made their own arrangements for going to Virginia, about which we know little, but the plans of Robinson's church are much better preserved. Some members argued enthusiastically for Guiana as a destination: being in South America, it was outside English jurisdiction, so they would be free of English religious law, and Walter Raleigh and Robert Harcourt had written alluringly of its fertility and warmth. They were put off by tropical diseases and the fear that, though the Spanish had not yet come near it, they were bound to once there was an English colony there. Virginia seemed safer, if the settlers were assured they would be allowed to practise their religion.

In 1617, the Robinson church sent two members to London: John Carver, merchant, deacon and Robinson's brother-in-law; and Robert Cushman, who had been a grocer in Canterbury and then a wool carder in Leiden. These men made contact with Edwin Sandys, Assistant of the Virginia Company, leading MP and son of the bishop who had been Brewster's landlord. Sandys was urgently recruiting new settlers to revive the fortunes of the Jamestown colony and 200 Separatists would increase their number by half.

Sandys assured the delegates there would be no problem obtaining a royal proclamation of freedom for their congregation, but he assumed their nonconformity lay in a few deviations from the Prayer Book, rather than an entirely different concept of church. When he asked for information about their religion, Brewster and Robinson sent him a brief, subtly worded summary in seven articles. These accepted the 39 Articles of the Church of England – which were a statement of Reformed theology – and affirmed that this teaching had saved many members of the Church of England with whom 'we do desire to keep spiritual communion'. This was a statement of Robinson's latter-day willingness to pray with people like Ames, but it sounded helpfully like a disavowal of Separatism. Similarly, they affirmed that it was acceptable for bishops 'to oversee the churches', but this was about their secular oversight of Christians, not, as it sounded, their right to dictate religion. As congregationalists, they were able to denounce the 'synod, classis, convocation or assembly' of presbyterians, without pointing out that their alternative was more radical still.[8]

Sandys was easily persuaded to support their plans, but obtaining the royal proclamation was harder. When told they would support themselves by fishing, the king replied, according to Winslow, 'So God have my soul, 'tis an honest trade, 'twas the apostles' own calling.' But James referred the question to the bishops and Privy Council.[9] Another leading member of the Virginia Company, the naval commissioner Sir John Wolstenholme, took the case to the Privy Council, who wanted to know the Leiden church's position on ministers, sacraments and the oath of supremacy. Robinson and Brewster wrote to Wolstenholme, via another church member, Sabine Staresmore, a successful merchant who had also worshipped with Jacob's congregation. The letter assured Wolstenholme they were happy to take the oath and that they were not Baptists, their theology of the sacraments being that confessed by the French Reformed Church. On the subject of ministers, they listed some trivial differences with the French Church, but Wolstenholme noticed a crucial evasion: 'Who shall make them?' he asked. Surprised into candour, Staresmore explained that the congregation has the authority to appoint ministers, all rival authority being derived from the popish antichrist. At this, Wolstenholme refused to take their answer to the Privy Council.

Instead, the Brownists met directly with the Secretary of State Sir Robert Naunton. He supported their cause, but told them the bishops would block it for fear that allowing nonconformity in overseas dominions would make it harder to enforce at home. The king, however, Naunton advised, was willing to ignore their nonconformity unofficially, so long as they caused no trouble. This indulgence was the best result they could hope for, he said, and it would only be endangered by pushing for an official response. Carver, Cushman and Staresmore got to work looking for investors to finance the expedition.

The first pilgrim

The Calvinist party in Holland consistently demanded a synod where the church could decide between them and the remonstrants, but Oldenbarnevelt refused to relinquish state control of the question, and so Holland gained its own Calvinist Separatist movement. After violence broke out between remonstrants and contraremonstrants, Oldenbarnevelt allowed towns to raise their own armies and command national Dutch troops stationed there. Four years before the truce with Spain was due to end, the Netherlands was on the brink of civil war. The English government was alarmed and the ambassador Sir Dudley Carleton pressed for a nationwide synod to unite the Netherlands, as did James himself. In 1618, Maurice of Orange, William's son, took troops into Holland, subdued it without a fight and had Oldenbarnevelt arrested.

A synod of the national church met in Dordrecht (or Dort) in November 1618. It became an international Reformed congress, with the enthusiastic support of James, as well as Dutch traditionalists such as Polyander. The synod condemned Arminianism and defined the Calvinism to be imposed on the Dutch Church. Episcopius was dismissed, Oldenbarnevelt executed and remonstrant preachers expelled from the Netherlands. Maurice prepared the country for war with Spain.

In January 1618, Francis Johnson died at the age of fifty-five. He was buried by the Dutch Reformed Church, perhaps at the behest of Matthew Slade, who reported on the funeral to the English ambassador. Slade mentioned that Johnson 'did, a few days before his death, publish a book wherein he disclaimed most of his former singularities'. It is tantalising to imagine Johnson's growing doubts about Brownism inspiring a 'deathbed recantation', as the Victorian historian Edward Arber believed, but the book was surely *A Christian Plea*. Though Slade was exaggerating the retreat Johnson made in that book, it was evident there; there is no trace of any further book by Johnson, and when Ainsworth wrote his last reply to him, after his death, it was entirely directed at *A Christian Plea*.[10]

It is likely that Johnson's followers had started their preparations to sail to Virginia by this point, expecting Johnson to take them there in a third attempt to lead his people across that sea. But it is also possible that it was the crisis of Johnson's death that made them decide to steal a march on Brewster and quietly make the crossing as soon as possible. Either way, they did not try to negotiate as a church with the English authorities, but planned to return secretly to London and arrange or join an expedition. Again they entrusted the organisation to Francis Blackwell, who had failed them the previous time.

A former member of Johnson's church apparently beat them all to it. The records are patchy, but it seems that Christopher Lawne, the whistleblower, crossed the Atlantic in charge of the *Marygold*, arriving in May 1618. He established a plantation across the James River from Jamestown, in Warascoyack Bay (now Burwell Bay), bringing a hundred settlers to work the land. He was one of twenty-two burgesses who attended the first General Assembly of Virginia, which met in Jamestown Church in July 1619, and he served as foreman of the jury in a murder case. That summer, disease swept his plantation and the residents were evacuated to the Charles City plantation, where Lawne was among those who died. The nearby Lawne's Creek still bears his name.

Among all the Separatists in the Netherlands, only Ainsworth's remnant had no apparent intention to go anywhere. Ainsworth and Thorp devoted their energies to their great series of books on the Hebrew scriptures, 1618 seeing the fourth instalment in three years, *Annotations upon the Book of Leviticus*; the next year brought Deuteronomy, Numbers and an omnibus of the five books of Moses. Their press was so busy with these renowned books that although Ainsworth found time to write the last word in his dispute with Johnson in 1618, it was not printed for two years.

John Paget of the English-language Dutch Reformed Church also put Ainsworth's arguments into print. The pair of them had been exchanging letters for eighteen months since Paget had lost a potential new member to the Ancient Church, and they debated Separatism, the Lord's Prayer and the use of ex-Catholic buildings. Paget printed the letters, with his final reply, in December 1618, binding with it a second book, attacking Ainsworth's Bible commentaries. Paget, a Hebrew scholar himself, was appalled that Ainsworth not only asked Rabbis about the meaning of Hebrew words but drew on their traditions of interpretation, and that Ainsworth was guided by the marginal notes of the Masoretic text, which Paget considered unbiblical. Ainsworth did not engage with Paget, but added a few pages, 'as the extreme infirmity of my body would permit', to his volume on Deuteronomy, explaining the principle of drawing from Jewish scholarship.

Brewster's press was still more prolific. Even while he was working to convince the English authorities to tolerate his church in their dominions, he printed perhaps seven books against the regime of the Church of England in 1618 alone. They included reprints of Robert Harrison and Thomas Cartwright and a new book by Robinson in defence of lay preaching. The Separatist books were secretly smuggled into England, but less radical ones, such as the anonymous puritan work *De vera et genuina Iesu Christi domini et saluatoris nostri religione*, were distributed more openly. In this way, Brewster came close to ruining his church's plans for America.

30

'Twixt cup and lip

AFTER THE FLURRY of puritan excitement that had greeted his coming to England fifteen years before, King James had seen the rule of bishops become broadly accepted in the southern kingdom. It worked well for him and he was keen to impose it more thoroughly on Scotland too. A series of reforms increased the power of bishops there, including the creation of a Court of High Commission. James sent bishops to be consecrated in England to ensure apostolic succession. When Presbyterian leaders tried to hold their General Assembly, he had them exiled for high treason, then re-established the Assembly under his own control. The 1616 Assembly obediently agreed to a new liturgy and confession of faith, and afterwards James tried to insert five articles into its canons introducing new ceremonies to the Kirk: kneeling at Communion, confirmation, feast days, private baptism and private Communion.

The five articles met resistance, even from the Archbishop of St Andrews, bringing the king to Scotland in 1617. He was accompanied by the Dean of Gloucester, a man already controversial in England for reviving rituals not seen since Mary Tudor, such as bowing to the altar. This was William Laud, who as Archbishop of Canterbury would be the architect of civil war. James introduced the English Prayer Book to Holyrood Chapel, along with organ and choir – though he was persuaded that statues were a step too far. And yet the king failed to get reforms through Parliament, and, after he left, the 1617 General Assembly passed only two of the articles, with modifications.

The struggle continued and the following year a Latin booklet appeared in England, *De regimine Ecclesianae Scoticanae*, which surveyed the state of the Kirk, presenting the king's policy in a very bad light. The tract was naturally anonymous and it outraged the king. This was no new Martin – the tone was serious and angry – but once again the search began for the mystery author and the outlaw press.

Investigation

The survivors of Johnson's church who were going to America with Francis Blackwell sailed for London in 1618. The need for colonists did not make England any safer for Brownists. Of course, they met for worship, and the representatives of Robinson's church joined them. So did the bishop's men, and Blackwell was among those arrested in the raid, while Staresmore escaped. According to Staresmore, Blackwell struck a deal with the bishop, betraying Staresmore in return for his own release. Staresmore was arrested and locked in the Wood Street Compter. Bradford says that Blackwell renounced his Separatism and at the High Commission the bishop not only acquitted him but praised him and pronounced a blessing on the voyage. Ensuing events, Bradford noted, demonstrate what wisdom there is in exchanging the Lord's blessing for the bishop's.

Blackwell's pilgrims arrived at Gravesend only to find that he had booked a large number of them on to a relatively small ship, presumably to maximise his own profits. Bitter recriminations followed in public – 'Thou hast brought me to this', 'I may thank thee for this!' – but the pilgrims set off nevertheless, 'packed together like herrings'.[1]

While Staresmore was stuck in prison, the Leiden agents' negotiations were further frustrated by the internal politics of the Virginia Company. Sandys had improved the company's processes and created the General Assembly in Virginia, to broad approval, but when he investigated the company's finances, he fell out with its chief officer Sir Thomas Smythe, who had amassed debts of more than £8,000. Smythe retired in April 1619, but when Sandys was elected in his place, Smythe challenged the election. Business such as granting land for the Leideners languished.

As the Netherlands got on a war footing, the Brownists there felt the impact. Independent churches were outlawed, private discussion of religion was forbidden, the state church took control of all provision for widows and orphans, and unauthorised books were banned. James offered military support on conditions including oversight of all English churches in the Netherlands.

The investigation into *De regimine Ecclesianae Scoticanae* turned to the Netherlands. The man in charge was Sir Robert Naunton, the Secretary of State who had been supporting Robinson and Brewster's application to the Privy Council for toleration. Having satisfied himself that the book was not printed in London or Edinburgh, Naunton concluded it must have come from the Netherlands, where Richard Schilders was still at work, fifty years into his career. In March 1619, Naunton sent a copy of the book to the ambassador, Carleton, asking him to complain to the Dutch authorities, confirm that the printer was Schilders, appeal for his punishment and the book's suppression, and discover the author.

Carleton found the Dutch sceptical of Schilders' guilt. He had, they pointed out, just that year taken a public oath to print no unlicensed book – though *De regimine* was printed before that. Under interrogation, Schilders swore he had nothing to do with the book.

Carleton had better luck tracing the author. A Scot living in the Netherlands showed Carleton a letter offering him a copy of the book. It was from the minister of Crailing in Roxburghshire, David Calderwood, who had been banished from Scotland for his outspoken opposition to bishops, but went into hiding instead. Scottish officials searched for Calderwood, but he had reliable friends and evaded capture.

In April 1619, the pages of Calderwood's second book attacking the king's reform of the Kirk arrived in Scotland, smuggled in French wine vats. Called, with unusual conciseness for the period, simply *Perth Assembly*, the book told the story of the previous year's General Assembly – through which James had forced the five articles – arguing that the Assembly was illegal and its resolutions invalid. Calderwood urged readers to refuse the reforms.

While the book was being secretly bound, Robinson's and Brewster's agents in London finally heard good news. The Virginia company internal dispute was resolved and their champion Sandys was in control, the first non-merchant to take charge of an English colonial venture. He saved the colony, sending 4,000 there over the next five years, most to their deaths. Now Brewster himself joined the men in London.

Dismal news reached England in May of the fate of Blackwell's expedition. It had suffered a slow Atlantic crossing of more than six months, and, like the Pilgrim Fathers two years later, they were blown far off course. Unlike them, they did not make do with their new destination, but headed up the coast. By the time they arrived in Virginia waters, the captain and six of the crew were dead, and it took the survivors a disastrously long time to find the small entrance to Chesapeake Bay. When the ship reached Jamestown in March 1619, according to Staresmore, 130 of the 180 passengers were dead. Francis Johnson's church was no more. Cushman feared this misadventure would put the Leideners off, and wrote to assure them that the London merchants were not dismayed, just determined to learn from Blackwell's mistakes.

The same week, *Perth Assembly* covertly went on sale in Edinburgh. In the uproar that followed, James ordered the arrest of both printer and writer. Having drawn a blank in Middelburg over the last book, he focused on Edinburgh, guardsmen searching the houses and stalls of official booksellers. One of them, James Cathkin, happened to be in London, and was arrested. He denied any involvement with the book, but confessed that Calderwood had recently been at his house. 'We have found the taed [toad]!' exclaimed James. Calderwood remained at large, however, and at the end of June Cathkin was released.[2]

A fresh lead came from Carleton in the Netherlands in July. Though he had not yet even heard of *Perth Assembly* from Britain, he became aware that it was circulating in Leiden and reported the book's 'scorn and reproach' for James's religious policy to Naunton. Carleton looked for the printer in Leiden, and so for the first time the actual culprit, William Brewster, was discovered.[3]

Carleton's breakthrough came when he saw a copy of *De vera et genuina Iesu Christi domini*, which Brewster openly printed and sold, and noticed the title page imprint was identical to the one in

De regimine Ecclesianae Scoticanae. Carleton could not yet prove that Brewster had also printed *Perth Assembly*, but he was certainly the man to help the Privy Council with their enquiries. So Carleton searched for Brewster, only to hear that he had left the country for London in the last few weeks.

Receiving this report in July 1619, Naunton searched for Brewster in London, only to hear that he had returned to Leiden. Naunton arrested some of his connections, and told Carleton to keep a look-out. Carleton replied that there was little to watch, as Brewster had already sold his house and moved his family out of the city.

The king was furious with their failure, telling Carleton that his majesty's friendship depended upon Brewster's apprehension. Brewster was becoming an international incident, and Leiden council told their bailiff to find him. It was a great relief when Carleton was able to report that Brewster had been arrested. And it was a huge embarrassment when Carleton then had to report that the bailiff, 'a dull drunken fellow, took one man for another', so the real Brewster was still at large.[4]

In fact the truth was even more embarrassing. Both Brewster and his business partner Brewer had come voluntarily to Leiden Town Hall. Brewster was held in the debtors' prison there and Brewer in the university, which was his right as a student, while the council awaited instructions on what to do with them. James insisted they be sent to London, but this alarmed the council. Considering the fate of Coppin and Thacker, and Barrow and Greenwood, repatriation could be a death sentence. The council thought highly of Robinson's church, so rather than abet the King of England, they pretended incompetence.

With Brewster at large, the king was all the more eager for Brewer to be brought to him, but the university, being an international community, was reluctant to repatriate students for crimes of opinion. The university confiscated Brewer's type, nailed shut the door to his lodgings, and kept him in the cell, but refused James's requests to send him home. It says something about the university's attitude that one of the men they appointed to deal with Brewer was Polyander, who as well as being Robinson's friend had written the preface to one of Brewer's books. With Polyander's mediation, Brewer agreed to go and meet

King James in return for a guarantee that he travelled as a free man, would not be punished, nor kept for long, and that his travel was paid for. Brewer was interrogated in England in December 1619, gave the authorities no useful information, and returned to Leiden.

Preparations and provisions

Two years after they first approached them, Cushman and Carver finally obtained the land grant from the Virginia Company on 9 June 1619. Thanks to the Brewster affair, the Brownists had to be more surreptitious than ever, taking the grant not in their own names, but in that of John Wincop, the puritan chaplain of the Countess of Lincoln, who planned to come with them. Carver then brought the papers to Leiden, along with their main investor and financial adviser, Thomas Weston, a London ironmonger, who helped them draw up contracts for other investors.

It was time to make some momentous decisions about which members of the church would go to America, so the church held a day of fasting to seek God's guidance. They could afford to send fewer than half of the church, they reckoned, and not everyone wanted to go, but still there were more volunteers than places, so they decided to send the younger and fitter ones. If the colony was a success, the others would follow later, subsidised by the first settlers; if not, the others would come back, subsidised by those who had stayed. Travellers who had not yet sold their Leiden property did so and pooled the money. They decided that Robinson would stay and pastor the larger part; Brewster would lead the travellers. And Brewster was at hand to agree, resourcefully and dependably hidden from view in Leiden by his friends.

With exasperating timing, now that the pilgrims finally had their Virginia land grant, another possibility opened to them. The New Netherlands Company invited them to join the Dutch settlement around what was to become Alderney, New York. The pilgrims were tempted by Dutch offers of free transport and cattle, but they had patriotic reservations and Weston advised that they would be better off dealing with London investors, and anyway Maurice of Orange denied permission.

Later, a third option emerged, and this one Weston recommended. A new English company was being created, the New England Council, claiming territory up to Nova Scotia. Weston and Robinson agreed that the fishing rights made the north more attractive than Virginia. The Leiden church disagreed about whether to go to Virginia or New England, while others still argued for Guiana. Some travellers refused to go to the wrong destination. In London their investors were equally divided, ready to withdraw their money if the wrong place was chosen. Then, despite the fact that the church could not take all their own number who wanted to go to America, Weston convinced them that for the expedition to be viable they needed to take a large company of passengers.

Carver brought the contracts they had written for investors to London, along with the capital released from selling houses in Leiden, and worked with Cushman raising funds from investors and buying supplies. They met up with Christopher Martin, a puritan merchant organising the passengers from Billericay who were to join the expedition – 'the strangers', as the Leideners called them. The three men salted meat and fish, pickled eggs, churned butter and baked biscuits for the journey, but Cushman and Carver were annoyed that Martin made the strangers' provisions separately, in Kent, without consulting them over quantities. And yet Carver made his provisions in Southampton ready to go straight on a ship, while Cushman worked in London eighty miles away, and they fell out themselves, Carver accusing Cushman of neglecting his job. 'There is fallen already amongst us a flat schism,' said Cushman. Weston was exasperated with these arguments and disjointed operations, warning they would, 'with going up and down, wrangling and expostulating, pass over the summer before [they] will go'. Had he not solemnly promised his help, Weston told them, he would abandon the venture. 'We have begun to build', Carver reckoned, 'and shall not be able to make an end.'[5]

They also had problems getting a ship. Weston insisted they could only afford to hire, while others would only invest if they bought a ship they could use for fishing in America. In May 1620, the congregation in Leiden bought a small ship called – reminiscent of the ships that took the Johnsons to Newfoundland – the *Speedwell*. This sixty-ton pinnace was not intended to contain all the settlers, but to take the Leideners to England, carry some of them across the ocean and then serve as a fishing boat. Weston ridiculed their decision, an attitude Robinson thought ill became a partner who had made so little progress in obtaining their main ship.

Despite all these troubles, the one other Brownist congregation remaining in the Netherlands now decided they wanted to join the American adventure too. Ainsworth's church talked to Robinson's about going with them, and the plan seems to have got far enough for the Amsterdamers to put money into it. Cushman was appalled at this prospect and at the clash of values he thought a joint expedition would suffer – a measure of how liberal, relatively, the Leideners' Brownism had become. 'I had thought they would as soon have gone to Rome as with us,' Cushman wrote; 'for our liberty is to them as ratsbane, and their rigour as bad to us as the Spanish Inquisition.' The plan came to nothing.[6]

The greatest conflict came over the terms that the Leiden church had drawn up for investors. These provided that, for seven years, the settlers would work two days a week for themselves and four for the investors. During that time, the land would belong to the investors; after seven years it would belong to the settlers. The investors were dissatisfied with these terms. The settlers had failed to get a fishing monopoly in either New England or Virginia, and without that, investors were looking at slim returns. Sir George Farrer and his brother, who had offered £500 each, withdrew, and Cushman and Carver feared they would lose everything. So Cushman changed the terms: the settlers would work entirely for the investors for seven years, after which the land would be co-owned equally with the investors.

The church back in Leiden heard about these new terms in June 1620 (by the Dutch calendar; May in England) and were appalled. Cushman had far exceeded his authority, subjecting the settlers to conditions that would make their lives in America vastly more difficult. They wrote to protest, refusing to honour the new terms, which were 'fitter for thieves and bondslaves than honest men'. This contract would prevent people building good houses, they said, and be particularly burdensome for poorer settlers. Cushman, the voice of proto-capitalism, replied that speculation was for the benefit of investors and the church could not embark upon it crying, 'Poor, poor; mercy, mercy!' 'Charity has its life in disasters, not in ventures.' On the other hand, he told them, they should be glad not to have good houses, which were an unnecessary indulgence. The extra two days a week, Cushman said, the investors would leave to the settlers' discretion and conscience, but sharing the final division of property was non-negotiable. If he had stuck to the original conditions, he insisted, they would have lost their funding, their transport and their land. The new terms were the only ones investors would accept, and 'if we will not go, they are content to keep their moneys'.[7]

The Leideners would not shift, and the impasse continued. The would-be migrants had no money left to stay at home, and no means to leave. Robinson regretted employing Cushman and doubted Weston. He told Carver that some members who had pledged money to their fund were refusing to pay up. 'Neither', he said, 'do I think there is a man here would pay anything, if he had again his money in his purse.'[8]

Cushman was on the point of abandoning the whole venture and returning to his wool combing in Leiden. When Weston heard about the contract dispute, he too was ready to quit. So much money had been sunk into the venture, though, that they agreed to rouse themselves for one last try. On Saturday 10 June (English calendar), they found a ship and took it for two days' trial. At 120 tons, it was affordable but smaller than they needed, which Cushman said would serve the Leideners right for being tight-fisted. They hired a pilot, John Clarke of Rotherhithe, who had sailed to Virginia twice, where he was captured by the Spanish and held for four years.

In the two days before Weston and Cushman had to pay for this ship, however, they came across the *Mayflower*. It had a capacity of 180 tons, so it was probably around ninety foot long with three masts and twelve guns.

Farewells

The Leiden pilgrims went to Delfthaven, on the mouth of the Nieuwe Maas, twenty miles south of Leiden, at the end of July, to board the *Speedwell*. The travellers included John Carver's wife Katherine,

329

William Bradford and his wife Dorothy, Edward and Elizabeth Winslow, and William Brewster – who had evaded arrest for a year – with his wife Mary and their younger sons Love and Wrestling. Their older children, aged between fourteen and thirty-three, stayed. Most of the church came to wave them off, along with the Ainsworth church. They had left Leiden after a day of impassioned, tearful prayer, solemn fasting, and a sermon from Robinson that lasted 'a good part of the day'. Winslow, twenty-five years later, recalled him telling them not to idolise what he had taught them but to receive new revelation, 'for he was very confident the Lord had more truth and light yet to break forth out of his holy word'. They talked throughout the night, and the next day a fair wind took them back to England.[9]

> Truly doleful was the sight of that sad and mournful parting; to see what sighs and sobs and prayers did sound amongst them … that sundry of the Dutch strangers that stood on the quay as spectators, could not refrain from tears … But the tide, which stays for no man, calling them away that were thus loth to depart; their reverent pastor, falling down on his knees, and they all with him, with watery cheeks commended them with most fervent prayers to the Lord and his blessing.[10]

A few days later, the *Speedwell* met up with the *Mayflower* at Southampton and with those it had brought from London, which included Cushman's second wife Mary and his eleven-year-old son Thomas. Weston brought the remainder of their money, but they had still not agreed about the two versions of their contract. The travellers insisted they would never honour the terms Cushman had agreed, so Weston told them they were on their own and kept the money. They had nearly £100 still to pay before they could leave Southampton, so they sold a couple of tons of butter, Carver and Martin having rather overdone it in their uncoordinated churning. They wrote a last letter to the investors offering as a compromise to keep working for them after the seven years if they had not made sufficient money by then. They said that they were leaving in serious straits, with 'not a sole to mend a shoe' and 'wanting many muskets', but willing to trust God and face the danger.[11]

The two ships left Southampton in early August. It was already worryingly late in the summer to be crossing the Atlantic, but within days, while they were still in the channel, the *Speedwell* started leaking. 'There was a board a man might have pulled off with his fingers,' Cushman said, 'two foot long, where the water came in as at a mole hole.' They had to turn back to Dartmouth for repairs.[12]

It took a week and a half for the workers to find and mend the leaks, while the travellers worried about the delay and the expense, neither of which they could afford. They were wasting a perfect wind and eating their supplies. The Brownists quarrelled with the strangers. Anxiety about the journey grew and, according to Cushman, Martin would not let the strangers ashore in case they ran away. Cushman wrote to London that everything pointed to their ruin and starvation: 'Prepare for evil tidings of us every day.' The ships set off again, leaving the English coast on 23 August, and by the following day, 300 miles past Land's End, the *Speedwell* was again leaking too badly to continue. They returned to Plymouth for another examination, watching the end of the month come and go. This time the workers found no particular leaks and told them the ship was simply letting in water all over.[13]

The pilgrims decided to abandon the *Speedwell*. They crammed what they could of its passengers and supplies aboard the *Mayflower*, but twenty people had to stay behind. Cushman was happy to be one of them. He returned to London. The *Mayflower* made its third departure for the New World on 6 September.

The Mayflower Compact

When the settlers sighted Cape Cod in November 1620, they had to make a decision about how they were going to run their colony. They had no leader and no system. Four months at sea together had underlined their diversity, their different religious outlooks, different reasons for coming, different social levels, different skills, in different groupings. If they were to survive, they needed a structure that would tie them together. If they had had a royal charter, it would have set this out for them, but they did not. Robinson had suggested some rules, but he was an authority for only half of the travellers.

The pilgrims had no experience of civic administration. They had no theory of government, certainly not a new theory. What they had was the experience of creating and maintaining a community through a mutual, conditional covenant, so they did that. The Mayflower Compact was drawn up, agreed and signed by the forty-one adult males. The settlement would be governed by consent. Forty years before, the first Brownists had created a church, without the decree of king or Pope but by their own agreement to be a church and to be answerable to one another; now, in the same way, they constituted 'a civil body politic' by mutual agreement. It was an idea with a future.

Epilogue: The long run

JOHN ROBINSON NEVER did take those left behind to join the pilgrims in Plymouth Plantation. Their investors were not eager to sink money into transporting those too frail to make the first journey, and when the pilgrims' first shipment of five hundred pounds' worth of beaver and otter skins, oak, walnut and sassafras was pirated off the coast of France, Robinson's hopes receded. Cushman went though, along with Jonathan Brewster, in 1621; Fear and Patience Brewster followed two years later. Robinson prayed for and sent encouragement to the settlers, especially when he heard that half of them died in the first winter. 'Oh! how grievous hath it been to you to bear, and to us to take knowledge of,' he wrote; 'which, if it could be mended with lamenting, could not sufficiently be bewailed; but we must go unto them, and they shall not return unto us.' They had died in battle, he said, and gained the victory. Robinson himself died on 1 March 1625 aged fifty.[1]

By then Henry Ainsworth had also crossed the greater ocean, dying in 1622. His last months were taken up with a dispute over his decision to admit Sabine Staresmore into membership despite his middle-way opinions, and, more happily, with the completion of his annotated translation of Song of Songs. The book was published in 1623, followed by a compilation in 1627, and he left unfinished work on Hosea, Matthew and Hebrews.

Both churches limped on for a while without their pastors. The Smyth group, though it still held English services, was absorbed into the Waterlander church. From the Baptists in England, the one faint sign of life was a petition to the king from Newgate in 1620 complaining about how many of them had died in prison. Jacob apparently did the opposite of Robinson, leaving his congregational church, and his wife, to go to Virginia in 1622, where he died two years later.

History would seem to be drawing a pretty firm line under the Separatist movement, but the truth was stranger. Not only did the Plymouth community survive, but in 1621 a minister called Hubbard quit the Church of England, founded a Separatist group in London, then led it into exile in Ireland. After he died, his followers returned to London and elected John Canne as their minister, and Canne went to Amsterdam in the early 1630s to lead the Ancient Church, as well as printing books, practising alchemy and selling brandy. In the Civil War, he was chaplain to the Leveller Robert Lilburne.

William Brewer returned to Kent, where he resumed printing and employed a candlemaker called Turner as a Separatist preacher. It was reported in 1626 that the Kent Brownists increased daily. Brewer wrote a book prophesying the destruction of England in three years, and was arrested in 1626, remained in prison for fourteen years and died a month after his release.

Jacob's church found a replacement minister, and grew considerably in the 1620s and 1630s. At least two groups broke away to form more thoroughly Separatist churches, but remained on good terms with the parent church. This 'Jacobite' group of churches had maybe a thousand members in total and they were home to a number of religious leaders of the English revolution.

Most surprisingly, the Baptists not only survived long enough in England to re-enter abortive negotiations with the Waterlanders in 1626, but did so on behalf of five churches, in London, Coventry, Lincoln, Salisbury and Tiverton, totalling 150 members. Then, in the 1630s, one of the Jacobite churches became Baptist. Unlike any of the Baptists with Amsterdam roots, they kept their Calvinist theology, so this was a second stream of Baptists, 'Particular' as opposed to 'General', and by 1644 there were seven Particular Baptist churches in London.

In 1631, the Bishop of Exeter reported 'there are eleven several congregations (as they call them) of separatists about the city (London), furnished with their idly pretended pastors, who meet together in brewhouses and such other places of resort every Sunday'. The unpopular high church policy of Charles I, enforced from 1633 by Archbishop Laud, gave it new impetus, and by 1641 Joseph Hall, now Bishop of Norwich, reckoned there were eighty Separatist churches in the London area, led by 'cobblers, tailors, felt-makers and suchlike trash'. More shocking still, a pamphlet that year named six female preachers. The radicalism of earlier Separatists had been overtaken; further light had broken.[2]

By this time, there were easily more than ten thousand congregationalists in North America, Laud's abominations inspiring even more immigration than separation. The Separatist settlement in Plymouth, though more than a thousand-strong itself, was swamped by the more successful Massachusetts Bay colony. Massachusetts was built on Jacob's non-separating congregationalism, the creed of a flood of puritans who had lost hope in presbyterianism without acquiring a taste for Brownism, removing themselves from the ever-worsening Church of England without formally ceding from it.

In England, Jacobism had seemed very much like a friendlier version of Brownism, founding reformed churches without damning those who worshipped elsewhere. In New England, it revealed itself for what it was, or what it also was: a design for a puritan state church. Massachusetts allowed no churches except congregational ones and it outlawed heresy, blasphemy and recusancy. The colony went so far as to allow only church members to vote, and strictly tested the orthodoxy and holiness of members. Dissidents such as Roger Williams and Anne Hutchinson were banished in the 1630s. They said they suffered for their conscience, but the Boston minister John Cotton disagreed: God communicates his truth perfectly, Cotton said in a twist of inquisitorial logic that could have shamed Bonner, so the heretic 'is not persecuted for cause of conscience, but for sinning against his own conscience'. Between 1659 and 1660, three Quakers, Marmaduke Stephenson, William Robinson and Mary Dyer, were executed in the puritan colony.[3]

Plymouth was not founded on such principles, but needing the protection and friendship of Massachusetts, its Separatism became subdued. In the longer term though, history and indeed geography were on the side of separation. The response of Williams and Hutchinson illustrated the fundamental difference between English and American persecution: they and others simply went to Rhode Island and formed a new settlement. They declared freedom of religion and the first American Baptist church was opened. However much control the new state churches had, they could not control what happened over the horizon, so their powers were as limited as the landscape was limitless. However many new Egypts sprang up, there was still plenty of Promised Land out there.

Meanwhile, in their more crowded territory and over an even longer timescale, the British slowly started to conclude, from the failure of every method of persuading the whole population to share a single outlook and identity, that they were going to have to learn to live with difference and accept their neighbours, whether Catholic or Baptist, Turk or Jew. The future belonged, of all people to give it to, to Thomas Helwys.

The Separatists had always been told that they were an unsuccessful-looking movement. Robinson's answer was that it was early days. Hus had preached the true gospel in the fifteenth century with meagre results – until Luther reaped the rewards a hundred years later. Now, said Robinson, the fields were so ripe they 'do promise within less than an hundred years (if our sins and theirs make not us and them unworthy of this mercy) a very plenteous harvest'. It was an unconvincing boast, but a century after the sailing of the *Mayflower* there were 340,000 dissenters in England, another 18,000 in Wales, totalling 6 per cent of the population. In America, they were a much larger proportion of a much smaller populace. Today, there are something like 2.5 million congregationalists in the world, and 40 million Baptists.[4]

There remains one loose end to the story: Brownism's great survivor – though perhaps not in a spiritual sense – who gave his name to the movement, to the dismay of everyone in it. Robert Browne was still living in his Achurch rectory, after Harrison and Cartwright, Barrow and Greenwood, Johnson and Ainsworth, Smyth and Helwys, Robinson and Jacob had all died. After Alice also died, Robert, aged sixty-two, married Elizabeth Warrener, but they did not get on, a fact that caused a stir in Achurch, and three years later, in 1615, he abandoned her and his job, though he kept the income. He seems to have felt the old itch, and over the next ten years held conventicles in the neighbouring village, Thorpe Waterville. He eventually returned to work at Achurch in 1626, was accused of not conforming to the Prayer Book, and sued his parishioners. Browne

was excommunicated in 1631 and removed from his post the following year. In August 1633, aged eighty-three, he was asked by his
godson, Robert Greene, the parish constable, to pay his rates; he
responded by assaulting Greene and found himself in Northampton
jail, where he died a month later.

The embarrassment Browne caused the Brownists was gigantic,
and the fact that he was treated as their figurehead seemed a gross
injustice. One certainly sees their point, and yet consider all that he
and the movement had in common: the extremism, the harshness,
the energy, the perversity, the ground-breaking radicalism, the quar-
relling, the inconsistency, the sacrifices, the moments of bravery, the
retreats, the flashes of genius, the reams of pedantry. For better and
for worse, they were all Brownists.

Notes

Introduction

1. Henoch Clapham, *The syn, against the holy ghoste* (Amsterdam, 1598), unpaginated.

Chapter 1

1. *The Acts and Monuments of John Foxe*, ed. Stephen Cattley (London, 1838),VI, 645.
2. *Foxe*, VI, 658.
3. *Foxe*,VI, 658.
4. Peter Marshall, *Heretics and Believers: A history of the English Reformation* (New Haven and London:Yale University Press, 2018); Joseph Lemuel Chester, *John Rogers* (London, 1861), 202n; *English Historical Documents: 1485–1558*, ed. C.H.Williams (London: Eyre & Spottiswoode, 1969), 839.
5. Ted Hughes, 'The Martyrdom of Bishop Farrar', *New Selected Poems 1957–1994* (London: Faber and Faber, 1995).
6. Eamon Duffy, *Fires of Faith: Catholic England under Mary Tudor* (New Haven and London:Yale University Press, 2009), 160.

Chapter 2

1. *The Writings of Robert Harrison and Robert Browne*, ed. Albert Peel and Leland Henry Carlson (London: George Allen & Unwin, 1953), 74.
2. *The Zurich Letters*, ed. Hastings Robinson (Cambridge, 1842–5) (2 vols), II, 160.
3. *Foxe*, VII, 322.
4. *Foxe*, VIII, 448.

5. John Strype, *Ecclesiastical Memorials* (Oxford, 1822) (3 vols), III, part 2, 133.
6. *Chronicles of the Pilgrim Fathers of the Colony of Plymouth, from 1602 to 1625*, ed. Alexander Young (Boston, 1841), 442.

Chapter 3

1. *The Writings of Henry Barrow 1587–1590*, ed. Leland H. Carlson (London: Allen & Unwin, 1962), 283.
2. *Harrison and Browne*, 74.
3. *Barrow 1587–1590*, 283.
4. *Zurich Letters*, II 30.
5. Richard Hooker, *Of the Laws of Ecclesiastical Polity* (London, 1821) (3 vols), I, 129–30.
6. *Elizabethan Puritanism*, ed. Leonard Trinterud (Oxford: OUP, 1971), 33.
7. Patrick Collinson, *The Reformation* (London: Weidenfeld & Nicolson, 2003), 114.
8. *Foxe*, I, 524.
9. *Correspondence of Matthew Parker*, ed. John Bruce and T.T. Perowne (Cambridge, 1853), 270.
10. *Zurich Letters*, I, 168.
11. *Zurich Letters*, I, 153, 141; *John Knox's History of the Reformation in Scotland* (London etc.) (2 vols), II, 200.
12. *The Oxford Handbook of the Early Modern Sermon*, ed. Peter McCullough, Hugh Adlington and Emma Rhatigan (Oxford: OUP, 2011), 377.
13. John Strype, *The History of the Life and Acts of Edmund Grindal* (London, 1710), I, 98.
14. *Three Fifteenth-Century Chronicles with Historical Memoranda by John Stowe*, ed. James Gairdner ([London]: Camden Society, 1880), 140.
15. *Zurich Letters*, I, 168.
16. *Zurich Letters*, I, 199, II, 4.
17. *The Remains of Edmund Grindal*, ed. William Nicholson (Cambridge, 1843), 203.

Chapter 4

1. *Remains of Grindal*, 202; *Zurich Letters*, 168; R.W. Dixon, *History of the Church of England* (Oxford: Clarendon Press, 1902), VI, 164.

2. *Remains of Grindal*, 211, 208, 212.

3. *Remains of Grindal*, 206.

4. Dixon, *History of the Church of England*, VI, 178-80; Albert Peel, *The First Congregational Churches* (Cambridge: CUP, 1920), 8–9; *Seconde Parte of a Register*, ed. Albert Peel (Cambridge: CUP, 1915), 79.

5. *Foxe*, VI, 576.

6. Peter Lorimer, *John Knox and the Church of England* (London, 1875), 298–300.

7. *Seconde Parte of a Register*, I, 587.

8. *Zurich Letters*, 201–2.

Chapter 5

1. *Seconde Parte of a Register*, I, 149.

2. Peel, *The First Congregational Churches*, 9; *Remains of Grindal*, 202.

3. *Remains of Grindal*, 317.

4. *Remains of Grindal*, 319.

5. Peel, *The First Congregational Churches*, 59, 60.

6. *Harrison and Browne*, 93; *Chronicles of the Pilgrim Fathers*, 442.

7. *Seconde Parte of a Register*, I, 625.

8. John Strype, *The Life and Acts of Matthew Parker* (Oxford, 1821) (4 vols), II, 283–5.

9. Peel, *The First Congregational Churches*, 23–4.

Chapter 6

1. Charles Wilson, *Queen Elizabeth and the Revolt of the Netherlands* (Berkeley: University of California Press, 1970), 1.

2. E.H. Kossman and A.F. Mellink, *Texts Concerning the Revolt of the Netherlands* (Cambridge: CUP, 1974), 60.

3. *Zurich Letters*, II, 169; J.A. Froude, *History of England from the Fall of Wolsey to the Death of Elizabeth* (London, 1866), III, 326.

4. *Zurich Letters*, II, 172; R. Keith, *The History of the Affairs of Church and State in Scotland* (Edinburgh, 1734) (3 vols), I, 429.

5. *Zurich Letters*, I, 211, II, 247.

6. Patrick Collinson, *The Elizabethan Puritan Movement* (Oxford: Clarendon Press, 1990), 101.

341

7. *The Works of John Whitgift*, ed. John Ayre (Cambridge, 1852), II, 104.

8. Samuel Clarke, *The lives of two and twenty English divines* (London, 1660), 26.

9. *Works of Whitgift*, II, 89; *Puritan Manifestoes: A Study of the Origin of the Puritan Revolt*, ed. W.H. Frere and C.E. Douglas (London: Society for the Propagation of Christian Knowledge, 1907), 30.

10. *Works of Whitgift*, I, 102.

11. *Puritan Manifestoes*, 9; *Seconde Parte of a Register*, I, 601, 586.

12. *The Works of John Smyth*, ed. W.T. Whitley (Cambridge: CUP, 1915) (2 vols), II, 441–2.

13. *Harrison and Browne*, 388–9; Albert Peel, *Tracts Ascribed to Richard Bancroft* (Cambridge: CUP, 2011), 72.

14. *Puritan Manifestoes*, 34; Christopher Hill, *Society & Puritanism in Pre-Revolutionary England* (London: Secker & Warburg, 1964), 205.

15. *Works of Whitgift*, 165.

16. *Zurich Letters*, I, 249; *Seconde Parte of a Register*, 82.

17. *Seconde Parte of a Register*, 79–80.

18. *Zurich Letters*, I, 237.

19. *Harrison and Browne*, 93.

20. Gāmini Salgādo, *The Elizabethan Underworld* (Stroud: Sutton Publishing, 2005), 185.

21. Peel, *The First Congregational Churches*, 33.

22. R.T. Jones, K. Dix, A. Ruston (eds), *Protestant Nonconformist Texts* (4 vols), I, 35–6.

23. *Zurich Letters*, I, 248–9.

24. *Seconde Parte of a Register*, I, 157–60.

25. *Harrison and Browne*, 93.

Chapter 7

1. *Puritan Manifestoes*, 21, 22, 26, 29, 31.

2. Daniel Neal, *The History of the Puritans* (London, 1732) (2 vols), I, 189.

3. Neal, *History of the Puritans*, I, 287.

4. Collinson, *Elizabethan Puritan Movement*, 144–5.

5. John Strype, *The Life and Acts of John Whitgift* (London, 1718), Appendix, 20; Strype, *Life of Parker*, II, 263, 240.

6. *Puritan Manifestoes*, 9.

7. *Seconde Parte of a Register*, 86.
8. *Seconde Parte of a Register*, 86.
9. Benjamin Brook, *The Lives of the Puritans* (London, 1813) (3 vols), I, 146n–148n; Neal, *History of the Puritans*, I, 317–21.
10. *Correspondence of Parker*, 461.
11. *Correspondence of Parker*, 464.

Chapter 8

1. Thielem J. von Bracht, *The Bloody Theatre, or Martyrs' Mirror*, trans. I. Daniel Rupp (Lancaster, Pennsylvania, 1837).
2. John Stow, *Annales of England* (London, 1605), 1149–50.
3. Bracht, *Martyrs' Mirror*, 916–17.
4. Thomas Crosby, *The History of the English Baptists* (London, 1738) (4 vols), I, 72–3.
5. Stow, *Annales of England*, 1151; Bracht, *Martyrs' Mirror*, 926.
6. Bracht, *Martyrs' Mirror*, 917; Albert Peel, 'A Conscientious Objector of 1575', *Transactions of the Baptist Historical Society*, VII (1920), 78, 112.
7. Peel, 'A Conscientious Objector of 1575', 79.
8. Peel, 'A Conscientious Objector of 1575', 96, 84, 76, 106, 103, 87.
9. Peel, 'A Conscientious Objector of 1575', 88–9, 87–8.
10. Strype, *Life of Grindal*, II, 570, 572.
11. *Puritan Manifestoes*, 10.

Chapter 9

1. Clarke, *Lives of two and twenty English divines*, 14.
2. *Harrison and Browne*, 404.
3. Strype, *Life of Parker*, II, 336–7.
4. Henoch Clapham, *Antidoton* (London, 1600), 25.
5. Stephen Ofwod, *An Advertisement to Jhon Delecluse and Henry May the Elder* ([Amsterdam?, 1632]), 40; John Strype, *Annals of the Reformation and the Establishment of Religion in the Church of England* (Oxford, 1824), II.2, 187; Thomas Fuller, *The church-history of Britain* (6 vols) (London, 1655), III, 166.
6. Browne's authorship is demonstrated in B.R. White, 'A Puritan Work by Robert Browne', *The Baptist Quarterly*, 18 (1959), 109–17.

7. *Harrison and Browne*, 59.

8. *Harrison and Browne*, 399.

9. 'A Brief Exposition of the One and Eternal Testament or Covenant of God', in *Fountainhead of Federalism: Heinrich Bullinger and the Covenant Tradition*, ed. Charles S. McCoy and J. Wayne Baker (Louisville: Westminster John Knox Press, 1991), 112.

10. *Harrison and Browne*, 422.

11. J.E. Neale, *Elizabeth I and her Parliaments* (London: Jonathan Cape, 1965) (2 vols), I, 391.

12. Richard Simpson, *Edmund Campion: A Biography* (London and Edinburgh, 1867), 161.

13. Strype, *Annals of the Reformation*, III.1, 22.

14. *Harrison and Browne*, 63; Strype, *Annals of the Reformation*, III.1, 22.

15. Stephen Bredwell, *The Rasing of the Foundations of Brovvnisme* (London, 1588), 128, 130.

16. Bredwell, *Rasing of the Foundations of Brovvnisme*, 137.

17. *Harrison and Browne*, 43, 68.

18. *Harrison and Browne*, 53

19. *Harrison and Browne*, 60.

20. *Harrison and Browne*, 63–4.

21. *Harrison and Browne*, 423.

22. Strype, *Annals of the Reformation*, III.1, 16.

23. *Harrison and Browne*, 424.

Chapter 10

1. William Bradford, *History of Plymouth Plantation, 1620–1647*, ed. Worthington Chauncey Ford (Boston: Houghton Mifflin Company, 1912) (2 vols), I, 28.

2. Timothy George, *John Robinson and the English Separatist Tradition* (Macon: Mercer University Press, 1982), 39.

3. *Harrison and Browne*, 164, 162, 415, 416.

4. *Harrison and Browne*, 164, 161, 266, 161, 162.

5. *Harrison and Browne*, 167, 155.

6. White, 'A Puritan Work by Robert Browne', 114; *Harrison and Browne*, 214–15.

7. *Harrison and Browne*, 257.

8. *Harrison and Browne*, 408, 207.

9. *Harrison and Browne*, 416.

10. *Tracts Ascribed to Richard Bancroft*, ed. Albert Peel (Cambridge: CUP, 1953).

11. *Harrison and Browne*, 149.

12. *Harrison and Browne*, 225.

13. *Harrison and Browne*, 93.

14. Patrick Collinson, *From Cranmer to Sancroft: Essays on English Religion in the Sixteenth and Seventeenth Centuries* (London: A & C Black, 2007), 124.

15. Keith L. Sprunger, *Dutch Puritanism: A History of English and Scottish Churches of the Netherlands in the Sixteenth and Seventeenth Centuries* (Eugene, Oregon: Wipf & Stock, 1983), 24; *Cartwrightiana*, ed. Albert Peel and Leland H. Carlson (London: Allen & Unwin, 1951), 48.

16. *Harrison and Browne*, 427.

17. George Johnson, *A Discourse of some Troubles and Excommunications in the Banished English Church at Amsterdam* (Amsterdam, 1603), 8.

18. *Harrison and Browne*, 428.

19. *Harrison and Browne*, 428.

20. *Harrison and Browne*, 253, 161.

21. *Harrison and Browne*, 428, 149.

Chapter 11

1. *Chronicles of the Pilgrim Fathers*, 427.

2. J. Waddington, *Congregational Martyrs* (London, 1861), 43–4; Ofwod, *An Advertisement to Jhon Delecluse and Henry May the Elder*, 40.

3. John Craig, *Reformation, Politics and Polemics: The Growth of Protestantism in East Anglian Market Towns, 1500–1610* (Abingdon: Routledge, 2016), 107.

4. *Harrison and Browne*, 538.

5. *Documents Illustrative of English Church History*, ed. H. Gee and J.H. William (London: MacMillan, 1914), 482.

6. Strype, *Life of Whitgift*, appendix, 45, 46, 47, 48.

7. Collinson, *The Elizabethan Puritan Movement*, 257.

8. Fuller, *Church-history of Britain*, III, 155; Strype, *Life of Whitgift*, 152.

9. James Calderwood, *The History of the Kirk of Scotland*, ed. Thomas Thomson (Edinburgh, 1842–9) (8 vols), IV, 2.

10. Calderwood, *History of the Kirk of Scotland*, IV, 3; James VI, *Basilikon Doron* (London, 1603), unpaginated preface, A4 verso.

11. *Harrison and Browne*, 519.

12. *Cartwrightiana*, 57.
13. *Harrison and Browne*, 447.
14. *Harrison and Browne*, 435; Bredwell, *Rasing of the Foundations of Brovvnisme*, 135.
15. Alison Plowden, 'Throckmorton, Francis (1554–1584)', *Oxford Dictionary of National Biography* (Oxford: OUP, 2004), LIV, 689.
16. *Zurich Letters*, II, 325.
17. Collinson, *The Elizabethan Puritan Movement*, 272.
18. Craig, *Reformation, Politics and Polemics*, 106.
19. Craig, *Reformation, Politics and Polemics*, 58.
20. Bredwell, *Rasing of the Foundations of Brovvnisme*, 39.

Chapter 12

1. Richard Bancroft, *Daungerous Positions and Proceedings* (London, 1593), 74.
2. P.W. Hasler, 'Job Throckmorton', in *The History of Parliament: The House of Commons 1558–1603*, ed. P.W. Hasler (London: The Stationery Office, 1981).
3. Neale, *Elizabeth I and her Parliaments*, II, 149.
4. Hasler, 'Job Throckmorton'.
5. Neale, *Elizabeth I and her Parliaments*, II, 163–4.
6. *Barrow 1587–1590*, 535; *Chronicles of the Pilgrim Fathers*, 433; *The Complete Writings of Roger Williams* (Eugene, Oregon: Wipf & Stock, 2007), II, 195; *The Writings of John Greenwood and Henry Barrow 1591–1593*, ed. Leland H. Carlson (London: George Allen & Unwin, 1970), 161; Richard Bancroft, *A survay of the pretended holy discipline* (London, 1593), 249.
7. *Chronicles of the Pilgrim Fathers*, 434.
8. *Barrow 1587–1590*, 64, 57.
9. Henry Ainsworth, *Covnterpoyson* ([Amsterdam], 1608), 23.
10. *The Writings of John Greenwood 1587–1590*, ed. Leland H. Carlson (London: George Allen & Unwin, 1962), 299.
11. *Greenwood*, 294; Peel, *Tracts Ascribed to Richard Bancroft*, 72.
12. *Barrow 1587–1590*, 54.
13. *Barrow 1587–1590*, 62.
14. *Barrow 1587–1590*, 55–6.
15. *Barrow 1587–1590*, 54.
16. *Greenwood*, 312.
17. *Barrow 1587–1590*, 91–100
18. *Barrow 1587–1590*, 102–4.

Chapter 13

1. Patrick McGrath, *Papists and Puritans under Elizabeth I* (New York: Walker & Co., 1967), 200.

2. Neil Hanson, *The Confident Hope of a Miracle* (New York: Knopf, 2005), 169.

3. Strype, *Life of Whitgift*, III, 212.

4. Strype, *Annals of the Reformation*, III.2, 11–12.

5. Hanson, *Confident Hope of a Miracle*, 410; Strype, *Annals of the Reformation*, III.2, 29; Anon, *A Skeltonicall salutation* (Oxford, 1589) [7].

6. *Barrow 1587–90*, 254.

7. *Barrow 1587–90*, 254; *Greenwood*, 314.

8. Fuller, *Church-history of Britain*, III, 167.

9. Bredwell, *Rasing of the Foundations of Brovvnisme*, 139, [vi].

10. Bancroft, *A Sermon Preached at Paules Crosse* (London, 158[9]) 76.

11. Champlin Burrage, *The 'retraction' of Robert Browne, Father of Congregationalism* (Oxford: OUP, 1907), vi; *Cartwrightiana*, 197f.

12. Bredwell, *Rasing of the Foundations of Brovvnisme*, 141, [xi, viii, viii–ix], 126.

13. Robert Some, *A godly treatise, wherein are examined and confuted ... H. Barrow and J. Greenewood* (London, 1589) (A2v).

14. William Pierce, *John Penry: His Life, Times and Writings* (London: Hodder & Stoughton, 1923), 167, 175.

15. *A Defence of Svch Points in R. Somes Last Treatise as M. Penry Hath Dealt Against* in *A Godly Treatise* (London, 1588; bound with *A Godly Treatise Containing and Deciding Certain Questions*), 55.

16. *Harrison and Browne*, 518.

17. *Harrison and Browne*, 529.

18. Benjamin Hanbury, *Historical memorials relating to the Independents or Congregationalists* (London, 1839) (3 vols), I, 24.

Chapter 14

1. *The Martin Marprelate Tracts: A Modernized and Annotated Edition*, ed. Joseph L. Black (Cambridge: CUP, 2011), 209.

2. *Martin Marprelate Tracts*, 8, 15, 29.

3. *An Introductory Sketch to the Martin Marprelate Controversy 1588–1590*, ed. E. Arber (Westminster, 1895), 107.

4. *Martin Marprelate Tracts*, 53.

5. Bancroft, *Sermon Preached at Paules Crosse*, 39, 83.

6. Bancroft, *Sermon Preached at Paules Crosse*, 77.

7. *Martin Marprelate Tracts*, 115, 126.

8. *Greenwood*, 277.

9. *Barrow 1587–1590*, 178–88.

10. *Barrow 1587–1590*, 202.

11. Anon, *Mar-Martine* [(London?, 1589)]

12. 'Mar-Martine', *Transactions of the Congregational Historical Society*, V (1912), 369; John Lyly, *A Whip for an Ape* ([London], 1589), 4.

13. *Martin Marprelate Tracts*, 147, 158.

14. *Martin Marprelate Tracts*, 153.

15. *Martin Marprelate Tracts*, 172.

16. *Introductory sketch to the Martin Marprelate controversy*, 116.

Chapter 15

1. *Martin Marprelate Tracts*, 198.

2. *Martin Marprelate Tracts*, 205.

3. Bancroft, *Sermon Preached at Paules Crosse*, 74; Pierce, *John Penry: His life, Times and Writings*, 268.

4. *Barrow 1587–1590*, 214, 216.

5. *Barrow 1587–1590*, 156, 228.

6. Christopher Lawne, *Brovvnisme turned the in-side out-ward* (London, 1613) [ii].

7. John Udall, *A demonstration of the trueth of that discipline which Christe hath prescribed* (East Molesley, [1588]), 2, 4, 2, 1.

8. *Martin Marprelate Tracts*, liv.

Chapter 16

1. *Greenwood 1587–1590*, 143.

2. *Greenwood 1587–1590*, 150–1.

3. *Greenwood 1587–1590*, 187.

4. *Greenwood 1587–1590*, 188–91.

5. *Harrison and Browne*, 530.

6. Strype, *Annals of the Reformation*, IV, 176.

Chapter 17

1. *Barrow 1587–1590*, 273–6.
2. John Calvin, *Institutes of the Christian Religion,* ed. John T. McNeil, trans. Ford Lewis Battles (Philadelphia: The Westminster Press, 1960), 4.1.13.
3. *Barrow 1587–1590*, 287.
4. *Barrow 1587–1590*, 281, 294, 299, 309, 316, 319, 328.
5. JG [Job Throkmorton], *M. Some Laid Open in his Coulers* ([?], 1588), 58.
6. *Barrow 1587–1590*, 423.
7. *Barrow 1587–1590*, 426.
8. *Barrow 1587–1590*, 443, 444.
9. Johnson, *A Discourse of some Troubles*, 205.
10. *The Works of John Robinson*, ed. Robert Ashton (London, 1851) (3 vols), II, 58.
11. George Gifford, *A short treatise against the Donatists of England* (London, 1590), 50; *The Writings of Henry Barrow 1590–1591*, ed. Leland H. Carlson (London: Allen & Unwin, 1966), 115.
12. *Barrow 1590–1591*, 370; *Chronicles of the Pilgrim Fathers*, 424–5.

Chapter 18

1. Richard Cosin, *Conspiracy for Pretended Reformation: viz presbyterial discipline* (London, 1699), 8, 9, 76.
2. Cosin, *Conspiracy for Pretended Reformation*, 44.
3. A.F. Scott Pearson, *Thomas Cartwright and Elizabethan Puritanism, 1535–1603* (Cambridge: CUP, 1925), 323.
4. Bancroft, *Daungerous Positions*, 154.
5. Cosin, *Conspiracy for Pretended Reformation*, 127.
6. *Greenwood and Barrow 1591–1593*, 101–3.
7. *Greenwood and Barrow 1591–1593*, 101.
8. George Paule, *The Life of John Whitgift* (London, 1699), 66; *Greenwood and Barrow 1591–1593*, 219.
9. Paule, *Life of Whitgift*, 64.
10. Matthew Sutcliffe, *An Answere to a Certaine Libel Supplicatorie* (London, 1592), 201–2, 78; Throkmorton, *The defence of Job Throkmorton against the slaunders of maister Sutcliffe*, Eii; Matthew Sutcliffe, *An Answere unto a certaine calumnious letter published by M. J. Throkmorton* (London, 1595), 74.

Chapter 19

1. Champlin Burrage, *The Early English Dissenters in the Light of Recent Research* (2 vols) (Cambridge: CUP, 1912), I, 138, 139.
2. *Greenwood and Barrow 1591–1593*, 295.
3. Neale, *Elizabeth and Her Parliaments*, II, 246.
4. Neale, *Elizabeth and Her Parliaments*, II, 249.
5. *Greenwood and Barrow 1591–1593*, 409, 411–12.
6. *Greenwood and Barrow 1591–1593*, 224.
7. *Greenwood and Barrow 1591–1593*, 275.
8. *Greenwood and Barrow 1591–1593*, 276.
9. *Greenwood and Barrow 1591–1593*, 277.

Chapter 20

1. *Martin Marprelate Tracts*, 181, 181n.
2. *Greenwood and Barrow 1591–1593*, 249.
3. *Greenwood and Barrow 1591–1593*, 250.
4. Neale, *Elizabeth and Her Parliaments*, II, 289.
5. *Greenwood and Barrow 1591–1593*.
6. Neale, *Elizabeth and Her Parliaments*, II, 290.

Chapter 21

1. Pierce, *John Penry*, 402.
2. Pierce, *John Penry*, 407.
3. John Waddington, *Congregational History, 1567–1700* (London, 1880), 93.
4. Burrage, *Early English Dissenters*, II, 95.
5. Pierce, *John Penry*, 476.
6. William Brereton, *Travels in Holland, the United Provinces, England, Scotland and Ireland* ([Manchester]: Chetham Society, 1844), 55–6.
7. Kirk R. MacGregor, 'Hubmaier's Concord of Predestination with Free Will', *Direction*, vol. 35, no. 2 (2006), 290.
8. Johnson, *A Discourse of some Troubles*, 97, 136.
9. Johnson, *A Discourse of some Troubles*, 95.
10. Johnson, *A Discourse of some Troubles*, 95.
11. Johnson, *A Discourse of some Troubles*, 97.

12. Johnson, *A Discourse of some Troubles*, 99, 100.
13. Francis Johnson, *A Treatise of the Ministery of the Church of England* ([?], 1595), 2.
14. William Lumpkin, *Baptist Confessions of Faith* (Valley Forge: Judson, 1969), 89, 90–1.
15. Lumpkin, *Baptist Confessions of Faith*, 92, 94–5.

Chapter 22

1. *Greenwood and Barrow 1591–1593*, 470.
2. Richard Hakluyt, *The Principal Navigations, Voyages, Traffiques & Discoveries of the English Nation* (12 vols) (Glasgow: J. MacLehose and Sons, 1903), VIII, 167.
3. Johnson, *A Discourse of some Troubles*, 109, 110.
4. Hakluyt, *Principal Navigations*, VIII, 179.
5. *Chronicles of the Pilgrim Fathers*, 441.
6. Henoch Clapham, *Theologicall axioms or conclusions* (Amsterdam, 1597), unpaginated, Examination 11; Clapham, *The syn, against the holy ghoste*, sixth page of Conclusion.
7. Henoch Clapham, *Antidoton* (London, 1600), 10, 33.
8. F.J. Powicke, *Henry Harrow, Separatist, and the Exiled Church of Amsterdam* (London: James Clarke, 1900), 226; *Complete Writings of Roger Williams*, II, 207.
9. [Francis Johnson], *Certayne letters* ([Amsterdam], 1602), 55.
10. Johnson, *A Discourse of some Troubles*, 76.
11. Sprunger, *Dutch Puritanism*, 53.
12. Francis Johnson, *An answer to Maister H. Jacob his Defence of the Churches and Ministery of England* ([Amsterdam], 1600), 28.
13. Ofwod, *An Advertisement to Jhon Delecluse and Henry May the Elder*, iv, 1.
14. Sprunger, *Dutch Puritanism*, 53–4.
15. Ofwod, *An Advertisement to Jhon Delecluse and Henry May the Elder*, 40n.
16. Johnson, *A Discourse of some Troubles*, 44.
17. Christopher Lawne, et al., *The Prophane Schisme of the Brownists* (London, 1612), 64.
18. Francis Johnson, *An Inqvirie and Ansvver of Thomas VVhite his Discoverie of Brovvnisme* ([Amsterdam], 1606), 29, 50.
19. Richard Clifton, *An advertisement concerning a book lately published by Christopher Lawne and others* ([Amsterdam, 1612]), 14; *Plymouth Church Records, 1620–1859* (New York: New England Society, 1920), I, 135.

Chapter 23

1. *Memoirs of the life of Robert Cary*, ed. Earl of Corke and Orrery (London, 1759), 147–8.
2. McGrath, *Papists and Puritans*, 364.
3. Adam Nicolson, *Power and Glory* (London: HarperCollins, 2003), 50.
4. Strype, *Life of Whitgift*, III, 408.
5. http://www.earlystuartlibels.net/htdocs/early_jacobean_section/B11.html#f1.
6. Miles Mickle-bound, *Mr Henry Barrowes platform* ([London?, 1611]), 131; Francis Johnson and Henry Ainsworth, *An Apologie or Defence of svch trve Christians as are commonly (vnjustly) called Brovvnists* (Amsterdam, 1604), 33.
7. McGrath, *Papists and Puritans*, 361.

Chapter 24

1. Burrage, *Early English Dissenters*, I, 286.
2. *The Works of John Robinson*, ed. Robert Ashton (London, 1851) (3 vols), II, 52.
3. Walter H. Burgess, *The Pastor of the Pilgrims: A Biography of John Robinson* (London: Williams and Norgate, 1920), 67; *Works of Robinson*, I, xviii.
4. Richard Bernard, *Plaine Euidences: The Church of England is apostolicall, the separation schismaticall* (London, 1610), 18.
5. Bernard, *Plaine Euidences*, 18.
6. *Chronicles of the Pilgrim Fathers*, 453.
7. *Works of Smyth*, II, 534, 331.
8. Richard Bernard, *Christian advertisements and counsels of peace* (London, 1608), 37; *Works of Smyth*, II, 535.
9. *Works of Robinson*, II, 8, 9.
10. *Works of Smyth*, II, 337; *Works of Robinson*, II, 52.
11. Burgess, *Pastor of the Pilgrims*, 81; Bernard, *Plaine Euidences*, 20.
12. Bradford, *History of Plymouth Plantation*, I, 22.
13. *Works of Smyth*, II, 575.
14. *Works of Robinson*, II, 101.
15. Lawne, *The Prophane Schisme*, 63.
16. *The Works of the Right Reverend Father in God, Joseph Hall* (London, 1808), IX, 457.

17. Henry Martyn Dexter and Morton Dexter, *The England and Holland of the Pilgrims* (Boston and New York: Houghton Mifflin, 1906), 393.
18. *Works of Smyth*, II, 526–8.
19. Young, *Chronicles of the Pilgrim Fathers*, 23.
20. *Works of Robinson*, III, 159.
21. Bradford, *History of Plymouth Plantation*, I, 26.
22. Burgess, *Pastor of the Pilgrims*, 79.
23. Bradford, *History of Plymouth Plantation*, I, 33.
24. Bradford, *History of Plymouth Plantation*, I, 33.
25. Johnson, *An inquirie and ansvver of Thomas VVhite*, 28; Thomas White, *A discoverie of Brownisme* (London, 1605), 11.
26. White, *A discoverie*, 26.
27. *Plymouth Church Records*, 139–40.
28. Bradford, *History of Plymouth Plantation*, I, 37, 40.
29. Ainsworth, *Covnterpoyson*, [iii].
30. Ainsworth, *Covnterpoyson*, 1.
31. Ainsworth, *Covnterpoyson*, 3–4.
32. Ainsworth, *Covnterpoyson*, 23, 22.
33. Ainsworth, *Covnterpoyson*, 10.
34. Ainsworth, *Covnterpoyson*, 29.
35. *Works of Smyth*, II, 335–6.

Chapter 25

1. *Greenwood*, 14.
2. *Works of Smyth*, I, 273, 315; Burrage, *Early English Dissenters*, II, 168.
3. *Works of Smyth*, II, 439–40.
4. *Works of Smyth*, II, 378.
5. W.P. Stephens, *Zwingli: An Introduction to his Thought* (Oxford: OUP, 1992), 91–3.
6. *Works of Robinson*, III, 168.
7. Francis Johnson, *A brief Treatise Conteyning Some Grounds and Reasons against two Errours of the Anabaptists* ([Amsterdam], 1609), 3; Henry Ainsworth, *A defence of the Holy Scriptures, worship, and ministerie, used in the Christian Churches separated from Antichrist* (Amsterdam, 1609), 121, 82; Richard Clifton, *The Plea for Infants and Elder People* (Amsterdam, 1610), 3; *Works of Robinson*, III, 197.
8. Bradford, *History of Plymouth Plantation*, I, 38.

9. *Works of Smyth*, II, 350; B.R. White, *The English Separatist Tradition* (Oxford: OUP, 1971), 133; B.R. White, *The English Baptists of the 17th Century* (London: Baptist Historical Society, 1983), 22–3.

10. *Barrow 1590–1591*, 108.

11. *Barrow 1590–1591*, 110.

12. M.M. Knappen, *Tudor Puritanism: A Chapter in the History of Idealism* (University of Chicago, 1939), 348.

13. *Works of Smyth*, II, 567.

14. White, *English Baptists of the 17th Century*, 24.

15. Johnson and Ainsworth, *An Apologie*, 109.

Chapter 26

1. *Works of Robinson*, II, 185.

2. Lumpkin, *Baptist Confessions of Faith*, 118.

3. Thomas Helwys, *An Advertisement or Admonition, unto the Congregations, which men call the New Fryesers, in the lowe Countries* (Amsterdam, 1611), 5; *Writings of Smyth*, II, 526.

4. Burrage, *Early English Dissenters*, II, 185.

5. *The Life and Writings of Thomas Helwys*, ed. Joe Early (Macon: Mercer University Press, 2009), 55, 57.

6. Walter Burgess, *John Smith, the Se-Baptist, Thomas Helwys and the First Baptist Church in England* (London: James Clarke, 1911), 201.

7. *Works of Smyth*, II, 759; Lawne, *The Prophane Schisme*, 56.

8. Burgess, *John Smith*, 197.

9. Burgess, *John Smith*, 197.

Chapter 27

1. Clifton, *The Plea for Infants*, [v].

2. Clifton, *The Plea for Infants*, 39.

3. *Works of Hall*, IX, 400.

4. Francis Johnson, *A short Treatise concerning the Exposition of those Words of Christ, Tell the Church* ([Amsterdam], 1611), A2 recto.

5. Collinson, *From Cranmer to Sancroft*, 141.

6. Henry Ainsworth, *An Animadversion to Mr Richard Clyftons Advertisement* (Amsterdam, 1613), 126.

7. *Works of Robinson*, III, 475.
8. *Works of Robinson*, III, 475.
9. Lawne, *The Prophane Schisme*, 42
10. *Life and Writings of Thomas Helwys*, 66.
11. Clifton, *An Advertisement*, 63–4.
12. Anon, *Persecution for Religion Judg'd and Condemn'd* ([London?], 1662), 35.
13. Ainsworth, *An Animadversion*, 49, 104.
14. Lawne, *The Prophane Schisme*, 15.
15. Clifton, *An Advertisement*, 117, 121.
16. Lawne, *The Prophane Schisme*, 17.
17. Lawne, *The Prophane Schisme*, 4.
18. Lawne, *The Prophane Schisme*, 25.
19. Lawne, *The Prophane Schisme*, 25, 21, 22,
20. Lawne, *The Prophane Schisme*, 10.
21. Clifton, *An advertisement*, 11, 12.
22. *Works of Robinson*, III, 95, 99.
23. Ainsworth, *An Animadversion*, 73, 74.
24. *Works of Smyth*, II, 754.
25. *Works of Smyth*, II, 753.
26. *Works of Smyth*, II, 758, 760.

Chapter 28

1. Thomas Helwys, *A short declaration of the mistery of iniquity* ([Amsterdam], 1612), 12, 130.
2. Helwys, *Mistery of iniquity*, 69.
3. Helwys, *Mistery of iniquity*, [i], 43.
4. Helwys, *Mistery of iniquity*, 46, 49.
5. Helwys, *Mistery of iniquity*, 209.
6. Helwys, *Mistery of iniquity*, 211, 205, 207, 208.
7. Helwys, *Mistery of iniquity*, [MS flyleaf].
8. Burrage, *Early English Dissenters*, I, 314.
9. *Works of Robinson*, 110, 114, 122.
10. *Plymouth Church Records*, 140; Edward Winslow, *Hypocrisie Unmasked*, ed. Howard Chapin (Massachusetts: Applewood, 1916), 93; Michael Watts, *The Dissenters: From the Reformation to the French Revolution* (Oxford: Clarendon Press, 1992), 51; *Works of Robinson*, III, 100.
11. *Works of Robinson*, III, 159.

12. Bradford, *History of Plymouth Plantation*, I, 89.
13. Burrage, *Early English Dissenters*, I, 255.
14. Leonard Busher, *Religions peace* (Amsterdam, 1614), 11, 3.
15. Anon, *Persecution for Religion Judg'd and Condmn'd* ([London], 1662), 16, 34.
16. Anon, *Persecution for Religion*, 46, 43.
17. Anon, *Persecution for Religion*, 26.
18. Anon, *Persecution for Religion*, 26.
19. Bradford, *History of Plymouth Plantation*, I, 50.
20. Winslow, *Hypocrisie Unmasked*, 99.
21. Keith Sprunger, *Trumpets from the Tower: English Puritan Printing in the Netherlands 1600–1640* (Leiden: E.J. Brill, 1994), 136.
22. Francis Johnson, *A Christian plea* (Amsterdam, 1617), 121.
23. Johnson, *A Christian plea*, 219.
24. Ofwod, *Advertisement to Jhon Delecluse and Henry May the Elder*, v.

Chapter 29

1. Bradford, *History of Plymouth Plantation*, I, 55.
2. Winslow, *Hypocrisie Unmasked*, 89.
3. Winslow, *Hypocrisie Unmasked*, 89.
4. Bradford, *History of Plymouth Plantation*, I, 40, 41, 124, 54, 56, 57.
5. Bradford, *History of Plymouth Plantation*, I, 60.
6. Henry Ainsworth, *A reply to a pretended Christian plea* (Amsterdam, 1618), 106; Johnson, *A Treatise of the Ministry of the Church of England*, 136.
7. Alec Ryrie, *Protestants: The Radicals Who Made the Modern World* (London: William Collins, 2017), 133; Bradford, *History of Plymouth Plantation*, I, 60.
8. Bradford, *History of Plymouth Plantation*, I, 72.
9. Winslow, *Hypocrisie Unmasked*, 90.
10. Edward Arber, *The Story of the Pilgrim Fathers 1606–1623 AD: As told by themselves, their friends, and their enemies* (London: Ward and Downey, 1897), 129–30.

Chapter 30

1. Bradford, *History of Plymouth Plantation*, 87–8.
2. Burgess, *Pastor of the Pilgrims*, 167.

3. *Letters From and To Sir Dudley Carleton, Knt, During His Embassy in Holland, from Jan. 1615/6 to Dec. 1620,* ed. Philip Yorke (London, 1757), 379.
4. *Letters From and To Sir Dudley Carleton,* 389.
5. Bradford, *History of Plymouth Plantation,* 118–19.
6. Bradford, *History of Plymouth Plantation,* 114.
7. Bradford, *History of Plymouth Plantation,* 112, 114.
8. Bradford, *History of Plymouth Plantation,* 107.
9. Winslow, *Hypocrisie Unmasked,* 97.
10. Bradford, *History of Plymouth Plantation,* 124–5
11. Bradford, *History of Plymouth Plantation,* 129.
12. Bradford, *History of Plymouth Plantation,* 142.
13. Bradford, *History of Plymouth Plantation,* 145.

Epilogue

1. *Works of Robinson,* I, lv.
2. Burrage, *Early English Dissenters,* I, 203–4; Watts, *Dissenters,* 80.
3. Roger Williams, *The Bloudy Tenent of Persecution for Cause of Conscience Discussed* (London, 1848), 20.
4. *Works of Robinson,* II, 66; Watts, *The Dissenters,* 509–10.

INDEX